Research Highlights in Technology and Teacher Education 2015

Senior Book Editors:

Leping Liu
David C. Gibson

Book Editors:

Leanne Cameron
Rhonda Christensen
Denise Crawford
Elizabeth Langran
John Lee
Marilyn Ochoa
David Rutledge
David Slykhuis
Joke Voogt
Melda Yildiz

Published by
AACE – Association for the Advancement of Computing in Education

Research Highlights in Technology and Teacher Education 2015
(ISBN: 978-1-939797-19-3) is published by
AACE, PO Box 719, Waynesville, NC USA
757-366-5606; Fax: 703-997-8760; E-mail: info@aace.org
© Copyright 2015 by AACE
www.aace.org
Available at http://www.aace.org/bookshelf.htm

Research Highlights in Technology and Teacher Education 2015

Foreword..5
Preface..7

TECHNOLOGICAL PEDAGOGICAL AND CONTENT KNOWLEDGE (TPACK)

TPACK as Shared Practice: Toward a Research Agenda..13
    David Jones, Amanda Heffernan and Peter R. Albion (Australia)

The Impact of Modeling and Mentoring on Pre-service Teachers to Use Technological Pedagogical Content
Knowledge..21
    Yehuda Peled and Anat Oster-Levinz (Israel)

Examining the Relationship between Self and External Assessment of TPACK of Pre-Service Special Education
Teachers..29
    Irina Lyublinskaya and Nelly Tournaki (USA)

TPACK for Teaching Mathematics and Science and Differentiation of Instruction: Case Study with Pre-service
Special Educators 37
    Nelly Tournaki and Irina Lyublinskaya (USA)

SCIENCE, TECHNOLOGY, ENGINEERING AND MATHEMATICS (STEM)

Teacher Dispositions toward Science, Technology, Engineering, and Mathematics (STEM) 45
    Gerald Knezek, Rhonda Christensen and Tandra Tyler-Wood (USA)

Lessons Learned from Creation of an Exemplary STEM Unit for Elementary Pre-Service Teachers: A Case Study 53
    Matthew Schmidt and Lori Fulton (USA)

Beginner Robotics for STEM: Positive Effects on Middle School Teachers 61
    Haihong Hu and Uma Garimella (USA)

Utilizing Wearable Technologies as a Pathway to STEM...69
    Bradley Barker, Jennifer Melander, Neal Grandgenett and Gwen Nugent (USA)

Computational Pedagogical Content Knowledge (CPACK): Integrating Modeling and Simulation Technology into
STEM Teacher Education..79
    Osman Yaşar, Jose Maliekal, Peter Veronesi, Leigh Little, and Soun Vattana (USA)

Pre-service Mathematics Teachers' Awareness of Social and Socio-Mathematical Norms during Technology-
Enhanced Lessons...89
    Tuğçe Kozaklı and Hatice Akkoç (Turkey)

3D Scanning of Fossils for Middle and High School Students: Science Teachers' Perspectives..............97
    Claudia Grant, Pavlo Antonenko, Jason Tovani, Aaron Wood and Bruce MacFadden (USA)

MOBILE TECHNOLOGY AND SOCIAL MEDIA

Engaging Students in Class through Mobile Technologies – Implications for the Learning Process and Student
Satisfaction 105
    Yair Zadok and Hagit Meishar Tal (Israel)

The Influence of Class Sets of Mobile Devices on Student Learning 113
    Nicholas J. Lux, Art Bangert, Miles McGeehan, Kathryn Will-Dubyak and Rob Watson (USA)

Beyond Professional Development: A Case Study of Implementing iPads in Early Childhood Education 121
    Ellen S. Hoffman, Elizabeth Park and Meng-Fen Grace Lin (USA)

"You are Here": Developing Elementary Students' Geography Skills by Integrating Geospatial Information Technologies 129
    Thomas Hammond (USA)

A Structural Equation Model for Understanding Intensive Facebook Uses of Preservice Teachers 137
    Ismail Celik, Ismail Sahin, Mustafa Aydin, Ahmet Oguz Akturk and S. Ahmet Kiray (Turkey)

ONLINE TEACHING AND LEARNING

Online Mentoring for Secondary Pre-service Teachers in Regional, Rural or Remote Locations 145
    Petrea Redmond (Australia)

Student Engagement: Best Practices in a K-5 Blended Learning Environment 153
    Cindy Prouty and Loredana Werth (USA)

Future Online Faculty Competencies: Student Perspectives 159
    Phillip L. Davidson (USA)

Feeling Anxious: Students' Perceptions and Emotions Relative to Online Assessments in College Courses 167
    Catherine F. Brooks (USA)

ASSESSMENT AND EVALUATION

Measuring 21st Century Skills in Technology Educators 175
    Rhonda Christensen, Gerald Knezek, Curby Alexander, Dana Owens, Theresa Overall, Garry Mayes (USA)

The Impact of Teacher Observations with Coordinated Professional Development on Student Performance: A 27-State Program Evaluation 183
    Kelly F. Glassett, Steven H. Shaha and Aimee Copas (USA)

A Performance Assessment of Teachers' TPACK Using Artifacts from Digital Portfolios 189
    Joshua M. Rosenberg, Spencer P. Greenhalgh and Matthew J. Koehler (USA)

WILL, SKILL AND TOOL DEVELOPMENT

A "Spot the Different Videos" Training Method to Build Up Teaching Skills Using ICT in Pre-service Teacher Education 197
    Minae Ogawa, Yasuhiko Morimoto, Takeshi Kitazawa and Youzou Miyadera (Japan)

A Preservice Secondary Education Technology Course: Design Decisions and Students' Learning Experiences 207
    Dawn Hathaway and Priscilla Norton (USA)

Teacher Comfort Related to Current and Future Technology Use 215
    Rachel Vannatta Reinhart, Toni Sondergeld, Savilla Banister and Sharon Shaffer (USA)

FOREWORD

SITE is proud to present the *2015 Research Highlights in Technology and Teacher Education*. This compilation represents some of the finest research presented at the 2015 SITE conference in Las Vegas, NV. Each article underwent two rounds of rigorous peer-review so the scholars featured in this book should be as proud of their accomplishments as we are to feature their work.

SITE is a broad-based organization of scholars from a wide variety of disciplines who are interested in the role of technology in teacher education. This book represents this wide range of interests so we trust that any SITE member will be able to find an article related to their research interests. At the same time, one of the best things about SITE is the opportunity to learn about research and innovation in areas outside of one's own specialization and to think creatively about the broader applications of technology.

Enjoy reading these research articles and experiencing the breadth and depth of research and innovation at SITE. Later this year, when submitting proposals for the 2016 Conference in Savannah, GA, we hope that you will consider also submitting your work for inclusion in the 2106 Research Highlights in Technology and Teacher Education.

David Slykhuis
SITE President

PREFACE

Research Highlights in Technology and Teacher Education is now in its seventh year of publication. Collections in this book series have continually presented the distinguished work by educators and researchers in the field, and are highlighted with contemporary trends and issues, creative methods, innovative ideas, theory and practice-based models, and effective use of research tools and approaches in the field of information technology and teacher education. This year, twenty-six chapters are included and organized into six themes: (a) Technological Pedagogical and Content Knowledge (TPACK), (b) Science Technology Engineering and Mathematics (STEM), (c) Mobile Technology and Social Media, (d) Online Teaching and Learning, (e) Assessment and Evaluation, and (f) Will, Skill and Tool Development

TECHNOLOGICAL PEDAGOGICAL AND CONTENT KNOWLEDGE (TPACK)

Over the past decade, TPACK (technology, pedagogy, and content knowledge) has been one of the most discussed themes in the literature on the use of information technology in teacher education. Theoretically and practically, it provides a framework for effective technology integration. Studies in this area have focused on exploring related issues and effective ways to use this framework to improve teaching and learning for teacher education students. This year, four chapters are included in this section.

In the first chapter, "TPACK as Shared Practice: Toward a Research Agenda," David Jones, Amanda Heffernan and Peter Albion from Australia describe challenges in integrating Information and Communication Technologies (ICT) into pre-service teacher education. These researchers argue that a distributed view of TPACK offers useful insights that can inform practitioners, researchers and policy makers as they explore practice and learn how to meet the technology integration challenge. A research agenda for TPACK is also proposed for further studies.

Authored by Yehuda Peled and Anat Oster-Levinz from Israel, Chapter Two "The Impact of Modeling and Mentoring on Pre-service Teachers to Use Technological Pedagogical Content Knowledge" presents an international study that examines the ability of pre-service teachers to integrate technological knowledge and pedagogical content knowledge (TPACK) into their teaching. Data are gathered from a large college located in the center of Israel and a small college in the northern part of Israel. Differences are found across these two institutions. The influence of lecturer and mentor teacher modeling on ICT integration is discussed, as well as necessary training components and the pre-service teachers' attitudes towards ICT and TPACK.

Next, in "Examining the Relationship between Self and External Assessment of TPACK of Pre-Service Special Education Teachers," Irina Lyublinskaya and Nelly Tournaki examine the relationship and differences between TPACK scores of lesson plans (external scores) developed by 150 pre-service special education teachers and scores of their self-reflections (self-scores) about teaching these lessons. Results suggest that both self and external TPACK scores improve significantly, while no significant differences are found between external and self TPACK scores for each lesson plan.

In the fourth chapter "TPACK for Teaching Mathematics and Science and Differentiation of Instruction: Case Study with Pre-service Special Educators," Nelly Tournaki and Irina Lyublinskaya address qualitative findings in the study introduced in chapter three with eight cases. The study describes how the quality of differentiation of instruction changes as TPACK improves and how strategies used for differentiation parallel the levels of TPACK achieved by each participant.

SCIENCE, TECHNOLOGY, ENGINEERING AND MATHEMATICS (STEM)

STEM continues to be one of the most discussed themes in the literature on teacher education. This year, seven chapters are included. Chapter five "Teacher Dispositions toward Science, Technology, Engineering, and Mathematics (STEM)," by Gerald Knezek, Rhonda Christensen and Tandra Tyler-Wood, presents a study in which dispositions of middle school teachers in an NSF-funded Innovative Technologies Project as well as teachers in two other STEM enrichment programs are compared with those of preservice educators from a midwestern university in the USA. Findings suggest that teachers from different regions of the US and in programs supported by the National Science Foundation or by state or corporate fund-supported programs have highly similar, positive attitudes toward Science, Technology, Engineering and Mathematics (STEM). Implications of these findings are discussed in terms of selecting new STEM teachers and factors that may encourage teachers to embrace and remain in STEM teaching.

In the study presented in chapter six "Lessons Learned from Creation of an Exemplary STEM Unit for Elementary Pre-Service Teachers: A Case Study" by Matthew Schmidt and Lori Fulton, a traditional inquiry-based unit on moon phases is transformed into a technology-rich STEM unit for pre-service teachers (PSTs), and the impact on PSTs' perceptions of inquiry-based science instruction is explored. Findings indicate that (a) PSTs hold absolutist beliefs and have a need for instruction on inquiry-based learning, and (b) explicit examples of effective and ineffective technology use are needed to impart an understanding of meaningful technology integration.

Haihong Hu and Uma Garimella, the authors of chapter seven "Beginner Robotics for STEM: Positive Effects on Middle School Teachers," introduce a 60-hour professional development program, in which twenty sixth through eighth grade math and science teachers are trained to integrate robotics into STEM-related curricula that aligns with Arkansas and the National Research Council's Science Standards. Findings from this mixed-methods study indicate that teachers improve significantly in STEM content knowledge, become more confident in using Robotics to enhance student interest and involvement in STEM activities, and successfully integrate robotics into STEM curriculum through the design of an inquiry-based lesson plan.

Chapter eight "Utilizing Wearable Technologies as a Pathway to STEM," authored by Bradley Barker, Jennifer Melander, Neal Grandgenett and Gwen Nugent, reports the findings of a pilot study that uses a wearable electronic technologies intervention as a way to improve attitudes towards science, technology, engineering and mathematics (STEM) content areas for students in grades four to six. The study uses a previously developed attitude instrument organized around constructs such as motivation, self-efficacy and learning strategies. Findings indicate that wearable technologies may indeed increase STEM attitudes and can be a viable way to increase participation in STEM for females.

In chapter nine: "Computational Pedagogical Content Knowledge (CPACK): Integrating Modeling and Simulation Technology into STEM Teacher Education," Osman Yaşar, Jose Maliekal, Peter Veronesi, Leigh Little, and Soun Vattana present a qualitative study in which pre-service teachers and in-service teachers are instructed in the use and basic operating principles of CMST (computational modeling and simulation technology) in an attempt to enhance its integration into teaching in a more permanent, constructivist, and tool-independent way. The results suggest that if teachers move beyond 'using' tools to learning their basic operating principles, they can construct authentic models, navigate among multiple tools that operate on the same principles, and as a result gain confidence in deciding which tools might better facilitate teaching of a topic.

With the emphasis in technology integration, there is a growing interest in research on teachers' and pre-service teachers' choices, strategies, views and norms related to using technology in the classroom. In chapter ten, "Pre-service Mathematics Teachers' Awareness of Social and Socio-Mathematical Norms during Technology-Enhanced Lessons," Tuğçe Kozaklı and Hatice Akkoç from Turkey explore exhibited norms among three pre-service mathematics teachers and examine their awareness of these norms during their technology-enhanced lessons. The findings indicate that participants can establish new classroom social learning norms during their technology-enhanced lessons.

It is believed that students are more engaged in science learning activities when given the opportunity to work on real world projects. Claudia Grant, Pavlo Antonenko, Jason Tovani, Aaron Wood and Bruce MacFadden present chapter eleven "3D Scanning of Fossils for Middle and High School Students: Science Teachers' Perspectives," which analyzes the potential of 3D scanning technology in middle and high school to scaffold the development of science literacy while contributing to broader 3D digitization and big data initiatives. Results indicate that teachers and students are not intimidated by the technology and, given adequate professional development and instruction, 3D scanning would be an important skill to develop in the classroom.

MOBILE TECHNOLOGY AND SOCIAL MEDIA

With the rapid development and increasing use of mobile technology applications and social media tools, studies in teacher education have formulated a new trend to explore appropriate ways to use those tools to improve teaching and learning. This year, five chapters are focused on this theme.

A study by Yair Zadok and Hagit Meishar Tal from Israel titled "Engaging Students in Class through Mobile Technologies – Implications for the Learning Process and Student Satisfaction" begins this section. This study inspects how students are using their mobile devices in class and whether lecturers can influence this usage to the benefit of learning. Findings suggest that students are more satisfied with the course and lecturer when they are actively engaged to use their mobile devices as study tools, indicating the possibility to turn what can be a distraction into a constructive means for improving the in-class experience of students and lecturers.

Nicholas J. Lux, Art Bangert, Miles McGeehan, Kathryn Will-Dubyak and Rob Watson introduce a study in chapter thirteen investigating "The Influence of Class Sets of Mobile Devices on Student Learning." The data related to student achievement including scores on district-wide reading and math assessments, keyboarding assessments, 21st century skills assessments, and attendance records are examined. Results strongly suggest the class sets of Chromebook devices significantly influence student learning. Research design and limitations are also discussed.

Chapter fourteen "Beyond Professional Development: A Case Study of Implementing iPads in Early Childhood Education," by Ellen S. Hoffman, Elizabeth Park and Meng-Fen Grace Lin, presents a mixed method study on implementing the use of iPads in Hawaii preschools by fifteen teachers. Findings suggest increasing concerns about how to best assist early childhood educators with the strategies required to respond to new affordances offered by touch-based tablets for young children. For professional development, participants prefer face-to-face collaboration and personalized training. Findings indicate that changing teachers' attitudes is as important as improving their skills.

The study introduced in chapter fifteen "You are Here: Developing Elementary Students' Geography Skills by Integrating Geospatial Information Technologies," explores the use of geospatial information technologies to develop third grade students' mastery of latitude and longitude and related geography skills. The author, Thomas Hammond, works with teachers and students at three elementary schools to develop and refine a week-long sequence for teaching latitude and longitude—along with map skills and geospatial awareness—incorporating GPS units, Google Earth overlays, and geospatially-embedded social media. Student learning outcomes are assessed, implications for geography education and teacher education are discussed, with recommendations for further research on the use of geospatial tools in elementary geography education.

With the increasing popularity of social networks, spending time on networking sites has become a part of a teacher's daily activities. The last chapter of this section "A Structural Equation Model for Understanding Intensive Facebook Uses of Preservice Teachers," by Ismail Celik, Ismail Sahin, Mustafa Aydin, Ahmet Oguz Akturk and S. Ahmet Kiray from Turkey, presents the intensive use of Facebook (FB) and the variables that directly and indirectly affect FB usage. The model shows that approximately 50% of the variance in intensive use of FB is predicted by other variables such as frequency of FB use, the time spent on FB, the number of FB friends, and the general use of FB.

ONLINE TEACHING AND LEARNING

Online teaching and learning for teacher education has been studied for decades. At various times, research and practice have focused on exploring: the use of new platforms or tools to deliver online instruction, theories and practice of instructional design for online learning, means of communicating and collaborating in an online learning environment, assessment and evaluation, online mentoring and advising, and online training for professional development. Four chapters are included in this section.

In chapter seventeen "Online Mentoring for Secondary Pre-service Teachers in Regional, Rural or Remote Locations," Petrea Redmond from Australia describes a project that investigates qualitative expressions in an online mentoring community involving secondary pre-service teachers and practising teachers. The practising teachers acted as online mentors to the pre-service teachers who are personally, professionally and geographically isolated due to being located in regional, rural or remote areas. The participants' posts in an invitational online space are coded using a content analysis framework, and outcomes from the online mentoring project are provided.

Cindy Prouty and Loredana Werth present a study in chapter eighteen, "Student Engagement: Best Practices in a K-5 Blended Learning Environment," aiming to investigate best practices in a K-5 learning environment and to determine if tablet usage in the classroom increases student engagement as observed through on-task conduct, homework completion, increased involvement in class activities, and fewer behavioral incidents. Some 250 students from a rural elementary school in the Pacific Northwest are observed in their classrooms and 30 certificated teachers participate in a survey and interviews. Results suggest that technology eliminates obstacles between casual and more prescriptive education practices.

Chapter nineteen "Future Online Faculty Competencies: Student Perspectives" introduces a qualitative descriptive study by Phillip Davidson that provides a better understanding of the dominant student perceptions of future competencies that online faculty might need in the future. A survey was issued to 500 college-level students. Results indicate that faculty communication, technical and computer skills, and patience with students are critical for success in future online classes.

Technology-based testing tools are being used in a variety of college course types, especially online courses. In the study described in chapter twenty "Feeling Anxious: Students' Perceptions and Emotions Relative to Online Assessments in College Courses" by Catherine F. Brooks, student experiences with online assessments, specifically timed exams and quizzes are analyzed. Findings suggest that students enjoy immediate feedback on their performance, but experience anxiety relative to online testing events and are often concerned about their teacher not 'being there' during online exams and quizzes.

ASSESSMENT AND EVALUATION

Assessment and evaluation have been major topics in the literature on using technology in teacher education. Researchers and educators have systematically developed technology-standard-based assessment methods, produced valid and reliable instruments and measurements, and performed appropriate data analysis. In this book, three chapters are included in this section.

A study by Rhonda Christensen, Gerald Knezek, Curby Alexander, Dana Owens, Theresa Overall and Garry Mayes titled "Measuring 21st Century Skills in Technology Educators" begins this section. In this study, data from 195 preservice and inservice teachers at four universities are analyzed to determine the suitability of the newly revised Technology Proficiency Self Assessment (TPSA C21) released for wide-scale distribution. The authors conclude that the TPSA C21 continues the reliable and valid measurement tradition of the TPSA spanning more than a decade, and extends that tradition with the addition of two scales designed to assess educator skills regarding emerging new technologies.

In chapter twenty-two "The Impact of Teacher Observations with Coordinated Professional Development on Student Performance: A 27-State Program Evaluation," Kelly F. Glassett, Steven H. Shaha and Aimee Copas report a study that examines a large number of schools and districts across the United States through systemic teacher observation aligning with professional development (PD). This study also describes a system wherein PD enables teachers to participate in a full range of activities from instructional videos on teaching techniques, to communities of other users, to posting and downloading PD-related materials. Results indicate that systemic observation coupled with aligned professional development impacts student achievement in reading and math.

In the study contributing to both TPACK and assessment knowledge described by Joshua M. Rosenberg, Spencer P. Greenhalgh and Matthew J. Koehler in chapter twenty-three "A Performance Assessment of Teachers' TPACK Using Artifacts from Digital Portfolios," the authors employ different methods of measuring teachers' Technological Pedagogical Content Knowledge (TPACK). The team tested the reliability of a performance assessment of the TPACK present in teachers' portfolio artifacts by focusing on two specific types of artifacts: Dream IT (a type of grant proposal), and a sustainable technology initiative. Reliability of attempts to code levels of

TPACK evident in these artifacts and development of more robust performance measures of teachers' TPACK are discussed.

WILL, SKILL AND TOOL DEVELOPMENT

The Will, Skill, Tool (WST) model of technology integration is originally developed by Knezek, Christensen, Hancock, and Shoho (2000). This model posits that educators' desire to use technology (will), training in use of technology (skill), and access to information processing hardware, software and support structures (tool), are all necessary for full integration of technology into the classroom environment. After fifteen years, this model still provides a useful framework for the practice of technology integration in the field of teacher education. This year, three chapters fall into this area.

In chapter twenty-four "A 'Spot the Different Videos' Training Method to Build Up Teaching Skills Using ICT in Pre-service Teacher Education," Minae Ogawa, Yasuhiko Morimoto, Takeshi Kitazawa and Youzou Miyadera from Japan introduce their study to establish an effective learning model for acquiring teaching skills using ICT (information and communications technology) in a teacher education course. A learning model is initiated and evaluated that involves a problem solving approach through "Spot the different videos" material to acquire knowledge and skills.

Dawn Hathaway and Priscilla Norton introduce a design-based research approach in course design. Chapter twenty-five "A Preservice Secondary Education Technology Course: Design Decisions and Students' Learning Experiences" examines the influence of three course design decisions on candidates' learning experiences. The three course design decisions are: to situate participants' study of technology in their disciplinary teaching field, to organize modules using disciplinary habits of mind, and to structure content and activities using a design pattern approach. Participants' reflections suggest that each course design decision is uniquely successful in focusing participants' learning on the *interaction* of technology integration concepts *and* discipline-specific contexts.

Lastly, the study Rachel Vannatta Reinhart, Toni Sondergeld, Savilla Banister and Sharon Shaffer present in chapter twenty-six "Teacher Comfort Related to Current and Future Technology Use," examines three variables – teachers' comfort with technology, value of learning new technology, and pedagogy in using technology for instruction – in relation to classroom technology use through a 1:1 pilot. Pre and post surveys are administered to 45 teachers. Multiple regression results indicate that only the variable "value of learning new technology" from pre survey significantly predict post (future) classroom technology use. In addition, teacher comfort, value, and pedagogy are not significantly different from pre to post.

Finally, we would like to take this opportunity to express our congratulations and our appreciation to the book review board, the book editors, and the authors of all the manuscripts contributed this year. We believe that this collection of papers is a welcome addition to the literature in the field of information technology in teacher education.

June 25. 2015

Senior Book Editors
Leping Liu
David C. Gibson

Reference

Knezek, G., Christensen, R., Hancock, R., and Shoho, A. (2000). Toward a structural model of technology integration. Paper presented to the Hawaii Educational Research Association Annual Conference, Honolulu, Hawaii.

SITE BOOK REVIEWERS 2015

Peter Albion, University of Southern Queensland, Australia
Cindy Anderson, Roosevelt University, United States
Leanna Archambault, Arizona State University, United States
Youngkyun Baek, Boise State University, United States
Sally Beisser, Drake University
Beth Bos, Texas State University, United States
Glen Bull, University of Virginia, United States
Livia D'Andrea, University of Nevada, Reno, United States
Niki Davis, University of Canterbury
Candace Figg, Brock University, United States
Mark Hofer, College of William and Mary, United States
Natalie Johnson, Arkansas State University, United States
Mary Kayler, University of Mary Washington
Kathryn Kennedy, International Association for K-12 Online Learning
Lin Lin, University of North Texas, United States
Lesia Lennex, Morehead State University
Cleborne Maddux, University of Nevada, Reno
Mahnaz Moallem, University of North Carolina Wilmington
Chrystalla Mouza, University of Delaware, United States
Priscilla Norton, George Mason University, United States
Blanche O'Bannon, University of Tennessee
Merryellen Schulz, College of Saint Mary, United States
Linyan Song, Towson University
Debra Sprague, George Mason University, United States
James Telese, University of Texas, Brownsville
Tandra Tyler-Wood, University of North Texas, United States
Hans van Bergen, Hogeschool Utrecht
Roberta Weber, Florida Atlantic University, United States
Lawrence Walker, University of Canterbury
Jana Willis, University of Houston-Clear Lake, United States
Thomas Winkler, Institute for Multimedia and Interactive Systems, Germany
Jeremy Wendt, Tennessee Tech University
Harrison Yang, State University of New York-Oswego, United States
Melda Yildiz, Kean University, United States
Hong Zhan, Embry-Riddle Aeronautical University

TPACK as shared practice: Toward a research agenda

David Jones
University of Southern Queensland, Australia
David.Jones@usq.edu.au

Amanda Heffernan
University of Southern Queensland, Australia
Amanda.Heffernan@usq.edu.au

Peter R. Albion
University of Southern Queensland, Australia
Peter.Albion@usq.edu.au

Abstract: The task of using Information and Communication Technologies (ICT) to effectively teach hundreds of pre-service educators, many of whom never attend campus, is a significant challenge, which is amplified by the need to do so in ways that model how they might use ICT in their own classrooms once they graduate. This paper analyses a collection of posts written across a teaching year on a group blog by three teacher educators as they explored their practice and attempted to learn how to meet this challenge. The analysis uses a distributed view of knowledge and learning to identify the barriers and enablers encountered, and how the teacher educators developed their distributed TPACK throughout the year. The paper argues that a distributed view of TPACK offers some interesting insights that can inform practitioners, researchers and policy makers as they explore practice and learn how to meet the technology integration challenge.

Introduction

The 30+ year goal of effective integration of technology into learning and teaching remains elusive (Brantley-Dias & Ertmer, 2013) regardless of the voluminous amounts of effort, research, and literature devoted to developing insights into how to achieve it. Belland (2009) critiqued the focus of researchers on teachers' beliefs and barriers to adoption of Information and Communication Technologies (ICT) for learning and teaching. Instead he suggested that the explanation for limited uptake of ICT by teachers in their classroom practice is related to their past experience and its effect upon teachers' habitus or dispositions to act in certain ways. He argued that, consistent with the observation that teachers very often teach as they were taught, the most powerful influence on the practices of teacher graduates would be their own experience as students in school. He cited examples of teacher educators professing constructivist beliefs but using teacher-directed approaches to prepare teacher candidates to adopt constructivist practices. For teacher education to be effective in overwriting the effects of conventional schooling to graduate teachers prepared to integrate ICT it must employ the strategies it promotes and allow teacher candidates to experience them as learners. The value of such modeling has long been recognized (LeBaron & Bragg, 1994) but not often achieved.

Technological Pedagogical Content Knowledge (TPACK)–one recent significant component of the literature–has become a popular framework for describing the knowledge required by teachers to successfully integrate technology and has underpinned attempts to measure and develop the TPACK of individual teachers (Di Blas, Paolini, Sawaya, & Mishra, 2014). As a consequence of the on-going growth in the perceived importance of ICT in education it has increasingly been seen as essential for teachers at all levels of education to build their TPACK (Doyle & Reading, 2012). Hence, teacher educators require knowledge in the domains of content, pedagogy, technology and their various intersections. Typically they are well prepared by education and experience in content and pedagogy but technology, and its intersections with the other forms of knowledge, presents significant challenges. Teacher educators are subject to their own *habitus* (Belland, 2009) and often have limited, if any, experience of the application of new ICT. Lankshear, Snyder and Green (2000) observed that, where teachers have limited experience of particular practices in the real world, they are challenged to design related authentic activities for the classroom. The protean nature of ICT, as discussed below, continually places teacher educators in the position of needing to model ICT practices that are not established parts of their repertoire. How then can teacher educators effectively model ICT integration so that the *habitus* of teacher candidates will be transformed? How can teacher educators develop the TPACK required for such modeling?

These were among the questions facing a group of teacher educators at the beginning of 2014. With a long history in the provision of distance education, the University of Southern Queensland has over recent years moved into online learning in a strategic way. The institution's strategic plan (USQ, 2012) seeks to "provide students with personalized adaptive learning support" through the use of "emerging technologies" that "enable collaborative teaching and individualized learning for students regardless of their location or lifestyle" (p. 6). For teacher educators this has meant that "by 2012, up to 70% of students in the 4-year Bachelor of Education were studying at least some subjects online" (Albion, 2014, p. 72) and struggling at times when the reality did not always match the institutional rhetoric.

Early in 2014 a private, shared blog was set up amongst a group of six teacher educators in an attempt to explore their shared practice and help bridge this reality/rhetoric gap. The blog provided a space to share stories about what frustrated, pleased, confused and surprised the teacher educators as they attempted to integrate technology into their teaching. Acting as a virtual water cooler, the blog evolved into a space where teacher educators at different stages of their careers could share practices; seek and provide support; and learn from each other.

Between February and October 2014, the six teacher educators shared a total of 82 posts and 150 comments, of which 77 posts (94%) and 111 comments (74%) were shared by three main contributors, who are the co-authors of this paper and, compared to other contributors, had higher levels of engagement with social media prior to initiation of the blog. All participants in the blog were invited to contribute to the paper but three declined for their own undeclared reasons on which we are unable to speculate. To avoid the complications of obtaining ethics approval and enlisting the other bloggers as research participants the analysis for this paper was restricted to the contributions of the co-authors who represented a range of experience and expertise. One teaches courses in ICT and Pedagogy and Networked and Global Learning with more than 20 years experience of university teaching and 3 years in teacher education. The second teaches courses in curriculum and pedagogy, rural and remote education, and teacher identity and professionalism and moved from school to teacher education 3 years ago. The third teaches courses in design and technology and online education and has more than 20 years experience in teacher education.

A focus on TPACK in the blog and the analysis for this paper was a natural consequence of the awareness of TPACK in Australian teacher education following a national Teaching Teachers for the Future project that used TPACK as its framework (Finger et al., 2013). One of the co-authors had been involved in that research and another teaches a course that explicitly seeks to develop the TPACK of teacher candidates making the focus on TPACK of teacher educators a natural extension. The same two co-authors have background in computing and a continuing interest in the potential for digital systems to be modified by their users acting as *digital renovators* (Jones, 2011).

Given the situated and distributed nature of the experience of using the shared blog, the paper draws upon a distributive view of learning and knowledge for this analysis. It begins by looking at recent writing around TPACK with a particular focus on perceived issues with TPACK and suggestions that a distributed view of TPACK might prove useful. Next, the paper describes four conceptual themes of a situated and distributed view of learning and knowledge. These themes are then used to identify and analyze the stories shared on the group blog. Finally, some initial questions for practitioners, teacher educators, researchers and policy makers are raised in the form of a proposed research agenda.

A distributive view of learning and knowledge

As noted by Di Blas et al. (2014), TPACK (the knowledge required to effectively integrate technology) "has consistently been conceptualized as being a form of knowledge that is resident in the heads of individual teachers" (p. 2457). The potential limitations of this perspective led those authors to draw on distributed cognition to explore the idea of distributed TPACK. Earlier, Putnam and Borko (2000) examined "new ideas about the nature of knowledge, thinking and learning" (p. 4), ideas which they labeled the "situative perspective" and included ideas such as situated cognition, distributed cognition and communities of practice. Phillips (2014) used these ideas in his investigation of the development and enactment of TPACK in workplace settings, implicitly recognizing the existence of TPACK as a form of shared practice embedded in context rather than knowledge held privately by individuals. Dron and Anderson (2014) suggest that the situative perspective of learning shares some common concepts and themes with a range of theoretical perspectives including heutagogy, distributed cognition, activity theory, Actor Network Theory, complexity theory and complex adaptive systems, Communities/Networks of Practice, and Connectivism. This range of perspectives has arisen from diverse disciplinary traditions.

Putnam and Borko (2000) developed three conceptual themes capturing the essence of these new ideas to examine the implications they may hold for how teachers design learning experiences, and learn about new ways of teaching. In the following we describe and use these three themes plus one other to analyze and draw implications from the stories shared on the blog.

Situated in particular physical and social contexts

The situated theme of learning and knowledge rejects the idea that context does not matter. Instead the entire context, understood as an interactive system including people, materials and representational systems, in which an activity takes place becomes "a fundamental part of what is learned" (Putnam & Borko, 2000, p. 4). The situated nature of learning means that an inappropriate context can limit transfer of learning into different contexts, a perspective that Putnam and Borko (2000) link to teacher complaints about professional development removed from the classroom being seen as "too removed from the day-to-day work of teaching to have a meaningful impact" (p. 6).

Social in nature

The social perspective of learning and knowing recognizes the important role of other individuals and of discourse communities beyond encouragement and stimulation. Instead, how we think and what we know arises from our on-going interactions with groups of people over time. The implication is that rather than learning being limited only to instruction in particular concepts and skills, it "is as much a matter of enculturation into a community's ways of thinking and dispositions" (Putnam & Borko, 2000, p. 5). The conception of schools as a powerful discourse community with established ways of thinking offers a partial explanation for the resistance to fundamental change of classroom teaching (Putnam & Borko, 2000).

Distributed across the individual, other persons and tools

The view of cognition as distributed proposes that the knowledge required to perform a task does not exist solely within an individual person, or just within groups of people. A distributed view sees cognition as requiring a contribution from a range of people and artifacts. The appropriate tools can enhance, transform and distribute cognition and through this expand "a system's capacity for innovation and invention" (Putnam & Borko, 2000, p. 10). This view offers lenses for exploring how technologies may be able to support and transform teaching and learning (Putnam & Borko, 2000).

Digital technologies are protean

Part of the argument for the addition of technology to Shulman's (1986) PCK (Pedagogical Content Knowledge) to form TPACK was that the rise of digital technologies had created "a very different context from earlier conceptualizations of teacher knowledge, in which technologies were standardized and relatively stable" (Mishra & Koehler, 2006, p. 1023). The rapid and on-going evolution of digital technologies means they never become transparent and it becomes important for teachers to continually develop technological knowledge (Mishra & Koehler, 2006). Though it has been suggested that, as digital technology use within schools becomes more common, "TPACK should, at least in theory, become embedded within other aspects of teachers' knowledge (Brantley-Dias & Ertmer, 2013, p. 117), the evolution of digital technologies will require corresponding changes in TPACK so that it is inherently unstable knowledge. With this theme we are seeking to explore two propositions. First, that technological knowledge should remain as a first class component of TPACK, for reason of its constant and rapid change. Second, that there may be benefits from changing the nature of the technological knowledge that is useful for teachers. As a result, this is a far more tentative theme than the previous three, but it also builds on the increased role technology plays in cognition suggested by those three themes.

Dron and Anderson (2014) quote Churchill (1943) as saying "We shape our buildings and afterwards our buildings shape us" (p. 50). But digital technologies are different, or at least they can be. Kay (1984) described the "protean nature of the computer" (p. 59) and suggested that it is "the first metamedium, and as such has degrees of freedom and expression never before encountered" (p. 59). However, experiencing the full protean nature of digital technologies requires the knowledge to manipulate them, particularly through (but not limited to) programming. If learning and knowledge are distributed across networks of people and objects – which in contemporary classrooms includes a significant proportion of digital technologies – then the ability to modify digital technologies appropriately would seem to be one approach to enhancing learning, especially given Shulman's (1987) view that the distinguishing knowledge of a teacher is the capacity "to transform the content knowledge he or she possesses into forms that are pedagogically powerful and yet adaptive to the variations in ability and background presented by the students" (p. 15). With digital technologies it is possible and desirable that we shape our technologies, then our technologies shape us, and then – as we learn - we shape our technologies some more.

Stories from the blog

Analysis of the data from the blog posts and comments was undertaken using these four conceptual themes as the framework. The use of a priori codes rather than a grounded approach was justified by our interest in a distributed understanding of TPACK as described above. The posts and comments from the co-authors were gathered in a single document and examined for fragments that resonated with the themes. These fragments were marked and collected with annotations that were used to prepare the following analysis of the stories shared on the blog.

Situated

A number of discussions on the blog focused on the challenges of centralized processes or communications that needed to be contextualized to our own circumstances. As noted previously, an inappropriate context can limit transfer of learning, and posts from the blog demonstrated that a similar limitation was found when communications or processes seemed less than an effective fit for our context.

An indication that the institutional units responsible for the technologies at the university are perhaps not working in exactly the same context as teaching staff is revealed through upgrade and maintenance work occurring at perhaps the worst possible times. For example, upgrades to the online assignment submission and management system were scheduled in the week major assignments were due to be submitted.

Senior academics responsible for learning and teaching adopted a communiqué model to encourage effective learning, teaching, and technology integration. This involved periodically sending identical email messages to all academic staff across the university. Due to their less than context-specific nature, the communiqués were limited to largely generic information. The lack of connection to the situated experience of teaching staff became a common concern about this model. For example, a communiqué including notice of decommissioning of the old Computer Managed Assessment process was sent to all academic staff, regardless of whether they made use of this function.

When considering the importance of situated knowledge and understanding of ICT, questions were raised in terms of how we are preparing our students for their future teaching contexts. The institution's use of a Learning Management System (LMS) and other tools that are unlikely to be found in many schools generated questions about the usefulness of these approaches in terms of preparing students to transfer their experience and skills beyond the context of university into their own teaching practices. Further consideration of this notion can also be found below in relation to the 'distributed' theme.

Discussion on the blog noted, in particular, the power of our shared context as a strength of the learning opportunities afforded by the collaborative nature of the space. Centralized support options by their very nature have to be neutral and accessible by any academic within the many disciplines offered by the university, with the support on offer being limited to the experiences of staff typically without any knowledge of the specifics of teacher education. In comparison, a blog shared by a group of teacher educators enabled the sharing of expertise developed through many years in various education sectors and systems. Moreover, that experience was grounded in attempting to develop and harness TPACK to enhance teacher education to the same cohort of students, thereby significantly increasing the relevance of the support provided to our own needs and those of our students. This is reflective of two themes, firstly as mentioned previously that the learning opportunities within the blog were situated in our contexts, but also the notion that distributed TPACK is social in nature.

Social

By its very nature the blog was an appropriate way of sharing information in ways that fit into our own schedules, likely more so than a traditionally scheduled meeting or forum might have been. Furthermore, the approach provided opportunities for participants to post comments and observations, or voice frustrations, at the time that they arose. This resulted in a wider range of issues being raised than might have been discussed had we waited for a scheduled meeting. Issues or points that might not have ordinarily warranted a specific email or phone call to other participants were quickly and easily posted to the blog. Fellow participants could then opt-in or -out of the conversation, depending on whether they were interested or experiencing a similar issue. Given that all three of us were comfortable in the interactive or social nature of online environments, the blog functioned well as a platform for discussion. That we contributed the majority of posts and comments on the blog does raise the question whether our colleagues found it an equally conducive platform.

One aspect of the blog that had significant rewards was the power of sharing practice, adding value to our teaching as a result. As a relative newcomer to tertiary teaching, Amanda was seeking to learn more about the ways colleagues were making use of the various functions afforded by Moodle, the LMS used by our institution. David provided access to the online environment for one of his courses, giving Amanda the opportunity to explore the ways of working initiated by a more experienced colleague who holds expertise in the field of ICT and education. One of the key themes explored earlier in this paper, the notion that TPACK is situated in particular physical and social contexts, was demonstrated by the blog in that it provided opportunities for learning that were contextualized to our field. This was particularly evident in the result of this collaboration, where Amanda was able to see the LMS being utilized in ways that she previously had not observed in other courses. In addition, this provided the opportunity to engage in informed discussions with David about the impact of certain tools and approaches being used in his course. An important aspect to note here is that this was provided in a context of teacher education courses as opposed to other, less contextualized, opportunities that may have been available through central support or elsewhere online. This resulted in a shift in practice for Amanda, adjustments to the online spaces, and more efficient ways of delivering learning experiences for students in her courses.

In the same vein, another significant discussion on the blog was about the delivery of course content and learning experiences for our students. Similar opportunities for shifts in practice resulted from discussions about processes for releasing course content, and even preferences for ways of recording lectures or vodcasts. The key opportunity here was the chance to discuss these approaches with people who had a shared context of teacher education, alongside the variety of levels of experience and expertise in different areas, which added a richness to the conversation. Interactions beyond the blog also benefited participants, with David and Peter's interactions in other online spaces such as Twitter providing solutions to challenges that David was facing with the LMS. The solution provided by Peter was identified as one that would not have been found as easily without these social networks.

Distributed

Stories from the blog are also illustrative of the notion that TPACK is distributed across the individual, other persons and tools. A number of the stories shared were identifying and sharing our responses to gaps in the complex assemblage of people, technologies and practices that make up learning and teaching, gaps that seemed to reduce the overall level of TPACK available across the system. One example of this problem was a new system for managing course documents that could support the use of only the Harvard referencing style, even though courses in teacher education and some other departments of the university courses require the use of the APA referencing style. Other examples of such gaps included issues with gaining access to computer labs, complexities of appointing casual teaching staff to work into courses, accessing the information necessary to create student groups, issues with the availability and performance of the LMS at the start of semester, and processes for contacting students who did not submit assignments, or checking in with students who had yet to engage within our courses. Discussion ranged from commiserating with our colleagues over having similar issues, to providing solutions which each of us had developed over time.

At times, though, these solutions became moot when systems changed unexpectedly and each of us identified some approaches that had worked in the past but were no longer possible for various reasons, either around submission of assessment, delivery and rollover of course content for ease of updating, or the continued use of an e-portfolio from a previous institution. While each of these issues was solved with workarounds, this was often a time sensitive exercise and the end result was not necessarily ideal. For example, Peter was working to modify course content from a previous semester and reached a solution, but "it took far longer than it needed to and finished in what seems an illogical arrangement".

The rise of Web 2.0 and the cloud has also seen a significant increase in the availability of a range of technologies (e.g., Google providing student email accounts) from providers outside of the institutional context. The use of Facebook and other social media as a means of working with students was also a pertinent discussion point at different times throughout the year. At times we discussed issues that had arisen on social media sites that were impacting upon the course (such as misinformation being disseminated and causing confusion for students), but we also discussed ways of trying to engage students on multiple platforms. Tensions sometimes emerged around this integration of 'outside' technologies. One example of note is the frustration voiced by an institutional learning designer at the direction they were given to encourage the use of formally approved technologies only. The discovery of a taxonomy separating technologies into core, supported, allowed and emerging is also worth noting here and harks back to the concepts discussed earlier in the situated theme, wherein we questioned how comprehensively we were preparing students for a world beyond our institutional tools and approaches.

This insular, institutional view of allowed systems is the reason why the closing of discussion forums on course sites just prior to and for 72 hours after an exam is seen as a practice that will prevent students being able to communicate inappropriately about the examination. This seems to be a moot practice, given the standard experience of each course having its own (and sometimes multiple) student-created and private Facebook groups, not to mention the other LMS provided forms of communication that are available to students.

All of these experiences with the problematic distribution of TPACK across and beyond the institution are perhaps a significant contributor to an observation shared after a discussion with other colleagues, for whom "it was just accepted as par for the course that there would always be fairly major problems with the technology". This acceptance of problems not only contributes to frustration, it also raises questions about the impact on innovation. Amanda posed the question "it makes me wonder. How many people would put [innovation] in the too-hard basket and go back to a tried-and-true method that has worked for them before?". What impact does this have on the ability to effectively integrate technology, if the knowledge of how to effectively integrate technology is distributed across artifacts that are seen as always having fairly major problems? This leads directly to the next theme, which concerns the rapidly evolving nature of technology and the importance of being able to work with/in and around limited tools.

Protean

One solution to the problematic distribution of TPACK across complex assemblages is the idea of 'digital renovation'. Rather than accept these problems, digital renovation draws upon the protean nature of digital technologies to adjust or enhance rigid and problematic systems to develop solutions. Digital renovation provides the opportunity to open up new educational possibilities, but only for those with the TPACK to engage in digital renovation. For example, David shared a pedagogical practice during a planning day and generated some significant interest from another teacher educator. However, the digital technologies provided by the institution do not provide sufficient capability to make this practice plausible within the context of a largish course (300+ students). While David was able to write Perl scripts that bridged the gap, this particular renovation was very specifically situated within the context of the renovator and could not be easily adopted by others. So, despite the interest in an effective practice, it could not be adopted more widely.

But not all such solutions suffer the same problem. Throughout the year the shared blog was used to share and discuss tools and shortcuts that had been developed to work around (or within) the limitations of institutional systems, providing timely solutions for challenges that were, at times, plaguing all of us. The blog's enabling of timely solutions is vital here, ensuring that while teachers may be 'perpetual novices' (Mueller et al., 2008) when it comes to rapidly changing technology and tools, these solutions were developed and shared responsively, providing collegial support and breaking down silos that may have existed. The blog, therefore, enabled us to collectively grow our own solutions to issues as they arose.

The inability to undertake appropriate digital renovation also creates gaps at the institutional level. It has often been reported that a major problem for students using the university's LMS was their inability to find required resources within course sites. The widely accepted reason for this difficulty within the institution is claimed to be the inconsistent and poor layout and design of individual course sites. However, it also points to the apparent inability of the institution to provide an effective search engine - the widely accepted method for finding resources online - that works within the bounds of the institutional LMS. Interestingly, a project is currently underway to streamline course sites to provide a consistent environment for students and apparently solve the discoverability issue. Discussion on the blog raised questions about the impact of this that also relates to previous themes reflecting the importance of context and specialized knowledge – an environment that works in one course may not be a good fit for another.

A final conversation worth noting in relation to the concept that digital technologies are protean was about the complexities of working in a recently updated system and the subsequent requirement of teaching staff adopting new, and as yet untested, processes. The difficulties faced in adopting these practices raised the question of whether the digital fluency of teaching staff was sufficient. Another perspective on these difficulties arose from one participant noting that the systems and processes being used were 'scarcely fit for purpose', raising questions about the digital fluency of the institution. While it was clear that those involved had reasonable ideas about what makes for good online learning practice, they did not always seem to have the digital fluency required to translate those ideas into efficient and effective practice.

The blog afforded us an interactive, low-pressure space to explore these ways of improving our practice, to engage in thoughtful and critical discussions, and to share the load of developing these understandings.

Conclusions and a proposal for a research agenda

Throughout 2014 a group of six teacher educators used a group blog to share the ups and downs of trying to effectively integrate technology into the education of pre-service teachers. Analysis of the 77 posts and 111 comments shared by three of those teacher educators using a distributed view of learning and knowledge was used to extract insights into how these educators developed and shared the TPACK necessary to effectively integrate technology into their teaching. The analysis has revealed that our TPACK was enhanced through the ability to engage in social discussion with colleagues from within the same context. Such situated collaborations helped overcome the limitations of organizational practices and technologies that were not always well suited to our context and aims. Knowledge of how to leverage the protean nature of digital technologies to overcome some of these limitations also helped.

In this light and assuming that "developing TPACK ought to be a critical goal of teacher education" (Mishra & Koehler, 2006, p. 1046) what have we learned? We began with two questions enunciated in the introduction above. How can teacher educators effectively model ICT integration so that the *habitus* of teacher candidates will be transformed? How can teacher educators develop the TPACK required for such modeling? Although we cannot claim to have a complete answer we believe that there is evidence that our sharing positively impacted the TPACK of each of us. Coupled with the evidence from other studies (Di Blas et al., 2014; Phillips, 2014) this suggests that there would be value in encouraging teacher candidates to engage in similar sharing of their experiences with ICT. Our courses already promote such sharing but the evidence here has confirmed the value of such sharing and each of us will continue to share and to model that behavior for students in our courses.

As is frequently the case in research, our work revealed more questions than it answered. Table 1 provides a list of research questions that make up an initial agenda for future work that maps out some potentially interesting directions.

Table 1: Proposed research questions for future research on TPACK as shared practice

Themes	Research questions
Situated	• How will a University-wide consistent structure for course sites impact the situated nature of learning?
	• How can institutional learning and teaching support engage with the situated nature of TPACK and its development?
	• How can University-based systems and teaching practices be closer to, or better situated in, the teaching contexts experienced by pre-service educators?
Social	• How can the development of TPACK by teacher educators be made more social?
	• How can TPACK be shared with other teacher educators and their students?
Distributed	• Is it possible to measure the digital fluency of a university, rather than focus on its teaching staff?
	• How can technologies specific to teacher education (e.g. lesson and unit plan templates) be enhanced to increase the capability and learning of teacher educators?
Protean	• Can the outputs of digital renovation practices by individual staff be shared?
	• How can institutions encourage innovation through digital renovation?
	• What are the challenges and benefits involved in encouraging digital renovation?

In framing this research agenda, it is important to keep in mind that the distributed view of knowledge drawn upon in this paper strongly suggests that there are significant limits to what teacher educators can achieve alone. The knowledge required is situated, distributed and social. Thus the success of such a research agenda will depend on how effectively all of the people and artifacts involved in teacher education can be involved in this research agenda.

References

Albion, P. R. (2014). From Creation to Curation: Evolution of an Authentic 'Assessment for Learning' Task. In L. Liu, D. Gibson, V. Brown, T. Cavanaugh, J. Lee, C. Maddux, M. Ochoa, M. Ohlson, D. Slykhuis & J. Voogt (Eds.), Research Highlights in Technology and Teacher Education 2014 (pp. 69-78). Waynesville, NC: AACE.

Belland, B. R. (2009). Using the theory of habitus to move beyond the study of barriers to technology integration. Computers & Education, 52(2), 353-364. doi: 10.1016/j.compedu.2008.09.004

Brantley-Dias, L., & Ertmer, P. A. (2013). Goldilocks and TPACK: Is the Construct "Just Right?". Journal of Research on Technology in Education, 46(2), 103-128.

Di Blas, N., Paolini, P., Sawaya, S., & Mishra, P. (2014). Distributed TPACK: Going Beyond Knowledge in the Head. In M. Searson & M. N. Ochoa (Eds.), Society for Information Technology & Teacher Education International Conference 2014 (pp. 2464-2472). Jacksonville, Florida, United States: AACE.

Doyle, H., & Reading, C. (2012). Building teacher educator TPACK: Developing leaders as a catalyst for change in ICT Education. In M. Brown, M. Hartnett & T. Steward (Eds.), Future challenges, sustainable futures. (pp. 272-282). Wellington, NZ: ascilite.

Dron, J., & Anderson, T. (2014). Teaching crowds: Learning and social media: Athabasca University Press.

Finger, G., Albion, P., Jamieson-Proctor, R., Cavanagh, R., Grimbeek, P., Lloyd, M., et al. (2013). Teaching Teachers for the Future (TTF) Project TPACK Survey: Summary of the Key Findings. *Australian Educational Computing, 27*(3), 13-25.

Jones, D. T. (2011). Residents and visitors, are builders the forgotten category? Retrieved from https://davidtjones.wordpress.com/2011/07/31/residents-and-visitors-are-builders-the-forgotten-category/

Kay, A. (1984). Computer Software. Scientific American, (September), 53-59.

Lankshear, C., Snyder, I., & Green, B. (2000). Teachers and Technoliteracy: Managing literacy, technology and learning in schools. Sydney: Allen and Unwin.

LeBaron, J. F., & Bragg, C. A. (1994). Practicing what we preach: Creating distance education models to prepare teachers for the twenty-first century. The American Journal of Distance Education, 8(1), 5-19.

Mishra, P., & Koehler, M. J. (2006). Technological Pedagogical Content Knowledge: A Framework for Teacher Knowledge. Teachers College Record, 108, 1017-1054.

Phillips, M. D. (2014). Teachers' TPACK enactment in a Community of Practice. Unpublished PhD, Monash University, Melbourne. Retrieved from http://arrow.monash.edu.au/hdl/1959.1/981787

Putnam, R. T., & Borko, H. (2000). What do new views of knowledge and thinking have to say about research on teacher learning? Educational Researcher, 4-15.

Shulman, L. S. (1986). Those who understand: Knowledge growth in teaching. *Educational Researcher, 15*(2), 4–14.

Shulman, L. S. (1987). Knowledge and teaching: Foundations of the new reform. Harvard Educational Review, 57, 1-22.

USQ. (2012). *USQ Strategic Plan 2013-2015*. Toowoomba, Qld. Retrieved from https://www.usq.edu.au/about-usq/about-us/plans-reports/strategic-plan

The impact of modeling and mentoring on pre-service teachers to use technological pedagogical content knowledge

Yehuda Peled
Western Galilee College, Israel
yehudap@wgalil.ac.il

Anat Oster-Levinz
Beit Berl College, Israel
anato@beitberl.ac.il

Abstract: The present study examines the ability of pre-service teachers from a large college located in the center of Israel and a small college in the northern part of Israel to integrate technological knowledge and pedagogical content knowledge (TPACK) into their teaching and compares the colleges. Significant differences were found between the two colleges concerning TPACK knowledge. The influence of lecturer and mentor teacher modeling on ICT integration is discussed, as well as the level of training components for technology integrated teaching and the pre-service teachers' attitudes towards ICT and TPACK.

Introduction

The Israeli Ministry of Education launched the IT National Initiative Program (ITNIP) in 2011 (Israeli Ministry of Education, 2011), in which part of the initiative focuses on teacher education and is called "Adjusting Teacher Training Colleges to the 21st Century" (ATTC21C) with the objective of transforming teacher education in order to meet the needs of the 21st century (Melamed, Mor, Harel, Peled, Shonfeld, & Ben-Shimon, 2011). The initiative focuses on teachers as agents of change, thus, on the need to teach pre-service teachers how to integrate ICT wisely into teaching and how to develop innovative pedagogy that will enhance learning and teaching processes. The present study focuses on two colleges of education that participate in the ATTC21C: a large college located in the center of Israel and a small college from the northern part of Israel. The study examines the ability of pre-service teachers to integrate technological knowledge with pedagogical content knowledge (TPACK) in their teaching.

Both colleges prepare pre-service teachers (undergraduate) in various disciplines. The colleges apply Ministry of Education policies concerning the ITNIP. The study compares the integration of TPACK in the large college to its integration in the small college and examines the ability of pre-service teachers to integrate TPACK into their teaching during the first year of their college's participation in the ATTC21C. Lovvorn and colleagues (2009) suggest that best practices often come from large institutions. They claim that small colleges looking for solutions need to adapt rather than implement these best practices for their institutional needs. Unlike large institutions with greater funding and larger student enrollment numbers, the challenges small colleges struggle with are naturally different.

Rural institutions located closer to population centers have a distinct funding advantage over community colleges serving strictly remote areas. Concerns were raised, however, regarding the ability of faculty to quickly integrate technology into their teaching curriculum. These concerns are certainly not unique to rural community colleges. However, they may be especially important to institutions serving the most remote, and traditionally most educationally under-served, regions of the country (Pennington, Williams, & Karvonen, 2006). ICT integrated learning environments enable the teacher to allocate time to support individual students or groups, thereby personalizing teaching methods in accordance with the learners' needs. However, research shows that although teachers are aware of the educational potential of integrating technologies in teaching, many use them in traditional ways, e.g., lectures and exercises, without promoting significant change in teaching and learning patterns (Kim, Kim, Lee, Spector, & DeMeester, 2013).

Mishra and Koehler (2006) formally defined a construct of knowledge that teachers possess when teaching with technology: the TPACK. They claim that technological knowledge (TK) should be added as a third domain of knowledge in the pedagogical content knowledge (PCK) framework described by Shulman (1986). It includes knowledge about standard technologies, such as blackboard, and more advanced technologies, such as the Internet. This domain of knowledge also includes the skills necessary to operate the technologies. Intersections between content knowledge (CK), pedagogical knowledge (PK), and technological knowledge (TK) include different types of knowledge that teachers should have in order to integrate technology in a meaningful manner in their teaching. Although the TPACK framework seems simple both in its text and diagram forms, it is fairly complex to grasp. TPACK is more than merely the sum of its parts; it enables a teacher to determine a "fit" between the curriculum focus, pedagogical strategies, and various technologies (Hofer & Grandgenett, 2012). With the increased use of these three types of knowledge, the use of TPACK has also increased in research and evaluation studies in K-12 as well as in higher education contexts (Lee & Tsai, 2010).

Pre-service teachers and TPACK

Pre-service teacher education is a specific context where the pre-service teacher's knowledge grows as a result of learning in courses, workshops and other pre-service experiences. TPACK can be applied within this context for developing cognitive awareness for the integration of TK in teaching (Bos, 2011). Numerous approaches have been suggested for understanding the development of TPACK and its use for preparing future teachers and for elucidating the impact of learning experiences and models (Abbitt, 2011). Research shows that most pre-service teachers have little knowledge or skills in the use of technology for teaching and learning (Tondeur, van Braak, Sang, Voogt, Fisser, & Ottenbreit-Leftwich, 2012), and that technology remains at the periphery of most teachers' practice (Lemke, Coughlin, & Reifsneider, 2009). This problem provides significant challenges to educational technology instructors, researchers, and teacher preparation programs.

Teachers who seek to integrate technology in their teaching find it complicated, since most technologies are not designed specifically for educational purposes. Integrating technology in teaching requires creative input from the teacher (Koehler et al., 2011), all the more so when considering pre-service teachers' rudimentary teaching experience. Therefore, teacher education programs seem to be the key factor in the preparation of new teachers to integrate technology into their teaching practice (Hofer & Grandgenett, 2012). In teacher preparation programs, pre-service teachers can develop their TPACK in a variety of ways. The three primary foci are (1) through a specific educational technology course; (2) content-specific teaching methods, or practicum courses; and (3) through the duration of coursework in a teacher preparation program (Hofer & Grandgenett, 2012). All three mentioned above are used in both colleges reported in this study.

Modeling and mentoring

Observational learning through modeling occurs when observers perform behaviors that they have not learned prior to exposure to the models (Bandura, 1969). Cognitive observational learning is enhanced when modeled displays contain explanation and demonstrations (Schunk & Usher, 2012). Cameron and Baker (2004) suggest that guidance, support and teacher modeling of "good" teaching are seen as key attributes of associate teachers. This is also significant when it comes to the use of technology in teaching as research shows that unless teacher education effectively integrates technology into its courses, pre-service teachers are unlikely to use technology effectively in their own teaching (Yilmazel-Sahin & Oxford, 2010).

The pre-service teachers described in this study meet lecturers in their college of education and mentor teachers in their practice at schools. The mentor teachers are the student teachers' direct and main instructors and serve as role models. Research shows that teacher mentoring has a positive effect on pre-service teachers' experience in teaching (Ingersoll & Strong, 2011). Our study examines the ability of pre-service teachers to integrate TPACK in two educational colleges and the impact of lecturers and mentor teachers' modeling on the integration of TPACK into the pre-service teachers' teaching.

Research Questions

Given the above analysis, we assume that the size and location of the colleges have an impact on the level and knowledge of the pre-service teachers; thus, the pre-service teachers in the small and remote college will show lower knowledge in TPACK integration. The following are the research questions that will be examined in this study: (1) Is there a difference in the ability of pre-service teachers from a small peripheral college to those from a large central college to integrate TPACK in their teaching? (2) Does modeling and mentoring affect pre-service teachers' technological knowledge with pedagogical content knowledge (TPACK) integration in their teaching?

Material and Methods

Participants: The study consisted of 280 pre-service teachers from the large college and 157 pre-service teachers from the small college. In both colleges 50% of the students are between 21 to 30 years old, 1% is under 20. Fifty percent of the students in both colleges are secular Jews; there is a difference in the number of observant Jews in the small and large colleges (20% and 5% respectively). The rest are non-Jewish students, mainly Muslim Arabs. There is also a difference in gender between the colleges: 72% of the students in the small college are female while at the large college 87% of the students are female.

Research Tools: The research tool is a self-assessment questionnaire that is part of a questionnaire that was found to be valid and reliable (Nagar et al., 2013). The questionnaire used in this research was re validated and re validated. The questionnaire includes statements in a Likert scale, multi-choice questions and three open-ended questions. Each of the statements and the questions were examined for reliability (the reliability of each question is stated in the findings).

Procedure: Data was collected through anonymous printed questionnaires which were distributed during classes. The introduction letter was read to the class. It emphasized that one can choose not to participate and/or stop participating at any given time without giving a reason. Classes were chosen according to availability of teachers. Surveys were coded and analyzed. Compliance in answering was high – approximately 97% of the participants answered all of the items in the questionnaires.

Findings

Difference between colleges regarding the components and knowledge of TPACK: Principal component analysis based on Varimax with Kaiser Normalization of the questionnaire's statements found that there are two groups of statements regarding TPACK. The TPACK components include five questionnaire statements concerning the ability of the pre-service teachers to design lessons with ICT, to teach with ICT and their ability to lead others to use ICT in teaching. TPACK knowledge includes two questionnaire statements concerning the way the students received this knowledge. In particular whether they learned it at the college or were exposed to it in their learning (modeling).

Five statements examine the level of TPACK components. The findings show that the level of TPACK components is moderate at both colleges: at the small college a score of 75 and at the large college a score of 74 on a scale from 1 to 100. The internal consistency reliability estimate based on the current sample suggested an adequate level of reliability (Cronbach's alpha of 0.87). No significant difference was found between the two colleges regarding the level of TPACK components. Two statements examine the level of TPACK knowledge. The results show that the level of knowledge is low at both colleges. The internal consistency reliability estimate based on the current sample suggested an adequate level of reliability (Cronbach's alpha of 0.85). There is a significant difference between the two colleges regarding TPACK knowledge, such that pre-service teachers at the small college are significantly higher in the level of TPACK knowledge ($M = 3.23$) than pre-service teachers at the large college ($M = 2.89$; $t_{(409, 0.99)} = 2.95$, $p < 0.01$). There is a significant moderate positive correlation between the TPACK components and the knowledge of TPACK ($r_p = 0.465$, $p < 0.001$). Such that the higher the level of TPACK components, the higher the level of TPACK knowledge. Pearson correlation between TPACK components and knowledge is -0.465 ($n = 224$, $p < 0.001$).

Lecturer and mentor teacher modeling

One open-ended question examined lecturer modeling. Only 80% of the students answered this question. It was found that the level of lecturer modeling at the small college is moderate – score of 75 and is low at the large college – score of 68 on a scale from 1 to 100. No significant difference was found between the colleges in lecturer modeling. In addition, only 8% of the pre-service teachers reported that in all their courses the lecturer effectively integrated ICT technology during class, 33% in most of the courses and 55% in some or few courses. All courses have a course website. For the question *to what extent have the course websites contributed to your learning?* 13% of the pre-service teachers claimed that it contributed very much, 38% and 32% a lot and quite a bit respectively, 13% a little and 4% not at all. Thirty-four percent participated in one distance-learning course, 42% participated in 2-3 courses, 9% in 4 or more and 15% of the pre-service teachers have not participated in any online course at all.

Chi-square analysis did not show a significant difference between colleges regarding effective integration of ICT during class, course website contribution to learning and participation in distance learning courses. It is important to note that most of the pre-service teachers (71%) believe that the use of ICT in teaching by college lecturers improves the quality of their learning.

One statement examined mentor teacher modeling. Over 60% of the students did not view an IT integrated lesson at the school they were observing. The level of mentor teacher modeling at both colleges is medium to low: at the small college – score of 60 and at the large college – score of 53 on a scale from 1 to 100. There is a significant difference between the colleges in the general sample ($t_{(223, 0.95)} = 2.29$, $p < 0.01$). Such that the mentor teacher modeling level at the small college is higher (M = 1.40) than that of the large college (M = 1.13; $t_{(420, 0.99)} = 2.62$, $p < 0.01$). There is no significant correlation between TPACK knowledge and mentor teacher modeling. There is a significant weak positive correlation between TPACK components and mentor teacher modeling ($r_p = 0.150$, $p < 0.05$). Such that the higher the level of TPACK components, the higher the mentor teacher modeling. Spearman correlations between mentor teacher modeling and TPACK components is 0.150 and -0.018 between mentor teacher modeling and knowledge. It is important to note that most of the pre-service teachers (73%) believe that the use of ICT in teaching by teachers at school improves the quality of their teaching.

Level of training components for technology integrated teaching

Fourteen statements examine the level of training components for technology integrated teaching. The results show (see Table 1) that the level of the training components is low in both colleges. At the small college – score of 45 and at the large college – score of 41 on a scale from 1 to 100. The internal consistency reliability estimate based on the current sample suggested an adequate level of reliability (Cronbach's alpha of 0.89). In addition, the results show that the training components are higher among students from the small college (M = 2.24) than among pre-service teachers from the large college (M = 2.03). This difference is significant ($t_{(420, 0.99)} = 2.97$, $p < 0.01$).

As can be seen in Table 1, there is a significant weak positive correlation in the general sample between the level of training components and the contribution of course websites to learning ($r_p = 0.162$, $p < 0.01$) and a weak positive correlation between the training components and the number of ICT courses a student takes in college ($r_p = 0.238$, $p < 0.001$). At the large college, there is a significant weak positive correlation between training components and contribution of course websites to learning ($r_p = 0.179$, $p < 0.01$) and a significant moderate positive correlation between training components and the number of ICT courses a student takes in college ($r_p = 0.318$, $p < 0.001$).
At the small college there is a significant weak positive correlation between training components and modeling of college lecturer ($r_p = 0.209$, $p < 0.05$), and there is a significant weak positive correlation between training components and the level of contribution of course websites to learning ($r_p = 0.170$, $p < 0.05$).

Table 1: Spearman correlations between the components of the technology integrated teacher training and ICT

	College	Modeling of college lecturer	To what extent did the course websites contribute to your learning?	How many ICT courses did you participate in?
Training components	Small college	0.209*	0.170*	0.088
	Large college	-0.005	0.179**	0.318***
	General sample	0.058	0.162**	0.238***

Note: n = 437, *p < 0.05, **p < 0.01, ***p < 0.001

Pre-service teachers' attitudes towards ICT and TPACK

There is a significant weak positive correlation between the TPACK components and the training components in the general sample ($r_p = 0.242$, $p < 0.001$) and a significant moderate positive correlation between the TPACK knowledge and the training components ($r_p = 0.369$, $p < 0.001$). At the small college there is a significant weak positive correlation between TPACK components and training components ($r_p = 0.192$, $p < 0.05$) and between the TPACK knowledge and training components ($r_p = 0.341$, $p < 0.001$). At the large college there is a significant weak positive correlation between the TPACK components and the training components (r_p = 0.284, p < 0.001) and a significant moderate positive correlation between TPACK knowledge and training (r_p = 0.423, p < 0.001) (see Table 2).

Table 2: Spearman correlations between the components of the training and pre-service teachers' attitudes towards ICT and TPACK

	College	Pre-service teachers' attitudes towards the integration of ICT in teaching	TPACK components	TPACK knowledge
Training components	Small college	0.055	0.192*	0.341***
	Large college	0.064	0.284***	0.423***
	General sample	0.050	0.242***	0.369***

Note: n = 437, *p < 0.05, **p < 0.01, ***p < 0.001

No significant correlation was found between the TPACK components of the general sample and modeling of college lecturer. There is a significant weak positive correlation between the TPACK components of the general sample and the contribution of course websites to pre-service teachers' learning (r_p = 0.248, p < 0.001). There is a significant weak positive correlation between the TPACK components of the general sample and the amount of distance learning courses pre-service teachers take in college (r_p = 0.143, p < 0.001) and a significant weak positive correlation between the TPACK components and the training components (r_p = 0.242, p < 0.001).

Five statements examined the attitudes of pre-service teachers towards the integration of ICT in teaching. The results indicate that the attitudes level is moderate at the small college with a score of 74 and at the large college a score of 76 on a scale from 1 to 100. The internal consistency reliability estimate based on the current sample suggested an adequate level of reliability (Cronbach's alpha of 0.77). No significant difference was found between the colleges.

Assignments focused on development of ICT teaching skills

Three statements examine the level of the assignments focused on the development of skills for ICT teaching (see Table 3); less than half of the responding pre-service teachers (44%) reported that preparation of ICT integrated teaching activities occurred in one or two courses they had taken and almost a third (28%) reported that this preparation did not occur in any of the courses they had studied. Furthermore, less than half (43%) reported that in none of the courses they had experienced actual instruction of ICT teaching units in the framework of the teaching experience. And finally, half of the respondents (49%) did not have any courses in which the teacher used learning management systems in a teacher's role. These findings show that the level of the ICT integrated assignments is low in both colleges. Cronbach's alpha for internal consistency reliability is 0.75. In addition, pre-service teachers at the small college received significantly more ICT integrated assignments (M = 2.20) than those at the large college (M = 1.91; $t_{(395,0.99)}$ = 3.10, p < 0.01).

Table 3: Distribution of the assignments focused on the development of skills variable

Question	None of the courses	1-2 courses	3-4 courses	5-6 courses	7 courses or more	Mean
Preparation of ICT integrated teaching activities	28%	**44%**	17%	7%	4%	2.15
Actual teaching of ICT teaching units in the framework of the teaching experience	**43%**	38%	11%	5%	2%	1.86
Using learning management systems in a teacher's role	**49%**	24%	10%	9%	8%	2.04

Discussion

In this research we examined the ability of pre-service teachers to integrate TPACK into their teaching, the parameters that influence this ability and whether there is a difference between the ability of pre-service teachers from a small college in the northern part of Israel and the ability of those from a large college situated in the center of the country. Pre-service teachers from both colleges claimed that they can integrate TPACK into their teaching. This is interesting as most of the pre-service teachers reported that they did not participate in an online course and most of them did not integrate ICT into their teaching as student teachers at school, meaning that there is a discrepancy between the actual TPACK teaching practice of pre-service teachers and their claims. A point of concern is the fact that only a very low percentage of the pre-service teachers claimed that they acquired their TPACK knowledge at college. This should be taken into account by the policy makers at those academic institutions, as it points to a somewhat hazy policy or TPACK training program.

Effective teacher modeling of ICT integration into various courses was reported by most of the pre-service teachers, but although research on teacher education shows that guidance, support and teacher modeling of "good" teaching are seen as key attributes of associate teachers (Cameron & Baker, 2004), the pre-service teachers do not attribute teacher modeling to their TPACK knowledge. Pre-service teachers who reported integrating ICT into their teaching emphasized that it was similar to the way they saw their lecturers teach in class – meaning they were "copying" their lecturers' teaching practices. It can be assumed that practical knowledge is acquired from observing teaching practices in class unintentionally by the pre-service teachers. Thus, lecturers at teacher education institutions should be aware of teacher modeling, discussing the specific practices they employ and directing the pre-service teachers' attention towards the specific practice, urging them to consider it as part of their "teaching toolbox."

Although research shows that teacher mentoring has a positive effect on pre-service teachers' experience in teaching (Ingersoll & Strong, 2011), most of the respondents had not had the opportunity to watch a mentor teacher integrate ICT into his or her teaching, which nevertheless has to be a factor for consideration when choosing a mentoring school and specifically mentoring teachers. Schools hosting pre-service teachers from the small college demonstrated more meaningful ICT integration modeling. This finding indicates that when choosing a host school for pre-service teaching experience, the college should include the schools' TPACK capability in its array of considerations. The college's message to its lecturers will eventually dictate the intensity and frequency of the ICT-based assignments that the pre-service teachers are asked to submit. Pre-service teachers at the small college reported a higher rate of ICT-based assignments as well as stating that their lecturers' modeling influenced their knowledge more than those at the larger college, which reflect the fact that the faculty members at the small college are required to participate in ICT integration workshops, and since last year they are required to integrate ICT into their teaching, thus there is a higher emphasis on ICT integration in class at the small college.

Summary and Recommendation

Although there is incompatibility between the pre-service teachers' beliefs and feelings regarding their ICT capabilities and their TPACK knowledge, their high self-esteem will enable them to take a further step and walk the extra mile towards truly meaningful TPACK integration in their teaching. Apparently, the determination of college management concerning ICT integration as part of the teaching–learning process is the most important factor controlling TPACK integration by pre-service teachers. It is neither the size nor the geographical location of the college.

We recommend a few strategies that could assist pre-service teachers in applying models and practices to effectively integrate technology into the pre-service teachers' future classrooms that strength the link between technology and pedagogy: (1) emphasizing the modeling of lecturers and mentor teachers and discussing authentic cases of teachers utilizing various technology resources in their classrooms; (2) providing pre-service teachers with opportunities to explore innovative technologies and integrate these technologies into rich learning activities; and (3) providing pre-service teachers with opportunities to implement activities that effectively utilize technology in authentic classroom settings.

References

Abbitt, J. T. (2011). Measuring technological pedagogical content knowledge in preservice teacher education: A review of current methods and instruments. *Journal of Research on Technology in Education, 43*(4), 281-300.

Bandura, A. (1969). Social-learning theory of identificatory processes. In D. A. Goslin (Ed.), *Handbook of socialization theory and research* (pp. 213-262). Chicago, IL: Rand McNally.

Bos, B. (2011). Teachers preparation using TPACK when Fidelity of treatment is defined. *Contemporary Issues in Technology and Teacher Education, 11*(2), 167-183.

Cameron, M., & Baker, R. (2004). *Research on initial teacher education in New Zealand: 1993-2004*. Wellington: New Zealand Council for Educational Research.

Collins, O. (2012). The use of ICT in teaching and learning of physical education. *Continental Journal of Education Research, 4*(2), 29-32.

Ertmer, P. A. (2005). Teacher pedagogical beliefs: The final frontier in our quest for technology integration? *Educational Technology Research and Development, 53*(4), 25-39.

Hofer, M., & Grandgenett, N. (2012). TPACK development in teacher education: A longitudinal study of preservice teachers in a secondary M.A.Ed. program. *Journal of Research on Technology in Education, 45*(1), 83-106. Retrieved from http://www.editlib.org/p/54946

Ingersoll, R., & Strong, M. (2011). The impact of induction and mentoring programs for beginning teachers: A critical review of the research. *Review of Education Research, 81*(2), 201-233.

Israeli Ministry of Education. (2011). *Adapting the education system to the 21st century: The national plan*. The official site of Israeli Ministry of Education (Hebrew). Retrieved from
http://cms.education.gov.il/EducationCMS/Units/MadaTech/englishsifria/AdaptingtheEducationSystemtothe21Century/Vision_and_rationale.htm

Jeong, H. (2013). Development of group understanding via the construction of physical and technological artifacts. In D. D. Suthers, K. Lund, C. P. Rosé, C. Teplovs, & N. Law (Eds.), *Productive multivocality in the analysis of group interactions* (pp. 331-351). New York, NY: Springer US.

Kidd, W. (2013). Framing pre-service teachers' professional learning using web 2.0 tools: Positioning pre-service teachers as agents of cultural and technological change. *Professional Development in Education, 39*(2), 260-272.

Kim, C., Kim, M. K., Lee, C., Spector, J. M., & DeMeester, K. (2013). Teacher beliefs and technology integration. *Teaching and Teacher Education, 29*, 76-85.

Koehler, M. J., Mishra, P., Bouck, E. C., DeSchryver, M., Kereluik, K., Shin, T. S., & Wolf, L. G. (2011). Deep-play: Developing TPACK for 21st century teachers. *International Journal of Learning Technology, 6*(2), 146-163.

Kolb, A. Y., & Kolb, D. A. (2012). Experiential learning theory. In N. M. Seel (Ed.), *Encyclopedia of the sciences of learning* (pp. 1215-1219). New York, NY: Springer US.

Lee, M. H., & Tsai, C.-C. (2010). Exploring teachers' perceived self-efficacy and technological pedagogical content knowledge with respect to educational use of the world wide web. *Instructional Science, 38*(1), 1-21.

Lemke, C., Coughlin, E., & Reifsneider, D. (2009). *Technology in schools: What the research says: An update. Culver City, CA*. Retrieved from
http://www.cisco.com/web/strategy/docs/education/tech_schools_09_research.pdf

Lovvorn, A., Barth, M., Morris, R., & Timmerman, J. (2009). Lessons learned from lessons learned: The fit between online education "best practice" and small school reality. *Online Journal of Distance Learning Administration, 12*(6). Retrieved from:
http://www.westga.edu/~distance/ojdla/winter124/lovvorn124.html

MacBrayne, P. S. (1995). Distance education: The way of the future for rural community colleges. In J. Killacky & J. R. Valadez (Eds.), *Portrait of the rural community college: New directions for community colleges* (no. 90, pp. 55-64). San Francisco, CA: Jossey Bass.

Melamed, O., Mor, N., Harel, S., Peled, R., Shonfeld, M., & Ben-Shimon, I. (2011). *Adjusting teacher training colleges to the 21st century*. Retrieved from http://cms.education.gov.il/NR/rdonlyres/6F257716-7C1A-4C2F-8CA9-046BD5C32BEB/132070/21CenturySkilsJuly2011.pdf

Mishra, P., & Koehler, M. J. (2006). Technological pedagogical content knowledge: A framework for integrating technology in teachers' knowledge. *Teachers College Record, 108*(6), 1017-1054.

Pennington, K., Williams, M. R., & Karvonen, M. (2006). Challenges facing rural community colleges: Issues and problems today and over the past 30 years .*Community College Journal of Research and Practice, 30*(8), 655-641.

Riechman, B., & Simon, E. (2013). Between pedagogy and technology: A two college case study-training Israel's teachers to meet the challenges of the 21st century. *International Journal of Digital Information and Wireless Communications, 3*(3), 10-25.

Schunk, D. H., & Usher, E. L. (2012). Social cognitive theory and motivation. In R. M. Ryan (Ed.), *The Oxford handbook of human motivation* (pp. 13-27). Oxford: Oxford University Press.

Shulman, L. S. (1986). Those Who Understand: Knowledge Growth in Teaching. Educational Researcher, 15(2), 4-14.

Stewart, V. (2013). Preparing teachers for globalization. CMU teacher preparation task force 2023. Transforming to a 21st century educator preparation program (pp. 82). College of education and human services Central Michigan University.

Nagar, G., Goldstein, O., Avidov-Ungar, O., Asaf, M., Oster-Levinz, A., Ganaeem, A., Forkosh-Baruch, A., Peled, R., Peled, Y., Sternlicht, O., Shonfeld, M. (2013). Evaluating the Implementation of the National Initiative in Israeli Teacher Education. *Changing Reality through Education, The 6th International Conference on Teacher Education.* 2-4 July, the Mofet institute. Retrieved from http://www2.kenes.com/davidyellin_he/program/ Documents/conference%20abstracts.pdf. [Hebrew]

Tondeur, J., van Braak, J., Sang, G., Voogt, J., Fisser, P., & Ottenbreit-Leftwich, A. (2012). Preparing pre-service teachers to integrate technology in education: A synthesis of qualitative evidence. *Computers & Education, 59*(1), 134-144.

Yang, C., & Chang, Y. S. (2012). Assessing the effects of interactive blogging on student attitudes towards peer interaction, learning motivation, and academic achievements. *Journal of Computer Assisted Learning, 28*(2), 126-135.

Yilmazel-Sahin, Y., & Oxford, R. L. (2010). A comparative analysis of teacher education faculty development models for technology integration. *Journal of Technology and Teacher Education, 18*(4), 693-720.

This research is part of the "Adjusting Teacher Training Colleges to the 21st Century" (ATTC21C) evaluation project. The research is supported by the Moffet Institute, Tel-Aviv, Israel.

Examining the Relationship between Self and External Assessment of TPACK of Pre-Service Special Education Teachers

Irina Lyublinskaya
College of Staten Island – The City University of New York, USA
inina.lyublinskaya@csi.cuny.edu

Nelly Tournaki
College of Staten Island – The City University of New York, USA
nelly.tournaki@csi.cuny.edu

Abstract: This study examined the relationship between TPACK scores of lesson plans (external scores) developed by 150 pre-service special education teachers and TPACK scores of self-reflections (self-scores) about teaching these lessons. The TPACK Levels Rubric (Lyublinskaya & Tournaki, 2012) was used to assess both types of TPACK. Results indicated that a) both, self and external TPACK scores significantly improved, and b) there was no significant difference between external and self TPACK scores for each lesson plan. In order to examine relationships between self and external scores, the participants were divided into three groups: close-estimators (self and external scores are within one standard deviation), over- and under-estimators (self scores are respectively higher or lower than external by more than a standard deviation) Correlational analysis conducted on self and external scores of TPACK revealed significant moderate to strong positive correlation between self and external scores.

Introduction

Technological Pedagogical Content Knowledge (TPACK) describes the teachers' body of knowledge needed for teaching with technology in specific content areas and grade levels. TPACK is identified with knowledge that relies on the interconnection and intersection of content, pedagogy, and technology (Mishra, & Koehler, 2006). The framework must be viewed as constituting more than a set of multiple domains of knowledge and skills that teachers require for teaching their students particular subjects at specific grade levels. Rather, TPACK defines a way of thinking that integrates the multiple domains of knowledge of subject matter, pedagogy and technology.

Assessing the complex construct of TPACK has been a challenge for the educational community. As a result, various types of data have been used in research to assess teachers' TPACK. Most commonly, researchers use self-reports. Self-report data are mostly collected through surveys, which are easy and cost-effective to administer, and provide the possibility to reach large samples of teachers (e.g., Archambault & Crippen, 2009; Lee & Tsai, 2010). A recent study (Tournaki, & Lyublinskaya, 2014) measured TPACK development of pre-service special education teachers through the use of the Survey of Pre-service Teachers' Knowledge of Teaching and Technology (Schmidt, Baran, Thompson, Mishra, Koehler, & Shin; 2009). Significant increases in TPACK were reported from pre- to post-surveys for pre-service teachers enrolled in a pedagogy course organized around the TPACK framework. However, when a survey is used to measure a construct there is always the possibility that teachers' perceptions might not always correlate with their teaching practices (Lawless & Pellegrino, 2007).

Another way to assess teachers' TPACK is through teaching artifacts e.g., lesson plans, curriculum materials, transcripts of implemented lessons, recordings of lessons. Koehler, Mishra, and Yahya (2007) used content analysis techniques for examining teaching artifacts and developed a coding protocol that identified the knowledge domains of the TPACK framework. The authors acknowledged the limitations of the analysis, including the possibility of subjectivity and bias in coding. Further, Groth, Spickler, Bergner, and Bardzell (2009) conducted a qualitative study in which they used teaching artifacts to develop a model for assessing teachers' TPACK. The first quantitative measure of TPACK for lesson plans was developed by Harris, Grandgenett & Hofer (2010) who modified the Technology Integration Assessment Instrument (TIAI) developed by Britten and Cassady (2005). This valid instrument measures three out of seven domains of TPACK framework, i.e., Technological Pedagogical Knowledge (TPK); Technological Content Knowledge (TCK); and TPACK. Further, Niess, et al. (2009) developed a model for progressive development of TPACK with detailed qualitative descriptors for the five levels of TPACK (recognizing, accepting, adapting, exploring, and advancing), and for each of the four components of TPACK (overarching conception, student understanding, curriculum, and instructional strategies). Based on Niess's model, Lyublinskaya and Tournaki (2012) developed and validated the TPACK Levels Rubric, a quantitative instrument that assesses teachers' TPACK in its development through the five progressive levels and the four components identified by Niess in her TPACK Development model. (Niess et al., 2009; Niess, 2011) This instrument was used to assess TPACK in the present study. Even though assessing teaching artefacts may not fully correlate with the quality of classroom instruction, this method of assessment is more objective than surveys as it does not rely on teacher's perceptions.

Theoretically, TPACK instruments are meant to assess different types of technologies used in different content areas and through a variety of artifacts. The purpose of this study was to examine the relationship between TPACK scores of lesson plans developed by pre-service special education teachers and TPACK scores of their self-reflections about teaching these developed lessons; the assessment of both types of TPACK scores was conducted using the same instrument. More particularly, the participants created two lesson plans that an external scorer evaluated using the TPACK Levels Rubric (Lyublinskaya & Tournaki, 2012) – the lesson plan scores will be referred as 'external' scores. Further, the participants taught each of the two lesson plans and at the end of the semester they wrote a self-reflective statement for each. The external scorer used the TPACK Levels Rubric to evaluate each statement – the self-reflections scores will be referred as 'self' scores. This study answered the following research questions: 1) How do lesson plan TPACK scores of special education pre-service teachers compare to their self-reflection TPACK scores measured by the same instrument? 2) Is there a relationship between lesson plan TPACK scores of special education pre-service teachers and their self-reflection TPACK scores?

Methods

Participants

150 pre-service special education teachers enrolled in a graduate pedagogy course designed to integrate technology into teaching mathematics and science to students with disabilities. There were eight sections of the course offered over four semesters. Males comprised 26% of the sample and females comprised 74%. 65% were between the ages of 23 and 26 years old, 7% were between the ages of 18 and 22, 17% between the age of 26 and 32, and 11% of the group were 33 years of age or older. The participants are referred to as pre-service teachers because they were enrolled in an initial certification program for special education. However, all of them completed initial certification in another area prior to enrollment in a graduate program: 43% of participants already held a license in general education childhood, 15% in early childhood license, 3% in adolescence English license, 1% in adolescence mathematics license, and 38% in adolescence Social Studies.

Instrument

The TPACK Levels Rubric constructed and validated by Lyublinskaya and Tournaki (2012) was used to assess lesson plans and self-reflection statements developed by the pre-service teachers. The structure of the rubric is based on the TPACK framework for assessing the development of teachers' classroom technology integration across five progressive levels [*Recognizing* (1), *Accepting* (2), *Adapting* (3), *Exploring* (4), *and Advancing* (5)] in each of the four components of TPACK as identified by Niess (2011).

Two performance indicators have been developed for each level of each component consistent with the qualitative descriptors developed by Niess (2011) and the principles for effective technology use (Goldenberg, 2000). The range of possible scores for each component is from 0 – 5, where the component score can be an integer (both performance indicators are met) or a half-integer (one out of two performance indicators are met). The score is assigned for each component independently. In order to achieve a particular level of TPACK, the teacher must meet both indicators of that level for each component. Thus, the teacher's TPACK level is determined by the lowest score across all four components.

The rubric was tested for inter-rate reliability and construct validity with in-service mathematics teachers using TI-Nspire technology (Lyublinskaya & Tournaki, 2012). Confirmatory Factor Analysis using varimax rotation with Kaiser normalization was completed to confirm construct validity of the rubric when applied to pre-service special education teachers. The procedure confirmed the four factors of TPACK for each set of lesson plans (Lyublinskaya & Tournaki, 2014).

Procedure

As part of a required graduate course on integrating technology into teaching mathematics and science to students with disabilities, participants developed two lesson plans that they taught in the field. The first lesson plan (LP1) was developed at the beginning of the semester while the second (LP2) at the end. Both lessons were taught towards the end of the semester and then participants developed a reflective statement for each lesson. The external scorer, a doctoral candidate in Mathematics Education trained to use the TPACK Levels Rubric, used the rubric to score the lesson plans and then the self-reflective statements. All information was given anonymously to the scorer to avoid bias.

Data analysis and results

Paired samples *t*-test compared LP1 with LP2 – submitted eight weeks apart – and indicated that both, self and external TPACK scores significantly increased with large effect sizes (see Table 1).

Table 1. Descriptive statistics and results of paired samples *t*-test for self and external TPACK scores

TPACK scores	Lesson Plan 1		Lesson Plan 2		N	t	Sig (2-tailed)	Cohen's *d*
	Mean	SD	Mean	SD				
Self	2.11	.854	2.80	.838	148	-8.120	$p < .001$	0.80
External	2.15	.750	2.69	.684		-7.862		0.75

Paired samples *t*-test was also used to compare self and external TPACK scores for each lesson plan. It revealed no significant differences between self and external scores for both lesson plans.

Pearson *r* bivariate correlation analysis performed on all self and external TPACK scores for both lesson plans revealed the following results:
1. moderate positive correlation between self and external TPACK scores for LP1 ($p < 0.001$, $r = .387$, $N = 148$)
2. no correlation between self and external TPACK scores for LP2
3. moderate positive correlations between self TPACK scores for LP1 and LP2 ($p < 0.001$, $r = .352$, $N = 148$)
4. moderate positive correlations between external TPACK scores for LP1 and LP2 ($p < 0.01$, $r = .288$, $N = 150$)

A series of analyses were performed in order to understand and interpret the relationship between self and external TPACK scores. The mean differences between self and external scores were very close to zero, which is consistent with the fact that there were no significant differences between these scores. The range of differences became larger with LP2 (see Table 2).

Table 2. Descriptive statistics for the difference between self and external TPACK scores on both lesson plans.

Difference	N	Range	Minimum	Maximum	Mean	SD
(Self-external) LP1	148	4.50	-2.50	2.00	-.020	.87
(Self-external) LP2	148	6.50	-3.50	3.00	.111	1.00

These descriptives suggest that there were three groups of participants for each lesson plan:

1. Participants whose self-scores were within one standard deviation from the external scores (close-estimators)
2. Participants whose self-scores were higher the external scores by more than one standard deviation (over-estimators)
3. Participants whose self-scores were lower than the external scores by more than one standard deviation (under-estimators).

As expected, paired samples t-test indicated a significant difference between self and external scores for over and under estimators for both lesson plans (see Table 3). For close-estimators there were no significant differences between self and external scores for LP1. Even though there was a significant difference between self and external scores for LP2, the effect size was small, $d = 0.14$. According to Cohen (1988), significant differences with effect size less than 0.2 are not meaningful.

Table 3. Descriptive statistics and results of paired samples t-test for self and external TPACK scores for each of the three groups

Group	Lesson Plan 1					Lesson Plan 2				
	Mean	SD	N	t	Sig (2-tailed)	Mean	SD	N	t	Sig (2-tailed)
Close estimators			90	.293	$p>.05$			95	2.222	$p<.05$
Self	2.14	.76				2.86	.58			
External	2.13	.69				2.78	.56			
Over estimators			28	20.463	$p<.001$			34	16.468	$p<.001$
Self	2.84	.56				3.41	.51			
External	1.61	.60				2.15	.62			
Under estimators			30	-15.661	$p<.001$			19	-9.458	$p<.001$
Self	1.45	.65				1.42	.87			
External	2.73	.63				3.24	.73			

In order to analyze patterns and relationships between self and external TPACK scores, participants were divided according to the three groups and Pearson r correlation analysis was performed for each group for each lesson (see Table 4).

Table 4. Results of correlational analysis of self and external TPACK scores for three groups of participants (close, over and under estimators)

Group	Lesson Plan 1						Lesson Plan 2					
	Mean	SD	N	r	R^2	Sig (2-tailed)	Mean	SD	N	r	R^2	Sig (2-tailed)
Close estimators			90	.881	.776	$p<.001$			95	.792	.627	$p<.001$
Self	2.14	0.76					2.86	0.58				
External	2.13	0.69					2.78	0.56				
Over estimators			28	.851	.724	$p<.001$			34	.705	.497	$p<.001$
Self	2.84	.56					3.41	.51				
External	1.61	.60					2.15	.62				

Under estimators			30	.752	.566	p<.001		19	.466	.217	p<.05
Self	1.45	.65					1.42	.87			
External	2.73	.63					3.24	.73			

Strong positive correlations between self and external TPACK scores were found for each group except for the under-estimators group on LP2 that had a moderate positive correlation. The amount of shared variance between self and external scores decreased from 77.6% on lesson plan 1 to 62.7% on lesson plan 2 for close estimators; from 72.4% on lesson plan 1 to 70.5% on lesson plan 2 for over-estimators; and from 56.6% on lesson plan 1 to 21.7% on lesson plan 2 for under-estimators.

Analysis of scatter plots for each group (see Figures 1 and 2) also revealed that for both lesson plans participants scored at all TPACK levels from *Recognizing* (1/5) to *Exploring* (4/5) in close-estimators and under-estimators. However, in over-estimators the external scores appeared only in the lower levels of TPACK, i.e., *Recognizing* (1/5) and *Accepting* (2/5) for LP1, and *Recognizing* (1/5), *Accepting* (2/5), and *Adapting* (3/5) for LP2.

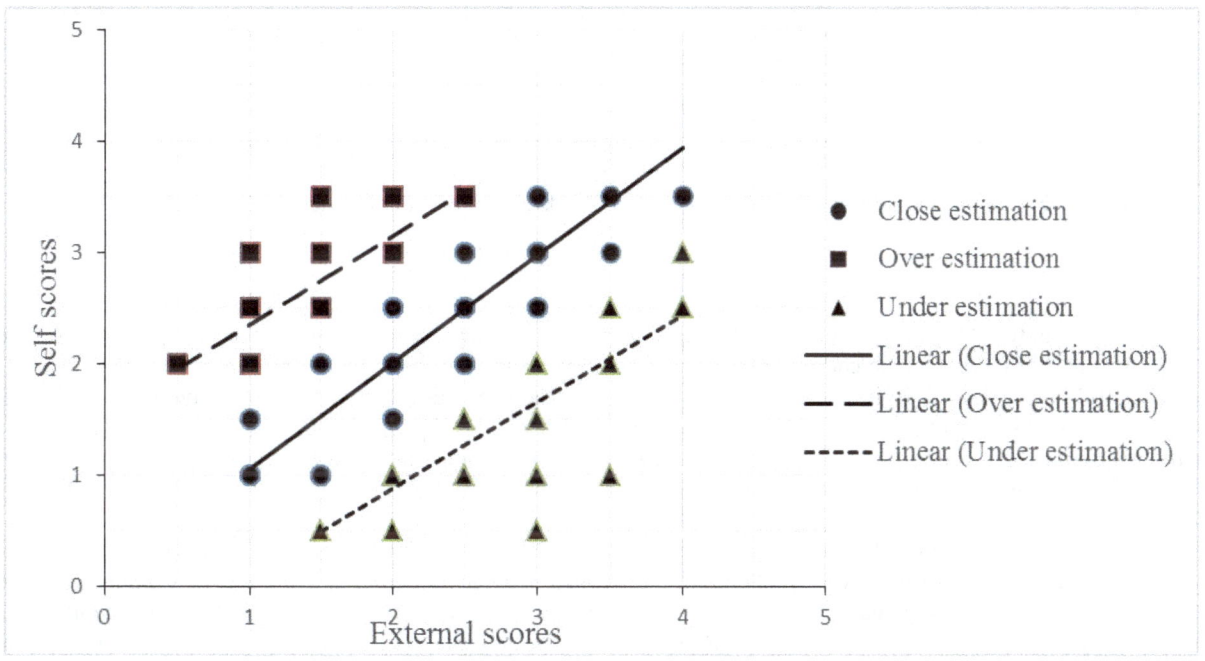

Figure 1. Correlations between self and external TPACK scores for the first lesson plan (LP1)

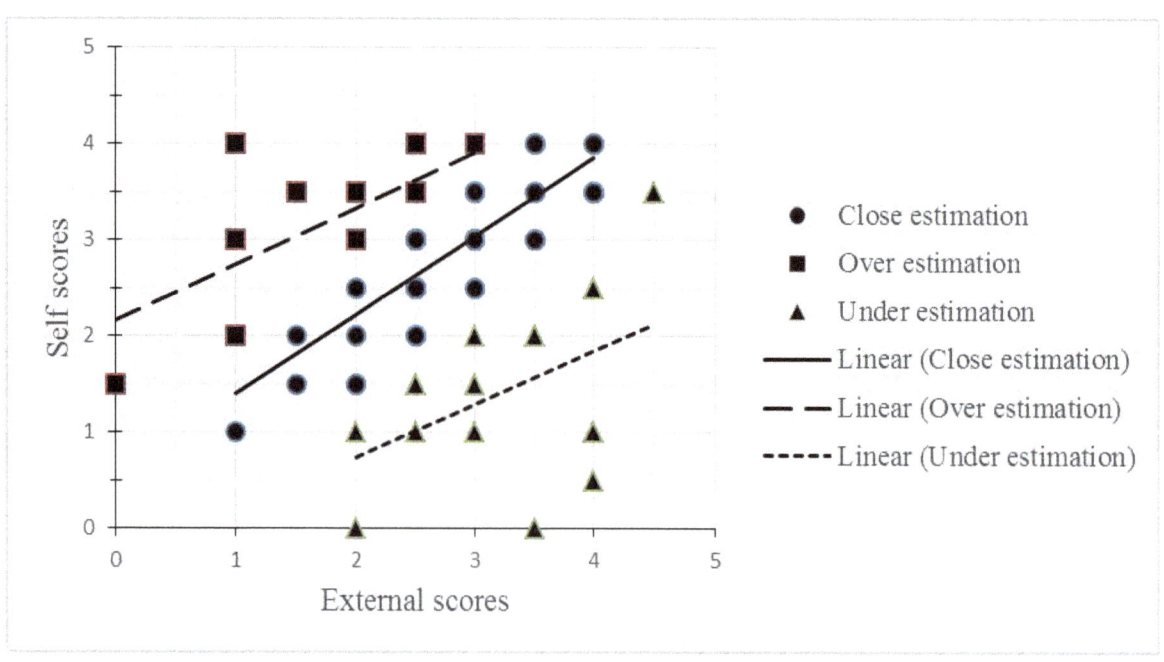

Figure 2. Correlations between self and external TPACK scores for the second lesson plan (LP2)

Discussion

The study collected and compared two different types of data produced by pre-service special education teachers as part of their graduate course on integrating technology into teaching mathematics and science to students with disabilities. These data included lesson plans that participants developed; taught in the field; and self-reflections that they wrote about these lesson plans and their teaching. The significance of this study was that the same instrument was used to assess participants' TPACK from both data sets and to compare external- and self-scores. This methodology allowed for meaningful examination of the relationship between external and self TPACK scores.

This study showed that a) both, self and external TPACK scores significantly improved from the first to the second lesson plan, and b) there was no significant difference between external and self TPACK scores for each lesson plan. The significant gains in external TPACK scores have been reported in a previous study by Lyublinskaya & Tournaki (2014). However, the findings about self TPACK scores have not been reported in the literature up to date therefore, the rest of the analysis focused on understanding and interpreting the relationship between external and self TPACK scores.

There was no significant difference between self and external TPACK scores on both lesson plans for the whole group. However, analysis of differences between self and external scores revealed that about 40% of participants on LP1 and about 35% on LP2 self-scored more than one standard deviation over or under the external score. Based on these results, we divided all participants into three groups in order to examine relationships between self and external scores in each group: close-estimators (self and external scores are within one standard deviation), over-estimators (self scores are higher than external by more than a standard deviation), and under-estimators (self scores are lower than external by more than a standard deviation). Descriptive statistics indicated that the majority of the participants (90/148 on LP1 and 95/148 on LP2) had very close self and external scores; that explains the fact that for the close-estimators there was no significant difference between self and external scores for LP1; while the significant difference in LP2 has such small effect size that it is not meaningful (Cohen, 1988). So the overall findings are indicative of the fact that the majority of participants were realistic in their perceptions of TPACK since their self-scores did not differ significantly from the external scores. Correlational analysis conducted on self and external scores of TPACK further confirmed this finding since there was a strong positive correlation between the two variables. Analysis of shared variance also indicated that the large part of the variability in self-scores can be explained by the variability in external scores for this group (77.6% on lesson plan 1 and 62.7% on lesson plan 2).

On the other hand, over-estimators' (28/148 on LP1 and 34/148 onLP2) and under-estimators' (30/148 on LP1 and 19/148 on LP2) self and external scores were significantly different with large effect sizes, which supported the procedure for selecting the groups. Further, strong to moderate positive correlations between self and external TPACK scores for over- and under-estimators on both lesson plans indicate consistency in pre-service teachers' self-scores to be higher or lower than external scores for all levels of TPACK. Analysis of shared variance for over-estimators showed results similar to close estimators: the large part of the variability in self-scores can be explained by the variability in external scores (72.4% on lesson plan 1 and 70.5% on lesson plan 2). However, for under-estimators, the shared variance between the self and external scores was significantly smaller than for the other two groups, leaving 43.4% of variability on lesson plan 1 and 78.3% of variability on lesson plan 2 still to be accounted for by other variables. These findings along with analysis of trends shown on scatter plots leads to the conclusion that these two groups exhibit different patterns .

Based on external scores, the highest level of TPACK achieved by over-estimators on LP1 was that of *Accepting*(2/5). The over-estimators at *Recognizing*(1/5) level had self-scores about two levels higher, while those at *Accepting*(2/5) level had self-scores only about one level higher. This trend shows that the difference between self and external scores for over-estimators is decreasing as their TPACK level increases. Similar patterns can be seen when comparing self and external scores for over-estimators on LP2. Based on external scores the highest level of TPACK for this group was that of *Adapting*(3/5). The self-scores for the pre-service teachers at *Recognizing*(1/5) level of TPACK were about two levels higher, while for those at *Accepting*(2/5) and *Adapting*(3/5) levels, the self-scores were only about one level higher than external. This trend could possibly explain why there were no high levels of TPACK in the over-estimation group: as external TPACK level increases, the difference between self and external scores decreases, so we can speculate that at *Exploring* (4/5) level the difference would be insignificant and therefore the pre-service teachers with higher levels of TPACK would be in the close-estimators group. In other words as teachers become more knowledgeable they also become more realistic about what they know which can be interpreted as gaining confidence; while the ones that are less knowledgeable believe they know more than they do – it is as though their perceived level of confidence does not correspond with reality. Empirical research has demonstrated that lack of teacher confidence is a major impediment to teaching and that content knowledge impacts the perceived confidence of teachers (Garbett, 2003; Kind, 2009; Murphy, Neil, & Beggs, 2007; Rivera, Manning, & Krupp, 2013). Finally, the size of the over-estimators group did not change from LP1 to LP2, which represents possibly the tendency in pre-service teachers to think higher of their teaching than external measurement suggests.The under-estimators group, however, had different trends. Based on external scores, the levels ranged from *Recognizing*(1/5) to *Exploring*(4/5) on LP1 and from *Accepting*(2/5) to *Exploring*(4/5) on LP2. At the lower levels of TPACK (*Recognizing* and *Adapting*) the pre-service teachers underestimated their levels by about one level. However, at higher levels of TPACK (*Adapting* and *Exploring*) the difference between external and self-scores increased to about two levels. It seems that as pre-service teachers in this group gained higher levels of TPACK, they became less confident about their level of knowledge on effective use of technology. Even though this group reduced its size to almost half from LP1 to LP2, about 13% of the sample presented this lack of self-confidence and tendency to over-criticize and under-evaluate the quality of their own teaching. According to Ertmer et al. (2012) lack of confidence could negatively impact technology integration. Our findings however, do not confirm the this suggestion since in this small sub-group the participants demonstrated high TPACK, therefore ability to integrate technology but low belief in possessing TPACK, therefore possibly low confidence. Future studies might want to actually assess psychological constructs of over and under estimators e.g., through surveys of self-confidence or self-efficacy in order to explore possible underlying factors that lead to false perceptions of competence.

The results of this study indicate that completion of an TPACK-based pedagogy course that provides an opportunity for pre-service teachers to develop, teach and reflect on their technology-infused lessons leads not only to significant gains in their TPACK, but also to development of a realistic view of their ability to effectively integrate technology. This is indicated by the fact that for the majority of pre-service teachers (about 62%) there is no significant difference between external and self-scores. Further, results show that the difference between self and external scores for over-estimators is decreasing as their TPACK level increases. That is, as pre-service teachers are gaining more TPACK they become more realistic in their self-reflections. On the other hand and where teacher educators need to be more attentive, there is a small group of under-estimators for whom the difference between self and external scores is increasing as their TPACK level increases. In this group as pre-service teachers gained higher levels of TPACK, they became less realistic about their ability of effective use of technology. The small number of participants (about 13%) that were left in this group at the end of the study were the ones that probably lacked self-confidence and had a tendency to over-criticize and under-evaluate the quality of own teaching. Teacher educators should be aware of such a minority in their students and attempt to support them in evaluating themselves realistically.

References

Archambault, L., & Crippen, K. (2009). Examining TPACK among K-12 online distance educators in the United States *Contemporary Issues in Technology and Teacher Education, 9*, 71-88.

Britten, J. S., & Cassady, J. C. (2005). The Technology Integration Assessment Instrument: Understanding planned use of technology by classroom teachers. *Computers in the Schools, 22*, 49-61.

Cohen, J. (1988). *Statistical Power Analysis for the Behavioral Sciences*, 2nd ed. Hillsdale, NJ: Erlbaum.

Ertmer, P. A., Ottenbreit-Leftwich, A. T., Salik, O., Sendurur, E., & Sendurur, P. (2012). Teacher beliefs and technology integration practices: A critical relationship. *Computers in Education, 59*(2), 423-435.

Garbett, D. (2003). Science education in early childhood teacher education: Putting forward a case to enhance student teachers' confidence and competence. *Research in Science Education, 33*(4), 467-481.

Goldenberg, P. (2000). Thinking (and talking) about technology in math classrooms. In *Issues in Mathematics Education*. Education Development Center, Inc. Retrieved from: http://www2.edc.org/mcc/pdf/iss_tech.pdf.

Groth, R. E., Spickler, D., Bergner, J., & Bardzell, M. (2009). A qualitative approach to assessing Technological, Pedagogical Content Knowledge. *Contemporary Issues in Technology and Teacher Education, 9*(4), 392-411.

Harris, J., Grandgenett, N., & Hofer, M. (2010). Testing a TPACK-based technology integration assessment rubric. In D. Gibson & B. Dodge (Eds.), *Proceedings of Society for Information Technology & Teacher Education International Conference 2010* (pp. 3833-3840). Chesapeake, VA: AACE.

Kind, V. (2009). A conflict in your head: An exploration of trainee science teachers' subject matter knowledge development and its impact on teacher self-confidence. *International Journal of Science Education, 31*(11), 1529-1562.

Koehler, M., Mishra, P., & Yahya, K. (2007). Tracing the development of teacher knowledge in a design seminar: Integrating content, pedagogy and technology. *Computers and Education, 49*(3), 740-762.

Lawless, K. A., & Pellegrino, J. W. (2007). Professional development in integrating technology into teaching and learning: Knowns, unknowns, and ways to pursue better questions and answers. *Review of Educational Research, 77*(4), 575-614.

Lee, M. H., & Tsai, C. C. (2010). Exploring teachers' perceived self-efficacy and technological pedagogical content knowledge with respect to educational use of the World Wide Web. *Instructional Science, 38*(1), 1–21

Lyublinskaya, I., & Tournaki, N. (2012). The effects of teacher content authoring on TPACK and on student achievement in algebra: Research on institution with the TI-Nspire handheld. In R. N. Ronau, C. R. Rakes, & M. L. Niess (Eds.), *Educational Technology, Teacher Knowledge, and Classroom Impact: A Research Handbook on Frameworks and Approaches* (295-322). Hershey, PA: IGI Global.

Lyublinskaya, I., Tournaki, N. (2014). A Study of special education teachers' TPACK development in mathematics and science through assessment of lesson plans. *Journal of Technology and Teacher Education, 22*(4), 449-470.

Mishra, P. & Koehler, M. J. (2006). Technological, pedagogical content knowledge: A framework for teacher knowledge. *Teachers College Record, 108*(6), 1017-1054.

Murphy, C., Neil, P., & Beggs, J. (2007). Primary science teacher confidence revisited: Ten years on. *Educational Research, 49*(4), 415-430.

Niess, M. L., Ronau, R. N., Shafer, K. G., Driskell, S. O., Harper, S. R., Johnston, C., Browning, C., Özgün-Koca, S. A., & Kersaint, G. (2009). Mathematics teacher TPACK standards and development model. *Contemporary Issues in Technology and Teacher Education, 9*(1), 4-24.

Niess, M. L. (2011). Investigating TPACK: Knowledge growth in teaching with technology. *Journal of Educational Computing Research, 44*(3), 299-317.

Rivera, M. A. J., Manning, M. M., Krupp, D. A. (2013). A unique marine and environmental science program for high school teachers in Hawai'i: Professional development, teacher confidence, and lessons learned. *International Journal of Environmental Science Education, 8*(2), 217-239.

Schmidt, D. A., Baran, E., Thompson, A. D., Mishra, P., Koehler, M. J., & Shin, T. S. (2009). Technological pedagogical content knowledge (TPCK): The development and validation of an assessment instrument for preservice teachers. *Journal of Research on Technology in Education, 42*(2), 83-87.

Tournaki, N. & Lyublinskaya, I. (2014). Preparing special education teachers for teaching mathematics and science with technology by integrating the TPACK framework into the curriculum: A study of teachers' perceptions. *Journal of Technology and Teacher Education, 22*(2), 243-259.

TPACK for Teaching Mathematics and Science and Differentiation of Instruction: Case Study with Pre-service Special Educators.

Nelly Tournaki
College of Staten Island – The City University of New York, USA
nelly.tournaki@csi.cuny.edu

Irina Lyublinskaya
College of Staten Island – The City University of New York, USA
inina.lyublinskaya@csi.cuny.edu

Abstract: In this paper, we argue that the Technological Pedagogical Content Knowledge framework (TPACK, Mishra & Koehler, 2006) can be used to develop excellence in teaching in a variety of classrooms that include differentiation of instruction. In order to examine how the quality of differentiation changes as TPACK improves, 150 lesson plans of pre-service special educators were assessed using the TPACK Levels Rubric (Lyublinskaya & Tournaki, 2012). Two lesson plans were randomly selected at each level of TPACK (with total of eight) and examined for evidence of differentiation of instruction. The study describes how strategies used for differentiation parallel the levels of TPACK that were achieved by each participant.

Purpose

The academic performance of students with disabilities is of concern to policy makers and educators since they exhibit poorer academic performance than their peers without disabilities (Wei, 2012). Therefore, teacher education programs need to be preparing effective special educators who will increase the achievement of their students. We argue that the TPACK framework (TPACK, Mishra & Koehler, 2006) can be used to develop excellence in teaching that includes differentiation of instruction. This framework claims that excellent teaching depends on teachers' technological, pedagogical and content knowledge. The participants in this case study were several pre-service teachers taking a graduate course on integrating instructional/innovative technology into mathematics and science. The purpose of the study was to determine the participants' level of TPACK then, to examine the quality of differentiation of instruction the participants used within the different levels of TPACK and finally to analyze the relationship between quality of differentiation and participants' TPACK level assessed through their lesson plans.

Theoretical Framework

TPACK describes the teacher knowledge needed for teaching with technology in various content areas, grade levels and classroom settings. TPACK identifies knowledge that relies on the interconnection and intersection of content, pedagogy, and technology (Mishra & Koehler, 2006). Lately, the TPACK framework has influenced professionals to re-structure teacher preparation programs (Chai, Koh, & Tsai, 2010; Niess, 2005, 2007). Such restructuring has led to some positive effects on preparation of general educators (Angeli & Valanides, 2009). However, very few studies address TPACK development of pre-service special education teachers. Marino, Sameshima, and Beecher (2009) offer an enhanced version of TPACK model that includes assistive technology in the technology domain of teacher knowledge. Benton-Borghi (2013) challenges teacher educators to further develop and improve TPACK by infusing UDL model. While both these models provide valuable suggestions for integrating TPACK into teacher education programs, they need authentic implementations in order to evaluate the effects of these models on pre-service teachers' knowledge for technology integration. To date only one TPACK-related research project has produced empirical results in relation to programs preparing special educators (Lyublinskaya & Tournaki, 2014; Tournaki & Lyublinskaya, 2014). This project assessed pre-service special education teachers' TPACK development through the five progressive levels and the four components identified by Niess in her

TPACK Development model. (Niess et al., 2009; Niess, 2011). The TPACK Levels Rubric (Lyublinskaya & Tournaki, 2012) used to assess teachers' TPACK level is described in the Instruments section below. The results of this research project indicated that participants' TPACK scores assessed through their lesson plans that were completed at the beginning and at the end of the semester, significantly increased. The purpose of the present case study was to examine lesson plans at different levels of TPACK and explore whether high levels of TPACK are associated with skillful differentiation of instruction.

Differentiated instruction "with the use of technology offers the opportunity for teachers to engage students in different modalities, while also varying the rate of instruction, complexity levels, and teaching strategies to engage and challenge students" (Stanford, Crowe, & Flice, 2010, p.1). So, differentiated instruction focuses on teaching strategies that give diverse students multiple options for taking in and processing information, making sense of ideas, and expressing learning (Tomlinson, 1999); and technology tools support such instruction since they offer personalized learning environments. Therefore, teachers with high levels of TPACK and ability to differentiate are what we look for in the 21st century classroom.

Methods

Study Context

The data were collected in a New York City public college over a period of four consecutive semesters in a required graduate pedagogy course designed to prepare pre-service special educators integrate technology into teaching mathematics and science to students with disabilities. The TPACK framework was used as the organizing framework for developing the course content and activities. The model of TPACK inherently addresses the needs of all students. Therefore, the focus of the course was not on the technology per se but rather on how the technology should be used to achieve subject-specific instructional goals and objectives and to meet the needs of all students, including those with disabilities. The course sequence included: 1) introduction to the theoretical aspects of technology integration into teaching and learning mathematics and science in the special education classroom; 2) exposure to different roles of technology, such as research and communication, visualization, problem solving, inquiry-based learning, technology for assessment, etc. that included hands-on lab experience with each technology tool followed by analysis of adaptations necessary to incorporate these activities in a special education classroom; and 3) evaluation and reflection on teachers' own professional practice. Throughout the course, discussions addressed adapting instruction with technology for students with disabilities, differentiated instruction, and assessment with technology.

Participants

A total of 150 pre-service teachers enrolled in the eight sections of the course agreed to participate in the study. The course was a requirement in the Master's program in Special Education. The participants are referred to as pre-service teachers because they were enrolled in an initial certification program for special education; however they have completed initial certification in general education at the undergraduate level. Males comprised 26% of the sample, females 74%. Sixty five percent were between 23 and 26 years old, 7% between 18 and 22, 17% between 26 and 32, and 11% were over 33. The participants completed a total of 20 hours of fieldwork and taught their two lessons in self-contained, Integrated Collaborative Teaching (ICT) or general education/inclusive classroom with minimum four students with IEPs. In all environments differentiation of instruction was necessary.

Description of Instrument

The TPACK Levels Rubric (Lyublinskaya & Tournaki, 2012), was used to assess lesson plans developed by the pre-service teachers. The structure of the rubric is based on the TPACK framework for assessing the development of teachers' technology integration across five progressive levels [*Recognizing* (1), *Accepting* (2), *Adapting* (3), *Exploring* (4), *and Advancing* (5)] in each of the four components of TPACK as identified by Niess (2011): 1) An overarching conception about the purposes for incorporating technology. 2) Knowledge of students' understanding, thinking, and learning with technology. 3) Knowledge of curriculum and curricular materials that integrate technology, and 4) Knowledge of instructional strategies and representations for teaching and learning with technologies.

All four components of TPACK fit the principles of effective differentiation of instruction, which imply that the teacher varies curricular content, the learning environment, learning activities, and products based on student readiness, interest or learning profile (Tomlinson, 1995).

The rubric was tested for reliability and validity with in-service mathematics teachers using TI-Nspire technology (Lyublinskaya & Tournaki, 2012). Factor Analysis using varimax rotation with Kaiser normalization confirmed construct validity of the rubric when applied to pre-service special educators (Lyublinskaya & Tournaki, 2014).

Data Analysis and Results

In this study the TPACK scores on the final lesson plan completed at the end of the semester were analyzed to determine the frequencies of scores within each level of TPACK. Scores ranged from 0 to 4.5, with 6% at *Recognizing* (1/5), the lower level; 53% at *Accepting* (2/5) level; 33% at *Adapting* (3/5) level; and 8% at *Exploring* level (4/5). (See Figure 1).

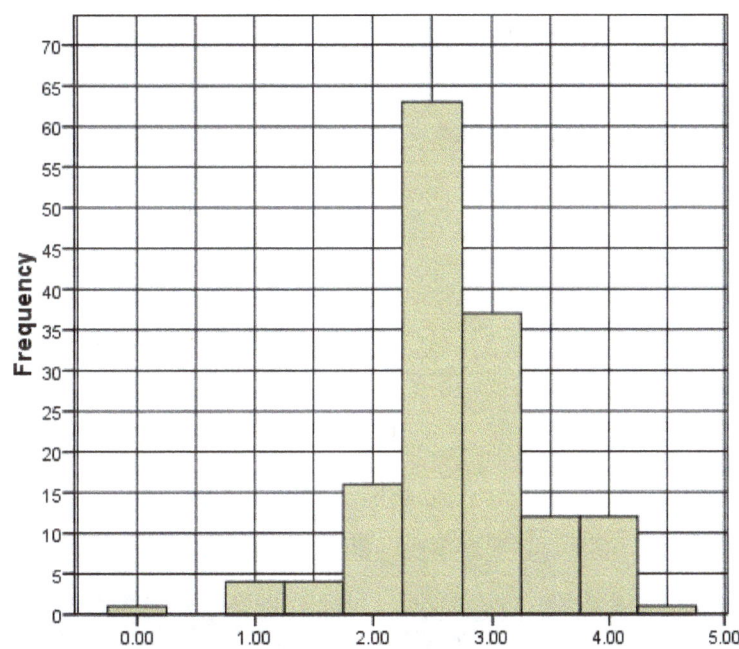

Figure 1. Distribution of frequencies of total TPACK scores on the final lesson plan.

To explore whether level of TPACK was associated with the use of strategies for differentiation of instruction, we divided the set of final lesson plans by the four levels of TPACK development and randomly selected two lesson plans from each level. In each lesson the quality of differentiated instruction, not including use of assistive technology, was then examined and discussed. The names used below are pseudonyms.

Case 1. Catherine - TPACK score 1/5. *Recognizing* level.

Catherine developed a 2nd grade mathematics lesson to teach students the value of coins and how to add money. In her lesson plan she included the lecture with all new information at the beginning of the lesson. After the lecture, she planned to have each pair of students on a computer play an on-line game that consisted of the following tasks: 1) matching coin values to the pictures, 2) adding coin values and checking their answers, 3) subtracting coin values and checking their answers. The game was a form of on-line worksheet with answers given immediately. The only differentiation provided by the teacher in this lesson was heterogeneous pairing of students with the intent that general education students will be helping students with disabilities during the practice. However, during the teaching of the lesson stronger students did all the work on computers, thus leaving students with disabilities without any practice.

Case 2. Gabrielle - TPACK score 1.5/5. *Recognizing* level.

Gabrielle developed a mathematics lesson for a 1st grade ICT classroom. The topic was the comparison of two-digit numbers. The lesson plan started with a lecture that presented facts and algorithms, as well as a song for memorization of comparison signs. The teacher developed two Smart Board interactive activities as part of the lecture and planned to call up one or two students to do the activities on the board. Technology was planned to be used mostly by the teacher for demonstration purposes and not by the students. There was no differentiation in this lesson, as the instruction was directed to the whole class.

Case 3. Nicole - TPACK score 2/5. *Accepting* level.

Nicole prepared and taught a 1st grade science lesson about the life cycle of a frog. She developed a multimedia tutorial using Microsoft Power Point software, which had non-linear structure, navigation, and self-assessment with immediate feedback (see Figure 2). This tutorial was intended to differentiate instruction by allowing students with disabilities to develop understanding of the topic on their own terms. However, the structure of the lesson and the quality of the content in the tutorial did not allow for full benefit of the technology-based activity. She started the lesson with a lecture. The information in the tutorial was a repetition of the lecture presented in a simplistic, non-interesting way, so the students became bored and distracted. The questions in the self-assessment section were focused on rote recall and memorization of facts and did not engage students either.

Figure 2. Sample slides of Nicole's multimedia tutorial demonstrating navigation and self-assessment features.

Case 4. Nikki – TPACK score of 2.5/5. *Accepting* level

Nikki developed a 1st grade lesson about states of matter for a self-contained classroom. She planned to start her lesson with assessment of prior knowledge that students had. The technology-based activity immediately followed and involved each student watching on-line video about the topic on their own computers and then completing a sorting activity in Smart Notebook software. She planned to conclude the lesson by providing all information to the students.

Case 5. Colleen - TPACK score 3/5. *Adapting* Level.

At *Adapting* level pre-service teachers adapt technology to replace traditional approaches. Colleen planned a 1st grade lesson about true and false mathematics statements. The lesson started with whole class discussion about the meaning of words "true" and "false", followed by teacher's modeling the mathematics statements using virtual manipulatives on the Smart Board. Students then individually completed an interactive activity in Smart Notebook that involved modeling several given mathematics statements, sorting mathematics statements, and answering questions in order to develop rules that explain when the statement is true or false. For students with Learning Disabilities, she planned to have calculators to figure out whether or not the mathematics facts were true or false. Colleen differentiated instruction based on specific needs of her students, and chose different strategies for students with different needs. However, the actual activities just use technology to replace traditional non-technology tasks.

Case 6. Danielle – TPACK score of 3/5. *Adapting* Level

In her 5th grade science lesson, Danielle asked her students to explore minerals in small groups. The whole class then discussed the general properties of the minerals. The technology-based activity involved pairs of students researching the internet about a given mineral and creating a blog entry with their findings. At the end of the lesson, the whole class read the blog created by each pair of students. In order to differentiate instruction, Danielle modified the activity for her students with Autism and ADHD by reducing the number of questions they had to answer for the blog. Again, this is an example of using technology to replace traditional non-technology tasks. Internet research replaced reading printed materials to gather information. Blog replaced poster presentations of findings.

Case 7. Ashley - TPACK score of 4/5. *Exploring* Level.

Exploring was the highest level achieved by some pre-service teachers. Ashley developed her lesson for a 4th/5th grade self-contained classroom to address the topic of polygons and their properties. Her lesson started with whole class discussion about properties of triangles, with the teacher modeling construction and dynamic exploration of triangles on the Smart Board using Geometer's Sketchpad software. Students then were placed in homogeneous pairs to construct and explore other polygons. Tasks and assessment were modified so low functioning students were only assigned to work with quadrilaterals, while higher functioning students worked with quadrilaterals and pentagons. The Geometer's Sketchpad software allowed students to construct the polygon, to move the vertices around to establish understanding of when the shape is a given polygon and when it is not. The choice of technology supported non-verbal visual learners. These students were able to observe changes in the shapes as they manipulated them on the computer screen.

Case 8. Erin - TPACK score of 4/5. *Exploring* Level.

Erin developed her lesson for a 1st grade self-contained classroom with six students classified with low functioning Autism. The topic was addition within 20. Erin developed an interactive Excel activity that included visual and numerical exploration of addition using spinners. This exploration helped students develop strategies for addition on their own (see Figure 3). The teacher coordinated the colors in numerical and graphical representations to help students develop understanding and strategies for addition. The second part of the activity included practice where students could apply the strategies they developed to complete given addition sentences. As they provided the answers, they received immediate feedback. The lesson plan involved students working in pairs with the Excel activity first and then presentation of the strategies to the whole class. Her differentiation strategies were strongly related to student needs.

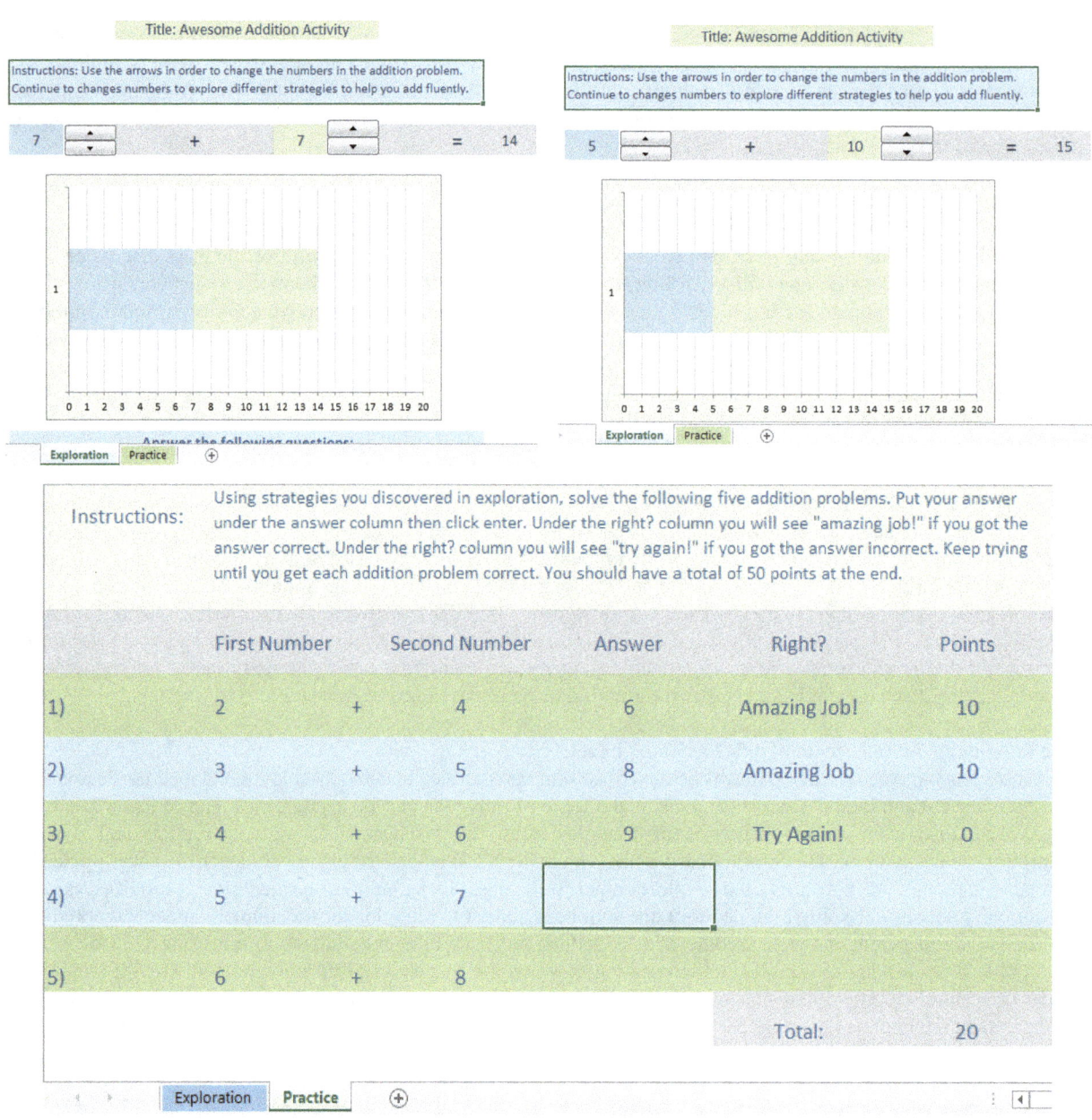

Figure 3. Erin's interactive Excel activity on addition

Discussion

The goal of this study was to examine how the quality of differentiation changes as TPACK improves. To achieve that goal we first, examined lesson plans of 150 pre-service special educators' and assessed their TPACK through the TPACK Levels Rubric (Lyublinskaya & Tournaki, 2012). Then, we randomly selected two lesson plans at each level of TPACK (with total of eight) and we looked at evidence of differentiation of instruction within these lesson plans and described how strategies used for differentiation parallel the levels of TPACK that were achieved by each participant. More specifically, the randomly selected cases illustrated that at the lowest level of TPACK (*Recognizing*) differentiation was either absent or limited and ineffective. Moving into the *Accepting* level of TPACK, we observed that the pre-service teachers planned to differentiate instruction by using an independent technology-based activity for students; however, they included direct instruction. We also noted that at this level of

TPACK pre-service teachers used the same differentiation strategies for all their students, independent of their specific disabilities. As TPACK scores improve, differentiation strategies also become more sophisticated; so at the *Adapting* level of TPACK the selected participants differentiated instruction in order to meet specific needs of their students e.g., provided accommodations such as calculators, for students with Learning Disabilities, or modifications such as reduced number of problems, for students with Autism. At the highest level of TPACK achieved by the selected participants of the study, that *Exploring*, the use of technology was quite sophisticated. One of pre-service teachers used dynamic geometry software such as Geometer's Sketchpad software in combination with Smart Board and another one developed original interactive Excel activity, both allowing for open-ended investigations. With such technology, adaptations can more easily address each student's needs – students are able to explore based on the level they are at and feedback can easily be individualized. We concluded that the analysis of the eight cases suggests that as teachers' TPACK scores increase (measured by TPACK Levels Rubric) so does the quality of their differentiation (based on qualitative analysis of lesson plans). In fact, the authors are currently working on the construction of a rubric that would measure, in a quantitative way, levels of teachers' differentiation. This way larger numbers of cases can be scored for level of differentiation which will then be related to levels of TPACK; through this process generalizable conclusions can be drawn.

Significance of the Study

While most studies in the field of TPACK deal with general educators, this study added to the very limited body of empirical studies (Lyublinskaya & Tournaki, 2014; Tournaki & Lyublinskaya, 2014) of TPACK development among special education pre-service teachers. With the rapid growth of technology, and the increasing number of students qualifying for special education services (Dillon, 2007; Federal Education Budget Project, 2009), it is challenging for special educators to gain and maintain the knowledge necessary for excellent teaching. Researchers might be able to demonstrate such proficiency of special educators through a strong correlation between teachers TPACK level and their ability to differentiate instruction – our study offered an initial exploration in this area.

Furthermore, the present study assessed pre-service special educators' TPACK through teaching artifacts, namely lesson plans. Such artifacts are considered more objective measures of TPACK than surveys given that surveys just reflect the opinions of the participants. It has been established that teachers' interactions with students may not be congruent with their responses to the surveys (Fang, 1996; Lyublinskaya & Tournaki, 2014).

Finally, equity and inclusivity cannot be achieved without the multimodal affordances that technologies provide through access, scaffolding, remediation, acceleration, and differentiation. Benton-Borghi and Chang (2010, 2012) suggested the lack of access to the curriculum is the hidden curriculum of inequity. One way to ensure that all students have access to the curriculum is through differentiation of instruction. To that extent this study is significant because it examined the use of differentiation of instruction in the lesson plans provided by the pre-service teachers and found that TPACK level could be an indicator of quality of differentiation of instruction. Therefore, in classrooms staffed with teachers with high TPACK and ability to differentiate, students will be offered with digital opportunities for representation and manipulation of content, expression of understanding and assessment of learning as well as engagement with content in a transformative way. In fact, effective integration of technology ends up simplifying and enhancing differentiation of instruction so the teachers can meet the ever increasing diversity of today's classroom (Stanford, Crowe, & Flice, 2010).

Future studies need to further examine this relationship between TPACK and differentiation levels. This study began the discussion by analyzing specific cases and indicating a pattern. To this date there are no studies that assess differentiation of instruction quantitatively – an assessment of such a complex process will prove invaluable since it will lead to generalizable findings. Finally, this type of study needs to be expanded to general education teachers who at this point also need to be differentiating instruction so that they can teach all the students in their classrooms.

References

Angeli, C. & Valanides, N. (2009). Epistemological and methodological issues for the conceptualization, development, and assessment of ICT-TPACK: Advances in technological pedagogical content knowledge (TPACK). *Computers & Education, 52*(1), 154–168.

Benton-Borghi, B. H. (2013). A universally designed for learning (UDL) infused technological pedagogical content knowledge (TPACK) practitioners' model essential for teacher preparation in the 21st century. *Journal of Educational Computing Research, 48*(2), 245-265.

Benton-Borghi, B. H. & Chang, Y. (2010, February). *Achieving inclusivity and equity for diverse student populations: Increasing teacher efficacy to teach every student using universal design for learning principles.* Paper presented at the 62nd Annual Conference of the American Association of Colleges for Teacher Education (AACTE), Atlanta, GA.

Benton-Borghi, B. H., & Chang, Y. (2012). Critical examination of candidates' diversity competence: Rigorous and systematic assessment of candidates' efficacy to teach diverse student populations. *The Teacher Educator, 47*(1), 29-44.

Chai, C. S., Koh, J. H. L., & Tsai, C.C. (2010). Facilitating preservice teachers' development of technological, pedagogical, and content knowledge (TPACK). *Educational Technology & Society, 13*(4), 63-73.

Dillon, E. (2007, July 17). Labeled: The students behind NCLB's "disabilities" designation. *Education sector.* Retrieved from http://www.educationsector.org/analysis/analysis show. htm?doc id=509392

Fang, Z. (1996). A review of research on teacher beliefs and practices. *Educational Research, 38*(1), 47-65.

Federal Education Budget Project. (2009). *Individuals with Disabilities Education Act—Cost impact on local school districts.* Retrieved from http://febp.newamerica.net/backgroundanalysis/individuals-disabilities-education-act-cost-impact-local-school-districts

Lyublinskaya, I. & Tournaki, E. (2012). The Effects of teacher content authoring on TPACK and on student achievement in algebra: Research on instruction with the TI-Nspire handheld. In R. Ronau, C. Rakes, & M. Niess (Eds.), *Educational Technology, Teacher Knowledge, and Classroom Impact: A Research Handbook on Frameworks and Approaches.* (pp. 295-322) Hershey, PA: IGI Global.

Lyublinskaya, I. & Tournaki, N. (2014). A Study of special education teachers' TPACK development in mathematics and science through assessment of lesson plans. *Journal of Technology and Teacher Education, 22(4),* 449-470

Marino, M. T., Sameshima, P., & Beecher, C. C. (2009). Enhancing TPACK with assistive technology: Promoting inclusive practices in preservice teacher education. *Contemporary Issues in Technology and Teacher Education, 9*(2), 186-207.

Mishra, P. & Koehler, M. J. (2006). Technological, pedagogical content knowledge: A framework for teacher knowledge. *Teachers College Record, 108*(6), 1017-1054.

Niess, M. L. (2005). Preparing teachers to teach science and mathematics with technology: Developing a technology pedagogical content knowledge. *Teaching and Teacher Education, 21*(5), 509-523.

Niess, M. L. (2007). Developing teacher's TPCK for teaching mathematics with spreadsheets. *Technology and Teacher Education Annual, 18*(4), 2238-2245.

Niess, M. L., Ronau, R. N., Shafer, K. G., Driskell, S. O., Harper, S. R., Johnston, C., Browning, C., Özgün-Koca, S. A., & Kersaint, G. (2009). Mathematics teacher TPACK standards and development model. *Contemporary Issues in Technology and Teacher Education, 9*(1), 4-24.

Niess, M. L. (2011). Investigating TPACK: Knowledge growth in teaching with technology. *Journal of Educational Computing Research, 44*(3), 299-317.

Stanford, P., Crowe, M.W., Flice, H. (2010). Differentiating with Technology. TEACHING Exceptional Children Plus, 6(4) Article 2. Retrieved on 1/11/2015 from http://escholarship.bc.edu/education/tecplus/vol6/iss4/art2.

Tomlinson, C. (1995). Differentiating instruction for advanced learners in the mixed ability middle school classroom. *ERIC Digest E536,* Eric Clearinghouse on Disabilities and Gifted Education.

Tomlinson, C. (1999). Mapping a route to differentiated instruction. *Educational Leadership,* 57(1), 12-16.

Tournaki, N. & Lyublinskaya, I. (2014). Preparing special education teachers for teaching mathematics and science with technology by integrating the TPACK framework into the curriculum: A study of teachers' perceptions. *Journal of Technology and Teacher Education, 22*(2), 243-259.

Wei, X. (2012). Does NCLB improve the achievement of students with disabilities? A regression discontinuity design. *Journal of Research on Educational Effectiveness, 5*(1), 18-42.

Teacher Dispositions toward
Science, Technology, Engineering, and Mathematics (STEM)

Gerald Knezek
University of North Texas, USA
gknezek@gmail.com

Rhonda Christensen
University of North Texas, USA

Tandra Tyler-Wood
University of North Texas, USA

Abstract: Dispositions of middle school teachers in an NSF-funded Innovative Technologies project as well as teachers in two other STEM enrichment programs are compared with those of preservice educators from a midwestern university in the USA. Comparisons are based on the preservice and inservice educators' completion of the same attitude instruments. Major findings are that teachers from different regions of the US and in programs supported by National Science Foundation versus state or corporate funds have highly similar, positive attitudes toward Science, Technology, Engineering and Mathematics (STEM), as well as STEM as a career. These findings can be contrasted with much less positive dispositions found in preservice teacher education candidates and in middle school students. Implications of these findings for selecting new STEM teachers, as well as factors that may encourage teachers to embrace and remain in STEM teaching, are discussed.

Introduction

As part of a US National Science Foundation-funded project called Middle Schoolers Out to Save the World (MSOSW), the authors spent six years developing instruments to measure STEM dispositions, implementing curricula to promote STEM content and careers, and providing teacher training to introduce classroom educators to the new opportunities made available through modern technologies (Tyler-Wood, Knezek, Christensen, 2010; Knezek, Christensen, Tyler-Wood, 2011; Knezek, Christensen, Tyler-Wood & Periathiruvadi, 2013). During the time span of this NSF-funded project, the instruments developed were administered to four distinctive groups of preservice and inservice educators as well as student groups involved in MSOSW and other externally funded projects. This paper provides comparisons and contrasts among the STEM dispositions of each of these groups, with a special focus on similarities among the inservice teachers, versus the disposition contrasts between teachers and the preservice and student groups. Implications for teacher education, based on established societal needs, are provided in the discussion section of this paper.

Research Questions

Three research questions were addressed in this study:

1. Are the STEM dispositions of MSOSW teachers comparable to those of teachers in other STEM enrichment programs?
2. Do higher STEM dispositions align with higher levels of technology integration?
3. How do preservice teacher STEM dispositions compare to those of practicing teachers who have volunteered to take part in STEM enrichment projects?

Literature Review

Science, Technology, Engineering and Mathematics (STEM) are important to the global competiveness of the United States (Banning & Folkestad, 2012; Holden, Lander, & Varmus, 2010). The United States is increasingly reliant on the STEM workforce to maintain leadership in the world economy (Banning & Folkestad, 2012). Improving the STEM workforce is a top priority for policy makers, practitioners and researchers who have goals to recruit and retain more students to work in STEM-related fields (Heilbronner, 2011), compete with the global competition, and most importantly improve STEM literacy for all students (Bybee, 2010). Research has shown that students have their dispositions toward disciplines like mathematics and science, shaped long before they begin college (George, Stevenson, Thomason, & Beane, 1992; Sadler, Sonnert, Hazari, & Tai, 2012).

For decades, researchers have studied the influence of teachers on their students and have concluded that teacher effectiveness is the most important factor in student achievement (Darling-Hammond, 2000; Hattie, 1987). More recently, researchers have focused on factors that increase student participation in STEM subject areas and have identified highly qualified teachers as a critical element for student success in STEM subjects (Museus, Palmer, Davis, & Maramba, 2011). Even students who are high STEM achieving students recognize that it is critical to have a high quality teacher in the classroom in order to improve STEM education in schools (Christensen, Knezek, & Tyler-Wood, 2014a).

Many programs currently focus on improving the STEM pipeline by preparing both teachers and students in engaging activities aimed at creating and increasing interest in STEM careers. In this paper, Going Green! MSOSW teachers are compared to those in two other STEM-related programs and to preservice educators. Similarities and differences among these groups will be addressed. All of these programs employed the same STEM disposition measures.

About The Going Green! Middle Schoolers Out to Save the World Project

Middle Schoolers Out to Save the World (MSOSW) spanned 2008-2013 and focused on sixth grade children using energy monitoring equipment to assess the amount of standby power consumed by their home entertainment devices and appliances when not performing any useful functions. Student-gathered data were used to build models of energy consumption in home environments – under the guidance of teachers – with a special focus on stand-by power and greenhouse gas emissions. Online and in-classroom communications, as well as cyber-infrastructure collaboration tools, data warehousing systems, visualization applications, and web site distributions, were used to help middle school students understand the relationship between energy, economics and climate change. Positive changes in dispositions toward science, technology, engineering, and mathematics were produced as a major outcome of the MSOSW project, with an especially significant effect on girls. The title revolved around 'SOS', emphasizing the critical importance of getting thousands of young people engaged in STEM learning. The world is indeed sending an 'SOS' in the form of news about global climate change, the need to find alternative ways to save energy, and the importance of creating new forms of global community and economy that build cultural as well as scientific understandings while solving important problems of our time. The project is based on the precept that middle school students, their teachers, and administrators need to recognize the importance of stimulating and encouraging students in response to this 'SOS'.

In 2013, the principal investigators of the original MSOSW project received a second NSF award to scale up the project to additional schools in diverse environments, with a special emphasis on interest in STEM careers. The project partnered with the *Whyville* online virtual educational environment to disseminate to a wider audience and emphasize this feature. STEM disposition data from this group of teachers was also gathered in the fall of 2013 and is included in the findings presented in this paper.

Instrumentation

The STEM Semantics Survey was the measurement instrument used in common in each of the programs discussed in this paper. The STEM Semantics Survey has been used in many projects across the country over the past several years and is reported to be one of the most widely-used student attitude instruments among those in the NSF Innovative Technologies instrument database (B. Schillaci, personal communication May 8, 2015). It is an instrument used to assess general perceptions of STEM disciplines and careers using Semantic Differential adjective pairs from Osgood's (1962) evaluation dimension. The STEM Semantics Survey is a 25-item semantic differential instrument based on Osgood's Evaluative Dimension and containing five scales assessing perceptions of Science, Technology, Engineering, and Mathematics, as well as STEM Careers.

Each of five scales on the STEM Semantics Survey consist of a target statement such as "To me, science is:" followed by five polar adjective pairs spanning a range of seven choices. For example, "To me, science is: exciting _ _ _ _ _ _ _ unexciting." Internal consistency reliabilities for participant perceptions of science, math, engineering, technology, and STEM as a career ranged from alpha = .85 to alpha = .95 for recent subjects. These numbers are in the range of "very good" to "excellent" according to guidelines provided by DeVellis (1991).

Participants

Three groups of inservice teachers participating in STEM-related projects, plus preservice teachers from a large Midwestern university in the USA were the primary participants in this research study. The ongoing NSF-funded MSOSW project described in the previous sections produced data for one group of inservice teachers over a time period spanning 2009-2012. In 2013 the authors were awarded a scale-up grant from the National Science Foundation to enhance and expand MSOSW activities for an additional four years. Data acquisition for teachers and students was renewed and proceeded during the fall of 2013 and late spring, 2014. In addition, during 2010-2012, the investigators for the MSOSW project were invited to assist in the evaluation of a US federal government stimulus fund initiative (ARRA) focusing on science and technology teacher development for middle school teachers in the State of Hawaii. Data acquisition from Hawaii STEM teachers took place in 2011, 2012, 2103 and 2014. During 2013-2014, the authors also assisted in the evaluation of the Communication in Science, Technology, Engineering, and Mathematics (CSTEM) Project centered in Houston, Texas and administered the same surveys to teachers whose students attended the end-of-year capstone STEM competition at the Houston Convention Center. Finally, over five years from 2009 through 2013, the authors replicated same-survey administrations to preservice educators enrolled in a technology integration course required of all E-8 teacher preparation candidates at a midwestern university graduating more than 500 certified teachers each year.

Specific attributes for the participants in this research from each of the data samples were as follows: 1. MSOSW subjects included middle school teachers from 11 schools across the US participating in a National Science Foundation (NSF) project focused on energy monitoring. 2. The Hawaii STEM Academy sample included middle school science teachers from the entire state of Hawaii participating in a state and federally funded STEM initiative. 3. The CSTEM group included teachers whose students were part of a STEM-focused afterschool program located throughout the greater Houston area; and 4. The preservice educator group hailed from a four-year university and were enrolled in a technology integration course required as one component of EC-8 teacher certification.

Data Collection Timetable

For the 2013-2014 school year, middle school teachers who were part of the Going Green! MSOSW project were asked to complete a battery of surveys regarding STEM attitudes as well as technology integration measures. Fourteen teachers from 11 schools provided data through the online survey administration system. During the Fall of 2014, 25 MSOSW middle school teachers completed the same STEM Semantic surveys as the other inservice and preservice teachers included in this study. During May of 2014, 48 STEM Academy middle school teachers from 23 Hawaii schools provided online data on the same survey instruments administered to the MSOSW teachers. Also during the spring of 2014, 33 CSTEM teachers provided data.

Activities of the Projects

The three STEM-related programs for which teacher data were collected using the same STEM Semantics Survey included the NSF sponsored Middle Schoolers Out to Save the World (MSOSW) project, the US government economic stimulus initiated Hawaii STEM Academy, and the foundation-funded Communication in Science, Technology, Engineering, and Mathematics (CSTEM) program. In the MSOSW project, teachers attend an institute to learn about an energy-related curriculum and how to implement the curriculum with their students. MSOSW teachers also are provided with energy monitors, web enhanced teaching opportunities, curriculum and ongoing support from the project personnel. In the Hawaii STEM Academy, teachers choose from a menu of professional development activities in areas such as aquaponics, energy monitoring, or digital fabrication and then receive a classroom set of laptops or tablet computers to help implement their newly acquired skills. The CSTEM program involves a year-long school-based afterschool program as well as a competition at the end of the school year. Students prepare during the school year for the C-STEM Challenge that engages students in multi-age groups to collaboratively solve six challenges that are designed by industry professionals. These challenges reflect national standards-aligned project-based learning activities. These programs are more fully described in detail in separate publications (Christensen, Knezek, & Tyler-Wood, 2014b; Knezek, Christensen, Tyler-Wood, & Periathuruvadi, 2013).

Analysis and Results

Data from the 2014 Hawaii STEM Academy teachers can be compared to MSOSW and CSTEM programs. An analysis of teacher perceptions is appropriate because all three programs focus on teachers integrating STEM enhanced activities for teaching and learning. As shown in Table 1 and illustrated in Figure 1, the NSF-funded MSOSW project teachers have dispositions comparable to the teachers in the Hawaii STEM Academy teachers as well as the CSTEM program teachers.

Table 1.
Comparison of Means for STEM Semantic Scales for Three Groups of Teachers Involved in STEM Enhancement Activities

	CSTEM teachers Spring 2014			MSOSW Teachers Fall 2013			Hawaii Teachers Spring 2014		
	N	Mean	SD	N	Mean	SD	N	Mean	SD
STEM Science	33	6.41	.89	14	6.67	.57	48	6.58	.72
STEM Math	33	5.42	1.43	14	5.26	1.10	48	5.40	1.33
STEM Engineering	33	6.25	1.00	14	5.81	1.01	48	6.14	1.13
STEM Technology	32	6.51	.80	14	6.13	.93	48	6.44	.93
STEM Career	33	6.32	1.09	14	6.67	.49	48	6.41	.96

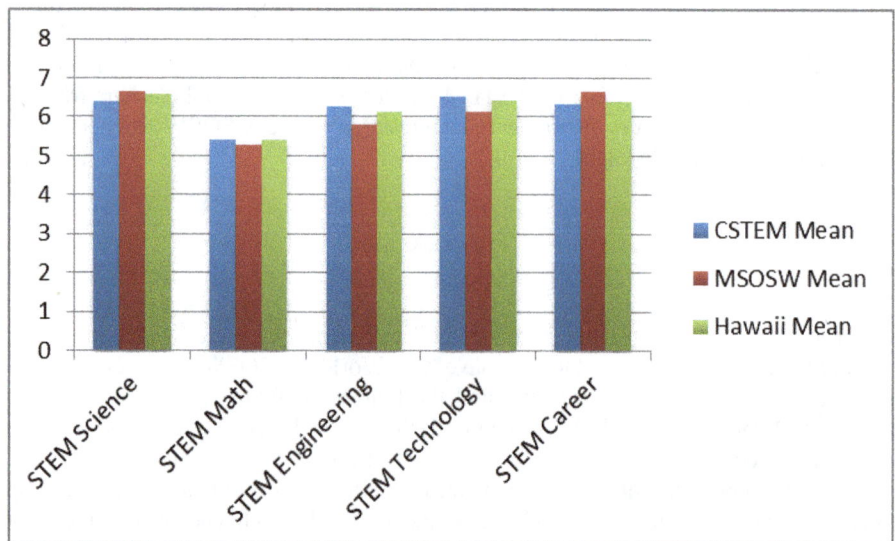

Figure 1. Middle school teachers' STEM dispositions from three STEM enhancement programs.

New data on the same instrument were gathered from 25 MSOSW teachers involved in the scale-up phase of the project during the fall of 2014. For additional comparison, data were also gathered from 30 leaders of technology-related professional associations attending the National Technology Leadership Summit in Washington, DC in September 2014. As shown in Figure 2, when viewed from a cumulative, layered perspective of STEM dispositions, the fourteen MSOSW teachers from 2013-14 and the 25 teachers in the project for 2014-15, possess high, positive STEM dispositions comparable to those of professional society leaders, CSTEM teachers supported by foundations awards for STEM enrichment, and STEM Academy teachers from Hawaii. Additional one-way analysis of variance procedures completed for the 2014 MSOSW teacher data revealed no significant differences in the dispositions of the 12 treatment teachers versus the 13 comparison group teachers for the 2014-15 school year. This provides an opportunity for the project research team to assess possible impacts of participation in project activities on teachers.

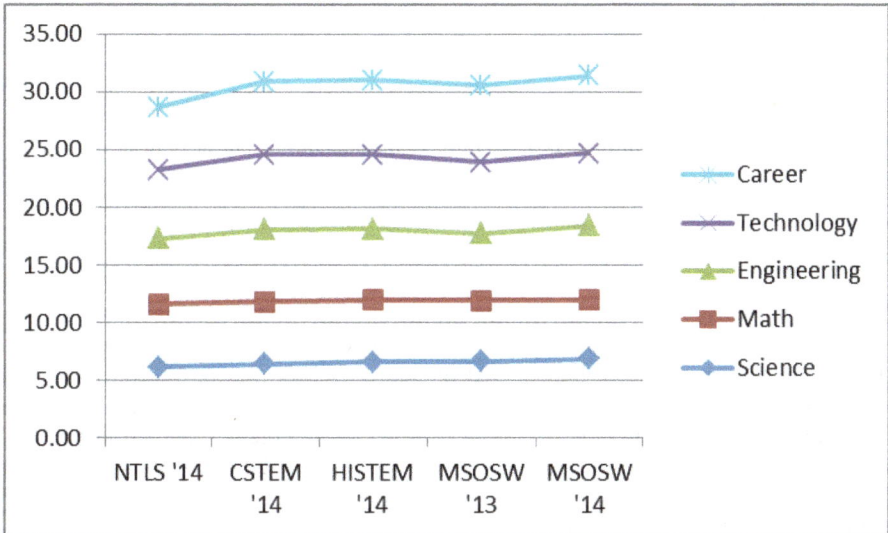

Figure 2. Middle school teachers STEM dispositions in the context of technology-society leader dispositions.

As illustrated in Figure 3, MSOSW sixth grade students (n = 175) displayed relatively high (well above neutral = 20) dispositions toward STEM measures on the same instruments; these are comparable to dispositions found in CSTEM students in a separate study (Christensen, Knezek, & Tyler-Wood, 2014b). However, as also shown in Figure 3, there is ample room for growth in the students before reaching the level of their teachers. If we expect students to exhibit positive attitudes toward and an affinity towards science, it is important that teachers possess high attitudes (Baldwin, 2014). Teacher attitudes have been shown to transfer to their students in areas such as technology (Christensen, 2002). We therefore can infer that the dispositions of the teachers in STEM programs are likely to have a positive impact on their students' dispositions toward STEM.

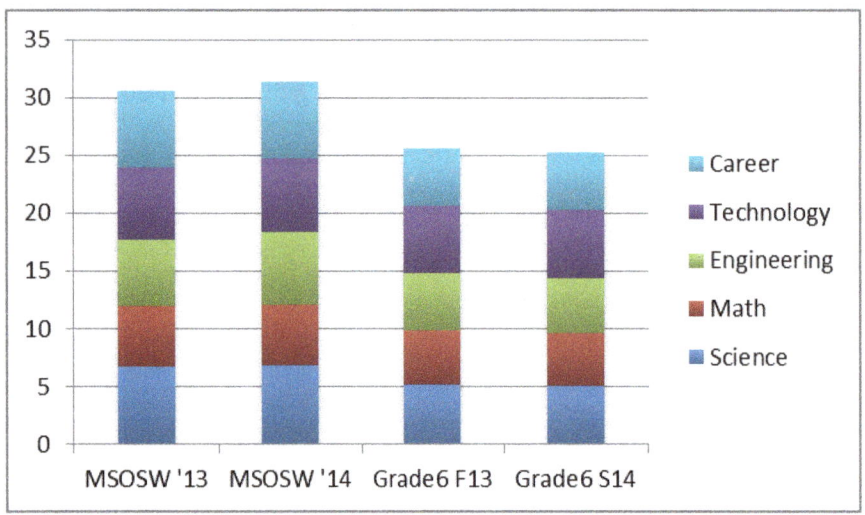

Figure 3. MSOSW middle school student STEM dispositions compared to their teachers.

Discussion

STEM Enrichment Educators

As shown in Figure 4, profiles for teachers in all three STEM programs examined in this paper are similar to persons in the category labeled STEM professionals. This latter category includes university faculty and research scientists who are National Science Foundation project principal investigators, as well as teacher educators and school district or statewide technology coordinators. The high alignment of the teachers surveyed from the three STEM programs examined in this paper, with the group labeled STEM professionals, indicates that perhaps a new group name, such as STEM enrichment educators, is needed for teachers like those in the three programs featured in this study. This new group would encompass K-12 educators who are focused on preparing the next generation of STEM professionals to participate in the STEM workforce of the future.

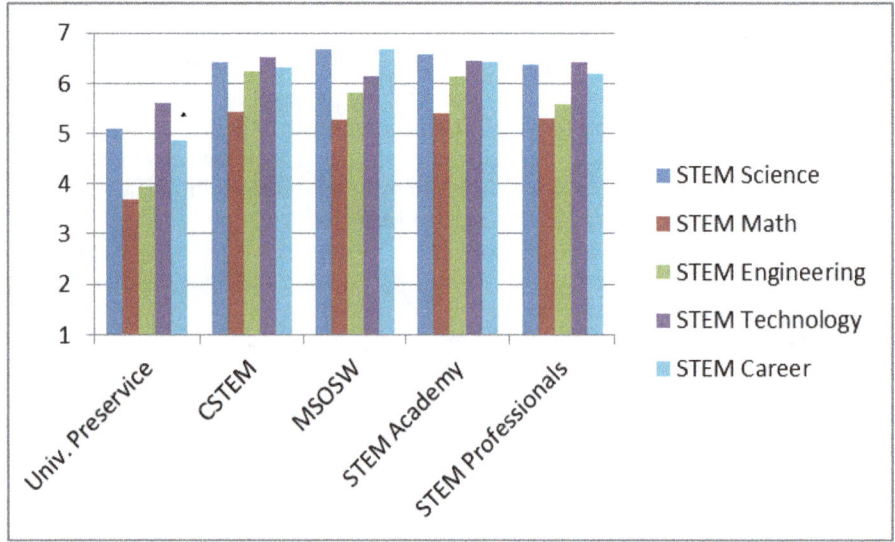

Figure 4. Distribution of STEM dispositions for preservice teacher candidates versus three groups of STEM enrichment educators.

Dispositions of Future Teachers

The university preservice students contributing data for one contrast group in this study were in their sophomore or junior year in teacher education programs. The levels of STEM dispositions for this group represented in Figure 4 have found to be stable in replication studies over four years (Knezek, Christensen, & Tyler-Wood, 2011). Most of the teacher candidates were planning to be elementary school teachers. Based on their relatively low dispositions toward STEM content areas and STEM as a career, it appears there is work to be done to prepare the candidates for their future classrooms if we expect them to display and transmit positive attitudes toward STEM when they teach the next generation.

Hope for STEM Enrichment Educator Retention

The Hawaii data set included demographic items asking those completing surveys if the training and technology access they received help keep teachers in teaching in general, and whether the respondent himself/herself was encouraged to stay in teaching? The answer provided by these STEM-training and STEM-equipped teachers was affirmative. By comparing the Hawaii program teachers' STEM dispositions to those of teachers participating in the MSOSW and CSTEM projects, we can infer that the rich training and activities related to the latter two programs may help retain teachers. This finding is consistent with the Will, Skill, Tool (WST) model of technology integration (Hancock, Knezek, & Christensen, 2003; Knezek, Christensen, Hancock, & Shoho, 2000) as broadly applied to STEM education in general. The model specifies that teachers require will (positive attitudes) in addition to the skill and access to resources and tools in order to become effective teachers of STEM. Teachers participating in all three STEM programs examined in this study clearly have high will – as indicated through their highly positive STEM dispositions.

Concerns for Our Society's Future

Elementary teachers in general are not all expected to be STEM teachers, so it may be that a selection issue creates bias for the contrasts presented in this paper. However, we have confirmed these preservice teachers often possess STEM dispositions less positive than current sixth graders (Knezek, Christensen, & Tyler-Wood, 2011). Therefore, whether these preservice educators remain in teaching or whether half leave the profession after 3-5 years as is now typical in the US – and then simply have the *first educator* title of "parents" after a few years – in either case these data provide cause for concern. We know the disposition profile of quality STEM teachers. We know they are very similar to STEM professionals. We know these are the likely dispositions of persons who aspire to STEM careers. If the parents and the majority of the EC-8 teachers of our future students have much less positive STEM dispositions than those typical of STEM Career Professionals, then we can have little hope that the children / students will have high dispositions and interest transferred to them by their parents or their teachers in school.

Conclusions

Teachers with positive STEM dispositions are not only more likely to transfer their love of STEM to their current students, but are probably more likely to stay in teaching, thus allowing experienced, enthusiastic teachers to prepare a pipeline of students for the STEM workforce of the future. Teachers in the STEM-enhanced programs examined in this paper are finding the necessary support and professional development to retain their enthusiasm for teaching STEM. Across the US we are confident there is a wide distribution of teachers who have high dispositions toward STEM and will transfer that enthusiasm to their students. Programs such as those described in this paper appear to be successful in fostering and maintaining positive dispositions in teachers regardless of whether they are state funded, federally funded or funded by corporate donations. These programs can serve as models for other educational entities seeking to enhance the education of students to fulfill the need for the STEM workforce of the future. However a word of caution is warranted regarding whether we can expect this trend to continue into the next generation of parents and teachers, who ironically are digital natives.

References

Baldwin, K.A. (2014). The science teaching self-efficacy of prospective elementary education majors enrolled in introductory geology lab sections. *School Science and Mathematics, 114*(5), 206-213.

Banning, J., & Folkestad, J. E. (2012). STEM education related dissertation abstracts: A bounded qualitative meta-study. *Journal of Science Education and Technology, 21*(6), 730-741.

Bybee, R. W. (2010). Advancing STEM education: A 2020 vision. *Technology and Engineering Teacher, 70*(6), 30-35. Retrieved from http://www.iteaconnect.org.

Christensen, R. (2002). Impact of technology integration education on the attitudes of teachers and students. *Journal of Research on Technology in Education, 34* (4), 411-434.

Christensen, R., Knezek, G., & Tyler-Wood, T. (2014a). Student perceptions of Science, Technology, Engineering and Mathematics (STEM) content and careers. *Computers in Human Behavior, 34*, 173-186. http://dx.doi.org/10.1016/j.chb.2014.01.046

Christensen, R., Knezek, G., & Tyler-Wood, T. (2014b). *C-STEM Teacher Report*. Denton, TX: Institute for the Integration of Technology into Teaching and Learning.

Darling-Hammond, L. (2000). Teacher quality and student achievement: A review of state policy evidence. *Education Policy Analysis Archives, 8*(1), January 2000. Available from http://www.washingtonstem.org/STEM/media/Media/Resources/Darling-Hammond-2000-Teacher-Quality-and-Student-Achievement.pdf.

DeVellis, R.F. (1991). *Scale development*. Newbury Park, NJ: Sage Publications.

Dwyer, D. C., Ringstaff, C., & Sandholtz, J. H. (1991). Changes in teachers' beliefs and practices in technology-rich classrooms. *Educational Leadership, 48*(8), 45-52. (ERIC Document Reproduction Service No. EJ 425 608).

George, P., Stevenson, C., Thomason, J., & Beane, J. (1992). *The middle school and beyond*. Association for Supervision and Curriculum Development. Alexandria, VA.

Griffin, D., & Christensen, R. (1999). Concerns-Based Adoption Model Levels of Use of an Innovation (CBAM-LOU). Adapted from Hall, Loucks, Rutherford, & Newlove (1975). Denton, Texas: Institute for the Integration of Technology into Teaching and Learning.

Hancock, R., Knezek, G. & Christensen, R. (2003). The Expanded Will, Skill, Tool Model: A step toward developing technology tools that work. World Conference on Educational Multimedia, Hypermedia and Telecommunications, Vol. 2003, Issue. 1, 2003, pp. 1415-1422.

Hattie, J. A. (1987). Identifying the salient facets of a model of student learning: A synthesis of meta-analyses. *International Journal of Educational Research, 11*, 187–212.

Holdren, J. P., Lander, E. S., & Varmus, H. (2010). *Prepare and inspire: K-12 education in science, technology, engineering, and math (STEM) for America's future.* (Executive Report). Washington, D.C.: President's Council of Advisors on Science and Technology.

Knezek, G., Christensen, R., Hancock, R. & Shoho, A. (2000). *Toward a structural model of technology integration*. A paper presented to the Hawaii Educational Research Association Annual Conference, Honolulu, HI.

Knezek, G., Christensen, R., & Tyler-Wood, T. (2011). Contrasting perceptions of STEM content and careers. *Contemporary Issues in Technology and Teacher Education 1(1)*. Retrieved from http://www.citejournal.org/vol11/iss1/general/article1.cfm

Knezek, G., Christensen, R., Tyler-Wood, T., & Periathiruvadi, S. (2013). Impact of environmental power monitoring activities on middle school student perceptions of STEM. *Science Education International, 21*(1), 98-123.

Museus, S., Palmer, R.T., Davis, R.J., & Maramba, D.C. (2011). *Racial and ethnic minority students' success in STEM education*. Hoboken: New Jersey: Jossey-Bass.

Osgood, C. E. (1962). Studies of the generality of affective meaning systems. *American Psychologist, 17*, 10-28.

Sadler, P.M., Sonnert, G., Hazari, Z., & Tai, R. (2012). Stability and volatility of STEM career interest in high school: A gender study. *Science Education, 96*(3), 411-427.

Tyler-Wood, T. Knezek, G. & Christensen, R. (2010). Instruments for assessing interest in STEM content and careers, *Journal of Technology & Teacher Education, 18*(2), 345-368.

Acknowledgement

This research was supported in part by the U.S. National Science Foundation Innovative Technology Experiences for Students and Teachers (ITEST) Grant #1312168, by the CSTEM Project of Houston, Texas, and by data from University of Hawaii.

Lessons Learned from Creation of an Exemplary STEM Unit for Elementary Pre-Service Teachers: A Case Study

Matthew Schmidt
University of Hawaii - Manoa
United States
matthew.schmidt@hawaii.edu

Lori Fulton
University of Hawaii - Manoa
United States
fultonl@hawaii.edu

Abstract: Preparing students with 21st Century Skills through STEM related teaching is needed; however, most teacher preparation programs do not focus on STEM education. We transformed a traditional inquiry-based unit on moon phases into a technology-rich STEM unit for pre-service teachers (PSTs). We describe lessons learned related to the development and implementation of this unit in an undergraduate elementary methods course and explore the impact on PSTs' perceptions of inquiry-based science instruction. Findings indicate that (a) PSTs held absolutist beliefs and had a need for instruction on inquiry-based learning and (b) explicit examples of effective and ineffective technology use are needed to develop an understanding of meaningful technology integration. While our design approach resulted in a successful modification of the unit, the usability of our digital instructional materials suffered. Findings suggest that inquiry-based STEM units can be implemented; however, development requires significant effort and testing of designs for successful implementation.

Introduction

There is a current shortfall of highly qualified STEM educators at the elementary level (Congressional Research Service, 2006; National Research Council, 2011). This is problematic because *exposing students to STEM topics early in their schooling increases the chances that those students will maintain interest and improve their abilities in related areas. Teacher preparation programs should focus on training teachers to meet the demand for qualified elementary STEM teachers, but existing programs are weak in STEM areas (Epstein & Miller, 2011). This means* many practicing teachers lack subject matter expertise (Congressional Research Service, 2006; Greenberg, McKee, & Walsh, 2013). We need to make changes to STEM teacher preparation programs, but *this poses challenges on many levels (see Atkinson & Mayo, 2010; Epstein & Miller, 2011; National Center for Education and the Economy, 2007; National Research Council, 2007). Top-down changes are particularly challenging; however, bottom-up reform efforts can empower individual educators to enact change within extant STEM teacher education programs. Bybee (2010) forwards a model in which STEM education reform is initiated by introducing short STEM instructional units into existing programs. These units can then serve as a model of exemplary STEM education for instructors, administrators, and parents; empowering educators to act as agents of change.*

In this spirit, the authors of this paper collaborated to create an exemplar moon investigation unit for a university teacher education STEM class. This article serves as a case study, which was guided by the following questions: 1) How does using an inquiry-based approach to teach science impact pre-service teachers' learning experience of the moon investigation unit? and 2) How does the integration of technology in the moon investigation unit impact pre-service teachers' learning experiences? For our project, we developed rapid prototypes of technology-enhanced instructional materials (including websites, instructional videos, and multimedia presentations) and evaluated each phase of our implementation.

Design approach

We opted for a rapid prototyping (RP) design approach because it allows designers to reduce development time and costs when creating instructional products (Desrosier, 2011; T. S. Jones & Richey, 2000; Tripp &

Bichelmeyer, 1990; Wilson, Jonassen, & Cole, 1993). This approach was appropriate for our project since we were implementing an instructional unit in a new way and did not have sufficient experience from which to draw. Drawing from Wilson, Jonassen, and Cole (1993), RP aligned with our overarching design objectives in that it allowed for both testing the "effectiveness and appeal of a particular instructional strategy" (p. 21.4) and quickly developing a model instructional unit. We performed four cycles of RP, illustrated in Figure 1 below.

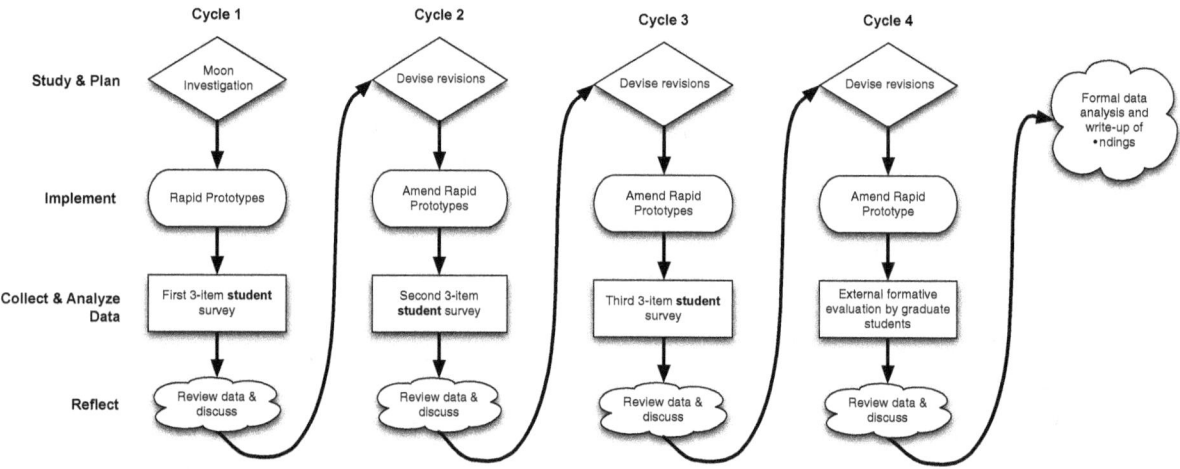

Figure 1. Iterative cycles of design, implementation, evaluation, and reflection.

Pedagogical framework

We adopted principles commonly used in high quality STEM programs to inform our pedagogical framework (for an overview, see Hanover Research, 2011). The instructional unit selected was the *moon investigation*, which was based on the popular, multi-week inquiry-based science activity described in Abell, Appleton, and Hanuscin (2010). In this activity, pre-service teachers (PSTs) learned about the moon individually and in groups by observing it on a regular basis over the course of the semester.

Inquiry-based science

Inquiry-based science is one approach to facilitating such learning. Minner, Levy, and Century (2010) describe inquiry as having "(1) the presence of science content, (2) student engagement with science content, and (3) student responsibility for learning, student active thinking, or student motivation with at least one component of instruction – question, design, data, conclusion, or communication" (p. 5). Recently the language of science has shifted from an inquiry-based approach to "science as a practice" (Osborne, 2014, p. 177). While engaging students in the practices of science is essential to developing a coherent science experience, elementary teachers claim to be uncomfortable teaching science in this way due to their limited content and pedagogical knowledge, negative experiences with science, management issues, and/or low levels of confidence (Appleton, 2007; Banilower, Heck, & Weiss, 2007; Davis, Petish, & Smithey, 2006; Howes, Lim, & Campos, 2009). Due to this discomfort many teachers avoid teaching science or rely on a textbook. This discomfort extends to the topic of the moon, as the moon phases and the relationship between the Earth, Sun, and Moon are challenging for adults and children alike (Lelliott & Rollnick, 2010; Mulholland & Ginns, 2008; Wisitsen, 2012).

Technological literacy

Technological literacy is defined as:

[T]he ability to effectively use technology (i.e., any tool, piece of equipment or device, electronic or mechanical) to accomplish required learning tasks. Technology literate people know what the technology is capable of, they are able to use the technology proficiently, and they make intelligent decisions about which technology to use and when to use it. (p. 47)

Students develop technological literacy by engaging in authentic problem solving that embeds technological tools. To promote technological literacy, computers can be used as "mindtools" to help learners engage in complex and authentic problem solving (Jonassen, 2000, 2011; Jonassen, Howland, Moore, & Marra, 2003). This allows students to think "deeply about the content that they are studying; if they choose to use these tools, they will facilitate their own learning and meaning-making processes." (Jonassen, Davidson, Collins, Campbell, & Haag, 1995, p. 20).

Methods

The nature of our research was qualitative (Creswell, 2012; Merriam, 2007; Stake, 1995). The purpose of our research was 1) to investigate the impact of a model STEM instructional unit on PSTs' perceptions of inquiry-based science instruction, as well as 2) to explore methodically methods and processes for meaningfully translating a traditional paper-and-pencil instructional unit into a multimedia-rich, technology-infused unit that could be delivered in an inverted format. The questions that guided our research were: 1) How does using an inquiry-based approach to teach science impact pre-service teachers' learning experience of the moon investigation unit? and 2) How does the integration of technology in the moon investigation unit impact pre-service teachers' learning experiences? Over one semester, we rapid prototyped instructional materials, making incremental improvements based on evaluation findings. Data were used to inform our progress, identify avenues for improvement, and establish best practices.

Research was performed in an undergraduate STEM teacher preparation course at a large Pacific university. Participants were 35 undergraduate students enrolled in the teacher preparation program (30 female, 5 male). Ages were between 20 and 25 years old. Data sources included field notes, minutes from weekly debriefs, and surveys. An external formative evaluation was conducted by students in a graduate-level instructional technology course and delivered to the researchers in the form of evaluation reports.

Data were analyzed using inductive and deductive axial coding (Charmaz, 2006; Strauss & Corbin, 1998). The survey data were stored in a spreadsheet for sorting and analysis. We developed a coding scheme for the data, individually coded the data, and then established inter-rater reliability. Reliability was established using a point-by-point estimate averaging 95% reliability, indicating high agreement between coders. Coded data were synthesized into three broad, overarching thematic areas. Representative artifacts from the data sources were identified and reviewed. Themes and excerpts were then organized, summarized and crafted into narrative.

Results

Three overarching themes emerged from coding: 1) challenges and successes related to engaging in inquiry learning, 2) the multidimensional nature of meaningful technology integration, and 3) design principles for transforming established practices for 21st century learners.

Challenges and Successes Related to Engaging in Inquiry Learning

PSTs were asked to observe the moon three times a week and to record information in a digital science notebook. This challenged many of the PSTs who were uncertain of what to record due to their perceived lack of factual knowledge. One PST stated, "Describing the moon is difficult because we do not have any knowledge about the moon." They wanted "more explicit instruction" asking specifically for instruction "on where we have to be standing exactly, and what time." Such a request removes the responsibility of the PSTs in the inquiry process and reduces their ability to learn this information through their own observations. Another challenging aspect for PSTs was engaging in the inquiry process. For many, this process was new and unsettling. Further, students wanted more instruction in applying this activity to themselves as teachers, specifically, "how to take a cool and awesome topic like this [and] make a lesson that is universal."

With challenges were also successes. It was evident in PST's comments that they were acquiring scientific understandings such as identifying the cycle of the moon: "I know the moon cycles now! When it is waning or waxing. Full moon by Friday!" Some PSTs were surprised to learn that the moon rises in the morning at times. Many PSTs commented about the unusual instructional approach we took with the assignment, saying such things as, "It is different than anything I have done so far." While PSTs struggled with inquiry, they appreciated "being forced" to actually look at the moon on a regular basis. As one PST summed it up, "I like the fact that we get to observe the moon in depth. I discover new things every time I do this assignment."

Multidimensional Nature of Meaningful Technology Integration

Pre-service teachers used technology and applied technology skills extensively, which were generally perceived positively. PSTs commented that they liked practicing using the technology tools and having their information available online for all to see and comment on. Some found the active approach was "a different, more engaging way to learn about technology" and facilitated them becoming an "active science learner." Others were challenged, however. One PST stated, "I am having major technical difficulty with the video imports. I don't know how to blog with my group at all, and I don't know how to know if it got saved and they see my comments when I do try to blog. I still to this day don't know if I blogged...." From an instructional perspective, we used technology to create and deliver instruction. Materials were created using a rapid prototyping approach. This approach allowed us to bring our materials online quickly, but caused the side effect that they were sometimes inconsistent and "confusing." We would make changes to new materials based on what we were learning, and these changes were not always reflected in the materials.

Design Principles for Transforming Established Practices for 21st Century Learners

Formative evaluation indicated that the directions for the assignment were clear and "the examples and background information in the instructional content [were] relevant to the instructional goals and context." Evaluators reported that multimedia "aids the instruction," was "easy to access ... through mobile devices," and was "excellent" in nature. In terms of degree of difficulty, the module was found to be "appropriate for the learner." The instruction was found to allow "teachers to step in to the role of learners of science, which will enhance their ability to teach science" as well as provide "sufficient practice and feedback opportunities." PSTs commented that they enjoyed observing the moon, they found the assignment intriguing, and that it had sparked their curiosity about the moon. They also commented about the ease of the assignment, stating, "It is not very difficult to do." Although findings indicate the module was effective in many ways, there were aspects of the module that need improvement. Both PSTs and external evaluators felt that the number of observations were excessive. A second area was cultural relevance, as the moon plays a significant role in the Pacific island culture in terms of navigation, farming, and fishing. We see opportunities in the future to build on this to make connections to home, cultural, and community experiences. A third area was site design. While rapid prototyping allowed us to quickly build materials, it also led to difficulties such as sections being too "wordy and confusing," instructions that were "excessive... and located in many different places," and navigation that was "not user friendly."

Overall, the moon module received high marks, indicating that the transformation of an established practice for studying the moon had been effective in meeting the needs of 21st century learners. This process will be strengthened through the identification and concentration on specific areas of improvement during the next iteration.

Discussion

Lessons Learned: Inquiry

While our inquiry approach was successful in fostering PSTs' knowledge and understanding of the moon, many struggled with the novelty of the inquiry process. Because of their lack of familiarity with the pedagogical approach, they had little background for evaluating their learning progress. The many requests to teach facts and to provide explicit instructions for exactly what to do for observing the moon provide evidence not only that PSTs struggled with the inquiry approach, but also gives some indication of their epistemological beliefs. Epistemological beliefs are generally conceived of as learners' personal views on the nature of knowledge and knowing (Hofer & Pintrich, 1997; Sandoval, 2005). Learners' epistemological beliefs generally fall into three stages of beliefs: 1) absolutist beliefs, 2) relativist beliefs, and 3) pluralist/evaluative beliefs (Hofer & Pintrich, 1997; Kuhn, 1999; Schraw, 2001). Drawing from Kuhn (1999), the absolutist view conceives of knowledge as coming from an external source, to be objective, and to be certain; the relativist view sees knowledge as subjective and a matter of opinion; and the pluralist/evaluative stance views knowledge as an ongoing process of evaluation and argument. PSTs' desire for facts and explicit directions suggests that students held largely absolutist epistemologies.

PSTs may express a desire for facts, but providing them with direct instruction is counterproductive to inquiry learning. Instead of directly teaching facts about a specific phenomenon such as moon phases, attention should be given to the inquiry-based approach itself. Students need guidance to grasp the principles of inquiry-based instruction and learning. Therefore, students should acquire an understanding of inquiry through shorter, guided inquiries and instruction on inquiry as an approach to learning prior to engaging in an extended, more open-ended inquiry. Opportunities to carry out shorter inquiry activities could include such experiences as creating and exploring coffee filter parachutes or "moon landers" from office supplies (see Riechert & Post, 2010). Building in opportunities for meaningful reflection (Abell et al., 2010; Anderson, 2010) throughout these experiences as well as throughout the extended moon investigation would provide students with the guidance they desire while allowing for concrete exploration and discussion of the concept of inquiry, based on experience gained in a short amount of time. Shorter activities will reduce uncertainty and increase trust in the approach since PSTs will be able to see the outcome of their work more quickly before engaging with a longer activity like the *moon investigation*. Also, instructors should focus on identifying and exploring PSTs' current epistemological beliefs (Chan, 2011; Fulmer, 2014). An awareness of PSTs current beliefs about knowledge provides a basis for exploring the nature of science. This can lead to a positive influence on PSTs' overall perceptions of science (Fulmer, 2014). PSTs' epistemological beliefs can impact their future teaching (Tanase & Wang, 2010) and can be influenced by culture. An awareness of how specific cultural elements might be influencing PSTs beliefs could be explored as part of the instructional sequence to promote higher stages of epistemological beliefs in culturally relevant ways.

Lessons Learned: Technology Integration

Just using technology is not an integrated experience. We wanted to use technology both as a conduit for learning and as a means of acquiring technological literacy. Having students use digital science notebooks is one example of a successful and appropriate use of technology for the *moon investigation* activity. However, not all uses of technology were equally appropriate. For example, some PSTs would use digital cameras in their cell phones or tablet computers for taking pictures of the moon, which were low resolution and did not sufficiently show moon phases. Others would download apps or use Google to locate information on moon phases or location of the moon and report that information in their digital notebooks with no real understanding of what the information meant. These examples show a lack of technological literacy, which is not only the ability to use technology, but also to know when to choose one technology over another or even when to not use technology at all (Davies, 2011).

Nowadays, technology is everywhere. We have instant access to information at any time. But having access to information with no context to interpret it is not useful. For instance, if a PST includes the azimuth and altitude of the moon in a journal entry, but does not know what those figures or terms mean, then the information itself is meaningless. We took many opportunities to model and explain appropriate technology use, but found that modeling and explanation was not enough to change PSTs' behaviors. Even when shown low-resolution photographs or when challenged to explain the meaning of information copied from a Google search, some PSTs continued to use these ineffective strategies. Explicit examples of effective and ineffective technology use are needed, and these examples should be presented frequently throughout the instructional sequence. Exploring examples of appropriate and inappropriate technology use to PSTs gives opportunities to collaboratively develop competencies. One way this could be scaffolded for PSTs would be to have them perform the first moon observation activity together as a whole class. This would allow them to not only explore concepts related to the moon, but also to explore strategies for using technology to record observations such as the benefits and limitations of using a camera, using apps to search for information, etc.

Lessons Learned: Instructional Design

Designing new instruction is complex and requires much planning in the selection of which technologies to use and the design of the instructional materials. We had no prior knowledge or experience upon which to base our design decisions and technology selection since we had never taught this unit before. For this reason, we opted for an RP approach. The RP approach provided a means for quickly developing and iterating our designs, but it also caused the user-friendliness of our digital instructional materials to suffer. The class website became cluttered and lacked a consistent look and feel. On the one hand, we see this as an indication of constant improvement to our materials and instructional approach. That is, the design of our materials became more refined and user-friendly over time, which is why materials at the end of the semester looked so different from those at the beginning. On the other hand, the lack of consistency impacted the learning experience, making it sometimes difficult to find things and to locate the latest, most accurate information. As noted in the literature on rapid prototyping, feature creep and constantly adding to designs can impact usability and effectiveness (Tripp & Bichelmeyer, 1990). In line with user experience heuristics (Nielsen & Loranger, 2006), simplifying the design of the materials and the web interface should be a priority, as should ensuring consistency. This includes reliably presenting the same types of information and media to users in similar ways. In addition to this, support could be provided via support channels for PSTs such as online discussion forums and one-on-one, helpdesk-like support.

Conclusion

If we as educators rely on top-down policy reform to shape STEM education, we may end up waiting for Godot. Winning the future starts today. Acting as local change agents within our locus of control is no naïve fantasy. Quality inquiry-based STEM instructional units can be successfully implemented in existing programs, but should not be seen as a quick-fix. Good design is complex and challenging. Quickly creating prototypes and testing them iteratively requires significant effort in terms of planning, implementation, and execution. As the case presented here illustrates, the process is colored by successes and challenges. While the process can result in very effective designs, it can also result in some components that fall short of expectations. It is therefore critical to ensure that failures are manageable (Desrosier, 2011). However, as Brown (2008) notes, "The goal of prototyping isn't to finish. It is to learn about the strengths and weaknesses of the idea and to identify new directions that further prototypes might take" (p. 87).

Acknowledgements

This material is based upon work supported by the grant *Project Laulima,* funded by the Office of Special Education Programs (OSEP). The authors gratefully acknowledge the assistance of Amelia Jenkins and Donna Grace, Co-Principal Investigators, without whose help this work would not have been possible.

References

Abell, S. K., Appleton, K., & Hanuscin, D. L. (2010). *Designing and teaching the elementary science methods course.* New York: Routledge..

Anderson, R. D. (2010). Inquiry as an organizing theme for science curricula. In S. K. Abell & N. G. Lederman (Eds.), *Handbook of research on science education* (pp. 807–830).

Appleton, K. (2007). Elementary science teaching. In S. K. Abell & N. G. Lederman (Eds.), *Handbook of Research on Science Education.* Mahwah, NJ: Erlbaum.

Atkinson, R. D., & Mayo, M. J. (2010). *Refueling the U.S. innovation economy: Fresh approaches to science, technology, engineering and mathematics (STEM) education.* Rochester, NY: Social Science Research Network.

Banilower, E. R., Heck, D. J., & Weiss, I. R. (2007). Can professional development make the vision of the standards a reality? The impact of the national science foundation's local systemic change through teacher enhancement initiative. *Journal of Research in Science Teaching, 44*(3), 375–395.

Brown, T. (2008). Design thinking. *Harvard Business Review, 86*(6), 84.

Bybee, R. (2010). Advancing STEM education: A 2020 vision. *The Technology and Engineering Teacher, September,* 30–35.

Chan, K.-W. (2011). Preservice teacher education students' epistemological beliefs and conceptions about learning. *Instructional Science, 39*(1), 87–108.

Charmaz, K. (2006). *Constructing grounded theory: A practical guide through qualitative analysis.* London: Sage.

Congressional Research Service. (2006). *Science, technology, engineering, and mathematics (STEM) education issues and legislative options* (No. RL33434). Washington, D.C.

Creswell, J. W. (2012). *Qualitative inquiry and research design: Choosing among five approaches.* London: Sage.

Davies, R. S. (2011). Understanding technology literacy: A framework for evaluating educational technology integration. *TechTrends, 55*(5), 45–52.

Davies, R. S., Dean, D. L., & Ball, N. (2013). Flipping the classroom and instructional technology integration in a college-level information systems spreadsheet course. *Educational Technology Research and Development, 61*(4), 563–580.

Davis, E. A., Petish, D., & Smithey, J. (2006). Challenges new science teachers face. *Review of Educational Research, 76*(4), 607–651.

Desrosier, J. (2011). Rapid prototyping reconsidered. *The Journal of Continuing Higher Education, 59*(3), 135–145.

Dove, A., & Dove, A. (2013). Students' perceptions of learning in a flipped statistics class (Vol. 2013, pp. 393–398). Presented at the Society for Information Technology & Teacher Education International Conference.

Dugger, W. E. (2001). Standards for technological literacy. *Phi Delta Kappan, 82*(7), 513–17.

Eisenkraft, A. (2010). Retrospective analysis of technological literacy of K-12 students in the USA. *International Journal of Technology and Design Education, 20*(3), 277–303.

Enfield, J. (2013). Looking at the impact of the flipped classroom model of instruction on undergraduate multimedia students at CSUN. *TechTrends, 57*(6), 14–27.

Epstein, D., & Miller, R. T. (2011). Slow off the mark: Elementary school teachers and the crisis in science, technology, engineering, and math education. *Education Digest: Essential Readings Condensed for Quick Review, 77*(1), 4–10.

Fulmer, G. W. (2014). Undergraduates' attitudes toward science and their epistemological beliefs: Positive Effects of certainty and authority beliefs. *Journal of Science Education and Technology, 23*(1), 198–206.

Fulton, L., & Campbell, B. (2014). *Science notebooks: Writing about inquiry*. Portsmouth, New Hampshire: Heinemann.

Glaser, B. (2000). The future of grounded theory. *Grounded Theory Review, 1*, 1–8.

Greenberg, J., McKee, A., & Walsh, K. (2013). *Teacher prep review: A review of the nation's teacher preparation programs*. National Council on Teacher Quality.

Hanover Research. (2011). *K-12 STEM education overview*. Washington, D.C.: Hanover Research.

Hofer, B. K., & Pintrich, P. R. (1997). The development of epistemological theories: Beliefs about knowledge and knowing and their relation to learning. *Review of Educational Research, 67*(1), 88–140.

Howes, E. V., Lim, M., & Campos, J. (2009). Journeys into inquiry-based elementary science: Literacy practices, questioning, and empirical study. *Science Education, 93*(2), 189–217.

Ingerman, Å., & Collier-Reed, B. (2011). Technological literacy reconsidered: a model for enactment. *International Journal of Technology and Design Education, 21*(2), 137–148.

ITEA. (2007). *Standards for technological literacy: Content for the study of technology* (3rd ed.). International Technology Education Association.

Jonassen, D. H. (2000). *Computers as mindtools for schools: Engaging critical thinking*. Upper Saddle River, NJ: Merrill.

Jonassen, D. H. (2011). *Learning to solve problems: A handbook for designing problem-solving learning environments*. New York: Routledge.

Jonassen, D. H., Davidson, M., Collins, M., Campbell, J., & Haag, B. B. (1995). Constructivism and computer-mediated communication in distance education. *American Journal of Distance Education, 9*(2), 7–26.

Jonassen, D. H., Howland, J., Moore, J., & Marra, R. M. (2003). *Learning to solve problems with technology: A constructivist perspective*. Upper Saddle River, NJ: Merrill.

Jones, A. (2013). The role and place of technological literacy in elementary science teacher education. In K. Appleton (Ed.), *Elementary Science Teacher Education: International Perspectives on Contemporary Issues and Practice*. Routledge, New York.

Jones, T. S., & Richey, R. C. (2000). Rapid prototyping methodology in action: A developmental study. *Educational Technology Research and Development, 48*(2), 63–80.

Kuhn, D. (1999). A developmental model of critical thinking. *Educational Researcher, 28*(2), 16–46.

Lelliott, A., & Rollnick, M. (2010). Big ideas: A review of astronomy education research 1974–2008. *International Journal of Science Education, 32*(13), 1771–1799.

Mason, G. S., Shuman, T. R., & Cook, K. E. (2013). Comparing the effectiveness of an inverted classroom to a traditional classroom in an upper-division engineering course. *IEEE Transactions on Education, 56*(4), 430–435.

Merriam, S. B. (2007). *Qualitative research and case study applications in education* (2nd ed.). San Francisco, CA: Wiley.

Minner, D. D., Levy, A. J., & Century, J. (2010). Inquiry-based science instruction—what is it and does it matter? Results from a research synthesis years 1984 to 2002. *Journal of Research in Science Teaching, 47*(4), 474–496.

Moravec, M., Williams, A., Aguilar-Roca, N., & O'Dowd, D. K. (2010). Learn before lecture: A strategy that improves learning outcomes in a large introductory biology class. *CBE Life Sciences Education, 9*(4), 473–481.

Mulholland, J., & Ginns, I. (2008). College moon project Australia: Preservice teachers learning about the moon's phases. *Research in Science Education, 38*(3), 385–399.

National Center for Education and the Economy. (2007). *Tough choices or tough times: The report of the New Commission on the Skills of the American Workforce*. San Francisco, CA: Wiley.

National Research Council. (2007). *Rising above the gathering storm: energizing and employing America for a brighter economic future*. Washington, D.C.: National Academies Press.

National Research Council. (2011). *Successful K-12 STEM Education: Identifying effective approaches in science, technology, engineering, and mathematics.* Washington, DC: National Academies Press.

Nielsen, J., & Loranger, H. (2006). *Prioritizing web usability.* Boston, MA: Pearson.

Pearson, G., Young, A. T., & others. (2002). *Technically speaking: Why all Americans need to know more about technology.* Washington, D.C.: National Academies Press.

Pierce, R., & Fox, J. (2012). Vodcasts and active-learning exercises in a "flipped classroom" model of a renal pharmacotherapy module. *American Journal of Pharmaceutical Education, 76*(10), 196.

Riechert, S. E., & Post, B. K. (2010). From skeletons to bridges & other STEM enrichment exercises for high school biology. *The American Biology Teacher, 72*(1), 20–22.

Sanders, M. (2009). Stem, stem education, stemmania. *The Technology Teacher, 68*(4), 20–26.

Sandoval, W. A. (2005). Understanding students' practical epistemologies and their influence on learning through inquiry. *Science Education, 89*(4), 634–656.

Schraw, G. (2001). Current themes and future directions in epistemological research: A commentary. *Educational Psychology Review, 13*(4), 451–464.

Stake, R. E. (1995). *The art of case study research.* Thousand Oaks, CA: Sage.

Strauss, A., & Corbin, J. M. (1998). *Basics of qualitative research: Techniques and procedures for developing grounded theory.* Thousand Oaks, CA: Sage.

Szalay, A., & Gray, J. (2006). 2020 computing: Science in an exponential world. *Nature, 440*(7083), 413–414.

Tanase, M., & Wang, J. (2010). Initial epistemological beliefs transformation in one teacher education classroom: Case study of four preservice teachers. *Teaching and Teacher Education, 26*(6), 1238–1248.

Tripp, S. D., & Bichelmeyer, B. (1990). Rapid prototyping: An alternative instructional design strategy. *Educational Technology Research and Development, 38*(1), 31–44.

Trundle, K. C., Atwood, R. K., & Christopher, J. E. (2002). Preservice elementary teachers' conceptions of moon phases before and after instruction. *Journal of Research in Science Teaching, 39*(7), 633–658.

Wilson, B. G., Jonassen, D. H., & Cole, P. (1993). Cognitive approaches to instructional design. *The ASTD Handbook of Instructional Technology, 4*, 21–21.

Wisitsen, Michele. (2012). Moon phases. *Planetarian, 41*(4), 14–22.

Worth, K., Winokur, J., Crissman, S., Heller-Winokur, M., & Davis, M. (2009). *The essentials of science and literacy: A guide for teachers.* Portsmouth, New Hampshire: Heineman.

Beginner Robotics for STEM: Positive Effects on Middle School Teachers

Haihong Hu
Uma Garimella
University of Central Arkansas
United States
hhu@uca.edu
UGarimel@uca.edu

Abstract: A "Beginner Robotics for STEM Teaching" professional development program was offered to 20 6th -8th grade math and science teachers in 2014. The program provided long-term, sustained high quality learning opportunities to Arkansas teachers, especially those in high need Local Educational Agencies. Participants were trained to integrate robotics into STEM-related curriculum that aligns with Arkansas and the National Research Council's Science Standards, and they went through a 60 hour training during which they built and programed robots through a collaborative and experiential learning program integrating concepts from various disciplines. Findings from a mixed-methods case study indicated teachers significantly improved in STEM content knowledge, became more confident in using Robotics to enhance student interest and involvement in STEM activities, and successfully integrated robotics into STEM curriculum through the design of an inquiry-based 5E lesson plan.

Introduction

The United State and the State of Arkansas both share a need to improve education in STEM subjects. In a Congressional Research Service Report, Kuenzi (2008) discussed an emergent concern that the United States was not educating an adequate number of students, teachers, and practitioners in the STEM areas. According to the Change the Equation non-profit agency (2013), business leaders in Arkansas cannot find the STEM talent they need to stay competitive. The critical reason identified was students' lagging performance in K-12; they are not exposed to challenging and engaging content. The average amount of time an elementary student spent on science was 2.5 hours/week in 2008. Only 24% - 35% of 8th graders in Arkansas school districts have math and science teachers whose undergraduate major was in the subject they teach by 2011. And, only 33%-58% of these 8th graders have science teachers who took 3 or more advanced courses in college by 2011. Thus, STEM subjects are the areas that await investment of finance and effort in K-12 education and teacher professional development.

It was found that providing effective technology professional development (PD) to STEM teachers had a positive effect on teacher and student learning outcomes (Elliot & Mikulas, 2012; Martin, Strother, Beglau, Bates, Reitzes, & McMillan, 2010). A report by researchers at the Institute of Education Sciences (Yoon, Duncan, Lee, Scarloss, & Shapley, 2007) finds from nine studies that teachers who receive substantial professional development, an average of 49 hours, can increase their students' achievement by about 21 percent.

Robotics has been found effective in enhancing middle school students' achievements (Barker & Ansorge, 2007) and learning motivation (Nugent, Barker, Grandgenett, & Adamchuk, 2010) in the STEM areas. It was reported (Barker & Ansorge, 2007) that the use of a science and technology curriculum based on robotics was helpful for increasing achievement scores of student who were 9-11 in an after school program. Another study (Nugent, Barker, Grandgenett, & Adamchuk, 2010) investigated the impact of robotics and geospatial technologies interventions on middle school students' learning of and attitudes toward STEM. Results indicated that a longer 40-hour summer camp led to significantly greater learning while a short-term 3-hour intervention mainly impacted learner attitude and motivation.

Therefore, a 60-hour professional development focused on a Robotics curriculum integrating Science, Technology, Engineering and Math can be especially beneficial to STEM teachers and K-12 students in Arkansas to improve achievement and enhance learner motivation.

Purpose of the Professional Development and Study

Engineering is prominently included in The Next Generation Science Standards (NGSS Lead States, 2013), as it was in the Framework for K–12 Science Education (National Research Council, 2012). To reflect the importance of understanding the human-built world and to recognize the value of better integrating the teaching and learning of science, math, engineering, and technology, it is important to incorporate engineering practices with natural sciences practices. A needs assessment survey was sent by email to select Arkansas school districts in

November 2013. Fifty-two teachers responded to the survey. When asked how interested they were in receiving PD in STEM areas, an overwhelming majority (96%) of teachers expressed interest in designing solutions to real world problems. Though 73% or more teachers indicated that they were interested in receiving training in all areas of STEM, 88% selected engineering content and design; more than 86% indicated engaging in argument with evidence and analyzing variables; 80% in developing new tools, and 76% in integration of science and engineering practices. The needs assessment data also revealed that 85% of teachers agreed that grade 6-8 students should have engineering based lessons. However, only 17% of the teachers had appropriate content knowledge, 25% knew how to facilitate and engage students in engineering lessons, while 17% knew an engineering faculty from a university. Thus, there is a noticeable need for assistance or training on how to teach the engineering design process.

Effective STEM instruction is characterized as capitalizing on students' interest and providing experience to engage students in the practice of science (National Research Council, 2011). This professional development was designed based on the theoretical foundations of Experiential Learning theory (Kolb, Boyatzis, & Mainemelis, 2000). In this professional development, the four-stage cycle for Experiential Learning: a) Abstract conceptualization (observing the modeling by PD instructors), b) Concrete experience (building and programming robots), c) Active experimentation (creating and presenting robotics lesson plans), and d) Reflective observation (daily journal writing) was implemented. The professional development program features real-world challenges for participants and their students to solve through conducting research, utilizing critical thinking and imagination. Design elements included the incorporation of multiple learning styles (auditory, visual, and kinesthetic components) and the use of a 5E lesson format (Bybee & Fuchs, 2006). Beside the STEM Content knowledge, effective use of Robotics and Cooperative Learning in Instruction were the other parts of the instructional content for the training. It was designed to prepare teachers to capture students' inherent inquisitiveness, to cultivate an interest in science and engineering, and to direct it toward discovering the possibilities of STEM-related careers. This professional development was intended to work as a model of STEM instruction best practices (National Research Council, 2011; Stohlmann, Moore, & Roehrig, 2012) in that it goes beyond the regular hands-on, inquiry-based real-world problem solving to the use of a performance assessment, which requires learners to justify their thinking in a cooperative environment, through the use of Robotics.

A mixed-method case study was conducted alongside the professional development to examine what participants learned from the training. The use of a case study method is considered appropriate as it can offer a thorough exploration of the event under investigation (Yin, 2003).

This study aimed to investigate whether a Robotics PD would positively influence K-12 teachers': 1) STEM content knowledge learning, 2) confidence in using Robotics to involve students in STEM activities, 3) integration of Robotics into STEM content through the design of cooperative learning lessons based on the National Science standards to implement strategies and methods that were modeled in the professional development sessions. Quantitative data sources included: pre- and post-assessment results and student attitudinal survey. Qualitative data included focus group and personal interviews, copies of 5E lesson plans and presentations, journals, and class observation notes.

Methods

The Beginner Robotics for STEM Teaching is a professional development program that consisted of a two-week summer institute (48 hours) with two follow-up days (12 hours) during the academic year. It was held on the campus of a university in central Arkansas. The university's Institute for STEM Professional Development and Education Research was the host of the PD, and it provides essential support to the university's mission in science and mathematics teacher education. It offers STEM educational opportunities through partnerships with local schools, professional development, research, K-12 outreach, and distribution of instructional resources (UCA STEM Institute, 2013).

Twenty (20) 6th-8thgrade teachers (16 female; 4 males) were selected into the robotics project. Thirteen of them were Caucasian; six were African Americans, and one was an American Indian. These teachers are from 10 schools in 7 school districts, within which 4 were high need LEAs. None of them reported that they had used Robotics prior to this PD. Within these teachers, eleven teach Science; two teach Mathematics and Science; two teach Math; two teach Science and English; two teach Vocational or Career Education; and one teaches Special Education. Regarding teaching experience, most of these teachers (15) have taught for 6 to 25 years. Only teachers who completed all the workshop procedures were included as participants in this study, and comparison between the pre- and post-intervention results were made on exactly the same set of individuals.

The Beginner Robotics for STEM Teaching sessions were content-intensive, and had a focus on integrating Robotics with STEM curriculum in middle schools so as to increase the probability of academic success for all students. The summer institute activities were tailored to address the stated training needs of partnering school district teachers based on the needs assessment. The project also afforded teachers the opportunity to build working relationships with university science and education faculty. During the PD, participants were trained to integrate robotics into STEM-related curriculum that aligned with Arkansas and the National Research Council's (2012) Science Standards, and they each actually built a LEGO Mindstorm NXT robot and programmed the robot using LEGO Mindstorms software NXT-G v2.0 through a collaborative and experiential learning program integrating concepts from various disciplines such as biology, physical science, mathematics, computer science and engineering.

The structure of the institute activities modeled the engineering design process used by scientists and engineers in industry. Each activity started with a design brief explaining the challenge, used videos of robots in action to make real world connections, and culminated in a final project (integration lesson plan) that can be shared and presented. Throughout the activities, learners gained and used knowledge of science, technology, and mathematics as they engineered a solution to the challenge. Project activities were designed to assist participants in designing the 5E Robotics integration lesson plans (Bybee & Fuchs, 2006), which can be implemented to help K-12 students develop 21st century, creative thinking, problem solving, teamwork, and communication skills required for success in school and beyond.

The two-week summer institute consisted of ten Monday- through- Friday sessions. Teachers were required to attend two Saturday academies in fall 2014 as part of the follow-up activities. During the fall semester, there were also classroom visits by the university faculty for classroom observations, lesson modeling, and teacher conferencing. The participating university faculty members provided continuous support to develop and implement STEM related lesson plans throughout the year.

Interviews were conducted towards the end of each week during the institute. Formative and summative assessments were conducted for each participant in the form of pre- and post-tests, respectively, to ensure that the professional development program's overall outcomes were achieved. A robotic workshop pre-and post-questionnaire was given to evaluate the participants' expectations of the institute as well as to gain insight into their prior knowledge of and attitude towards robotics technology.

Results & Findings

Participants' data on (1) STEM content knowledge, 2) confidence in integrating Robotics to involve students in STEM activities, and 3) integration of Robotics into STEM content through the design of 5E cooperative learning lessons were collected using paper-pencil assessments, questionnaires and electronic submissions. Quantitative data were analyzed using descriptive statistics and qualitative data were analyzed using content analysis.

STEM Content Knowledge

The Beginner Robotics for Education Assessment was given to participants on June 23, 2014 to assess knowledge levels in robotics as well as to enhance teaching and learning. The exact test was administered as a post-test on July 11, 2014. It is a 25- question, multiple choice instrument (please see Table 1 for sample assessment items) to measure STEM content knowledge related with Robotics. It measures knowledge in 4 areas, including: a) Science, such as motion and stability (NGSS: MS-PS2-1): Forces and interactions (e.g., Learn to control speed and power of a robot using a motor); b)Technology, such as understanding and using technology systems (ISTE:S,6,a) (e.g., Program and control input and output devices of a robot); c) Engineering, such as developing a model to generate data for iterative testing and modification of a proposed object, tool, or process such that an optimal design can be achieved (NGSS: MS-ETS1-4.) (e.g., Choose a robot challenge, build it, test it, evaluate it, and revise it); d) Mathematics, such as using data involving distance, time, turning angle, degrees of rotation, sound volume, and gear ratios to solve problems (CCSS.Math.Content.6.RP.A.1) (e.g., Use data from specialized sensors such as rotation, sound, light, ultrasonic, and touch). Summary statistics of the pre- and post-test scores are located in Table 2.

Table 1. Sample Assessment Items

Science item:	*Engineering item:*

1. One way to increase acceleration is by
    A. Increasing mass.
    B. Decreasing force.
	3. Engineering at its fundamental level is:
	    A. Math

C. Decreasing mass. D. Increasing both force and mass proportionally.	B. Problem solving C. Science D. Art

Technology Literacy item:
2. The process of repeating the design process over and over again is known as:
    a. Refining
    b. Repetition
    c. Ideate
    d. Iteration
	Math item:
	4. How do you calculate the Circumference of a wheel?
	    A. Radius/2 x Pi
	    B. Diameter x 2 x Pi
	    C. Radius x Pi
	    D. Diameter x Pi

Table 2. Summary Statistics of Pre- and Post- Test Scores

Test	Sample Size	Mean	Standard Deviation	Standard Error	Minimum	Maximum
Post	20	61.8000	7.396	1.654	48	76
Pre	19	55.7895	8.791	2.017	40	68

A one-tailed paired t-test of pre- and post-test scores yielded a *t*-statistic = 3.347 with 18 degrees of freedom and *p-value* = 0.0041. Given an α = 0.05 level of significance, there is sufficient evidence to suggest that the average post-test score is significantly greater than the average pre-test score. Only scores of participants who completed both pre and tests were included in the paired analysis.

Confidence in Integrating Robotics

A Robotic Workshop Pre-and Post-Questionnaire was given to participants' to gain insight into their attitude towards robotics technology. On the (5-point Likert-type scale) items that assess participants' confidence in integrating Robotics into the STEM curriculum, there were measurable increases (please see statistics in Table 2). The number of participants who planned to use educational robotics kits after this training rose from 10 in the pre-questionnaire to 17 in the post-questionnaire.

Table 3. Confidence in Integrating Robotics into the STEM Curriculum

Items on Confidence	Pre-Questionnaire Mean	Pre-Questionnaire Mode	Post-Questionnaire Mean	Post-Questionnaire Mode
1. Supporting students participate in robotics competitions	2.37	3	2.90	3
2. Preparing youth to use Robotics in learning STEM	2.42	3 3	3.14	3
3. Using computers to teach youth about robotics	2.63	1	3.29	3
4. Implementing Robotics Curriculum	2	1	3	3
5. Utilizing sensors in robotics	1.74	1	3.05	3
6. Building robots using LEGO® MINDSTORMS® NXT Kit	1.95	1	3.52	4
7. Programming LEGO® MINDSTORMS® NXT Robots	1.74	1	3.19	3
8. Helping student design and build their own robot	2.16	1	3.24	3
9. Utilizing robotics as a vehicle for youth engagement	2.05	1	3.24	4
10. Implementing the Engineering Design Process with students	1.84	1	2.95	3

In addition to general conversation, participants were personally interviewed. All participants possessed no prior formal robotics training. At the conclusion of the institute, teachers' confidence increased. They began to understand what students could learn via robotics and how they could apply this technology to various subjects and reach all students. One teacher said, "The workshop will assist [her] with getting students who are uninterested in science or engineering to engage them in learning new and exciting things about the world around them." "I did not think I would be able to incorporate robots in but now I am comfortable with the programming and finding lessons that integrate robots into our standards," was another teacher's comment. She is now looking forward to it. Because the teachers completely enjoyed themselves and received a "tremendous wealth of resources and practical ways to implement the robotic technology into the curriculum and manage it," as one teacher stated, their classroom will be reenergized resulting in more student engagement and involvement.

Integration of Robotics through the design of a lesson plan

Participants attended a ten-day summer robotic institute that afforded them the opportunity to interact with STEM education instructors to carry out the main goal of the project. At the end of the PD, each of the 20 participant created a Robotics Integration Lesson Plan using the 5E template, addressing the strategies to engage, explore, explain, elaborate, and evaluate. Participants created lesson plans to cover the topics such as how to make a faster robot verses a more powerful robot; torque and speed, and determine which combination of large and small gears is more suitable for each; understanding of the fields of engineering, design, creating models, and the engineering design process; proportional Relationships between Distance and Time; demonstrating Newton's Second Law of Motion by programming NXT robots to explore two different variables, mass & acceleration, and their relationship to force, etc. In their lesson plans, participants designed a great variety of active, learner-centered activities to take advantage of the unique features of Robotics for STEM instruction.

Figure 1 & 2: Photos of participants building and experimenting with robots actively.

Teachers were very responsive when asked during the focus group interview how they plan to incorporate the information they gained during the institute into their respective classrooms. One participant stated that she had "successfully completed a lesson on calculating speed depending on the gears." Another teacher added that her robotic lessons "involved measurement, speed/velocity, distance, time, and other standards that students seem to perform the lowest." An additional idea expressed during the conversation was that robotic technology could be used as bell ringer. The robot could perform a function and the students will have to utilize their critical thinking skills to create the program for that particular function and then test their program. After lesson plans were created using the 5E lesson plan template, participants designed presentations integrating robotics to demonstrate their lesson to their fellow participants. Teachers were able to share ideas with one another through presentations, and could access all 20 lesson plans, which were submitted via Google Drive to a collaborative folder.

With the professional development training all participants received, they will confidently enter their classrooms and execute what they have learned using the hands on materials such as the Mindstorm NXT kit and binders that included information about the robots and the 5E lesson planning. Teachers' energetic attitudes will transfer to their students to enhance their interest and overall involvement in robotic activities.

Discussion

Overall, participants in this study positively incorporated Robotics as a useful and effective tool for STEM teaching and learning, they improved measurably in their STEM content knowledge, confidence in integrating Robotics into the STEM curriculum, and were able to effectively apply their knowledge and skills in the design of a lesson plan to actively engage students in learning activities and assessments.

As to STEM content knowledge, participants from this study reported significantly higher means for learning at the end than at the beginning of the study. Concerning confidence in integrating Robotics into the STEM curriculum, participants reported higher means in the post-test than in the pre-test of the study. These are comparable to findings from studies providing technology professional development (PD) to STEM teachers in that they also found a positive effect on teacher learning outcomes and motivation (Elliot & Mikulas, 2012; Martin, Strother, Beglau, Bates, Reitzes, & McMillan, 2010).

Participants' successful integration of Robotics through the design of a lesson plan could have been attributed to how the PD was designed. This Professional Development can be considered effective in improving participants' integration of Robotics into STEM content through the design of 5E cooperative learning lessons, and confidence in integrating Robotics to involve students in STEM activities because it went through a rigorous instructional design process and is consistent with a framework by Martin et al. (2010) for connecting instructional technology PD to teacher and student outcomes. This connection involved: (a) modeling instruction(the Robotics demonstrations modeled the instructional techniques that were presented); (b) community building (participants were engaged in activities such as self-introduction, iterative experiments, and lesson plan sharing that supported collaborative learning and community building); (c) technology utilization (the target technology was used to support the instruction and participants' practice with the Robotics challenges); and (d) connection to practice (the PD content was applied in the lesson plan process and associated with participants' regular instructional standards and objectives).

This study's results may not reliably apply to other populations due to relatively small sample size, and the nature of voluntary summer professional development. However, this project can provide valuable information to consider in the instructional design of future technology and pedagogy PDs.

Conclusion

Overall, this Robotics professional development for K-12 STEM teachers have been a positive and fruitful experience for participants allowing them to advance their knowledge and skills in teaching and learning, explore with emerging technologies, and cultivate their readiness for teaching engineering design process in the STEM fields. They had active experience with Robotics through experiential learning and were able to design hands-on lesson plans integrating the robots in inquiry-based, cooperative learning activities and assessments to achieve STEM-related outcomes. The participants have learned to use the robots as a vehicle for best practices in STEM instruction, and they have updated their Technological, Pedagogical, and Content knowledge (TPACK).

References

Barker, B.S. & Ansorge, J. (2007). Robotics as Means to Increase Achievement Scores in an Informal Learning Environment. *Journal of Research on Technology in Education, 39*(3), 229- 243. Retrieved December 19, 2013 from http://www.editlib.org/p/100758.

Bybee, R., & Fuchs, B. (2006). Preparing the 21st century workforce: A new reform in science. *Journal of Research in Science Teaching, 43*, 349-352.

Change the Equation Agency. (2013). Vital Signs measure the health of the K-12 STEM learning enterprise, state by state. Retrieved from: http://vitalsigns.changetheequation.org/#ar-Arkansas-Overview

Elliot, S. & Mikulas, C. (2012). Improving Student Learning Through Teacher Technology Training: A Study of the Effectiveness of Technology Integration Training on Student Achievement. In P. Resta (Ed.), *Proceedings of Society for Information Technology & Teacher Education International Conference 2012* (pp. 1759-1766). Chesapeake, VA: AACE. Retrieved from http://www.editlib.org/p/39842 .

Kolb D., Boyatzis, R. & Mainemelis, C.(2000) "Experiential Learning Theory: Previous Research and New Directions". In R. J. Sternberg and L. F. Zhang (Eds.), *Perspectives on cognitive, learning, and thinking styles*. NJ: Lawrence Erlbaum, 2000.

Kuenzi, J. J. (2008). Science, Technology, Engineering, and Mathematics (STEM) Education: Background, Federal Policy, and Legislative Action. Congressional Research Service Reports. Paper 35. Retrieved from:

Martin, W., Strother, S., Beglau, M., Bates, L., Reitzes, T., & McMillan Culp, K. (2010). Connecting instructional technology professional development to teacher and student outcomes. *Journal of Research on Technology in Education, 43*(1), 53.

National Research Council. (2011). *Successful K-12 STEM Education: Identifying Effective Approaches in Science, Technology, Engineering, and Mathematics.* Committee on Highly Successful Science Programs for K-12 Science Education. Board on Science Education and Board on Testing and Assessment, Division of Behavioral and Social Sciences and Education. Washington, DC: The National Academies Press.

National Research Council. (2012). A Framework for K-12 Science Education: Practices, Crosscutting Concepts, and Core Ideas. Washington, DC: The National Academies Press.

NGSS Lead States. (2013). Next Generation Science Standards: For States, By States. Washington, DC: The National Academies Press.

Nugent, G., Barker, B. S., Grandgenett, N., & Adamchuk, V. I. (2010). Impact of Robotics and Geospatial Technology Interventions on Youth STEM Learning and Attitudes. *Journal of Research on Technology in Education. 42*(4), 391–408. ©2010 ISTE www.iste.org.

Stohlmann, M., Moore, T. J., & Roehrig, G. H. (2012). Considerations for Teaching Integrated STEM Education, *Journal of Pre-College Engineering Education Research (J-PEER)*: 2(1), Article 4. http://dx.doi.org/10.5703/1288284314653

UCA STEM Institute. (2013). Mission and vision. Retrieved from: http://uca.edu/steminstitute/mission-and-vision/

Yin, R. K. (2003).Case study research: Design and methods (3rd ed.). Thousand Oaks: Sage.

Yoon, K. S., Duncan, T., Lee, S. W.-Y., Scarloss, B., & Shapley, K. (2007). Reviewing the evidence on how teacher professional development affects student achievement (Issues & Answers Report, REL 2007–No. 033). Washington, DC: U.S. Department of Education, Institute of Education Sciences, National Center for Education Evaluation and Regional Assistance, Regional Educational Laboratory Southwest. Retrieved from http://ies.ed.gov/ncee/edlabs

Acknowledgement

This project was supported by a U. S. Department of Education grant provided through the No Child Left Behind program for improving the quality of teaching and instruction in Arkansas. It was channeled through the Arkansas Department of Higher Education (ADHE). The authors of the paper wish to express their sincere thanks for the opportunity to participate in the project. This paper reflects the research of the members of the project and does not necessarily represent the work of U. S. Department of Education or the No Child Left Behind program, or their expressed beliefs. The researchers wish to also thank the members of the project team as well as members of the ADHE project leadership.

Utilizing Wearable Technologies as a Pathway to STEM

Bradley Barker
University of Nebraska-Lincoln
United States
bbarker1@unl.edu

Jennifer Melander
University of Nebraska-Lincoln
United States
jmelander5@unl.edu

Neal Grandgenett
University of Nebraska at Omaha
United States
ngrandgenett@unomaha.edu

Gwen Nugent
University of Nebraska-Lincoln
United States
gnugent1@unl.edu

Abstract: The purpose of this paper is to report the findings of a pilot study that utilized a wearable electronic technologies intervention as a way to increase attitudes towards science, technology, engineering and mathematics (STEM) content areas for students in grades 4 to 6. The study utilized a previously developed attitudinal instrument that examined eight constructs around motivation, self-efficacy and learning strategies. The findings indicate that wearable technologies may indeed increase STEM attitudes and could particularly be a viable way to increase participation in STEM for females.

Introduction

The wearable technology field, including electronic textiles (e-textiles), promises to be an excellent interdisciplinary STEM context and technology-rich learning experience because it relies upon principles of engineering design, electricity, circuitry, and computer programing while combining fashion design and aesthetics for the creation of innovative wearable products. For example, a wearable technologies product like the OMsignal biosensor shirt (http://www.omsignal.com/) captures the wearer's heart rate, breathing, and activity levels through almost invisible sensors within the shirt and shares the information through a mobile device. It is anticipated that this shirt will provide critical biological information to the wearer and to doctors regarding health and wellness issues. In another example, Google X-Labs recently announced the development of a contact lens that will monitor glucose levels in tears and have the capability to transmit that information (Landen, 2014). This technology is intended to alert the wearer when glucose levels are elevated, which is important in cases when immediate medical assistance is either needed or might also be immediately prevented. While these and other new products like the Apple Watch and Samsung's Galaxy Gear are becoming increasingly prominent, they are only the tip of the iceberg when it comes to the potential of wearable technology, and sales of wearable technologies are expected to grow from US $750 million in 2012 to over $5.8 billion by 2018, with many wearable devices devoted to health and physical activity (Wei, 2014).

Seemingly, e-textiles (including those that can be worn) provide an ideal hands-on learning space for students because such a learning environment is both exciting and personally relevant, especially for females who tend to be more interested in textiles and fashion design than their male counterparts. With wearable e-textiles, technology that is normally hidden becomes visible, and computing becomes personally relevant when it is combined with textiles that the maker can actually use. E-textiles bring together engineering and computing to make computers that are "soft, colorful, approachable, and beautiful" (Buechley, Peppler, Eisenber & Kafai, 2013, p.1).

These wearable electronic inventions contain embedded computational devices and electronic elements that transform them into 'smart' objects.

Traditionally, the development of wearable electronic textiles has been reserved for scientists, textile engineers, health professionals, and pioneers in the arts and fashion design (Buechley et al., 2013). However, with the development of small, relatively low-cost programmable microcontrollers like the LilyPad Arduino, students can now design, build, and program their own devices. The LilyPad Arduino is a compact programmable microcontroller based on the popular Arduino board. The LilyPad was made to look like a futuristic water lily, with a purple circular printed computer board (PCB) with conductive holes around the edges that move electricity through silver nylon thread. This conductive thread can be connected to input, output, and a wide range of sensory devices and is used to connect a power supply to the LilyPad. The LilyPad can be purchased relatively inexpensively as a kit with the conductive thread, LED lights, sensors, motors, and switches (Buechley et al., 2013) necessary to create wearable technology items. Computer programming is an important component of wearable e-textile design when considering its educational potential, and the LilyPad can be programmed to control the electrical signals sent through the thread-based circuitry.

Current Project

In the fall 2014 the Wearable Technologies (WearTec) project, as facilitated by a team of faculty from the University of Nebraska-Lincoln's Mechanical and Materials Engineering Department, the Department of Biological Systems Engineering, 4-H Youth Development, the Nebraska Department of Education, and the University of Nebraska at Omaha's Department of Teacher Education piloted approximately 10 hours of instruction centered on wearable technologies. The goal of the WearTec project was to develop an intervention that focuses on solving real world problems and practicing the engineering design process while immersed in the innovative area of wearable technologies. The engineering design process was incorporated through direct instruction in early lessons followed by probing questions and scaffolding on guided implementation of the process. In addition, for each lesson students were asked to record information in an engineering design notebook. The lessons use various versions of the LilyPad microcontroller and compatible light and temperature sensors, LEDs, buttons, switches, motors, power supplies and sound devices, which are all connected with conductive thread. Specifically, the lessons included: a) building electrical circuits, b) engineering design, c) building a bracelet or pennant, d) programming the LilyPad, and e) building an interactive toy. For the bracelet/pennant lesson the LilyTiny microcontroller (a smaller, preprogrammed version of the Lilypad Arduino) was used, along with LEDs and a 3-Volt battery. The lesson provided an opportunity for students to integrate the LilyTiny and LEDs with multicolored felt fabric to create wearable bracelets or pennants embellished with flashing LEDs. For the programming activity the project used the LilyPad ProtoSnap Development Board, which consists of the LilyPad microprocessor connected to LEDs, sensors, switches and other components on a PCB. For the final activity, students used a standalone LilyPad Arduino microcontroller and related components to design and create a textile-based product in the form of a small toy monster. Like other technology-focused interventions the cost to implement the activities with youth are a consideration and costs for the current intervention are estimated at $100 to $150 per student. However, some components like the LilyPad ProtoSnap Development Board, which consists of a microprocessor prewired with LEDs, buzzers, sensors and other components could be reused thereby reducing the costs of the intervention over time. Other components are consumable and most likely would have to be purchased for each of the iterations of the intervention.

Theoretical Background

The theoretical basis for using wearable technologies in education, which includes the design, development, and building of wearable computer-based electronic artifacts, is firmly situated in the constructivism theory of learning (Piaget, 1972). This theory purports that youths' new knowledge is actively constructed from the world around them through experiential practice and by independent/guided research to integrate new knowledge and to arrive at a deeper understanding. Problem-based learning (PBL) is a constructivist learning model that uses ill-structured problems that invite multiple approaches to develop a solution (Husain, 2011). Like constructivism, PBL is student-centered, which allows students to determine what they need to solve the instructional challenge with minimal facilitator input and limited guidance (Klegeris & Hurren, 2011). Also, rather than focusing exclusively on a single discipline, PBL typically requires students to engage in interdisciplinary thinking that is foundational to STEM learning and application (Carnevale Smith & Stoll, 2010; Nicholl & Lou, 2012; Wiznia, et al., 2012).

From these two well-recognized theoretical perspectives, wearable electronic textiles that combine computing with aesthetics can be thought of as cognitive tools (Jonassen, 2000) that enhance the learning process and allow students to creatively and collaboratively problem solve while drawing on computer programming, mechanical and textile design, and other STEM content. In addition, the wearable technologies for learning are closely aligned with components of engineering design that have been shown to support the study of science and its collaborative problem solving (Riskowski et al., 2009). These components include: 1) interaction - collaboration between team members and groups to design build-test artifacts, 2) artifact development that fosters the individuals and teams knowledge, and 3) critical analysis, a process of continual iterative design. The Next Generation Science Standards (NGSS) also support the use of engineering as a framework to engage students in disciplinary core ideas and as an instructional point of entry to pique students' curiosity, capture their interest, and motivate their continued study. The insights gained help students recognize that the work of scientists and engineers is a creative endeavor - one that has deeply affected the world in which they live (NRC Framework, 2012, p. 218). Several studies support the combination of engineering design, PBL, and design-based science as effective means to increase understanding of STEM with long-term retention of learning and to decrease the achievement gaps between groups (Hmelo, et al., 2000; Mehalik, et al., 2008).

Current Research

Few studies have specifically examined wearable technologies in education. However, there are related studies that have examined the effectiveness of programs that use manipulatives with interactive capabilities similar to e-textiles like educational robotics. These studies suggest that participation in robotics activities increases interest in STEM, improves workplace and life skills, and inspires youth to enter STEM careers (Melchior et al., 2005; Nugent, Barker, & Grandgenett, 2012). Unlike standard robot kits, however, the LilyPad and associated electronic components are not hidden behind plastic coverings. The exposed components must be treated carefully to avoid problems like shorting the circuit. At the same time the exposed components become an exceptional opportunity for youth to develop skills in circuit planning and arrangement of components. In addition, unlike entering STEM through robotics, which has been traditionally dominated by males, wearable technologies offer an alternative pathway to STEM through textiles and computing that may be more closely aligned with the typical societal experiences of some females. Past research suggests that creating designs with the LilyPad helps learners to better understand underlying electrical structures and processes that are normally hidden (Peppler & Glosson, 2013). Peppler and Glosson (2013) found that middle school students in an out-of-school time (OST) club learned about electrical current, battery polarity, circuit conductivity, and diagramming series circuitry through the use of LilyPad kits. Youth in the project built persistence of vision (POV) wristbands using the LilyPad and LEDs connected to a power supply. In another study Kafai, Fields, and Searle (2013) delivered an e-textile workshop to high school students looking specifically at the intersection of coding, circuitry, and crafting. Like Peppler and Glosson (2013) they concluded that making the technology visible to students provided a better understanding of the circuits and computer programming. Creating wearable computation devices involves identifying, debugging, and solving problems in coding, circuitry, and crafting (Kafai, Fields & Searle, 2013). These design problems help learners develop inquiry skills, including observation, hypothesis generation, testing, and evaluation of solutions (Sullivan, 2008). When building artifacts, concepts like electrical voltage, current, resistance, and polarity are reinforced for students. When working with wearable technologies, getting the artifact to work is not enough. Peppler, Sharpe, and Glosson (2013) argue that another important aspect of wearable technologies is the aesthetics that reflect the voice of the designer. The intersection of STEM and art in wearable technologies reinforces the computing, circuitry, and engineering while unlocking the creativity and artistry of design. We believe that this learning intersection is particularly promising.

This pilot study specifically examined the effect of the wearable technologies intervention on student's attitudes toward science, technology, engineering, and mathematics (STEM) content areas utilizing curricular lessons focused on wearable e-textiles. Participants completed a pre attitudinal survey prior to beginning the intervention and a post session survey immediately afterwards. The actual intervention for the study included the building of electronic textiles (bracelets, t-shirts with LEDs and sensors, and stuffed toys) in two afterschool programs using the LilyPad components (microprocessors, LEDs, sensors and conductive thread). The program was delivered in-person by university faculty, certified teachers, and afterschool educators for approximately 1.5 hours weekly for seven weeks. The intervention aligned with problem-based learning and the instruction was facilitated by two university instructors and one certified teacher while building toward the context of a specific engineering solution. For example, students were charged with developing a t-shirt design that provides high visibility in low-light situations. All participants were given engineering notebooks and encouraged to draw their designs and document their progress within the notebook for later consultation. A paired sample t-test was used to compare the pre and post survey means.

Description of the Participants and Context

The sample for the pilot group consisted of 43 students ranging in age from 8 to 14 with a mean age of 11.49 years. Nearly 28% of the participants were from under-served populations as determined by student demographics. For the pilot 17 (39.5%) males and 26 (60.5%) females participated in the intervention. Participants were recruited from the 21st Century Community Learning Centers (21st CCLC) grant programs and through the Nebraska 4-H youth development program in the Southeast portion of Nebraska. The 21st CCLC program is a federally funded, competitive grant program designed to support the establishment of community learning centers serving students attending high-need schools.

Instrumentation

The attitude instrument was adapted from a previous instrument used and validated for an educational robotics intervention (Nugent, Barker, Grandgenett, & Adamchuk 2009). The instrument consists of 33 Likert scale items modeled after the Motivated Strategies for Learning Questionnaire (Pintrich, Smith, Garcia, & McKeachie, 1999). The questionnaire included two sections focusing upon: a) motivation and b) the use of learning strategies (see Appendix for survey questions). The motivation component included questions measuring youth self-efficacy in circuitry and wearable technologies. Self-efficacy is derived from Bandura's (Bandura, 1977) theory of self-efficacy that is based on one's belief in their ability to cope with a task. Self-efficacy has also been shown to be correlated with achievement outcomes (Sorge, 2007). The self-efficacy scales (circuitry and wearable technologies) focused on youths' self-appraisal of their confidence in performing certain circuitry and wearable technologies tasks, such as "I am confident that I can program a computer to blink LED lights." The motivation section also included questions on students' perceived educational value of mathematics, science, technology and wearable products. These task value scales strive to measure youth's evaluation of the importance, usefulness, and interest of a task. Research has shown that an early interest in STEM topics is a predicator for later learning and/or eventual career interests and choices (OECD, 2007). Sample items included, "It is important for me to learn how to conduct a scientific investigation," and "I like learning new technologies such as e-textiles."

The learning strategies section of the assessment focused on problem solving and teamwork. The problem solving scale measured the degree to which students use specific problem solving approaches to successfully accomplish the wearable tasks. Our anecdotal observations of the students had shown that they appeared to use a variety of problem-solving approaches, including trial and error, with little pre-planning and problem analysis. Sample survey items included, "I use a step by step process to solve problems" and "I make a plan before I start to solve a problem." The teamwork scale was included because a major goal of the project was to encourage teamwork, getting students to work with their peers to solve problems. A sample item included "I like being part of a team that is trying to solve problems."

Similar to the original study by Nugent, Barker, Grandgenett, & Adamchuk (2009) the overall Cronbach alpha reliability for the post survey was 0.95. A repeated measures design was used for the pilot using the identical survey for the pre and posttest. Educators leading the program administered the survey on the first day of the intervention and then again on the last day.

Results

To determine if significant differences existed between the pre and post attitudinal instruments mean scores a repeated measures *t*-test was run for each attitudinal scale. The mean scores for the pre and posttest are presented as well as the standard deviation and the significance in Table 1. In addition a Cohen's *d* was calculated to indicate the relative effect size for each scale. Accordingly, a small effect size (d) = 0.2, 0.5 is a medium effect, and 0.8 would constitute a large effect size. The overall mean scores showed an increase from pre ($M = 4.19$, SD = 0.32) to post ($M = 4.31$, $SD = 0.45$). The difference was not significant $t(20) = 1.80$, $p = .088$; however it did represent a medium effect size, $d = 0.65$. The science task value was the only scale to show a significant increase from pre ($M = 4.11$, $SD = 0.48$) to post ($M = 4.36$, $SD = 0.55$), $t(20) = 2.84$, $p = .010$, and represented a medium effect size. It is important to note that the problem approach scale actually decreased from pre ($M = 4.21$, $SD = 0.49$) to post ($M = 4.13$, $SD = 0.63$). The difference was not significant $t(20) = 0.96$), $p = 0.347$.

Table 1: Pre and post comparisons for attitudinal scales

Measure	M_{pre}	M_{post}	t (df)	Std. Dev.	Sig. (2-tailed)	Cohen's d
Motivation						
Science Task Value	4.11	4.36	2.84 (20)	0.40	.010*	0.62
Mathematics Task Value	4.15	4.33	1.70 (20)	0.49	.103	0.37
E-Textiles Task Value	4.40	4.50	0.92 (20)	0.55	.367	0.18
Technology Task Value	4.43	4.53	1.48 (20)	0.32	.156	0.31
Self-efficacy						
E-Textiles	4.11	4.12	.075 (20)	0.73	.941	0.013
Circuitry	3.96	4.20	1.30 (20)	0.84	.208	0.29
Learning Strategies						
Problem Approach	4.21	4.13	0.96 (20)	0.41	.347	(0.20)
Teamwork	4.15	4.38	1.40 (20)	0.74	.175	0.31
Overall Mean Score	4.19	4.31	1.80 (20)	0.32	.088	0.40

Note: * p < .05

Discussion

This pilot project has documented the impact of a wearable technologies project on the attitudes of students towards STEM content areas from using a pre to post survey instrument. Wearable technologies including electronic textiles are similar to other digital manipulatives like education robotics and yet different enough that it would seem a natural way to increase interest and engagement amongst female participants. Wearable technologies allow participants to combine computing technology, circuitry and aesthetics to create projects that are personally meaningful. This pilot study specifically examined the impact of a wearable technologies intervention on the attitudes of participants using a revised version of the instrument reported by Nugent, Barker, Grandgenett, and Adamchuk (2009). Two constructs of the instrument were modified to reflect questions on e-textiles and technology as opposed to robotic and GPS technologies in the original instrument.

The results of the pilot study indicate that participants overall reported increases in their attitudes towards STEM. However, it should be noted that only 21 out of the 43 total participants completed both the pre and post surveys, which considerably reduces the power of the study and therefore the potential to detect significant differences. Additional studies with larger sample sizes need to be conducted to determine effectiveness of the intervention. In addition, it should be noted that participants reported mean pretest scores nearing 4.0 on a 5.0 scale introducing a potential ceiling effect for the posttest scores. This is especially true when the scores are divided by gender with females reporting a higher overall pretest score ($M = 4.26$, $SD = 0.32$) compared to males ($M = 4.09$, $SD = 0.46$). One area of concern is the small changes in the e-textiles self-efficacy scale. Again, when broken down by gender males actually reported a higher pre ($M = 4.17$, $SD = 0.61$) than post ($M = 4.08$, $SD = 0.79$) while females had a slight increase from pre ($M = 4.06$, $SD = 0.73$) to post ($M = 4.15$, $SD = 0.87$) on the e-textiles self-efficacy scale items. One possible reason for the decrease in scores for males was their potential overestimation of their abilities in sewing and stitching using conductive thread to complete a circuit. Some males may lack prior knowledge in sewing and therefore may have not realized the difficulty of the task. Most females had some experience in sewing although many had used machines and never hand stitched and therefore may have more accurately reported their efficacy on the pre survey items. In addition, since these questions were modified from the original version of the survey and additional psychometric analysis should be done to assure reliability and validity. Again, because of the small sample size a confirmatory factor analysis was not run (Tabachnick & Fidell, 2013).

While the results of this study are not significant overall it is important to note that the intervention did have a medium effect size on the attitudes as indicated by the overall Cohen's $d = 0.40$. In addition, it is important to note that 60.5% (26) of the participants all of whom self-selected into the program were females. More female students participated proportionally in the wearable technologies program when compared to similar programs like educational robotics where only 30% of participants are females (Nugent, Barker, Grandgenett & Welch, 2014). A trend also reported by Martin et. al., (2011) with a participation ratio of male to female students of 2:1 or greater. The results of the study support the assumption that unlike entering STEM through robotics, which has been traditionally dominated by males, wearable technologies may well offer an alternative pathway to STEM through textiles and computing that may be more closely aligned with the typical societal experiences of some females. While the program exhibited promising results the project team expects that by expanding the curricular lessons and providing students additional experiences in wearable technologies, the students would display increases in attitudes towards STEM content areas. Finally, our team has been generally encouraged by these pilot study results, and we believe that wearable technologies may well be able to positively contribute to the growing educational efforts to better engage and interest students in STEM instruction, while perhaps representing a powerful new intersection of computing, electronics, and engineering while also unlocking the creativity and artistry of design for many students.

Limitations of the Study and Recommendations for Future Research

The main goal of this study was to pilot newly developed lessons centered on wearable electronic textiles for late elementary and middle school students. While the results were promising, the study was limited by the small sample size, and underpowered at $n=21$. Potentially due to the low statistical power a significant difference was not detected from pre to post tests and the results cannot be generalized to the target population as a whole. Additional studies with larger samples and appropriate statistical power are needed to better understand the effect of the intervention on student learning and attitudes towards STEM. In addition, future studies might want to focus on teacher and educator preparation to implement programs that involve wearable technologies looking specifically at implementation strategies, student to teacher ratios, efficacy and how such an intervention could fit into the school day to support STEM learning.

References

Bandura, Albert. 1977. Self-efficacy. The Exercise of Control. New York: Freeman.
Buechley, L., Peppler, K., Eisenberg, M., Kafai, Y. (2013). Textile Messages: Dispatches from the World for e-Textiles and Education. New York, NY: Peter Lang.
Carnevale, A.P., Smith, N., & Melton, M. (2011). STEM. Available from Georgetown University Center on Education and the Workforce website: http://cew.georgetown.edu/STEM
Hmelo, C. E., Holton, D., & Kolodner, J. L. (2000). Designing to learn about complex systems. *Journal of the Learning Sciences, 9*, 247-298.
Husain, A. (2011). Problem-based learning: A current model of education. *Oman Medical Journal, 26*, 295.
Jonassen, D. (2000). *Computers as mindtools for schools. Engaging critical thinking* (2nd ed.). Saddle River, NJ: Prentice-Hall.
Kafai, Y., Fields, D., Searle, K. (2013). Making connections across disciplines in high school e-textiles workshops. In L. Buechley, K. Peppler, M. Eisenberg, Y. Kafai (Eds.), Textile Messages: Dispatches from the World for e-Textiles and Education. New York, NY: Peter Lang.
Klegeris, A., & Hurren, H. (2011). Impact of problem-based learning in a large classroom setting: Student perception and problem-solving skills. *Advances in Physiology Education, 35*, 408–415.

Landen, R. (2014) Google lens for monitoring glucose has hurdles to clear before hitting market. *Modern Healthcare*. http://www.modernhealthcare.com/article/20140117/NEWS/301179919 (last accessed 10-21-2014).

Martin, F., Scribner-MacLean, M., Christy, S., Rudnicki, I., Londhe, R., Manning., C., Goodman, I. (2011). "Reflections on iCODE: using web technology and hands-on projects to engage urban youth in computer science and engineering." *Autonomous Robots*, **30**(3), pp. 265–280, DOI: 10.1007/s10514-011-9218-3.

Mehalik, M. M., Doppelt, Y., & Schunn, C. D. (2008). Middle-school science through design-based learning versus scripted inquiry: Better overall science concept learning and equity gap reduction. *Journal of Engineering Education, 97*, 71–85.

Melchoir, A., Cohen, F., et al. (2005). More than Robots: An Evaluation of the FIRST Robotics

Competition Participant and Institutional Impacts. Waltham, MA, Center of Youth and Communities, Heller School for Social Policy and Management, Brandeis University. Milestones in Computer Development. (n.d.) Retrieved August 8, 2007 from http://www.cis.usouthal.edu faculty/daigle/project1/timeline.htm

National Research Council. (2012). *A framework for K-12 science education: Practices, crosscutting concepts, and core ideas.* Washington, DC: The National Academies Press.

Nicholl, T. A., & Lou, K. (2012). A model for small-group problem-based learning in a large class facilitated by one instructor. *American Journal of Pharmaceutical Education, 76*(6), Article 117. doi:10.5688/ajpe766117

Nugent, G. C., Barker, B., Grandgenett, N., & Welch, G. (2014). Robotics camps, clubs, and competitions: Results from a US robotics project. In J. Lee, P. Martinet, M. Strand, S. Ghidoni, & M. Munaro (Eds.), Proceedings of 4th International Workshop Teaching Robotics, Teaching with Robotics &5th International Conference Robotics in Education Padova (Italy) July 18, 2014 (pp. 11–18).

Nugent, G., Barker, B., & Grandgenett, N. (2012). The impact of educational robotics on student STEM learning, attitudes and workplace skills. In B. S. Barker, G. Nugent, N. Grandgenett, & V. I. Adamchuk (Eds.), *Robotics in K–12 education: A new technology for learning.* Hershey, PA: IGI Global.

OECD. 2007. PISA 2006 Science Competencies for Tomorrow's World. Volume 1: Analysis.

Peppler, K., & Glosson, D. (2013). Learning about circuitry with e-textiles in after-school settings. In M. Knobel & C. Lankshear (Eds.), *The new literacies reader.* New York, NY: Peter Lang Publishing.

Peppler, K., Sharpe, L., & Glosson, D. (2013). E-Textiles and the new fundamentals of fine arts. In L. Buechley, K. Peppler, M. Eisenberg, Y. Kafai (Eds.), Textile Messages: Dispatches from the World for e-Textiles and Education. New York, NY: Peter Lang.

Pintrich, Paul, David Smith, Teresa Garcia, and William McKeachie. 1999. A Manual for the Use of the Motivated Strategies for Learning Questionnaire. Ann Arbor: University of Michigan.

Piaget. Jean. 1972. The Child's Conception of the World. Towota, NJ: Littlefield Adams.

Riskowski, J., Todd, C., Wee, B., Dark, M., & Harbor, J. (2009). Exploring the Effectiveness of an Interdisciplinary Water Resources Engineering Module in an Eighth Grade Science Course. *International Journal of Engineering Education*, 25 (1), 181-195.

Sorge, C. 2007. "What Happens: Relationship of Age and Gender with Acience Attitudes from Elementary to Middle School. Science Educator. Vol 16, pp. 33-37.

Sullivan, F. R. (2008). Robotics and science literacy: Thinking skills, science process skills and systems understanding. *Journal of Research in Science Teaching, 45*(3), 373-394.

Tabachnick, G.G. and Fidell, L.S. (2013). Using Multivariate Statistics (sixth ed.). Pearson, Boston

Wiznia, D., Korom, R., Marzuk, P., Safdieh, J., & Grafstein, B. (2012). PBL 2.0: Enhancing problem-based learning through increased student participation. *Medical Education Online, 17*. doi:10.3402/meo.v17i0.17375

Wei, J. (2014). How Wearables Intersect with the Cloud and the Internet of Things: Considerations for the developers of wearables. Consumer Electronics Magazine, 3(3), 54-56. doi: 10.1109/MCE.2014.2317895

Acknowledgements

This material is based upon work supported by the National Science Foundation under Grant No. ITEST #1433822 awarded to the University of Nebraska-Lincoln. Any opinions, findings, and conclusions or recommendations expressed in this material are those of the author(s) and do not necessarily reflect the views of the National Science Foundation.

Appendix

Statement	Strongly Agree	Agree	Neither Agree nor Disagree	Disagree	Strongly Disagree
1. It is important for me to learn how to conduct a scientific investigation.	5	4	3	2	1
2. It is important for me to learn about technology.	5	4	3	2	1
3. It is important for me to learn how to use appropriate tools and techniques to gather, analyze and interpret data.	5	4	3	2	1
4. It is important for me to learn about computer science.	5	4	3	2	1
5. It is important for me to learn how to use mathematical formulas to help solve practical problems.	5	4	3	2	1
6. It is important for me to learn how to make accurate measurements to help solve mathematical problems.	5	4	3	2	1
7. It is important for me to be able to record measurements and calculations into tables and charts.	5	4	3	2	1
8. It is important for me to learn how to collect and interpret data to verify a prediction or hypothesis.	5	4	3	2	1
9. It is important for me to understand basic engineering concepts (e.g. design tradeoffs, circuits, power) related to e-textiles.	5	4	3	2	1
10. It is important for me to learn how to program a computer.	5	4	3	2	1
11. It is important for me to learn about how technology works.	5	4	3	2	1
12. I like learning new technologies such as e-textiles.	5	4	3	2	1
13. I like using the scientific method to solve problems.	5	4	3	2	1
14. I like using mathematical formulas and calculations to	5	4	3	2	1

Statement	Strongly Agree	Agree	Neither Agree nor Disagree	Disagree	Strongly Disagree
solve problems.					
15. I like learning new technologies like Google glass.	5	4	3	2	1
16. I use a step-by-step process to solve problems.	5	4	3	2	1
17. I make a plan before I start to solve a problem.	5	4	3	2	1
18. I am confident that I can program a computer to blink LED lights.	5	4	3	2	1
19. I try new methods to solve a problem when one does not work.	5	4	3	2	1
20. I carefully analyze a problem before I begin to develop a solution.	5	4	3	2	1
21. In order to solve a complex problem, I break it down into smaller steps.	5	4	3	2	1
22. I am certain that I can build e-textile following instructions.	5	4	3	2	1
23. I am certain that I can fix a broken circuit in an e-textile that does not behave as expected.	5	4	3	2	1
24. I am certain that I can design a soft circuit.	5	4	3	2	1
25. I am confident that I can program a sensor to react to light or heat.	5	4	3	2	1
26. I am confident that I can sew an electric circuit.	5	4	3	2	1
27. I am confident that I can make a parallel circuit	5	4	3	2	1
28. I am confident that I know what causes a short-circuit.	5	4	3	2	1
29. I like listening to others when trying to decide how to approach a task or problem.	5	4	3	2	1
30. I like being part of a team that is trying to solve a problem.	5	4	3	2	1
31. When working in teams, I ask my teammates for help when I run into a problem or don't	5	4	3	2	1

Statement	Strongly Agree	Agree	Neither Agree nor Disagree	Disagree	Strongly Disagree
understand something.					
32. I like to work with others to complete projects.	5	4	3	2	1
33. I like learning new technologies such as soft circuits.	5	4	3	2	1

Computational Pedagogical Content Knowledge (CPACK): Integrating Modeling and Simulation Technology into STEM Teacher Education

Osman Yaşar, Jose Maliekal, Peter Veronesi, Leigh Little, and Soun Vattana
The College at Brockport, State University of New York
Brockport, NY 14420, United States
oyasar@brockport.edu

Abstract: Making judicious choices of when, what and how specific tools and pedagogies to use in the teaching of a topic can be improved with the help of curriculum inventories, professional development, and practice but such resources and experience do not often transfer to new circumstances, particularly those involving computational modeling and simulation technology (CMST) tools. This article presents a qualitative case study in which pre-service teachers and in-service teachers are prepared about not just the use but also basic operating principles of CMST in an attempt to enhance its integration into teaching in a more permanent, constructivist, and tool-independent way. The results suggest that if teachers move beyond 'using' tools to learn their basic operating principles, they can construct authentic models, navigate between multiple tools that operate on the same principles, and as a result gain confidence to more judiciously decide under different circumstances as to what tools might better facilitate teaching of a topic.

Introduction

Challenges in technology education have brought education and computing communities together. Computer scientists' challenge is the current crisis of underproduction and underrepresentation of students. It has triggered a major K-12 outreach to help boost interest in computing by addressing learning difficulties of computing concepts and principles (Fincher & Petre 2005) and improve the teaching of these concepts in the context of applications (CC 2005). Educators' challenge is how to improve technological pedagogical content knowledge (TPACK) of teachers (Mishra & Koehler 2006). Teaching with technology is complex; not only does it often require customization but also the technologies themselves must be content specific and pedagogically suitable (Koehler & Mishra, 2008). Teachers need help, through professional development (PD), to deploy appropriate technologies in the classroom, stay up-to-date with emerging technologies, and assess efficacies of different pedagogical approaches (Loucks-Horsley *et al.*, 2010). However, due to frequent changes in available tools and their increasing capacity; curriculum inventories and teacher PD content do not often transfer to new circumstances. While latest technologies offer more capacity, their optimum utilization may necessitate knowledge of underlying principles for easier transfer into new circumstances and better integration (Koehler & Mishra 2005, 2008; Niess 2005; Flick & Bell 2000).

Computational modeling and simulation technology (CMST) offers a way to potentially address some of the problems mentioned above. There is enough evidence in the literature about effectiveness of computer simulations as a tool (Bell & Smetana 2008; Wieman *et al.* 2008; Rutten, van Jolingen, van de Veen 2012; Smetana & Bell 2012; Maeng *et al.*, 2013) but difficulties remain regarding its current use, spread and integration into classroom instruction (Koehler & Mishra 2008). While readymade computer simulations can be considered as effective tools that allow learners to manipulate variables, test hypotheses or develop relationships between variables in the context of a topic, design-based modeling and simulation tools offer more features to also manipulate mathematical and computational accuracy of simulations and the laws of nature that are embedded in the model.

For the past decade we have been promoting the use and integration of design-based CMST tools (such as Interactive Physics, AgentSheets, Excel, STELLA, TI-84 graphing tools, Project Interactivate (PI), and Geometer's Sketch Pad (GSP)) into secondary school instruction. Through support from the National Science Foundation's Math and Science Partnership (MSP) program, we offered a 3-tier (beginner, advanced, and expert) summer workshop from 2003 to 2010, serving 188 STEM teachers from a high-needs urban (Rochester City) school district (SD) and a high-achieving affluent suburban (Bright Central) SD. The beginner-level workshop was meant to teach them technology knowledge (TK); the advanced-level training targeted their technological content knowledge (TCK) development, involving use of these tools to construct curriculum modules and lesson plans in their subject areas; and the expert-level workshop focused on teaching them CMST principles while demonstrating how this particular technology interacts with specific instructional methods to improve their technological pedagogical content knowledge (TPCK, or TPACK). Despite its favorable impact, curricular, structural, and technology access barriers made it difficult to sustain its success, use, and spread with the same intensity after funding for the program ended in 2010. In an exit survey, many teachers complained about not having adequate number of available curriculum modules and not having enough time to gain tool proficiency in order to construct new models and simulations in their subject areas, or even understand readymade lesson plans that used such models.

Structural and curricular barriers will be hard to overcome until teaching and learning of computational skills are fully implemented as a result of the new state and national student learning outcomes. However, to address PD and inventory needs, we developed a comprehensive database of curriculum modules (see www.brockport.edu/cmst) using the tools listed above. The beginner-level in-service PD was transferred into a methods course in natural sciences (NAS), namely NAS 401/501 CMST Tools, serving more than 300 hundred in-service and pre-service teachers from 20 school districts since 2008. No data was collected on how this methods course impacted both groups because of the high number of teachers and SDs, lack of funding to collect and analyze data, and the cumbersome process and protocols to follow up with a school district to collect data. A second methods course (NAS 402/502 CMST Principles) was developed two years ago to go beyond tool use and teach fundamental principles and pedagogical aspects of modeling and simulations.

Informed by findings and resources of our work in the past decade with inservice teachers from Rochester City SD (RCSD) and Brighton Central SD (BCSD) as well as the preservice teachers from our recent Robert Noyce Scholarship program, we are currently exploring *how a deep knowledge of the workings of CMST tools improves development of teachers' TPACK skills to judiciously know what, when, and how to use such tools in the teaching of a topic.* This work has also been inspired by a recent study (Maeng *et al.* 2013) to contribute to the ongoing TPACK research. In that study, authors investigated technology-enhanced inquiry instruction and TPACK preparation of 27 secondary school preservice science teachers in the context of a 2-year Master of Teaching program. While our preservice Noyce Scholars similarly took 3 courses (educational technology, NAS 401/501 & NAS 402/502 methods courses) and did a capstone project, there are some distinctions between our studies. Their investigation included general technologies, such as digital images, videos, online computer simulations, animations, probeware, spreadsheets, and so on; our focus is only on a particular technology — i.e., design-based computational modeling and simulation technology. The second distinction is about research methodology. While their research included classroom observations during student teaching, we had no data from classrooms of the preservice Noyce Scholars yet — this is part of future plans. What follows in the sections below is how CMST can be considered within the general TPACK framework; background knowledge about CMST principles and pedagogy; and a discussion of qualitative data collected from pre/post activity surveys and focus group interviews.

Computational Pedagogical Content Knowledge (CPACK)

Figure 1 illustrates interaction among CMST's multiple knowledge domains (mathematics, computer science, and sciences). This interaction has given rise to a new content domain as witnessed by establishment of many bachelor's, master's, and doctoral programs in computational science and engineering (CSE) in the past two decades (Swanson 2002; Yaşar *et al.* 2000; Yaşar & Landau 2003). Emerging of a new knowledge domain from interaction of multiple domains stands testimony to what has been advocated by Mishra and Koehler (2006) and other educators about the unique nature of TPACK when technology, pedagogy, and content closely interact. Adapting a saying by Aristotle to our case, we can perhaps say "the whole is different from its parts." The interaction of math, science, and computing technology has also given rise to a particular pedagogy as described in Yaşar & Maliekal 2014a-b, Yaşar *et al.* 2006a-b, and Yaşar 2004. This is even more interesting than the emergence of a content (CSE) domain, because pedagogy was not even among the constitutive domains of CMST to start with. In the context of the TPACK framework, CMST may be understood as Computational Pedagogical Content Knowledge (CPACK) as it only involves the computational technology whereas TPACK is more general and inclusive. CMST's link to K-12 teaching pedagogies was not obvious initially and it took a long time for it to evolve to this point as explained below. The declining number of high school students entering college STEM programs (Augustine 2007) as well as the prerequisite knowledge needed in such an interdisciplinary field led to K-12 outreach activities by CSE educators, including the authors. Close collaboration with teachers created clear benefits of using computer simulations, animations, and images coming from national labs, NASA, and the academic scientific computing community. Compounding this later was the increasing capacity, friendliness and easy-to-use feature of new software tools that made it possible to replicate in the classroom the inquiry process a scientist followed in his/her research practice. Scientists often start with a statement, a hypothesis, an experiment, or a computer model (a simplified version of reality). They, then, deductively dig further to gather evidence using theoretical scenarios, experimental trials, or simulations. Finally, putting the pieces of the puzzle together after much searching and sorting, they inductively arrive at some conclusions. In this two-way process (top-down and bottom-up) as shown in Fig. 2, if the new conclusions formed inductively from detailed evidence are different from the initial assumption, understanding, or model, then one can say that a *conceptual change* has taken place (Carey 2000). In case of a study that uses a computer model, new findings provide feedback to modify the initial model. Since learning theories suggest that students learn science by practicing it the way scientists do (Bransford, Brown, and Cocking 2000; Donovan & Bransford 2005), then recent design-based modeling and simulation tools offers just that; not only by bringing the scientific inquiry process to the classroom but also representations of systems that are too big (e.g., solar system), too small (e.g., molecules), too dangerous (e.g., fire), or expansive to access physically.

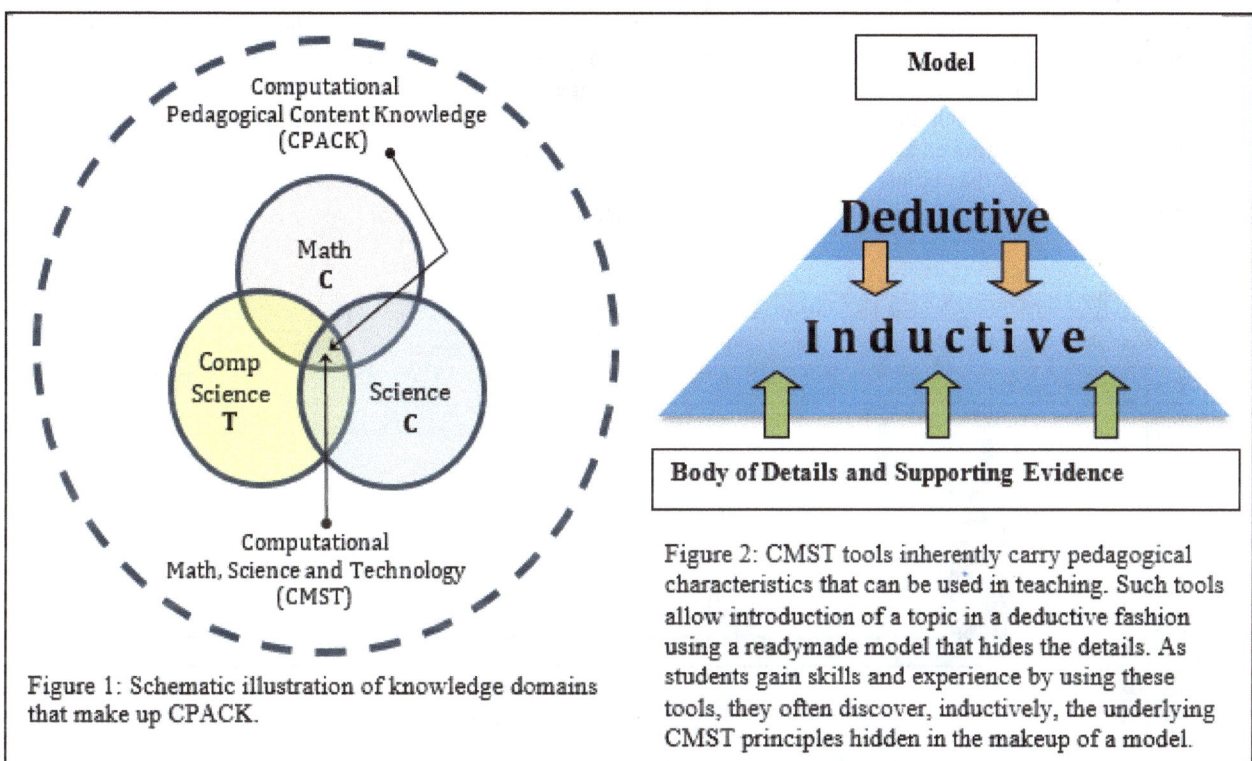

Figure 1: Schematic illustration of knowledge domains that make up CPACK.

Figure 2: CMST tools inherently carry pedagogical characteristics that can be used in teaching. Such tools allow introduction of a topic in a deductive fashion using a readymade model that hides the details. As students gain skills and experience by using these tools, they often discover, inductively, the underlying CMST principles hidden in the makeup of a model.

Recent advances in computer software have alleviated many of the hurdles that once stood in the way of model construction. Through advanced software tools, such as the Interactive Physics (IP), young students can construct a model (e.g., a pool table, a rollercoaster, or a spring experiment as seen in Fig. 3) and conduct simulations without having to initially know the mathematical, computational, and scientific principles embedded in the model. Actually, regardless of whether these models are created by students or introduced by teachers, this deductive approach engages students as it hides threatening details and boring aspect of science (Augustine 2007). Once a model is constructed by selecting from a drop-down menu and drawing appropriate connections, a series of controlled simulations can lead to changes to the model and seeing the consequences to the simulations. This process is more than just establishing a relationship between variables as it is done with online simulations. The more control the user wishes to have over the design and modification of the model, the more interest it might generate about the underlying principles and facts used in the model construction by the tool itself. A teaching method consisting of model construction and subsequent simulations might, then, create a dynamic cycle — one in which learners would be at the center of constructive learning to test a hypothesis or principles surrounding a model via controlled experiments, then analyze and evaluate results to go back to improving the model. Anyone who learns in this deductive/ inductive fashion (see Fig. 2) would, in fact, be practicing the craft of scientists (Hammond 2001). In so doing, learners may be guided to reconcile the difference between their own preconceptions and simulation results, resulting in deep, as opposed to shallow, learning. The efficacy of this has been evidenced in a project-based afterschool program (Yaşar *et al.* 2014, MSPNET 2005-2006).

Mathematical and Computational Principles of CMST

A core principle of scientific modeling and simulation is that differential equations are solved to predict a system's new behavior based on its old behavior and the change that took place. We do this because the nature often talks to us in the language of change, such as $dy/dx = 2x$, instead of revealing a direct relationship that we so desire, such as $y = x^2$. Mathematicians call dy/dx a differential equation, derivative, or simply the rate of change as it is known in secondary schools. One can often infer a direct relationship, $y=f(x)$, by summing up (or integrating) the incremental changes in y; i.e., $y_{new} = y_{old} + dy = y_{old} + 2x \cdot dx$ (the change in y depends on x and the change in x). We can manually do this summation until we cover the range of interest in x by updating it similarly as $x_{new} = x_{old} + dx$. It often can be done mathematically, too, via a simple rule: increase the power of x by 1 in the expression for dy and divide it by the new power — i.e., $y = \int dy = \int 2x \cdot dx = 2 \cdot (1/2) \cdot x^{1+1} = x^2$. However, the problem is that finding an analytical answer this way is not always possible; especially when there are multiple variables and higher-order derivatives (derivatives of derivatives) describing the change. Examples include climate change, spread of fire, population dynamics, and nuclear reactions, etc. What we do under those conditions is to do it manually (numerically), as mentioned above, by using a simple algebraic equation (*new = old + change*) for x and y over and over. A table of *new* data points (x_n, y_n) can be constructed using the *old* data points (x_{n-1}, y_{n-1}) as shown in Table 1 and Table 2 where we arbitrarily chose the initial conditions as *(0, 0)*, a range for x as *($0 \leq x \leq 5$)*, and a value for dx as *1*.

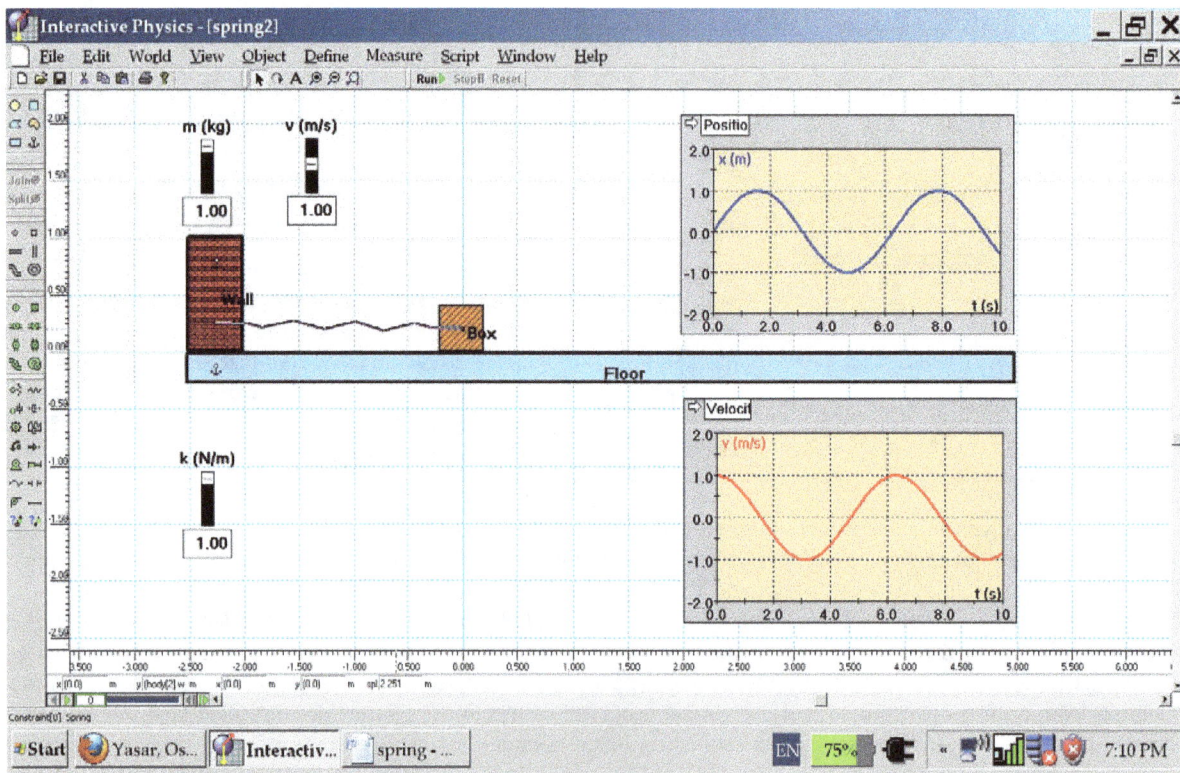

Figure 3: Design of a box and spring experiment from scratch by a 9th grade student using Interactive Physics (MSPNET 2006). Control buttons (m-mass, k-spring stiffness, and v-initial velocity of the box) allow both manipulation of variables and monitoring of the harmonic oscillation. Buttons on the left help create objects and those at the top allow the user to change computational accuracy of the simulation as well as the external forces such as friction, air resistance, or gravity that are acting on the objects.

X	$X_1 = 0$	$X_2 = X_1 + dx$	$X_n = X_{n-1} + dx$
Y	$Y_1 = 0$	$Y_2 = Y_1 + 2 \cdot X_1 \cdot dx$	$Y_n = Y_{n-1} + 2 \cdot X_{n-1} \cdot dx$

Table 1. Steps to build an (X, Y) table based on initial conditions, known range of x, and chosen value for dx.

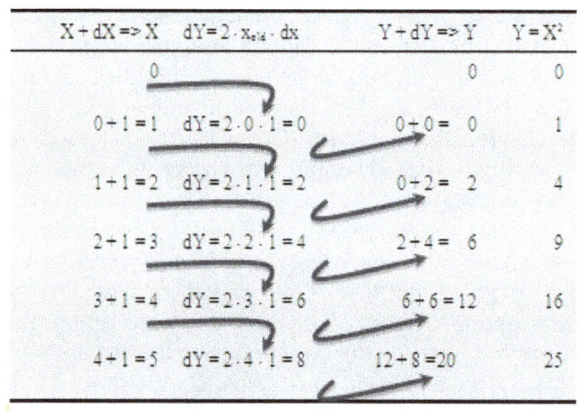 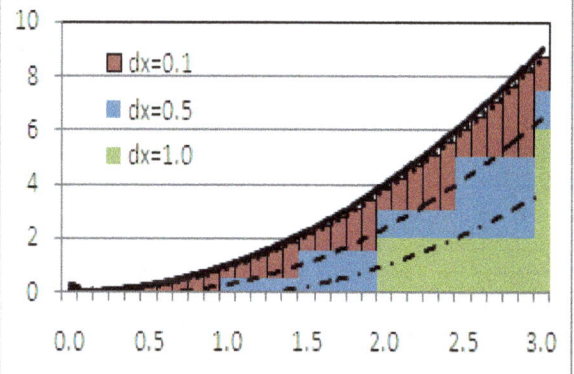

Table 2. Hands-on illustration of the algebraic scheme.   Figure 4: Numerical results (dashed lines) are compared to the analytic solution (solid line).

Numerical integration constitutes a major aspect of computational modeling and simulations. The mathematical method for updating and the choice for the step size (dx) affect the accuracy of computations. While tools such as IP provide a way to control these parameters, a user may not want to deviate from default methods and values. However, when doing it manually either by hand or a spreadsheet the user gets to have full control over them. In so doing, at least three important lessons are learned. For example, when results for different dx values are compared to the analytic solution ($y = x^2$) using a graph (see Fig. 4), a correlation between the step size (dx) and the accuracy of the results becomes obvious right away – i.e., *the smaller the dx, the more accurate the answer*. Secondly, the cost of accuracy become obvious as more accuracy means more data points. Furthermore, the need for automation becomes obvious when the number of data points increase. While a human can calculate a few data points by hand when dx is 1, or 0.5, for smaller dx values such as 0.1 or 0.05 one would have to move to Spreadsheets, such as Excel, to automate the calculation and to graph $y = f(x)$ curves. But for much smaller increments (dx), such as 0.0001, or 0.000001, spreadsheets would not be much help to handle and monitor such a large data set – a million steps would be needed in the above example for $dx = 0.000001$. This is where the need for computer programming becomes obvious.

In an after-school project initiated by the authors, several 9th graders (see MSPNET 2005-2006) from Brighton High School (NY) were able to replicate Interactive Physics simulations in Fig. 3 using Excel and later with Fortran programming language to compute the position ($x_{new} = x_{old} + dx$) and velocity ($v_{new} = v_{old} + dv$) as a function of time, where $dx = v \cdot dt$ and $dv = a \cdot dt$, and $a = F/m$ *(acceleration=Force/mass)*. Since change is caused by external forces, all they needed was a formula for the forces. As a result, computation of *change* motivated them to learn basic laws of physics. For example, the force applied by a spring onto an attached object in Fig. 3 is $F = -k \cdot x$, where k is the stiffness coefficient of the spring and x is the displacement of the object from the equilibrium position. Once they learned the process and understood these basic mathematical, computational, and scientific principles, they transferred their skills and knowledge to other circumstances. To simulate planetary motion all they had to know was the formula for the interplanetary gravitational force ($F = G \cdot M \cdot m / x^2$; where G is a Universal Constant, M and m are masses of the planets separated by distance x), which governs the orbital motion of a planet around the Sun.

Discussion of Results

The work reported here involves: 1) 26 preservice Noyce Scholars from our secondary math and science certification programs, and 2) 188 inservice teachers from Rochester City and Brighton Central SDs. Out of the 26 preservice teachers, only 12 had taken both NAS 401/501 CMST Tools and NAS 402/502 CMST Principles and Pedagogy course at the time of data collection: we will call them PST2. The remaining 14 (PST1) had only taken NAS 401/501 CMST Tools course. Of all 188 inservice teachers who attended MSP summer training, 110 teachers attended the training once which only involved CMST tools training with some experience with developing modules and lesson plans to use those modules; we will call them IST1. 78 inservice teachers attended 2 summer sessions with additional training on two tools of choice and development of modules and lesson plans; we will call them IST2. 43 inservice teachers (namely IST3) attended 3 summer sessions that included those above plus some knowledge of CMST principles (excluding text-based computer programming) as well as a capstone project. Data collected include pre/post activity surveys, interviews and artifacts (lesson plans, modeling and simulation examples, and class assignments) because of its relative recent start. The analysis of data on inservice teachers for this study also included classroom observations and student responses to technology. Details of other data sources and their analysis for inservice teachers can be found in Yaşar *et al.* (2014). Authors used a simple descriptive statistic to analyze Likert-scaled pre/post activity surveys and an inductive approach (Creswell 2009) to analyze participants' responses to the open-ended questions and interview transcripts. The transcripts were independently analyzed and coded around common themes by two researchers and an external evaluator. Data from artifacts were used to triangulate the results.

Inservice Teachers (ISTs): Exit surveys showed that usage of the tools in the classroom was directly linked to the amount of PD teachers received. All trained teachers reported that on a daily base they used laptops for presentations, graphing calculators for math instruction, and electronic smart boards for interactive lessons. 60% of group IST1 teachers reported occasional use of one or more CMST tools in their classrooms. On the other hand, 50% of IST2 teachers and 78% of IST3 teachers reported regular use of one or more tools. Additional data from IST3 demonstrate their TPACK skills (what, when, and how to use a tool). While both math and science teachers took the same training and were exposed to the same tools, usage profiles and purpose of usage per subject area reflect judicious thinking: Math (6% drill, 12% demo, 18% modeling and simulation; and 64% other purposes), Science: (0% drill, 8% demo; 87% modeling and simulation; and 23% other purposes). Usage profiles also changed per grade level as shown in Table 3 below. Another indicator that demonstrates their TPACK is that 60% stated that they occasionally search for free tools and use them at least one time to teach a topic. Once someone found a tool, it was quickly propagated to the whole group.

Subject/Grade	Daily	Weekly	Bi-weekly	Special Projects
Math, 7-8th	Laptop, smartboard	Power Point, PI, TI tools, GSP, Excel, Flash	AgentSheets (AS)	Interactive Physics (IP), Stella, GIS/GPS, Java
Math 9-12th	Laptop, smartboard, TI graphing calculators	Power Point, Project Interactivate (PI)	Excel, Flash	Interactive Physics, Stella, GIS/GPS, Java
Science 7-8th	Laptop, smartboard, Power Point	AgentSheets, Excel, Project Interactivate (PI)	Interactive Physics (IP), GIS/GPS, Flash, Java	Stella, GSP
Science 9-12th	Laptop, smartboard	Flash, Excel, Power Point	Interactive Physics, TI tools, GPS, Java	Stella, AgentSheets, GIS, PhET

Table 3: CMST tool usage profile by inservice teachers according to the grade level taught.

Furthermore, 94% of IST3 teachers agreed that training made them more effective in the classroom; 87% agreed that it strengthened their pedagogical skills; 73% agreed that it strengthened their content knowledge; 100% agreed or strongly agreed that training strengthened their skills related to modeling and simulation; 86% reported that they continue to use the hardware, software and curriculum inventory made available through project in their classrooms; and 80% believed that their participation served to build their school leadership skills. As far as assessing the impact on student learning using data on achievement scores see Yaşar *et al.* (2014), but here we will briefly mention how students in different subject areas responded. 90% of teachers who did use modeling and simulation tools and smart boards agreed that it increased student engagement and made STEM concepts more comprehensible. Student reaction to modeling was found to be 97% favorable in math and 77% in science classes. Observed improvement in problem solving skills was reported by 72% of math and 31% of science teachers. While science classes utilized technology less due to limited access and lack of science-related modeling examples, in instances where it was utilized, a deeper understanding of science topics was achieved, compared to math topics (83% vs. 76%). Finally, students in higher grade levels found modeling and simulations more engaging in both math classes (grades 7-8: 77% vs. grades 9-12: 90%) and science classes (grades 7-8: 75% vs. grades 9-12: 85%). It was even found helpful to non-traditional (special education) learners; again the higher the grade level the higher the engagement: math classes (grades 7-8: %76 vs. grades 9-12: 100%) and science classes (grades 7-8: 75% vs. grades 9-12: 85%).

Pre-service Teachers (PSTs): The data for preservice Scholars include surveys, open-ended questions, and focus group interviews. We examined their evolution from stage 1 (1st summer-NAS 401/501 CMST Tools) to stage 2 (2nd summer- NAS 402/502 CMST Principles and Pedagogy). Just like the inservice teachers, responses changed with the amount and content of training. The data for stage 1 include groups PST1 and PST2 while data for stage 2 includes only PST2. At stage 1: 65% strongly liked and 35% somehow liked learning new tools; 57% said they definitely want to learn CMST principles and pedagogy while 43% said OK; 100 % liked project-based learning; 10 % reacted unfavorably to group work (because we mixed them with interns who were not at the same par); 20% wanted more time and help for lesson development. Although there was no classroom data to show how judiciously they would choose what, when, and how to use CMST tools, their inclinations towards some tools were obvious as 50% found Interactive Physics difficult to use and understand and 100 % loved AgentSheets and Excel. While Interactive Physics is generally very intuitive and easy to use, the threatening aspect of physics overtook them (because they did not take it in high school!). This definitely changed at stage 2 as they figured out how it worked. We saw them going from not knowing much about computer simulations to wanting to learn more about mathematical modeling and computer programming. Some indicated a desire to teach computer science once they start a teaching job. Below are some common themes from each stage in the form of statements from students.

Themes emerging from interviews at the end of 1st (intro level) summer coursework:
- It was beneficial to work with someone in a different content area
- It was nice taking a specific science subject and trying to see how one can fit mathematics into that subject but the reverse situation is also equally beneficial where one takes mathematics and sees what real life applications, what science applications one can put to this, instead of the other way around.
- While it is a struggle to deal with equations and variables as far as how they relate to one's content area, the level of simplicity in which they are introduced make them more bearable as new skills are developed.
- It is beneficial to see the transition into simplicity. The hands-on approach and simplicity of usage engage students and increase learning.
- Excel is a great CMST tool. It is simple and it explains the CMST principles well. It can be used with students to apply equations, graph the relationships and then really apply mathematics to real life.

Themes emerging from interviews at the end of 2nd (advanced) summer coursework:
- Creating a model from scratch encourages the learners to seek an understanding of the underlying details.
- Full utilization of CMST tools necessitates an understanding of underlying mathematical, computational, and scientific principles. Use of such technology offers a chance for teachers to get an exposure to other fields. Such exposure is found to be invaluable as it enables teachers to connect multiple fields in a meaningful way as they are applied to the solution of a problem or to the teaching of a topic.
- Computer programming is easy and enjoyable with graphical tools such as Scratch and Processing. While boring aspects of typing and likelihood of making syntax errors are eliminated, algorithmic skills are fostered through a user-friendly graphical interface. Learning programming has been found to be phenomenal, because it allows the students to see what's going on a little bit better. Sharing and adaptation is made easier through a vast source of programming examples available to public.

Conclusion

There are several barriers blocking full utilization of new technologies and pedagogies in teaching. Curricular constraints often leave little or no room for experimentation with an effective, research-based pedagogy in a classroom setting. Another barrier is that not all technologies, pedagogies, and content can be integrated. Teachers need long-term assistance in developing knowledge of such intricate interactions. This study focuses on a specific case of TPACK based on the use of CMST tools. The study provides evidence that integrating CMST into teaching and learning situations engages both teachers and students because of its constructivist approaches and authentic experiences that mimic how scientific inquiry and science processes are done. It also argues that CMST has a significant warrant to be considered as a knowledge domain in its own right rather than just a teaching tool. Making this kind of fundamental shift will help teachers more judiciously decide how to integrate their CPACK into their classrooms. Future work will include collection and analysis of further data from observations of classroom instruction by teachers involved in this study.

References

Augustine, N. (2007). Is America Falling Off the Flat Earth? Washington, D.C.: The National Academic Press.
Bell, L. R and Smetana, L. K. (2008). Using Computer Simulations to Enhance Science Teaching and Learning. In Technology in the Secondary Science Classroom (Eds. Bell et al.). Washington, DC: NSTA Press.
Bransford, J., Brown, A. and Cocking, R. (2000). How People Learn. National Academy Press, Wash., D.C.
Carey, Suzan. (2000). Science Education as Conceptual Change. *Journal of Applied Deve Psych*, 21(1): 13-19.

Creswell, J. W. (2012). Educational Research. 4th Edition. Pearson Education, Inc.

Computing Curriculum (CC). 2005. ACM, AIS, and IEEE Computer Society. http://www.acm.org.

de Jong, T., & van Joolinger, W. R. (1998). Scientific Discovery Learning with Computer Simulations of Conceptual Domains. *Review of Educational Research*, 68(2), 179-201.

Donovan, S. and Bransford, J. D. (2005). How Students Learn. The National Academies Press, Wash, D.C.

Fincher, S. and Petre, M. (2005). Computer Science Education Research. Taylor and Francis e-Library.

Flick, L. and Bell, R. L. (2000). Preparing tomorrow's science teachers to use technology: guidelines for Science educators. *Contemp Issues Technol Teach Educ* 1: 39-60.

Hammond, L-D., Austin, K., Orcutt, S. and Rosso, J. (2001). How People Learn: Introduction to Learning Theories. Stanford University. http://web.stanford.edu/class/ed269/hplintrochapter.pdf.

Koehler, M., Shin, T. S., Mishra, P. (2011). How Do We Measure TPACK? Let Me Count the Ways. In R. Ronau, C. Rakes, and M. Niess (Ed.). Education Technology, Teacher Knowledge, and Classroom Impact.

Koehler, M. J., and Mishra, P. (2008). Introducing TPCK, in Handbook of Technological Pedagogical Content Knowledge (TPCK) for Educators, Routledge Press, New York & London.

Koehler, M. J., and Mishra, P. (2005). What happens when teachers design educational technology? The development of technological pedagogical content knowledge. *J Educ Computing Research*, 32(2), 131-152.

Loucks-Horsley, S., Stiles, K. E., Mundry, S., Love, N., Hewson. (2010). Designing professional development for teachers of science and mathematics. Third Edition, Thousand Oaks, CA: Corwin Press.

Maeng, J. L., Mulvey, B. K., Smetana, L. K., and Bell, R. L. (2013). Preservice Teachers' TPACK: Using Technology to Support Inquiry Instruction. *J. Science Education Technology*, DOI 10.1007/s10956-013-9434-z

Mishra, P., Koehler, M. J. (2006). Technological pedagogical content knowledge: A framework for integrating technology in teacher knowledge. *Teachers College Record*, 108 (6), 1017-1054.

MSPNET (2005). Mathematical and Computational Tools to Observe Kepler's Laws of Motion. Yaşar, P., Kashyap, S., and Roxanne, R. NSF MSPNET Library, http://hub.mspnet.org/index.cfm/14566.

MSPNET (2006). Limitations of the Accuracy of Numerical Integration and Simulation Technology. Yaşar, P., Kashyap, S., and Taylor, C. NSF MSPNET Library. http://hub.mspnet.org/index.cfm/14568.

Niess, M. (2005). Preparing teachers to teach science and mathematics with technology: Developing a technology pedagogical content knowledge. Teaching and *Teacher Education*, 21, 509-523.

Rutten, N., van Joolingen, R., and van der Veen. (2012). The Learning Effects of Computer Simulations in Science Education. *Computer & Education*, 58; 136-153.

Smetana, L. K. and Bell, R. L. (2012). Computer Simulations to Support Science Instruction and Learning: A critical review of the literature. *Int. J. Science Education*, 34 (9); 1337-1370.

Swanson, Charles. (2002). A Survey of Computational Science Education. *http://cssvc.ecsu.edu/krell/Computational%20Science%20Education%20Survey%20Paper.htm*

Wieman, C., Adams, W., Perkins, K. (2008). PhET: Simulations That Enhance Learning. *Science*, 332; 682-3.

Yaşar, O. (2014). A Pedagogical Approach to Teaching Computing Principles in the Context of Modeling and Simulations. *J. Computing Teachers*, Winter Issue.

Yaşar, O. and J. Maliekal. Computational Pedagogy. (2014a). *IEEE J. Comp. in Sci & Eng*, 16 (3), 78-88.

Yaşar, O. and Maliekal, J. (2014b). Computational Pedagogy Approach to STEM Teaching and Learning. In M. Searson & M. Ochoa (Eds.), *Proc of Soc for Info Tech Conf 2014* (pp. 131-139). Chesapeake, VA: AACE.

Yaşar, O., J. Maliekal, L. little, and P. Veronesi. (2104). An Interdisciplinary Approach to Professional Development for Math, Science, and Technology Teachers. *Journal of Comp in Math and Sci Teaching*, 33 (3).

Yaşar, O. (2013a). Computational Math, Science, and Technology (C-MST) Approach to General Education Courses. *J. Computational Science Education*, 4 (1), 2-10.

Yaşar, O. (2013b). Teaching Science through Computation. *J. Sci. Tech. and Soc.*, Vol. 1 (1), 9-18.

Yaşar, O., Maliekal, J., Little, L. and Jones, D. (2006a). A Computational Technology Approach to Education. *IEEE Comp. in Sci. & Eng.*, **8** (3), 2006, pp. 76-81.

Yaşar, O., Little, L. J., Tuzun, R., Rajasethupathy, K., Maliekal, J. and Tahar, M. (2006b). CMST: A Strategy to Improve STEM Workforce & Pedagogy to Improve STEM Education. *Lect Notes in Comp Sci*, 3992, 169-176.

Yaşar, O. (2004). CMST Pedagogical Approach to Math & Science Education. *Lect Notes in Comp Sci*, Vol. 3045, 807-816.

Yaşar, O. and Landau, R. (2003). Elements of Computational Science & Engineering Education, *SIAM Review*, 45; 787-805.

Yaşar, O., Rajasethupathy, K., Tuzun, R., McCoy, A. and Harkin, J. (2000). A New Perspective on Computational Science Education, *IEEE J. Comp. in Sci & Eng*, **5** (2).

Pre-service Mathematics Teachers' Awareness of Social and Socio-Mathematical Norms during Technology-Enhanced Lessons

Tuğçe Kozaklı
Faculty of Education
Uludağ University, Bursa, Turkey
tkozakli@uludag.edu.tr

Hatice Akkoç
Faculty of Education
Marmara University, Istanbul, Turkey
hakkoc@marmara.edu.tr

Abstract: As a result of the emphasis on technology integration, there is a growing need for research on teachers' and pre-service teachers' choices, strategies, views and norms related to using technology in the classroom. This study aims to explore social and socio-mathematical norms constituted by three pre-service mathematics teachers and to examine their awareness of these norms during their technology-enhanced lessons. For each participant, four lessons were observed and video-taped, followed by semi-structured interviews. To investigate participants' awareness of social and socio-mathematical norms, they watched the selected sections of their own lesson videos. The findings indicated that participants both intentionally and unintentionally established new norms during their technology-enhanced lessons. Furthermore, feedback during the interviews promoted awareness and identification of new norms.

Introduction

With the advances in computer and communication technologies, teaching of mathematics has been dramatically changed (Gawlick, 2005). Especially for over two decades, various technological tools in mathematics teaching have been widely used (Artigue, 2002) and the potential of digital technologies have been highlighted for mathematics education (Drijvers, 2012). NCTM's (2000) "Principles and Standards for School Mathematics" document emphasized that "Technology is essential in teaching and learning mathematics; it influences the mathematics that is taught and enhances students' learning" (p.3).

The ways teachers teach with technology is crucial for successful technology integration. Recently, teachers' behaviours in integrating technology into instruction and relationship between using technology and pedagogy have been investigated through "Technological Pedagogical Content Knowledge" (TPCK or TPACK) framework. TPCK is defined as the knowledge required for effective technology integration (Mishra & Koehler, 2006) and has been used in mathematics education research to investigate in-service and pre-service mathematics teachers' technology-enhanced practices (Penglase & Arnold, 1996 as cited in Goos, 2003; Niess, et al., 2009; Ozgun-Koca, Meagher & Edwards, 2010; Yigit, 2014).

Teachers' practices are considered as an important factor determining why technology 'works' or 'why it does not work' in mathematics teaching (Kendal & Stacey, 2002). However, teachers do not have enough experiences in using technology for teaching mathematics and they encounter some difficulties. Therefore, mathematics teachers should be prepared for the arrangement of learning environments using technological tools and resources (Drijvers, 2012). There is need for investigating ways of supporting teachers to effectively use technological tools (Maracci & Mariotti, 2009). In order to help teachers to integrate technology into mathematics teaching, it is important to focus more on teaching techniques and practices that emerge in technology-enhanced lessons and how these relate to the role of technology (Drijvers et al., 2010).

When learning and teaching approaches are directed from the traditional lessons to technology-enhanced lessons, teachers' experiences and practices become important factors for explaining the role of technology in teaching mathematics and whether their classroom interaction (e.g., behaviour and communication) has changed or not (Monaghan, 2001). When using technology, teachers develop new norms and constitute classroom strategies for these established norms. A new environment can generate new classroom norms (Tabach, 2008; Ruthven, 2009). Therefore, it is necessary to focus on teachers' roles in the teaching process (Drijvers, 2012). This leads us investigating teachers' choices, behaviours and norms they constitute in technology-enhanced learning environments.

Teachers should be aware of classroom culture that is an indispensable part of learning mathematics occurred in a specific socio-cultural environment. It is essential for teachers to understand the interrelations between classroom norms and mathematics learning for constructing an appropriate learning environment (Even & Tirosh, 2008). When effects of teachers' norms in technology integration are considered, identifying teachers' awareness about these norms becomes an important factor since norms are mostly outside teachers' awareness (Voigt, 1985 as cited in Yackel, Cobb & Wood, 1991). Therefore, this paper focuses on norms which are constituted by pre-service mathematics teachers and their awareness of these norms in technology-enhanced learning environments.

Theoretical Framework

The need to understand teachers' actions as they teach mathematics in a computerized environment using suitable technological tools and resources is greater than ever (Tabach, 2013). When investigating this new classroom environment, *emergent perspective* (Cobb & Yackel, 1996) is considered in terms of understanding teachers' practices and determining social perspectives (social norms and socio-mathematical norms).

In this paper, we focus on social and socio-mathematical norms in emergent perspective developed by Paul Cobb and Erna Yackel (1996). The two constructs of social norms and socio-mathematical norms bring to the fore two aspects of the classroom culture. Taken together, these constructs form a framework for describing the classroom culture that is together constituted by the teacher and students in the course of their interactions (Bowers, Cobb & McClain, 1999). Norms established and evolve through the interactions in the classroom, are taken into account in technology-enhanced teaching processes and pre-service teachers' awareness of these norms are investigated.

Social and Socio-mathematical Norms

Integrating technology into the classroom environment constructs a new classroom culture. To investigate this classroom culture, individual perspectives (beliefs and values) and social perspectives (social norms and socio-mathematical norms) need to be addressed (Cobb & Yackel, 1996). In this paper, social and socio-mathematical norms that are constituted by pre-service mathematics teachers and their awareness about these norms are discussed.

"Norm" is a sociological construct and not a rule that prescribes individual actions. Rather, it is a collective notion. Norms are based on expectations that are constituted as participants interact with each other (Yackel, 2000). These norms are not static orders but are instead regularities in the process of interaction (Voigt, 1985 as cited in Yackel, Cobb & Wood, 1991).

Related literature makes a distinction between social and socio-mathematical norms. Social norms are not specific to mathematics and deal with the general structure of classroom activity. They can be applied to any subject matter area. To give an example, students should challenge others' thinking and justify their own interpretations in science or literature classes as well as in mathematics. On the contrary, socio-mathematical norms are obligations and expectations that are related to a mathematical activity (Bowers, Cobb & McClain, 1999). For example, the social norm can be introduced to set an expectation in the classroom which encourages students to question each other's thinking and explain their ways of thinking. However, socio-mathematical norms are the normative understandings of what counts mathematically different, sophisticated and efficient in a classroom (Yackel & Cobb, 1996). The obligation to resolve disagreements by the given arguments is a general social norm, whereas the standards established by the classroom community to evaluate these arguments are socio-mathematical norms (Bowers, Cobb & McClain, 1999).

Teachers develop social and socio-mathematical norms when using new technologies, and constitute classroom strategies for establishing and maintaining these norms (Ruthven, 2009). In line with this point, this paper focuses on the following questions with regard to technology integration in general and questioning norms in technology-enhanced learning environments in particular:
1. What kinds of social and socio-mathematical norms are constituted by pre-service mathematics teachers during technology-enhanced mathematics lessons?
2. To what degree pre-service teachers are aware of social and socio-mathematical norms in technology-enhanced mathematics lessons?

Methodology and Context of the Study

A case study was conducted to investigate norms and awareness of norms during technology-enhanced lessons (Cohen, Manion & Morrison, 2007). Participants of the study are three pre-service mathematics teachers in a teacher preparation programme in a state university in Bursa, Turkey. It was a seven-month program which awards its participants a certificate for teaching mathematics in high schools for students aged between 15 and 18. The courses in this programme are in the scope of education and mathematics education. The study was conducted during "Instructional Technologies and Material Development" and "Teaching Practice" courses. The aim of the former course was to develop technological pedagogical content knowledge. The course focused on two software, namely Geogebra and Cabri Geometry. Participants were involved in hands-on activities in front of a computer and prepared teaching materials using these software programs. Participants also taught lessons in partnership schools during "Teaching Practice" course. The data collection methods are observation and semi-structured interviews. The first author of this paper observed four lessons of each participant. For each participant, the last two lessons were technology-enhanced. A total of twelve lessons were video-recorded. Lessons were analyzed using an observation form which aims to reveal social and socio-mathematical norms. Participants were also interviewed to better understand their constituted norms, were asked to explain how they planned to integrate technology into their lessons and compare their technology-enhanced lessons to their traditional lessons. To investigate participants' awareness of their norms, they watched the selected sections of their lesson videos. These sections were chosen by the researchers based on the analysis of the videos. At least one section was selected to exemplify each norm. Participants were asked to discuss and reflect on these distinct moments to discover their awareness. The first two lessons in which they did not use technology were analyzed for the purpose of triangulation to discover how their norms in these lessons differ from their norms in technology-enhanced lessons.

Findings

Data analysis revealed various social and socio-mathematical norms. Norms that are presented in Table 1 were distinguished based on the observations of pre-service teachers' lessons. The awareness of norms was investigated through post-lesson reflection processes. For some of the norms, participants did not make any reflections. These norms are out of the scope of this paper.

Findings will only focus on a set of common norms which were observed in all three pre-service teachers' lessons. Table 1 summarizes norms constituted by participants.

	Ata's Norms	Filiz's Norms	Kader's Norms
SN	Examples are provided to help students understand the topic.	Examples are provided to help students understand the topic.	Examples are provided to help students understand the topic.
SN	After each explanation, question of "Is there any point not understood?" is directed.	After each explanation, question of "Is there any point not understood?" is directed.	After each explanation, question of "Is there any point not understood?" is directed.
SN	After students solve problems, solutions are repeated briefly by teacher.	After students solve problems, solutions are repeated briefly by teacher.	After students solve problems, solutions are repeated briefly by teacher.
SN	In case students do not understand something, it is revised in different ways until it is understood.	In case students make mistakes, the teacher steps in and corrects them immediately.	Students' mistakes are corrected immediately and only the correct solution is focused.
SMN	Students try to solve problems with clues which are given by the teacher.	Students try to solve problems with clues which are given by the teacher.	The teacher expects students know the rules and formulas, at the same time promotes an understanding of reasons behind them.

SMN	Justification and proving processes are important.	It is expected that students explain their ideas and make discussions by guiding questions like "How can you do this, do you have any idea about this?"	During technology-enhanced lessons, group work and guidance are emphasized.
SMN	Software is used for justification, proving and visualization.	Software is used for justification, proving and visualization.	Software is used for justification, proving and visualization.

Table 1: Norms constituted by pre-service teachers (SN: Social Norm, SMN: Socio-Mathematical Norm)

In technology-enhanced teaching processes, three socio-mathematical norms were observed for each pre-service teacher. Pre-service teachers had also taught lessons without integrating technology into their teaching. Socio-mathematical norms which are presented in Table 1 were not observed in these lessons. In other words, these socio-mathematical norms emerged from the integration of technology into teaching. On the other hand, the four social norms as summarized in Table 1 were both observed in technology-enhanced and traditional lessons.

In the next sections, findings regarding pre-service teachers' awareness of their norms will be presented through excerpts from their reflections.

Pre-service Teacher Ata

Ata had four lessons two of which were on the Pythagorean Theorem. One of these lessons was technology-enhanced. During this lesson he used Geogebra software which was run on PC and projected onto the board. The pre-service teacher first explained how to use the software using both demonstration and hands-on-activities. He solved the problems first by writing on the board then by justifying their solutions with the software.

During the interview he mentioned that he had some difficulties during this lesson since it was his first technology-enhanced lesson. He found it hard to coordinate himself between the board and the computer. He also emphasized that he focused on the proof of the Pythagorean Theorem especially in this lesson, but not in his previous lesson where he did not use the software:

Researcher: You first gave the theorem on the board, and then you illustrated it through the software. What was the reason for this choice?
Ata: Yes, I first proved it in an ordinary way. I gave the written proof on the board while I demonstrated a visual proof through the software. These two proofs were different. In my opinion, students understood better with the software. This is obvious from my lesson's video that they understood better when I used the software. They didn't understand anything when I taught them directly.
Researcher: Can we say that you give great importance to proofs?
Ata: Proof is important, generally speaking yes. In my opinion, it should be given at high school after all. Because, students should know where things come from…I do not prefer to use technology for the purpose of justification too much. It seems to me that it makes students excluded from the lesson; therefore, I don't think of using it too often. Actually, it will be a wrong choice to use technology for every topic. Therefore, technology may be more effective if it is used for teaching new things.

As can be understood from his excerpt above, he is aware of the socio-mathematical norm "Software is used for justification, proving and visualization". It was also evident in his reflections that the socio-mathematical norm "Justification and proving processes are important" emerged in a technology-enhanced learning environment.

As a result of focusing on proving and justification, he said that there was a discussion in his lesson for the first time. He mentioned that integrating technology into his teaching and establishing a visual proof created a discussion in the classroom. Upon watching of his videos, on the other hand, he realized that he remained passive during these discussions:

Researcher: For instance, you came up with a discussion when using the software.
Ata: But, I remained a bit passive, anyway. Students were discussing, but I couldn't give any reactions.

Researcher: Well, there were students who gave wrong answers, but you didn't dwell on them. Did you wait for them to see the solution?

Ata: Actually, nothing came to my mind in the heat of the moment. As you might notice watching the videos, I was standing silent while students were discussing.

Pre-service Teacher Filiz

Filiz had four lessons two of which were technology-enhanced. One of these lessons was on "Fundamental elements of circles" and the other was on "Angles in Circles". She used Geogebra software which was run on PC and projected onto the board. She used Geogebra just for justifying the properties of a circle. She first explained them on the board followed by a demonstration through the software. Compared to her first two lessons in which she did not use technology, she focused on justification and proof in her technology-enhanced lessons. Filiz had watched a segment of her lesson video in which the socio-mathematical norm "Software is used for justification and visualization" was dominant and she made reflections on her teaching as follows:

Researcher: Now, you give all of the properties on the board. Then, you demonstrate them one by one through the software. You never mentioned where these properties come from in your previous lessons, but you explained them using the software.

Filiz: It was like proving. Well, it seems that I started preferring to show where the rules come from, why they work, instead of giving the rules directly.

She not only used the software for justification and proving, but also for solving geometry problems. After students solved the problems and exercises on the board, she constructed the solutions through the software. When students made mistakes in their solutions, Filiz demonstrated the solution through Geogebra and spotted the mistakes. This approach is considered as the social norm "In case students make mistakes, the teacher steps in and corrects them immediately". As she was watching her lesson video, she reflected on this norm as follows:

Researcher: If you notice, the student made a mathematical mistake here and you immediately intervened and corrected it using the software.

Filiz: Shouldn't I have corrected? Actually, it would have been suitable if I hadn't intervened and given him an opportunity to realize his own mistake. I should have let him solve the question and show that the result was wrong. Instead I directly corrected him, I did wrong, that is, I should have given him a chance.

A can be seen from the excerpt above, Filiz became aware of the norm and discussed alternatives to her approach. Another social norm in her approach was "After each explanation, question of 'Is there any point not understood?' is directed". This norm was evident in all of her four lessons. After watching her lesson videos, she developed an awareness of this norm. She mentioned that she started to understand her students' reactions to this approach:

Researcher: You always asked students the question of "Is there anything that you couldn't understand?" after each problem solving activity.

Filiz: I always ask this question as a teacher. Even if I forget to ask that question, my students started to say "We couldn't understand" or "We understood every thing, let's move on". They got into a routine thinking that "The teacher will ask anyway, then let's give an answer before she asks".

Researcher: Well, do you think that it is sufficient to ask this question for every student?

Filiz: No, it is not because not every student does tell. Actually, it is not sufficient, but... What can be done? What kind of a method can be followed? I don't know.

As can be understood from the excerpt above, Filiz is aware of her approach but could not develop an alternative to better evaluate students' understandings.

Pre-service Teacher Kader

Kader had two technology-based lessons in two different classes on the same topic: Area of a triangle. She first taught the topic at the board then she drew the triangles using Geogebra. Students worked in groups and drew the triangles using their tablets. Organized in groups, students got the chance to hold discussions and; therefore, "their voice raised too much" in Kader's words.

Compared to her first two lessons which were more traditional, new kinds of norms were observed in her technology-enhanced lessons. Norms towards classroom setting, roles of students and the teacher, and teaching techniques changed with the integration of technology. More importantly, a new socio-mathematical norm has emerged with the existence of technology, namely "During technology-enhanced lessons, group work and guidance are emphasized":

Researcher: You were generally next to the board in your other lessons. Students would stand up to solve problems. But, whenever the technology came into existence, students began to study in groups and you walked through the classroom dealing with each group.

Kader: I have just noticed that now... from time to time I was not aware of how I behave, but there was a great change in my classes with the use of technology anyway. The students figure out the rule by themselves. This way, we drew, worked and the rule came out automatically. When we give them a rule, they can not comprehend where the rule comes from. Technology has contributed much to this problem. They can comprehend better when they do themselves. It sticks in their minds as well.

As can be seen from the excerpts above, the pre-service teacher became aware of the change in her teaching approach. Although she did not organize group work in her traditional lessons, she guided students to discover rules themselves during group discussions in her technology-enhanced lessons. With this regard, the socio-mathematical norm "The teacher expects students know the rules and formulas, at the same time promotes an understanding of reasons behind them" revealed itself in different ways. In some cases Kader gave the rules directly, in other cases she tried to construct the rules using students' works in Geogebra. However, in either case, a socio-mathematical norm "Software is used for justification and visualization" has emerged and she showed why the rules worked using the software. The pre-service teacher's awareness of these norms is evident in the following excerpt:

Researcher: Should the rules be given by the teacher all the time? What is your opinion about this?

Kader: Yes. I don't know why I did so but I did. I was not even aware of it; of course, it is better to let them figure out the rule. But I don't know why I did so. I give the rule when I think it is suitable, but I want them to figure out the rule in due course. They tried to find it using Geogebra, it's better for them. I thought it would be better.

Researcher: Firstly, you gave your explanations on the whiteboard, and then you used the software to make verification based on your explanations or students' explanations.

Kader: I used the technology with the purpose of justification mainly. We should never neglect that if the students had not got tablet computers at their hands, the class would probably have been monotonous. There would have been no difference in using the technology, possibly a little or no difference. The direct participation of the students was more crucial, otherwise presenting rules would have no effect.

The way Kader used the software for the purpose of verification was evident from her reflections. She also emphasized the importance of having tablets in the classroom to promote students' active participation.

Discussion

In this study, social and socio-mathematical norms were investigated in the context of technology-enhanced teaching. Considering the gap in the literature concerning awareness of social or socio-mathematical norms, a qualitative analysis of three pre-service mathematics teachers' reflections was carried out.

The pre-service teachers watched their video-taped lessons and had discussions on those videos to reveal their awareness of norms throughout the interviews. One of the key findings is that participants had already been aware of some of the norms determined by the researchers and behaved in the expected way on purpose. With this regard, they mentioned that they did so "conspiratorially and intentionally". Another important finding which revealed itself so many times is that participants realized some of the norms upon watching their own lesson videos. They reported that they were not conscious of their actions beforehand.

One of the remarkable findings is the emergence of new norms with the existence of technological resources in the classroom. Among those norms, one particular norm is common in all three participants' lessons: Software is used for justification, proving and visualization. Considering the fact that pre-service teachers did not give importance to proofs in their traditional lessons, their emphasis on proofs in their technology-enhanced lessons becomes crucial. As they watched their lesson videos, they developed an awareness of this situation through their reflections. Participants also mentioned about the feedback effect of the interviews. At the end of the interviews, they declared that they got such feedback for the first time and they were given an opportunity to realize the situations that they had never thought over.

To the extent that classroom norms constrain and enable learning, it is possible for teachers to estimate which norms they might wish to foster (Yackel, 2000). In the classroom, it is the teacher who initiates and guides the constitution of norms. Since the pre-service teachers' norms play an important role in their teaching approaches, it becomes prominent to train them with awareness about these norms in teacher education programs. To be able to guide pre-service teachers for successful technology integration, teacher educators should pay attention to what kinds of social and socio-mathematical norms they have. A new environment can generate new classroom norms (Tabach, 2008; Ruthven, 2009); therefore, teacher education programs should guide teachers and pre-service teachers developing awareness of these norms.

References

Artigue, M. (2002). Learning mathematics in a CAS environment: The genesis of a reflection about, instrumentation and the dialectics between technical and conceptual work. *International Journal of Computers for Mathematical Learning*, 7(3), 245-274.

Bowers, J., Cobb, P., & McClain, K. (1999). The evolution of mathematical practices: A case study. *Cognition and Instruction*, 17(1), 25–64.

Cobb, P., & Yackel, E. (1996). Constructivist, emergent, and sociocultural perspectives in the context of developmental research. *Educational Psychologist*, 31, 175-190.

Cohen, L., Manion, L. & Morrison, K. (2007). *Research in mathematics education* (6th ed.). New York: Routledge.

Drijvers, P., Doorman, M., Boon, P., Reed, H., & Gravemeijer, K. (2010).The teacher and the tool: instrumental orchestrations in the technology-rich mathematics classroom. *Educational Studies in Mathematics*, 75(2), 213-234.

Drijvers, P. (2012). Digital technology in mathematics education: Why it works (or doesn't). *Proceedings of the 12th International Congress on Mathematical Education Program* 8 July – 15 July, 2012, COEX, Seoul, Korea

Even, R., & Tirosh, D. (2008). Teacher knowledge and understanding of students' mathematical thinking and knowledge. In L. English (Ed.), *Second handbook of international research in mathematics education* (pp. 202-222). NY: Routedge.

Gawlick, T. (2005). Connecting arguments to actions–dynamic geometry as means for the attainment of higher van Hiele levels. *ZDM, The International Journal on Mathematics Education*, 37(5), 361-370.

Goos, M. (2003). Learning to teach mathematics with technology: A study of beliefs in context. In L. Bragg, C. Campbell, G. Herbert, & J. Mousley (Eds.), *Mathematics education research: Innovation, networking and opportunity. Proceedings of the 26th Annual Conference of the Mathematics Education Research Group of Australasia* (pp. 404-411). Sydney: MERGA.

Kendal, M., & Stacey, K. (2002). Teachers in transition: Moving towards CAS-supported classrooms. *ZDM, The International Journal on Mathematics Education*, 34(5), 196–203.

Maracci, M., & Mariotti, M.-A. (2009). The teacher's use of ICT tools in the classroom after a semiotic mediation approach. *Paper presented in WG9, Cerme6 Conference*, 28 January–1 February 2009, Lyon, France.

Monaghan, J. (2001). Teachers' classroom interactions in Ict-based mathematics lessons. In M. van den Heuvel (Ed.), *Proceedings of the 25th International Conference for the Psychology of Mathematics Education, Vol. I* (pp. 383-390). Utrecht, The Netherlands.

Mishra, P., & Koehler, M. J. (2006). Technological pedagogical content knowledge: A new framework for teacher knowledge. *Teachers College Record*, 108(6), 1017-1054.

National Council of Teachers of Mathematics (2000). Principles and standards for school mathematics. Reston,VA: NCTM.

Niess, M. L., Ronau, R. N., Shafer, K. G., Driskell, S. O., Harper S., Johnston, C., Browning, C.,Ozgun-Koca, S. A., Kersaint, G. (2009). Mathematics teacher TPACK standards and development model. *Contemporary Issues in Technology and Teacher Education*, 9(1), 4-24.

Ozgun-Koca, S., Meagher, M., & Edwards, M. T. (2010). Preservice teachers' emerging TPACK in a technology-rich methods class. *Mathematics Educator*, 19(2), 10-20.

Ruthven, K. (2009). An investigative lesson with dynamic geometry: A case study of key structuring features of technology integration in classroom practice. *Paper presented in WG9, Cerme6 Conference*, 28 January–1 February 2009, Lyon, France

Tabach, M. (2008). Learning beginning algebra in a computer intensive environment (CIE). *The Journal of Mathematical Behavior, 27*(1), 48-63.

Tabach, M. (2013). Developing a general framework for instrumental orchestration. *Eighth Congress of European Research in Mathematics Education* (CERME 8).

Yackel, E., Cobb, P., & Wood, T. (1991). Small-group interactions as a source of learning opportunities in second-grade mathematics. *Journal for Research in Mathematics Education*, 22, 390-408.

Yackel, E., & Cobb, P. (1996). Sociomathematical norms, argumentation, and autonomy in mathematics. *Journal for Research in Mathematics Education*, 27, 458-477.

Yackel, E. (2000). Creating a mathematics classroom environment that fosters the development of mathematical argumentation. *Paper presented in WG1 Mathematics Education in Pre and Primary School, of the Ninth International Congress of Mathematical Education*, Tokyo/Makuhari, Japan.

Yigit, M. (2014). A review of the literature: How pre-service mathematics teachers develop their technological, pedagogical, and content knowledge. *International Journal of Education in Mathematics, Science and Technology, 2*(1), 26-35.

Acknowledgement

This study is part of a MA thesis entitled as "Interaction between Orchestration Types Emerged During Technology-Enhanced Mathematics Teaching and Social and Socio-Mathematical Norms" in Marmara University, Turkey.

3D Scanning of Fossils for Middle and High School Students: Science Teachers and Students' Perspectives

Claudia Grant, University of Florida, cgrant@flmnh.ufl.edu
Pavlo Antonenko, University of Florida, p.antonenko@coe.ufl.edu
Jason Tovani, Delta High School, jtovani@deltaschool.org
Aaron Wood, Iowa State University, awood@iastate.ed
Bruce MacFadden, University of Florida, bmacfadd@flmnh.ufl.edu

Abstract: Students are more likely to engage in science learning activities when given the opportunity to work on a real project, particularly a project that will have a meaningful impact in society (Reiser, 2004). This study analyzes the potential of 3D scanning technology in middle and high school to scaffold the development of science literacy while contributing to broader 3D digitization and big data initiatives. Middle and high school science teachers were invited to participate in a two-day pilot workshop where they were introduced to the technology and the science concepts associated with the scanned specimen. High School students were also invited to a demonstration of the process while learning about the wide range of possibilities 3D technologies have to offer. Our results indicate that teachers and students are not intimidated by the technology and given adequate professional development and instruction, 3D scanning would be an important skill to develop in the classroom. K-12 educators and students can be important stakeholders in 3D digitization process and contribute to virtual museum collections and archives while learning about evolution, extinction, biodiversity and climate change.

Introduction

Science education in the United States is changing towards a more inquiry☐based approach that will allow students to develop 21stcentury skills resulting in better preparation for the workforce of today and tomorrow. Following a national effort to integrate the Next Generation Science Standards (NGSS), the Florida Museum of Natural History (FLMNH) has started an initiative to incorporate 3D scanning and printing technology in middle and high schools in California and Florida. Scientists and engineers have been using 3D technologies for many years now and have made breakthrough discoveries in fields of medicine (Rengier et al., 2010), engineering (Campbell et al., 2011), and manufacturing (Berman, 2012) among many others.

Natural History museums and universities have started to digitize their collections (e.g., iDigBio and Morpho Source in the U.S.) for research, but in so doing these become available to downstream users, i.e., anyone who has access to the Internet. "These collections are public assets. They play an important role in promoting public health and safety, homeland security, trade, and economic development, medical research, resource management, education, and environmental monitoring" (Stebbins, 2014). Some examples of digitized fossil collections include the GB3D Type Fossils, which is digitizing their specimens of microfossil species and subspecies (3d☐fossils.ac.uk), the Smithsonian X 3D (3d.si.edu), which aims to share 3D models of iconic objects, as well as natural history specimens from their collections and partner institutions, and Fossil Insect Collaborative (fossilinsects.colorado.edu) to help better understand climate change. For scientists, this is an important step forward, because specimens that were not suitable for loans can now become available through 3D technology for further studies. K12 teachers and students can be important stakeholders in the 3D digitization process and contribute to virtual museum collections and archives while learning about evolution, extinction, biodiversity, anatomy, and climate change in addition to the technical skills they develop along the way.

This paper describes a project aimed at introducing 3D scanning technology in secondary science classrooms. Because 3D technologies are not present in the current curriculum, we had to ask science teachers and students about their perceptions in using this type of technology. We specifically focused on curriculum enhancement and possible learning outcomes, computer requirements and server space, issues related to time, scaffolding of the different components, professional development for teachers and contributing to big data. In addition, we added students' perceptions on the technology, learning of science, and potential interest in STEM careers as a result of interaction with 3D technology. Our goal was to determine whether this type of technology is suitable for a K12 environment and what the potential benefit to students would be.

Conceptual Framework

The table below conceptualizes the technology being used, a proposed method of instruction and science standards to be implemented in addition to teacher professional development and active role in activity design. A list of possible outcomes is proposed based on research and study results.

Table 1: Conceptual framework

3D Technology: Scan, Print, Digitization, and Database Integration
• Teacher Professional Development and Curriculum Design: Implementation and Testing   • Next Generation of Science Standards: Inquiry Based Learning   • Problem/Project Based Learning (PBL)   • STEM Integration
K12 Educational Outcomes
• Increased Student Motivation   • Science Career Interests   • 21st Century Skills   • Teacher Preparation

Project Goals

This project was designed based on two goals. First, increase student motivation and engagement in science learning and scientific inquiry, and to increase or awaken interest in science careers. By fostering integration of new and emerging technologies and allowing for opportunities to contribute in a meaningful way to science, students will experience feelings of self-efficacy, competence, higher levels of interest, and the need for accomplishing goals. Those are components that motivate students in the classroom (Pintrich, 2003), and by being derived from science practices students will be step closer to science research enjoyment and potential science career selection. Boredom in the classroom is common but studies suggest that Problem Based Learning (PBL) engages students in school activities (Krajcik, 2006). Creative freedom emphasized through the use of guided PBL as venue for students to present the results of their inquiries is a goal to prevent boredom and increase student engagement.

Second, support secondary science educators in conceptualizing learning experiences that meet NGSS. The proposed activities cover almost all NGSS science and engineering practices and crosscutting concepts, and a wide range of core ideas especially in life, earth sciences, and engineering recommended by the National Academies (National Research Council, 2012). These activities are designed for students to make connections between the different disciplines (life sciences, earth sciences, technology, engineering and mathematics) and to understand how these disciplines interact with each other. High quality teacher training in technology and science content knowledge rooted in current research and best practices is essential and a core goal.

Participating Schools

In partnership with Pajaro Valley Unified School District (Watsonville, CA), Santa Cruz City Schools (Santa Cruz, CA), P. K. Yonge Developmental School (Gainesville, FL), and Kanapaha Middle School (Gainesville, FL), the FLMNH hosted a two-day 3D scanning workshop for middle and high school teachers. Thirteen participating teachers from CA and FL had the opportunity to immerse themselves in the 3D scanning technology, scan fossils from the Museum's Vertebrate Paleontology Collection and to brainstorm possible classroom integration ideas. Teachers' feedback was crucial to understand the limitations, workflow, professional development, and overall needs in order to successfully integrate in the classroom.

A 3D scanning demonstration was also conducted at a local charter high school in CA. Seventeen students participated in the demonstration and had the opportunity to scan a fossil and to go through all different stages to finally end with a partial or completed 3D model.

Research Questions

Teachers. We collected in-depth qualitative data (n=13) on the science teachers' perspectives regarding the potential of 3D scanning technology for enhancing the relevance and rigor of science instruction. Specifically, we explored teachers' perspectives regarding the following questions:
1. What is the potential of 3D scanning for improving science education at the middle and high school level?
2. What type of professional development, technical support, and instructional design scaffolds would be required for science teachers?

High school students. For the group of high school students (n=17) who participated in the 3D scanning demonstration, we collected qualitative data on the potential of 3D scanning technology in their career preferences and asked them the following questions:

1. What did you find interesting and/or engaging about the 3D technology?
2. How might 3D printing technology relate to careers you are interested in?
3. Would you be interested in creating high quality digital fossil models for scientists and other students to use?

Method

We had a range of participant teachers from multiple middle and high school teaching levels. In order to protect teachers' identity pseudo names have been assigned. Teacher 1, Jane, teaches 8th grade integrated science, and her motivation to participate on this activity relates to the connections that can be made between 3D scanning and NGSS. "I think that being able to think and work in 3D is an important skill for students to learn, and it's related to our NGSS, Common Core and College and Career Readiness standards. It could also increase student engagement" (Jane). Teacher 2, Angela, teaches grades 9th – 12th on the topics of biology, marine biology and integrated science. Her motivation to participate on the study comes as a consequence of understanding the potential of 3D models in the classroom and how the possibility for students to touch and measure specimens that would not be available otherwise, can make a difference in her curriculum and instruction. "After learning scientists' thoughts and ideas, I began to understand some of the amazing, practical applications of having 3D objects in a classroom" (Angela). Angela also mentioned that 3D technology could be especially helpful to English learners who are the majority of the student population at her school. Teacher 3, Peter, teaches integrated science 10th – 12th grades and his motivation to participate relates to the difference of teaching a concept without a specimen versus teaching the concept with the specimen. We have previously mentioned that rare and/or delicate fossils might never be available to a K12 audience, but 3D technologies change that limitation and open doors for classroom investigations that were not seen before. "I saw the relevance and value of 3D technology for teaching science. Science is about stuff; it's about actual living and non-living things that take up space - or influence that space - around us. So, to teach science well, educators need to give kids access to that 'stuff.' I recognize that 3D technology - scanning and printing - open up access to that stuff in ways that may not be possible at all without it" (Peter). Teacher 4, Mary, who teaches biology, integrated environmental science, and AP environmental science, mentioned that her motivation to participate in this workshop relates to providing opportunities for engagement. She thinks having students focused on a 3D scanning task can open the doors for deeper classroom discussions about the specimens being scanned and the environment where they lived. Teacher 5, Carla, who teaches art tutorial leadership after school and who is also credentialed to teach 7th and 8th biology also sees an opportunity for not only student engagement, but also to open the dialogue with students on possible careers associated with 3D scanning skills. "I want my students to learn to participate in technology-based learning and, in the future, careers and conversations" (Carla). 6th grade science teacher, Marta, was motivated by this project because she is always looking for ways to incorporate technology that can support her science instruction. Marta believes that 3D scanning is innovative and an ideal technological tool that can naturally support science.

The participant high school is an alternative charter high school that serves students that have not been successful in larger comprehensive schools, and as such has a unique and challenging student population. When invited to learn about 3D modeling and printing, about 15% of the entire student population signed up to attend the session in lieu of attending a career panel discussion, indicating that whatever they know about 3D modeling and printing is interesting to them. Their interest and engagement was apparent from the moment they walked in the room and saw the equipment; scanners, computers, stands, fossils, etc. After the presentation, as they were allowed to begin manipulating the hardware, it became clear that they were somehow well prepared to do so. They easily grasped the same concepts that took the teachers longer to understand. Some students even progressed on their own, as if they had known the software for weeks. This was inspiring, and leads us to believe that these students would be ready and interested in more opportunities to learn about and explore 3D modeling, whether embedded in a math or science course or as a stand-alone 3D modeling class. This would be a great way for the school to increase the relevance of high school math and science content for students that have struggled with more traditional approaches to these subjects. The curricular freedom as an independent charter school means that such a class could be implemented as soon as it is developed, and this is definitely something being considered.

Procedure
3D Scanning Teacher Training and Student Demonstration

A 3D scanning expert provided an introduction to the 3D scanning and printing technology. This activity was conducted three times: once for teachers in FL, once for teachers in CA and once for high school students in CA. The expert first explained the acquisition of 3D data via automatic triangulation and photo processing performed by a NextEngine™ scanner. By providing visual examples of previously scanned fossil specimens, the expert showed how and when missing data are present and directed teachers to identify it. Color contrast and intricate shapes were presented as challenges to gathering comprehensive 3D data from specimens. Limitations related to specimen size were discussed. Teachers and students exhibited a great interest in learning how scientists scan large objects or specimens that cannot be extracted from the field. Processing power and memory capacity of the desktop or laptop computer connected to the scanner hardware was also discussed as a potential limiting factor. The image files produced by the scanner can be rather large, meaning that large and/or complicated specimens might lead to computer issues if the computer does not have the appropriate memory and processor.

Time is an important factor to be considered when scanning specimens. The expert explained the times required to scan 3 different types of fossil horse bones that varied in overall size and complexity. This information was useful for determining the time needed for learning activities in the classroom. The expert and the teachers then discussed the stitching process, preparing the file for the printing procedure, and computer storage requirements. Teachers had the opportunity to create their first 3D model of an upper-right fossil horse tooth and to refine it for the final print process. The first step was to properly prepare the fossil for the scanning process. Depending on the characteristics of the specimen, some of them being shinier than others, talc powder is applied to the fossil to reduce light reflectance that might interfere with the scanning process.

The second step was to properly align the specimen on the NextEngine™ scanner base. This process varies depending on the shape and size of the fossil being scanned. Teachers and students had the opportunity to set it up multiple times based on the different views needed in order to create the final 3D model. Once the specimen was placed and secured, teachers and students were introduced to the initial scan settings. After all scans were made, any excess data not belonging to the actual specimen (e.g., clay or scanner platform) was removed and scan faces were stitched together. The resulting 3D model could be viewed in multiple formats, such as textured (natural look) and solid color among other settings that allow for proof and polishing the final product.

In addition to the tools provided by NextEngine ScanStudio HD™ software, teachers and students experienced the process of uploading the final model to a Microsoft™ cloud service that repairs and refines 3D models before being printed. Once the model repair was done, teachers in FL took the final .STL file to the University of Florida – College of Architecture's Fab Lab, where they experienced the process of plotting the file to the printer and seeing the actual model being printed. Teachers in CA, took the .STL file to a technology classroom in the local high school where the workshop was conducted. For high school students, experts brought 3D printed specimens to pass them around for students to manipulate.
The printed 3D model was enlarged to twice the size of the original fossil specimen to demonstrate how scan data can be manipulated to facilitate specific lesson plans. In this case, shape differences in the teeth of 2 fossil horses of very different sizes could be compared after scaling the small horse to the size of the larger horse, potentially serving as a lesson in critical observation skills.

Data Collection Process

Once teachers were able to print the model they scanned, a focus group (Creswell, 2012) was conducted in order to explore ideas on best practices to implement this activity in the classroom. The focus group was unstructured and mostly lead by teachers emphasizing the areas where they saw possible technical challenges and to reflect on ways to move forward. Most of the participant teachers, based on their classroom size, saw potential challenges relating to classroom management. However, all indicated that with a proper roll out, adequate professional development and careful instructional design, they could overcome challenges. Logistics and classroom management often confront the use of technology in the classroom. Still, once teachers' thoughts moved beyond challenges and started to explore the potential 3D scanning has for enhancing science curriculum, student motivation and skills, new ideas emerged that lead us to believe there is promise and that we should pursue this idea further.

Discussion

Possible Learning Outcomes and 3D Scanning as a Tool for Curriculum Enhancement

An opportunity for student-lead Citizen Science projects was one of the emerging themes. Many teachers thought of the possibility of having students to collaborate with a local natural history museum or nature centers where they could access fossils or bones to be scanned. These student-lead scans would then become part of the national effort to digitize natural history collections. "I know that there is a lot of effort right now going into the digitization of specimens in natural history museum collections so that they can be cataloged and made available to researchers and maybe students through easily accessible cloud storage. I would want my students to be a part of that process" (High School Teacher). All other teachers agreed that having students contributing to science would be the ultimate engaging strategy.

Visualization was a second emerging theme as a strong component of student learning. Teachers pointed out that having students design their own objects in response to inquiry activities could be a powerful tool for discussion and understanding of key concepts while keeping the engagement level high. For those students who can better grasp concepts by looking and touching, this would be a definite game changer, teachers stated.

Observations and Comparisons was a third emerging theme where teachers thought of 3D specimens as a powerful tool to compare the actual specimen with 3D scanned specimen, and 2D image. Questions such as: what are the advantages of one over the other? Can digital fabrication be a successful tool to support biological sciences? Teachers thought these would be good questions for students to raise, investigate and respond. Because there are not very many institutions that would let students manipulate specimens, there are not enough studies done and this could constitute an incredible opportunity for student-lead research.

Another potential area of study is whether students learn the concepts better when analyzing the bone or fossil in the screen while going through the stitching process versus learning about it through book instruction. For example, can students better learn the name of the bones on any specific animal by scanning, stitching and creating a 3D model of each bone? Would this detail-oriented activity enhance student learning? Further studies need to be done, but there are multiple areas where learning outcomes could be measured while using a 3D scanning activity as a learning tool.

Computer Requirements, Server Space and IT Support

One of the concerns is the file size of each specimen. Image size can be upwards of several Giga Bytes and as such, an alternative to Dropbox or local computer space should be proposed. For example, some of the participant schools in CA require teachers and students to have a Gmail account, and therefore all Google products (including storage) can be available for file transfer and storage. It is also important to point out that each school within the same district would have a different policy, and each scenario should be studied on a case-by-case basis.

Participating teachers suggested that at least one IT representative should be available. This person would know how the scan process works and would have extensive knowledge on equipment troubleshooting. In addition, teachers suggested having technology and science content support via phone during a determined set of hours. Alternatively, students could interact with a scientist via Skype or a similar technology. One of the ideas they suggested was to have a system of teaching assistants, who have been trained in the technology, working with teachers providing the support needed.

Time

The time it takes to scan one specimen, particularly a larger one, is much greater than one, two or even three class periods. This appeared to be the greatest issue brought up by teachers. However, they all agreed that finding the right strategy would be an easy to overcome obstacle and they brainstormed on possible scenarios based on the number of students and existing technology in their schools. They thought of mobile labs with 10-15 scanning stations where students can navigate from station to station experiencing all the different stages of the scanning process until the 3D model is ready for print. The actual technology setting will ultimately depend on what is available in terms of technology and budget, how many students will be involved and how many teachers per school will share the technology.

Scaffolding

Teachers proposed that one way to introduce the stitching process would be to ask the students, to draw a fossil specimen on a piece of paper. Once the drawing is final, wrap it into or around a simple shape, such as a cylinder or cube. The shape could be a household object, like a toilet paper roll or an aluminum foil ball that approximates the overall size of the fossil specimen they will eventually scan. This step will not only help them identify the stitching points easily, but will also incorporate scientific illustration concepts to the activity.

Teachers also suggested that assessments will be measured in a different way based on understanding of bigger ideas, rather than a standardized or multiple choice test, which leads student to focus on conceptual understanding, rather than bits of information.

Professional Development

Given that 3D scanning and printing technology is largely untested in K12 classrooms, teachers were concerned with professional development. This conversation centered around two main themes:

Professional development on 3D scanning and printing technology. Although teachers did not express discomfort with the learning of the technology, they emphasized the need for ongoing professional development, not a single workshop approach. Teachers requested a refresher lesson every time a new fossil specimen would be introduced as an activity. Refresher lessons or workshops would provide opportunities for teachers to practice different scanner settings and scenarios, ask questions and become more proficient.

Professional development in science content for all specimens to be scanned. Teachers need to be able to understand the technology but also, to have content knowledge in order to make the connections between science and technology (Chiu, 2013). Teachers indicated that although they may have sufficient content knowledge within biology and earth sciences, they would require consistent collaboration with researchers on developing lesson plans related to active, on-going research in areas such as: ecology and extinction, evolution in the fossil record, ancient and modern biodiversity and ancient and modern climate change.

Contributing to Big Data in National Collections

While teachers confirmed that some of their students would feel intimidated and lose interest in the activity, they also indicated that a great number of students would be engaged and grasp the concepts to successfully create a high-fidelity model that could ultimately be useful for a scientific study. For those students who demonstrate enthusiasm and feel they can master the skill, opportunities could be given to accurately scan a specimen and to finally upload to a cloud where the specimen could be used by other students, artists and scientists around the world.

When high school students were asked the question: Would you be interested in creating high quality digital fossil models for scientists and other students to use? All students who volunteered to answer the survey (n=5) responded positively. Some students even thought of the possibility and benefits of scanning fossils in the field. "Scientists could scan out in the field and send the data into the cloud for students and schools to then print and use without worrying about damaging it" (High school student). This observation is valuable and accurate because scientists have done this is the past. For example, Dr. Nicholas Pyenson, at the Smithsonian Institution, 3D scanned a group of fossil whales found at the Atacama Dessert in Chile (Pyenson, 2014). In addition, teachers suggested that contributing to real-life projects would increase their students' engagement and enthusiasm in the topic being studied.

Students Perceptions

Seventeen participating high school students experienced scanning activities. While their demonstration was shorter than teachers', they spent around three hours imitating the same process as teachers did. Students had the opportunity to experience the technology and to experiment with the scanner and software features in a risk-free environment. They also had multiple opportunities to ask questions about fossil science and 3D technology. The results overwhelmingly show that students liked the activity and would like to pursue further education in the topic.

Students were asked specific questions about how the technology will benefit them on a personal level: In what ways would 3D scanning & printing technology help you learn science concepts? "3D printing would help me very much in class by giving us a strong visual and something to hold and move around with our own hands. An actual replica of the object or subject we're learning about" (High school student).

The results demonstrate that 3D scanning technology should be introduced in the classroom. Schools would have to navigate ways around limitations, such as costs of hardware, software licenses and teacher training, but these are merely financial limitations that can be lifted with a grant proposal or through fundraising. Students at the participating high school are more than ready for this kind of innovative instruction. During the demonstration session, several students shared the reasons for their interest in this technology, and these reasons were as diverse as they were - fashion, engineering, video game design, medicine, and sports among others. It would be exciting to see what they would do with a solid foundation in 3D modeling at such a young age.

Broad Significance to SITE Membership and Society

This research advances our understanding of the potential efficacy of the recently developed 3D scanning technologies in K12 science learning. This approach to integrating 3D technologies in K12 can potentially improve both the relevance of educational practices in our schools and broaden the impact of ongoing digitization efforts of paleontological research collections. K12 students can provide and make significant contributions to the national digitization effort while learning about the concepts outlined on their curriculum. In addition, it advances our knowledge of teacher professional development, especially focused on technology, providing initial understanding on length and intensity of training needed to develop successful STEM integration experiences.

This project is designed with the idea of excitement in mind by providing access to specimens that can only be seen at museums and to foster real-life experiences to engage students in the process of science. This project is a transferable model that can be adopted by other higher education and K12 institutions and expand the scope to many other STEM-related topics. Content knowledge training also provides an opportunity for teacher-scientist collaborations where both parties learn from each other's expertise. Partnerships are crucial to these activities because the results are reflected "not only in high-quality professional development experiences for teachers but also in an improved capacity of all partners to advance common reform goals." (Butler Khale & Woodruff, 2014, p. 79).

References

Chiu, J.L., Bull, G., Berry III, R. Q., Kjellstrom, W.R. (2012). Teaching Engineering Design with Digital Fabrication: Imagining, Creating, and Redefining Ideas. *Emerging Technologies for the Classroom*. Springer Science+Business Media New York 2013.

Butler Khale, J., Woodruff, S. B. (2014). Ohio's 30 Years of Mathematics and Science Education Reform: Practices, Politics, and Policies. *Models and Approaches to STEM Professional Development*. Virginia: NSTA Press.

Krajcik, J. S., & Blumenfeld, P. (2006). Project-based learning. In R.K. Sawyer (Ed.), *The Cambridge handbook of the learning sciences*. New York: Cambridge University Press.

Pintrich, P. R. (2003). A motivational science perspective on the role of student motivation in learning and teaching contexts. *Journal of Educational Psychology,* 95, 667-686.

Pyenson, N. D., Gutstein, C. S., Parham, J. F., Le Roux, J. P., Chavarría, C. C., Little, H., A. ... Suárez, E. (2014). Repeated mass strandings of Miocene marine mammals from Atacama Region of Chile point to sudden death at sea. Proceedings of the Royal Society B: *Biological Sciences* 281 20133316.

Stebbins, M. & Lieberman, E. (2014). Fossils, seeds, and space rocks: Improving the management of and access to the nation's scientific collections. Retrieved from http://www.whitehouse.gov/blog/2014/03/20/fossils-seeds-and-space-rocks-improving-management-and-access-nation-s-scientific-co

National Research Council. (2014) *Literacy for science: Exploring the intersection of the Next Generation Science Standards and Common Core for ELA Standards: A workshop summary.* Washington, DC: The National Academies Press, 2

National Research Council. (2012) *A Framework for K-12 Science Education: Practices, Crosscutting Concepts, and Core Ideas.* Washington, DC: The National Academies Press.

Engaging Students in Class through Mobile Technologies – Implications for the Learning Process and Student Satisfaction

Dr. Yair Zadok
Dan School of Hi-Tech Studies
College for Academic Studies in Or Yehuda, Israel
yair_z@mla.ac.il

Dr. Hagit Meishar Tal
HiT- Holon institution of Technology
Hagitmt@hit.ac.il

Abstract: This study inspects how students are using their mobile devices in class and whether lecturers can influence this usage to the benefit of learning. Two groups of students studied in the same program with the same lecturer. In the first group, the lecturer actively engaged students to use their mobile devices as study tools, and in the other group the lecturer taught in the usual frontal style but use of mobile devices by the students wasn't forbidden. While both groups used their devices in a distractive fashion, e.g. email or browsing non-class related sites, the study demonstrates a significant reduction in such distractive uses in the intervention class. Moreover, students in this class were more satisfied with the course and the lecturer. These findings suggest the possibility of a true paradigm shift. If faculty can go beyond current thinking and proactively engage their students through use of mobile devices, they may be able to turn what is currently clearly a distraction into a constructive means for improving the in-class experience of students and lecturers alike.

Introduction

Over the past few years many students are attending class with personal mobile devices (e.g. laptops, tablets and/or smartphones) and are making use of them during class sessions. Part of this usage positively supports learning such as taking notes of class materials, taking pictures of whiteboards, browsing websites that support learning, and part of the usage is not related to classwork such as answering emails, sending SMS messages, browsing non-class related websites, etc.

Studies that observed the influence of personal mobile devices on actual learning and on the concentration levels of students, suggested that the benefit derived from the use of such devices is smaller than the harm that is hidden in this usage. Students who possess such devices tend to be overly distracted, which can hurt their own academic achievements, as well as the attention of other students in the classroom who are not using such mobile devices (Christensen, C. M. & Horn, M , 2008; Barkhuus, 2005; Baiyun. & DeNoyelle, 2013; Gehlen- Baum & Weinberger , 2012; Fried, 2008; Kraushaar & Novak, 2010).

Presumably, this state of affairs should lead to the conclusion that students should be prevented from using such tools during class sessions, as they would cause harm to themselves and to their classmates if they did use them. However, this possibility is not acceptable for a number of reasons. One reason is that use of personal mobile devices is becoming an inseparable part of our day to day habits, and enforcing a ban on use of such devices in class is a virtual impossibility. A second argument is rooted in the fact that constructive use of mobile devices in the classroom can make lessons more interesting and engaging for students, increase their motivation and improve participation (Barak, 2006; Mifsud, et al., 2013). Mobile instruments afford internet access to information relevant to the classwork at hand and allow use of online tools to increase in-class interaction and constructive and cooperative learning by students (Meishar-Tal & Kurtz, 2014). These new circumstances, i.e. usage of mobile devices in the classroom, require a new framework for learning from students and from lecturers whose goals are to minimize damage caused by distractions, and to enhance benefits derived from constructive use of mobile devices.

This paper describes an attempt to harness mobile technologies possessed by students to the benefit of in-class learning and examines the effectiveness of employing mobile related activities to support learning and to contribute to the reduction of distractive in class actions.

Research Methodology

This research is an intervening research. For the sake of this research, two groups of students were selected. Both groups of students studied in the same program, the same subject and with the same lecturer. The first group (Group1) was the group where an intervention was made. In this group the lecturer made extra use of mobile technologies in order to engage the students during classes. In each class session, the students were exposed to uses and methods to leverage mobile instruments in class, and were given assignments that incorporate use of cellular phones for learning. Simultaneously, the control group (Group 2) studied in accordance with the "regular" class format, i.e. with frontal teaching that does not incorporate use of mobile technologies in class. Students that brought mobile instruments to class were allowed to make use of them, without specific guidance from the lecturer.

The most prevalent uses of mobile telephones made by the intervention group were:
1. Use of Facebook as an alternative channel for in-class communications (backchannel).
2. Use of cameras to document learning processes, to photograph whiteboards, etc.
3. Incorporation of video clips into assignments and deliverables.
4. Engaging students through interactive surveys and use of QR codes.
5. Storing and sharing of files in Cloud environments such as Dropbox and Google Drive.

The goal of the research was to observe the differences between the two groups in three areas:
1. The manner in which students in each of the groups made use of personal mobile technologies during classes – the degree of constructive use versus the degree of distractive use.
2. The levels of satisfaction with the course of both groups.
3. The levels of achievement at the end of the course.

To compare between the groups' manners of usage, levels of usage and students' feelings towards usage of mobile phones, two questionnaires were constructed and given to both groups simultaneously:
1. A preliminary questionnaire (pre) in which the students from both groups were asked to answer background questions (age, gender, personal mobile equipment at their disposal in class and their degree of computer literacy), and questions dealing with their views regarding use of mobile devices in class.
2. A summary questionnaire (post) in which the students reported on the actual use they made of mobile devices in class.
3. In addition, the results of the standard feedback questionnaires given by the College were analyzed and compared for both groups and a comparison was made between the results of the identical test given to both classes at the end of the course.

Research Population

Both questionnaires were answered by 135 students divided into two groups as follows:

Table 1: Characteristics of the Research Population

	Number of Respondents	Average Age	Degree of Computer Literacy (scale of 1-5)	% Women	% Men
Group 1	72	29.3	3.65	84.70%	15.30%
Group 2	63	28	3.65	88.90%	11.10%

From Table 1 we see that both groups are similar in age, levels of computer literacy reported by the students and in gender distribution.

Table 2: Types of Mobile Devices at the Students' Disposal

	Laptop	Tablet	Smart-phone	Tablet & Laptop	Laptop & Smartphone	Smartphone & Tablet	All Three	None
Group 1	5.6	1.4	62.5	0	18.1	1.4	1.4	9.7
Group 2	3.2	0	65.1	0	15.9	7.9	0.7	7.9

In terms of the types of mobile devices at the disposal of the students, the situation was similar in both classes: The most common devices were smartphones, followed by combinations of smartphones and laptops. In the second group more tablets were found at the expense of laptop computers.

Also compared were the initial, pre-research views of the students from both groups regarding the impact of mobile device usage on learning. No significant differences between the groups were found. Table 3 describes the initial views of the students using T tests of statistical significance.

Table 3: Initial, pre-research views of the students from both groups regarding the impact of mobile instruments on learning.

	Group 1		Group 2	
Positive Views	Average	Standard Deviation	Average	Standard Deviation
Contribute to documentation of learning processes	3.51	0.14	3.25	0.14
Contribute to organization of personal knowledge	3.38	0.14	3.16	0.16
Contribute to inter-student sharing and collaboration	3.32	0.14	3.33	0.17
Make learning more interesting	3.14	0.15	3.08	0.15
Contribute to an atmosphere of learning	2.93	0.14	3.00	0.14
Contribute to increased student class participation	2.60	0.14	2.56	0.15
Negative Views	Average	Standard Deviation	Average	Standard Deviation
Ease boring periods in class	3.25	0.14	3.46	0.16
Act as a factor that distracts from classwork	3.11	0.15	3.25	0.16
Negatively impact student concetration levels	2.96	0.14	2.97	0.15
Negatively impact student privacy	1.94	0.12	1.81	0.13

Findings

I. Levels of Usage Constructive to Learning and Levels of Distractive Usage

The first research question dealt with the examination of the differences between the intervention group and the control group in terms of levels constructive use and levels of distractive use. To assess the differences, the students were asked to report on the degree to which they employed mobile instruments in class for constructive uses (Table 4) and for distractive uses (Table 5).

Table 4: Differences between the Groups in Levels of CONSTRUCTIVE Usage

	Group 1	Group 2	t (133)
Perform internet investigations of ambiguous, class related terms	3.89	2.63	6.3 ($p<0.01$)
Search the internet for materials that can help with topics studied in class	3.71	2.68	5.65 ($p<.001$)
Take notes and write summaries	2.89	1.94	4.1 ($p<.001$)
Add personal notes to lecturer presentations	2.25	1.68	2.36 ($p<.05$)
Average	**3.17**	**2.23**	**5.69 ($p<.001$)**

The results show that there is a statistically significant difference between the groups in levels of distractive usage and in levels of constructive usage. The levels of constructive usage of the students in the intervention class were significantly higher.

Table 5: Differences in Levels of DISTRACTIVE Usage between the Groups

	Group 1 Average	Group 2 Average	t (133)
Distractive Uses - Communications Related			
Sending and receiving emails	3.08	3.11	Not Significant
Sending SMS messages	2.85	3.08	Not Significant
Visiting social network sites	2.79	2.98	Not Significant
Chatting with students in class	2.69	2.83	Not Significant
Average, Communications Related	**2.85**	**3.00**	**Not Significant**
Distractive Uses - Content Related			
Browsing news sites	1.86	2.56	3.56 ($P<.05$)
Browsing entertainment sites	2.01	2.60	2.93 ($P<.05$)
Working on tasks / homework from other courses	2.08	2.19	Not Significant

Playing computer games	1.57	1.84	Not Significant
Average, Content Related	**1.88**	**2.30**	**2.72 (p<.01)**

In the case of distractive usage, the respondents were given a list of distractive uses of two types: distractive uses related to "communications" (activities of communicating with other parties both outside and inside the classroom, not related to the classwork), and distractive uses related to "content" (including uses where students browse online content that is not related to the classwork) (Table 5). The findings give evidence to the notion that in general, distractive uses related to "communications" are more common than distractive uses related to "content", in both groups (t(134)=26.18 p<.001) (Figure 1). This finding underpins findings from previous studies (Kurtz and Meishar-Tal, 2014) that indicate differences between students in levels of distractive usage related to "communications" and distractive uses related to "content".

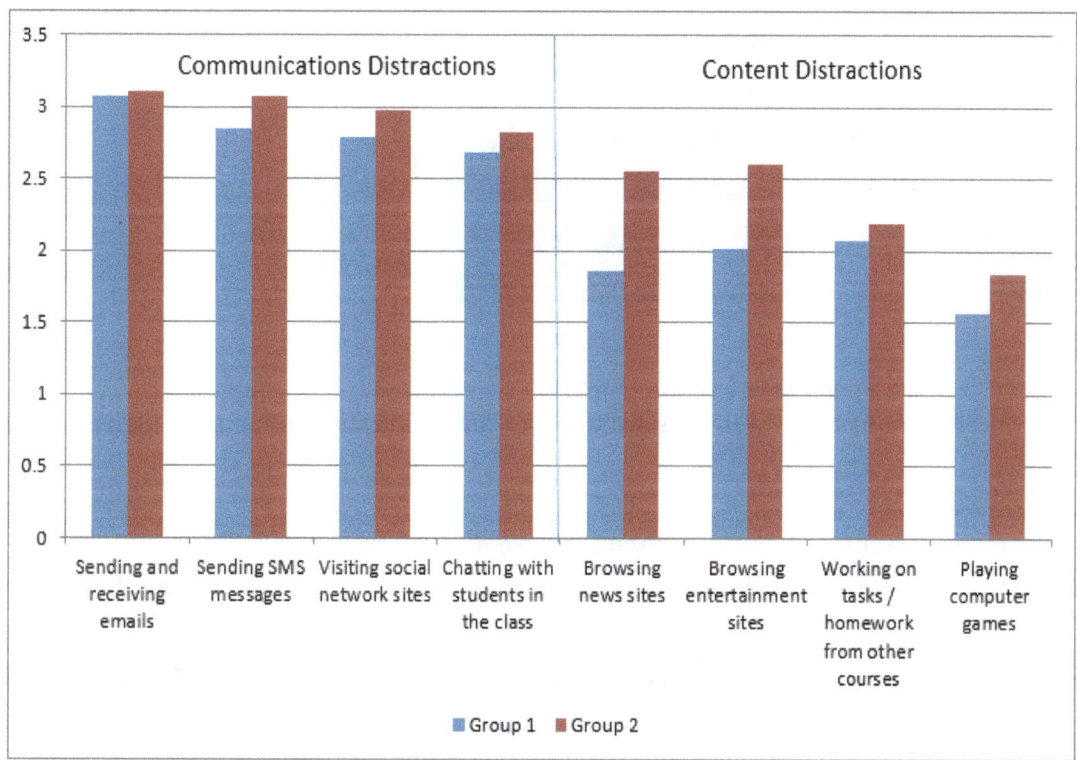

Figure 1: Differences in levels of distractive uses between the two groups

In the case of "Communications Distractions", the differences between the groups are not large and are not statistically significant, i.e. students from both groups reported that they conducted "communications" related distractive activities during class and no statistically significant difference was found between the groups as relates to these activities. The statistically significant differences were found in the volume of browsing to sites with distractive content such as news and entertainment sites. The students from the intervention group visited such sites less often than their counterparts from the second group. This finding implies that it is in a lecturer's capacity to affect a reduction in "content" related distractive activities by increasing constructive activities and by engaging the students in their classes. When a lecturer does not engage his / her students, they turn to channels that distract from learning and they consume distracting content. Conversely, when students are required to take part in constructive activities by means of mobile devices, this activity comes at the "expense" of distractive "content" related activities. Then again, "communications" related distractive activities are harder to constrain. No reduction in distractive "communications" activities was found, even amongst the students in the intervention group, despite the students having been engaged in constructive activities with mobile devices.

II. Differences in Levels of Satisfaction between the Groups

The second research question addressed the differences in students' levels of satisfaction in both groups. The findings are derived from the standard satisfaction survey distributed to students at the end of every course taught at the College. The data given to the lecturer is summary data that does not allow for statistical testing rather it affords only presentation of theories (Figure 2).

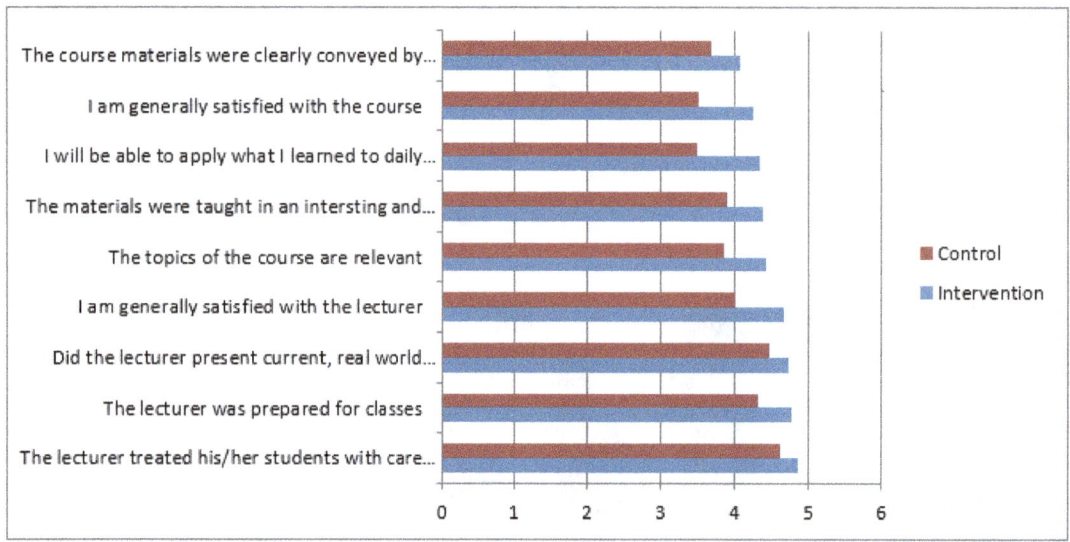

Figure 2: Satisfaction with the lecturer and the course

From Figure 2 we can learn that the levels of satisfaction of the intervention group were higher for all aspects of the survey.

III. Differences in Final Exam Achievements between the Groups

At the end of the course the participants were given the same final exam. The exam focused on course materials and did not test the skills acquired by the intervention group during the course. The exam was a closed book exam that included 34 multiple choice questions. The average grade of the intervention group was 77.9 and of the control group was 78.2. No statistically significant difference was found between the grade point averages of the two groups.

Discussion

The goal of this research was to study how intentional engagement of students by a lecturer by means of personal mobile technologies, impacts usage of these devices by students in manners constructive to learning and distractive to learning. For this purpose, two groups were chosen, identical in their characteristics, where one was instructed with methods incorporating mobile technologies and the other was instructed using standard frontal teaching. A comparison made between the two groups at the end of the course showed that amongst the intervention group, the level of constructive usage was higher than the level in control group. This finding is not surprising, as the students in the intervention group were asked to perform a great deal of constructive activities. Moreover, they were given tools geared towards increasing the level of constructive activity in the classroom.

The more remarkable findings are those that indicate that side by side with the gap between the groups in constructive activity, a difference also existed in the levels of distractive activity. The study demonstrates that distractive activity of the type "distracting content" was statistically less prevalent in the intervention group than in the control group. This portends that it is in the power of a lecturer that engages his / her students by means of the mobile devices in their possession, to decrease, in this indirect fashion, both the distracting influence they are subject to, and the potential damage that might be inflicted upon them from these distractions. With that said, the findings also give evidence that engaging students via mobile instruments did not succeed in being a moderating factor for distractions of the "communications" type, that include sending emails, visiting social network sites and the sending and receiving of SMS messages. It seems that the lure of keeping lines of "communications" with the world open during class is too great a temptation and it will be very hard to overcome.

The research also shows that use of mobile devices in class can greatly contribute to the satisfaction of students from their course studies. This usage positively impacts the learning experience, generates interest in classwork and makes classes more enjoyable, even if it does not help to improve student achievements.

Summary

This study contributes to the growing body of research on the topic of use of personal mobile technologies in academic instruction. The findings of this research suggest that lecturers, who make deliberate use of learning technologies, add to processes that support learning and reduce a portion of the distracting activities. In addition, such use contributes to student satisfaction and to a positive and enjoyable learning experience. Student use of personal mobile technologies in class is a phenomenon that will further increase over time. It therefore requires of lecturers to change their style of classroom instruction in order to stay relevant to their students and to help them prevail over the distractions mobile technologies have the potential to create.

References

Kurtz, G. and Meishar-Tal, H (2014) Personal Mobile Devices in Lectures: Uses and Implications for the Learning Process, *Chais conference proceeding*. Retrieved June 10, 2014 from: http://www.openu.ac.il/innovation/chais2014/download/F2-3.pdf

Baiyun, C. & deNoyelles, A. (2013). Exploring Students' Mobile Learning Practices in Higher Education. *EDUCAUSE Review.* . Retrieved October 10, 2013 from: http://www.educause.edu/ero/article/exploring-students-mobile-learning-practices-higher-education?utm_source=Informz&utm_medium=Email+marketing&utm_campaign=EDUCAUSE

Barak, M., Lipson, A., & Lerman, S. (2006). Wireless laptops as means for promoting active learning in large lecture halls. *Journal of Research on Technology in Education, 38*(3), 245-263.

Barkhuus, L. (2005). Bring your own laptop unless you want to follow the lecture: Alternative communication in the classroom. In *Proceedings of the 2005 international ACM SIGGROUP conference on supporting group work* 140-143.

Christensen, C. M. & Horn, M. (2008), *Disruptive class: How disruptive innovation will change the way the world learns* NY: McGraw Hill,

Fried, C.B. (2008). In-class laptop use and its effects on student learning. *Computers & Education 50*(3), 906–914.

Gehlen-Baum, V. & Weinberger, A. (2012). Notebook or Facebook? How Students Actually Use Mobile Devices in Large Lectures. In A. Ravenscroft, S. Lindstaedt, C. D. Kloos, & D. Hernández-Leo (Eds.) *21st Century Learning for 21st Century Skills (Volume 7563)* (pp 103-112). Berlin Heidelberg: Springer-Verlag.

Kraushaar, J.M., & Novak, D.C. (2010) Examining the Effects of Student Multitasking with Laptops during the Lecture. *Journal of Information Systems Education 21*(2), 11.

Meishar-Tal, H. & Kurtz, G. (2014) The Laptop, the Tablet, and the Smartphone Attend the Lecture" in: Keengwe , J. & Maxfield M. (ed.) Advancing Higher *Education with Mobile Learning Technologies: Cases, Trends, and Inquiry-Based Methods.* Hershey, PA: IGI Global.

Mifsud, L., Anders I. Mørch, A. I. & Lieberg, S. (2013): An analysis of teacher-defined activities with mobile technologies: predecessor and successor tool use in the Classroom. *Learning, Media and Technology, 38*(1), 41-56.

The Influence of Class Sets of Mobile Devices on Student Learning

Nicholas J. Lux
Montana State University
United States
nicholas.lux@montana.edu

Art Bangert
Montana State University
United States
abangert@montana.edu

Miles McGeehan
Bozeman School District
United States
miles.mcgeehan@gmail.com

Kathryn Will-Dubyak
Montana State University
United States
kathryn.willdubyak@montana.edu

Rob Watson
Bozeman School District
United States
robert.watson@bsd7.org

Abstract: This quantitative study, part of a larger mixed-methods study, focused specifically on investigating the influence on student achievement of class sets of Chromebook computers. In this case, a class set differs slightly from the more common 1:1 design; class sets of devices means that students have the device at their disposal throughout the entire school day, but do not take them home after school. Devices were provided to elementary and middle school classrooms across a medium-sized school district in the Pacific Northwest, and researchers examined data related to student achievement including scores on district-wide reading and math assessments, keyboarding assessments, 21st century skills assessments, and attendance records. Results from the study strongly suggest the class sets of Chromebook devices significantly influenced student learning. However, research design and other limitations preclude any overstated connections between the integration of devices and outcomes of the pilot.

Introduction

Digital learning tools have potential to provide rich, relevant, and situated learning experiences. Instruction situated within technology-rich learning environments that support this kind of learning is becoming more and more commonplace as teachers work toward active and engaged learning partnerships between students and teachers (Rosen & Beck-Hill, 2012). Technology-rich environments have demonstrated the ability to increase student achievement, enhance differentiation in teaching and learning, raise student attendance, and decrease disciplinary actions (Moyer-Packenham & Suh, 2012; Pulford, 2009; Rosen & Beck-Hill, 2012). However, this landscape is continually shifting. Teachers are now expected to interact with new technologies in new ways to deliver appropriate pedagogy to meet the learners' needs (Kang, Heo, Jo, Shin, & Seo, 2010-11). This technology and pedagogy connection is often the source of scrutiny, and many argue a transformation is afoot with changes coming to the institution of curriculum-based instruction (Bidarra & Martins, 2010-11). These changes include shifts in the instructional focus to emphasize contribution, creativity, innovation, problem solving, communication, collaboration, and global awareness (Lu, 2011; AACTE & P21, 2010). As a result, teaching and learning practices are changing to accommodate these new perspectives and adapt to a world of digital natives (Funkhouser & Mouza, 2013).

Further complicating matters is that teachers are now required to constantly negotiate new technical innovations and skills as current technologies and approaches become obsolete (Shieh, 2012). Despite these challenges, teachers still recognize that technology integration provides them certain affordances otherwise not possible like more instructional time for learning and exploration, increased motivation, engagement, and interest, and opportunities for students to more readily share work and collaboratively solve problems (Neiss & Gillow-Wiles, 2013). Further, technology-rich environments are not necessarily the "silver bullet" to educational woes. Personal devices and software are merely tools in the classroom, which could be used to enhance education or possibly hinder it. Teachers may also focus solely on technology-centric approaches to learning without sensitivity to how people learn (Salomon & Perkins, 2005).

Twenty-first century standards coupled with college and career demands have been putting pressure on school districts across the nation to introduce ubiquitous computing in earlier grades. One-to-one (1:1) computing has shown the capacity to enhance curriculum resulting in increase student achievement, engagement, learner satisfaction, new differentiation possibilities, and create opportunity for student-centered learning environments (Rosen & Beck-Hill, 2012). Additionally, 1:1 computing has demonstrated reductions in absenteeism and behavioral problems (Rosen & Beck-Hill, 2012). It is important to point out that all 1:1 initiatives do not provide identical results. Many suggest some positive trends in the findings, but little report all of the potential benefits listed above. Results demonstrating increased engagement, student satisfaction, improvements in 21st century skills, and enhanced differentiation opportunities stand out most frequently (Abell Foundation, 2008). Increased achievement is common but some contradictory results exist, especially when it comes to standardized test scores (Abell Foundation, 2008). School administrators point out that 1:1 designs may not aptly prepare students for multiple choice testing that routinely focuses on lower level depth of (Abell Foundation, 2008), however this should not reduce the credibility of the educational benefits 1:1 environments provide.

Purpose

Following the approval of a technology levy at the local level, a medium-sized school district in the Pacific Northwest committed to piloting one classroom set of Chromebooks for each elementary and middle school throughout the District in order to investigate the influence of class sets of devices in the classroom. With the assistance of educational researchers at a local university, the district intended to investigate the systemic influence of class sets of devices in the classroom. Researchers conducted a large mixed-methods study to examine the overall influence of the Chromebook devices on teaching and learning. This included studying quantitative data related to student achievement, as well as closely examining qualitative data focused on classroom practice, teachers' perceptions about the devices, and students' perceptions about the devices.

Despite the broad nature of the larger effectiveness study, this particular study focused on the potential influence of the Chromebook devices as it relates directly to the quantitative data related to student achievement in math, reading, keyboarding, and 21st century skills, and other quantitative metrics like attendance data. Better understanding the potential influence of class sets of Chromebook computers on student learning might provide unique insight into how technology could better support teaching and learning processes. Therefore, this pilot study investigated the influence of class sets of Chromebook computers on student learning. The researchers used the following research question to guide the inquiry: How did student use of Chromebooks influence student achievement?

The Study

The context for this study was a school district serving approximately 6400 K-12 students located in the Pacific Northwest. The district contained mostly Caucasian students from a wide variety of socio-economic backgrounds. More than 20% of the families served were classified below the poverty line, while a majority of families were considered middle class. It should be noted that the school district purposefully did not employ a true 1:1 design due to resource constraints and other logistical considerations. Instead, the pilot provided a class set of devices that remained in the classroom throughout the school day, where each student had their own device. The distinct difference between this model and a true 1:1 model is that students in this pilot were not allowed to take the devices home with them after school; the devices stayed at school.

Multiple data sources were employed for this quantitative investigation. Again, the intent was to study the overall possible influence of the Chromebook devices on student learning. This included closely examining quantitative data related to student achievement in math, reading, keyboarding, and 21st century skills, and other metrics like attendance data. Table 1 includes a breakdown for teach of the data sources.

Table 1
Data Matrix: Description of sequence and methods of procedures

Instrument	Data Collection Methodology and Information
District Achievement Data	Researchers were granted access to district provided achievement data for math and reading assessments.
Keyboarding Assessments	Researchers were granted access to district provided assessment data for a keyboarding assessment taken by all 3rd, 4th, and 5th grade students.
Attendance Data	Researchers were granted access to district provided attendance data for all students within the district.
21st Century Skills Assessment	Participating teachers administered a technology skills assessment to participating students in a pre/post capacity two times during the academic year (beginning, end).
Free & Reduced Lunch and IEP Status	Researchers were granted access to district provided data related to students on free and reduced lunch, and those with IEPs.

Findings

The following section provides an overview of the initial findings from quantitative measures used to collect data during the Chromebook pilot. Data analysis has provided some noteworthy findings. Results have been broken down by potential influence on student achievement data, keyboarding assessments, attendance, 21st century skills assessment, and free and reduced lunch count and IEP status, and shared thusly.

Student Achievement Data

Independent-samples T-tests were conducted to compare the scores on district-wide math and reading assessments for students that participated in the Chromebook pilot and those that did not participate in the pilot. Elementary students (Grades 3, 4, and 5) completed the district-wide math and reading comprehension assessments three times during the school year (Fall, Winter, and Spring). For the purposes of this study, the spring scores on each of these assessments are the focus of the analysis.

Results from these tests suggest that the spring scores for elementary (Grades 3, 4, and 5) Chromebook pilot participants were significantly higher from non-Chromebook pilot participants on both math ($p < .001$) and reading assessments ($p < .001$). However, it should be noted that the computed Cohen's d effect size for the significant findings was in the upper-region of what is generally considered small (Cohen's d standard of .2 or lower = small; Cohen's d standard of .5 - .3 = medium; Cohen's d standard of .8 or higher = large). Results for this analysis have been provided in Table 2.

Inspection of the two group means indicated that the average math achievement score for Chromebook pilot participants (M = 33.69) was significantly higher than the mean score (M = 31.49) for non-Chromebook pilot participants. The Cohen's d was approximately .48. This was just below the threshold for what is considered a "medium" effect size. In addition, analysis of the group means also indicated that the average reading comprehension score for Chromebook pilot participants (M = 23.08) was significantly higher than the mean score (M = 21.84) for non-Chromebook pilot participants. The Cohen's d is approximately .43, again just slightly below the commonly accepted threshold considered a medium effect size. Results for this analysis have been provided in Table 2.

Table 2

Comparison of Chromebook participants and Non-Chromebook participants on Math and Reading Comprehension Assessments

Variable	M	SD	t	df	p	d
Math - Spring			7.51[a]	456.2[a]	<.001*	.48
Chromebook Participants	23.08	2.08				
Non-Chromebook Participants	21.84	3.09				
Reading Comprehension – Spring			6.71[a]	443.5[a]	<.001*	.43
Chromebook Participants	33.69	4.15				
Non-Chromebook Participants	31.49	5.97				

[a] The *t* and *df* statistics were adjusted because variances were not equal
* Significant at the .005 level

Keyboarding

A series of one-sample T-tests were conducted to compare the scores on district-wide keyboarding assessment completed at the end of the school year. All students in the district completed this assessment, not just those participating in the Chromebook pilot. The t-tests compared Chromebook participants' scores on the keyboarding assessment to the mean grade level scores on the keyboarding assessment calculated from scores for all students in the district. Results from these tests suggested that the keyboarding assessment scores for elementary (Grades 3, 4, and 5) Chromebook pilot participants were significantly higher from non-Chromebook pilot participants ($p < .001$). Results from these tests also indicated that the keyboarding assessment scores for middle school (Grade 8) Chromebook pilot participants were not significantly different from non-Chromebook pilot participants. The Cohen's *d* for each of grade scores indicating significant differences were quite high, ranging from .75 to 1.92, all considered large effect sizes. Results from the keyboarding assessment are provided in Table 3.

Table 3

Comparison of Chromebook participants score on Keyboarding Assessment Compared to District Mean Scores

Grade Level	District M	Sample M	SD	t	df	p	d
3rd Grade	13.13	15.64	6.28	2.71	52	.009*	.75
4th Grade	21.14	25.06	8.97	5.33	148	<.001*	.87
5th Grade	24.36	33.42	9.57	5.27	30	<.001*	1.92

*Significant at the .005 level

Attendance

There were no significant differences measured in attendance, defined as total days missed, between Chromebook pilot students and non-Chromebook pilot students at the start of the school year. However, Chromebook pilots had significantly less mean days missed between the start of the pilot and the end of the school year (11/1/13 - 6/11/14). Inspection of the mean days missed for the two groups show Chromebook pilot students (M = 7.48) was significantly lower than the mean days missed for the non-Chromebook students (M = 9.05). However, it is very important to note that the Cohen's d effect size was quite low (d = .20), indicating a small effect size of the difference. It is likely that the very large sample size contributed to the significant difference in the attendance rates after the pilot began. Additional research is needed to determine this more conclusively. Results from the attendance analysis are provided in Table 4.

Table 4

Mean days of school missed before and after the start of the pilot for Chromebook pilot students (n=282) and Non-Chromebook pilot students (n=1884)

Students	M	SD	t	df	p	d
Before the start of pilot (8/27/13-10-/31/13)			-1.39	2164	.166	.09
Chromebook Pilot Students	1.68	2.18				
Non-Chromebook Pilot Students	1.92	2.79				
After the start of pilot (11/1/13-6/11/14)			-3.61 [a]	464.62 [a]	<.001*	.20
Chromebook Pilot Students	7.48*	6.40				
Non-Chromebook Pilot Students	9.05*	8.97				

[a] The *t* and *df* statistics were adjusted because variances were not equal
Significant difference at the .005 level

21st Century Skills & Technology Assessment

In efforts to measure participating students' growth in 21st century technology skills, a pre- and post-technology assessment was administered. This test was only administered to those students in Chromebook classrooms. Therefore, all resulting data is only relevant to Chromebook students; there was no control group, and no resulting data about 21st century skills for students not enrolled in the pilot. Results should be interpreted thusly. The intent of the assessment was to provide insight into students' proficiencies with critical 21st century skills including creativity, innovation, information fluency, critical thinking, decision-making and digital citizenship. A paired samples t-test was conducted to determine if elementary students' post-assessment scores were significantly higher than pre-assessment scores. Results suggests that elementary students' post-assessment scores (M = 336) were significantly higher than their pre-assessment scores (M = 336), $t(185)$ = -16.613, p <.001. The Cohen's *d* effect size was .76, which is just below the commonly accepted threshold (.8) for a large effect. Results from this analysis are provided Table 5 and Figure 2.

Table 5

21st century skills and technology assessment district overall proficiency levels for elementary participants (Pre-assessment n=194; Post-assessment n=218)

Score	Pre-Assessment Mean	Post-Assessment Mean	p	d
Overall Score	276	336	<.001*	.76

*Significant at the .005 level

Figure 2

21st century skills and technology assessment district overall mean scores for participants

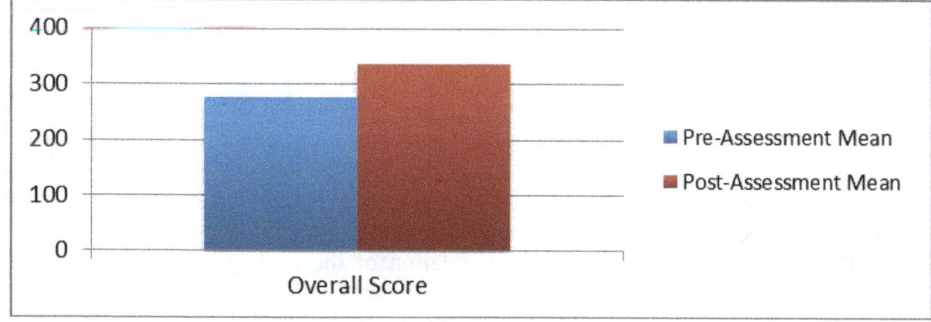

Free and Reduced Lunch and IEPs

In the interest of examining the possible influence of the pilot on closing the achievement gap, we conducted an analysis to determine if those Chromebook students with IEPs, and those eligible for free and reduced lunch, did significantly different than those students not in the Chromebook pilot. Therefore, we isolated those students with IEPs, and those students eligible for free and reduced lunch, and used a Mann-Whitney U test. We used the non-parametric Mann-Whitney U test because of the small sample size for those in the pilot as compared to the much larger sample size of those students not in the pilot. It should be noted that we did not isolate for grade level with this analysis. As a result, mean scores comparisons are across all grade levels for those students that take those tests. In other words, the analysis is for mean scores across grades three, four, and five.

From this analysis, significant differences were detected for the comparison of students eligible for free and reduced lunch and mean scores. Students eligible for free and reduced lunch and in the Chromebook pilot ($M = 22.61$) scored significantly higher on the spring reading comprehension assessment than those students eligible for free and reduced lunch and not in the pilot (M = 20.62), $U = 2798$, $p = <.001$, $r = .23$. And those students eligible for free and reduced lunch and in the Chromebook pilot (M = 32.31) scored significantly higher on the spring math assessment than those students eligible for free and reduced lunch and not in the pilot (M = 28.76), $U = 3113$, $p = .003$, $r = .18$. However, the effect sizes for these differences were small ($r = .23$, $r = .18$ respectively). Results for this analysis have been provided in Table 6.

Table 6

Comparison of mean scores on spring assessments for students eligible for free and reduced lunch

Assessment Mean Score	Chromebook Students	Non-Chromebook Students
Reading Comprehension	22.61*	20.62
Math Mean	32.31*	28.76

*Significantly higher at the <.005 level

Summary of Findings

In regard to math and reading achievement, results from this study indicate that elementary Chromebook pilot participants scored significantly higher than non-Chromebook pilot participants for both the math and reading assessments. Technology literacy was also a focus of our analysis on student achievement. All students completed the 21st Century Skills Assessment. At the start of the pilot, 37% of elementary students scored "proficient" or "advanced" on the nationally-normed 21st Century Skills and Technology Assessment, while 66% scored "proficient" or "advanced" on the post-assessment given at the end of the year. Data for middle school students is a bit more complicated.

As researchers, we also looked at student engagement. It has been suggested that school attendance might serve as one indicator of student engagement. In regard to school attendance, Chromebook pilot students had significantly less mean days missed between the start of the pilot and the end of the school year (11/1/13 - 6/11/14). However, there was no significant difference between Chromebook students and non-Chromebook students in the period of time before the pilot began. This might suggest that students in Chromebook pilot classrooms were more motivated to attend school once the pilot began (8/27/13 – 10/31/13).

Limitations

Several limitations restrict the interpretation of the findings that have emerged from this evaluation. The following section provides a brief analysis of those limitations, and includes suggestions for further research that might address them. It should not be implied that the limitations provided here are the only limitations of the study. However, we submit that this is not a finite list. We recognize a number of logistical constraints beyond what are listed have possibly limited the study, and results should be considered as such.

A key limitation of this evaluation restricting the interpretation of the findings was the lack of a true experimental design. We must be careful to not overstate any possible connections between the integration of devices and outcomes of the pilot, and instead recognize that results simply suggest that there might be a connection between the integration of the class set of devices and these changes in students learning and teacher practice. Therefore, a more rigorous experimental research design, including randomization, to better understand these connections is an important suggestion the research teams hopes the school district might consider for future research.

We also recommend that a more rigorous experimental design would help control for pre-implementation differences among students. Consequently, findings in this evaluation report do not account for those pre-pilot differences, including a wide variety of confounding covariates like prior technology skill or access to technology at home. It is recommended that any future research on the implementation of Chromebooks include such a focus, and better understand the variety of contextual factors that might influence.

Thirdly, the lack of a control group for the 21st century skills assessment limits interpretation of the results. Although a randomized control group is not necessarily critical, having a group of students not in the Chromebook pilot complete the 21st century skill assessment could provide considerable insight into the real growth of students' technology literacy as a result of the pilot. In other words, next steps might include either a district-wide technology skills assessment, or at the very least, a technology assessment give to a randomized sample of the population who are not in classrooms with class sets of devices. These pre- and post-data could then be compared to that of students in classrooms with class sets of devices in an effort to determine if there is significant growth in those technology skills that might influenced by the presence of the class set of devices.

And lastly, we recognize that the evaluation is somewhat limited in scope. We looked at results that emerged only after a small one-year pilot. Although findings were compelling, what remain to be understood are larger scale ramifications. These include aspects such as the long-term impact of the class sets of devices. What happens to students' achievement and technology skills the year following participating in a Chromebook classroom? What happens if they are in a class without the class set of devices? What happens to teacher practice in the second, third, or fourth year? Common sense would lead one to believe that, given ongoing support and professional development, teachers would continue to innovate their practice and the integration of technology? Therefore, we recommend that the district engage in an extended examination of these questions.

Although significant differences were found across the evaluation, some with considerable implications for the interpretation of the results, it is very important that readers keep the resulting effect size in mind. As indicated in the findings, although some analyses detected significant differences suggesting a possible influence of the devices on learning and teaching, the resulting small effect size in some of those analyses needs to be considered. Therefore, future research should focus precisely in those domains of research on class sets of devices where significant results were detected with an accompanying small effect size. Better understanding if a truly significant difference is really occurring in the phenomenon, rather that results simply being influenced by the very large sample size, would help researchers and practitioners better understand the phenomenon and results themselves.

Conclusion

In summary, despite evidence that indicates the class sets of Chromebook devices significantly influenced student learning and teacher practice, it must be noted that the research design, and lack of a true experimental approach to the study, precludes any overstated connections between the integration of devices and outcomes of the pilot. In other words, we recognize, and urge readers of this report, to not over-interpret findings. This evaluation design did not control for any initial group differences. We used intact groups (classrooms) as the sample. Most importantly, readers should keep in mind that results simply suggest that there might be other underlying connections between the integration of the class set of devices and these changes in students learning and teacher practice. Therefore, readers should not over-interpret the data and findings, and make claims suggesting that the Chromebooks are responsible for the pilot outcomes. A more rigorous experimental research design would be required to make such assertions.

Notwithstanding, results from this study are certainly encouraging, and do in fact, serve as reason to further study the impact of the class sets of Chromebooks on student achievement. Coupled with a more rigorous research design in which group differences are more carefully controlled, further investigation could be conducted to better understand the influence of the devices on teaching and learning. Further, findings from this study certainly align with previous research that also indicates 1:1 computing environments can positively influence student achievement (Moyer-Packenham & Suh, 2012; Pulford, 2009; Rosen & Beck-Hill, 2012), including metrics for engagement like absenteeism (Rosen & Beck-Hill, 2012). And as evidenced by the scores on the 21st century learning assessments, it could be argued that a class set of devices could lead to increased performance in regard to those skills like critical thinking, problem-solving, and collaboration (Lu, 2011; AACTE & P21, 2010). Based on these findings, and their alignment with previous research, it would be prudent to further study the influence of class sets of devices, but doing so and addressing the concerns expressed in the limitations of this study. Doing so could inform many of the factors related to technology integration, including purchasing, professional development, and integration methodologies.

References

Abell Foundation (2008). *One-to-one computing in public schools: Lessons from "laptops for all" programs.* Retrieved from The Abell Foundation website: http://www.abell.org/pubsitems/ed_onetoone_908.pdf

American Association of Colleges of Teacher Education (AACTE) & Partnership for 21st Century Skills (P21). (2010). *21st century knowledge and skills in educator preparation.* Washington, DC: Author.

Bidarra, J., Martins, O. (2010-11). Exploratory learning with Geodromo: Design of emotional and cognitive factors within an educational cross-media experience. *Journal of Research on Technology in Education, 43*(2), 171-183.

Kang, M., Heo, H., Jo, I., Shin, J., Seo, J. (2010-11). Developing educational performance indicators for new millennium learners. *Journal of Research on Technology in Education, 43*(2), 157-170.

Lu, L. (2011). Art Education Avatars in Action: Preparing Art Teachers for Learning and Teaching in a Virtual Age (for Special issue Digital Games and Simulations in Teacher Preparation). *Journal of Technology and Teacher Education, 19*(3), 287-301.

Moyer-Packenham, P. & Suh, J. (2012). Learning Mathematics with Technology: The Influence of Virtual Manipulatives on Different Achievement Groups. *Journal of Computers in Mathematics and Science Teaching, 31*(1), 39-59.

Niess, M. & Gillow-Wiles, H. (2013). Advancing K-8 Teachers' STEM Education for Teaching Interdisciplinary Science and Mathematics with Technologies. *Journal of Computers in Mathematics and Science Teaching, 32*(2), 219-245.

Pulford, P. (2011). The influence of advice in a virtual learning environment. British Journal of Educational Technology, 42(1), 31-39.

Rosen, Y., & Beck-Hill, D. (2012). Intertwining digital content and a one-to-one laptop environment in teaching and learning: Lessons from the time to know program. *Journal of Research in Technology Education, 44*(3), 225-241.

Salomon, G., & Perkins, D. N. (2005). Do technologies make us smarter? Intellectual amplification with, of, and through technology. In D. D. Preiss & R. Sternberg (Eds.), Intelligence and technology (pp. 71–86). Mahwah, NJ: LEA.

Shieh, R. (2012). The impact of Technology-Enabled Active Learning (TEAL) implementation on student learning and teachers' teaching in a high school context. Computers & Education, 59. 206-214.

Beyond Professional Development: A Case Study of Implementing iPads in Early Childhood Education

Ellen S. Hoffman
University of Hawaii-Manoa
USA
ehoffman@hawaii.edu

Elizabeth Park
Chaminade University of Honolulu
USA
epark@chaminade.edu

Meng-Fen Grace Lin
University of Hawaii-Manoa
USA
gracelin@hawaii.edu

Abstract: This mixed methods case study reports results from a project on implementing iPads by fifteen teachers from Hawaii preschools. We found that previous assumptions about professional development need to be updated. Rather than questions of should technology be used which have dominated past discourse for early childhood teaching, increasingly the concern is how to best assist early childhood educators with the strategies required to respond to new affordances offered by touch based tablets for young children. For professional development, participants preferred face-to-face collaborations and wanted training personalized to skill levels. Further, changing teachers' attitudes was as important as improving skills.

Multiple studies and meta-analyses have been done examining effective practices in professional development (PD) to enhance implementation of educational reforms (Desimone, 2009, 2011), particularly in terms of use of digital technologies in classrooms (Lawless & Pellegrino, 2007). Despite such increased understanding of best practices, the costs, resources, and time needed for ideal PD are generally difficult for most schools to sustain. When viewed from the broader perspective of adoption theory, the conditions for change are only partly impacted by PD, further complicating any expectations of reform implementation based on professional development.

In this multiple methods case study, we examined the impacts of a PD program aimed at helping teachers implement tablet computing in preschool teaching and learning. By viewing change within a broadened context provided by adoption theory, we were able to better understand how PD affected the teachers. The data for the study came from a larger, multiple methods evaluation of two grant projects related to implementing iPads for assessment in Hawaii preschools. The focus here is on the PD components of the project. We note briefly those areas that agree with earlier studies and focus on the findings that raise questions about or expand on extant research. In particular, our results suggest that a rapidly changing technology landscape requires updates to some of the previous assumptions about technology use, attitudes, and affordances in early childhood education (ECE).

Background

Numerous studies have found that despite increases in access and ease of use of digital technologies, teachers have not embraced these for teaching and use remains limited in classrooms. Results from both large-scale surveys and smaller case studies show an interplay among real and perceived barriers as well as personal and external factors in adoption, including teacher beliefs, knowledge and skills, support, and PD (Ertmer, Ottenbreit-Leftwich, Sadik, Sendurur, & Sendurur, 2012; Inan & Lowther, 2010; Kim, Kim, Lee, Spector, & DeMeester, 2013; Kopcha, 2012; Mueller, Wood, Willoughby, Ross, & Specht, 2008; Ottenbreit-Leftwich, Glazewski, Newby, & Ertmer, 2010).

While these adoption factors influence use in early childhood education, there are also additional factors that impact the process. The early learning environment is a unique context that is different from other school settings, not only in the developmental levels of young children but also in relation to structure, regulation, and teacher credentialing (Blackwell, Lauricella, Wartella, Robb, & Schomburg, 2013; Guernsey, 2014). As noted by Blackwell et al. (2013), there are fewer empirical studies on preschool educators' technology adoption than for those in K-12. Using data from a large-scale survey of members of the National Association for the Education of Young Children (NAEYC) in 2012, the authors examined barriers from the perspective of Unified Theory of Acceptance and Use of Technology (UTAUT) (Venkatesh, Morris, Davis, & Davis, 2003), as well as the relationship among first- and second order barriers revealed by applying a more education focused adoption model (Ertmer, 1999). UTAUT variables include performance expectancy, effort expectancy, social influence, and facilitating conditions. First-order barriers are those extrinsic factors such as time, access, training, and support, while second-order barriers are intrinsic, including social, cultural, and psychological factors impacting teacher beliefs, experiences, and confidence (Ertmer & Ottenbreit-Leftwich, 2010). Blackwell et al. found a complex interplay among the variables. In a further path analysis of the same data, the authors found that the strongest indicators of use among the surveyed ECE population were attitudes towards children's learning and confidence, but they noted that the first-order barriers, particularly support and technology policy, had a dynamic relationship with these second-order barriers (Blackwell, Lauricella, & Wartella, 2014). This parallels earlier findings from an interview study which found that use was more influenced by personal concerns related to impacts on teachers over student or parent concerns (Wood, Specht, Willoughby, & Mueller, 2008).

The adoption of technology in preschool settings is additionally confounded by conflicting advice and research findings on the impact of digital technologies on young children (Guernsey, 2014). There is uncertainty over what developmentally appropriate technology integration means and how to assist teachers to understand and implement technology integration successfully for young children (NAEYC & Fred Rogers Center, 2012; Parette, Quesenberry, & Blum, 2010). Further, teachers may have ambivalent attitudes with both positive and negative concerns held concurrently as a result of conflicting advice from experts, mixed recommendations from research, and media hyperbole about the dangers of extensive use with young children (Lindahl & Folkesson, 2012; Lynch & Redpath, 2012). At the same time, teachers recognize the need for digital age literacies and citizenship (Guernsey, 2014).

With the changing mobile technology environment, these devices are not only rapidly being used by most adults but new studies of uses of mobile technologies such as iPads are suggesting that gesture-based navigation and non-textual interfaces are beginning to provide new understandings of the affordances of these technologies for early learners (Beschorner & Hutchison, 2013; Neumann & Neumann, 2014). As such, the context for understanding technology in ECE is changing rapidly and potentially impacting attitudes.

Professional development is generally proposed as a critical element in changing teachers skills and interest in applying technology in teaching. PD can be seen as having identified best practices in general (Desimone, 2011; Penuel, Fishman, Yamaguchi, & Gallagher, 2007), as well as that specific to technology integration (Lawless & Pellegrino, 2007). Specific strategies have been identified for early childhood educator PD that parallel professional development for other teachers but also recognize the unique needs of this population (Mitchell & Cubey, 2003; Snell, Forston, Stanton-Chapman, & Walker, 2013; Zaslow, Tout, Halle, Whittaker, & Lavelle, 2010), including an emphasis on collaboration, modeling, demonstration by instructors, and feedback to participants both during workshops and classroom-based interventions. Given constraints on time and budgets for PD on technology integration for early childhood educators, McManis and Gunnewig (2012) suggested providing built-in support within software and creating effective learning communities. Parette et al. (2010) argued that there needs to be a more focused effort on changing attitudes about the imperatives of technology integration in ECE. This would include training not only for operational competency but in establishing an understanding of why particular tools are important to young children and how to use these tools effectively in classroom contexts.

The Study

The study reported here was focused on PD for technology integration among preschool educators. Four teachers from a single Hawaii preschool participated in the 2013 pilot project, *iPad for Teacher's Educational use At Children's Habitat* (iTEACH). In the following year, the initial four were joined by eleven more teachers representing four additional preschools in an expansion of the project, *iTEACH Connect*. Both projects were funded by the Samuel N. and Mary Castle Foundation. Each teacher received an iPad for use in their school and participated in workshops covering iPads for classroom and administrative uses. Target areas were using a student assessment app for IPad from Teaching Strategies GOLD™ and using the IPad for parent communication in addition to more general uses.

Data were collected through surveys, interviews, observations, focus groups, and social media postings via *Instagram*. The data reported here are from the second year evaluation. A particular strength of this research is that the evidence goes beyond the many self-reports in earlier studies of professional development and technology use, with classroom observations providing context and sometimes contradictions to the teacher survey responses and interview conversations. While the study covered a small number of teachers in a constricted geographical region, it follows the recommendations of Yin (2014) in applying multiple methods to provide depth and rich description through an exploratory case study that can contribute to theoretical generalization.

Participants and Setting

Of the 15 participating teachers, all but one were female. In terms of age, five teachers were between 30-39 while three were 40-49 and six teachers were between 50-59 range; one teacher reported being over 60. One teacher held a high school diploma, one had an associate degree, nine had bachelors degrees, while four had earned a masters. One teacher reported having a professional diploma in early childhood. All were highly experienced preschool teachers: the youngest with three years teaching, while the others had from 7-37 years. Of the group, six were currently teaching classes for four year olds and pre-kindergarten, five taught two and three year olds, three had mixed classrooms, and one was an administrator without a regular classroom assignment. Ten teachers, including one assistant teacher, were from two private pre-schools that were part of a larger consortium, while four teachers along with one administrator were from a second consortium of schools. Two of the schools were selected because of the high number of students from low socioeconomic status (SES) households and all schools had high ethnic diversity reflective of Hawaii as a whole.

At the start of the project, all teachers had technology experience but they varied in self-rating of computing skills: five as proficient, six as intermediate, and four as novices. All had used some type of mobile device, including eight with iPods and ten with smartphones. There was slightly less proficiency with iPads than general computing skills prior to the project, with five proficient, six intermediate, and five novice. Four had not used iPads, while seven had two or more years experience and four had a year or less. Six found it somewhat easy to learn new technologies, but the rest rated their ability to learn technology as average or somewhat difficult.

Findings

The findings are summarized in two broad areas: teacher response to PD strategies within the project and the impacts of changing attitudes.

Professional Development Strategies in Relation to Best Practices

Seven PD workshops for project participants were held in the preschools between January and June 2014 which included an initial orientation workshop, four GOLD® assessment training workshops, and two workshops by the Fred Rogers Center for Early Learning and Children's Media at Saint Vincent College. The four GOLD® training workshops included curricula provided by the vendor but taught by a local trainer. The workshops presented by the Fred Rogers Center focused on parent communication for selected teachers and digital media literacy in the early years for all participants. A wrap-up workshop was held in November 2014.

Based on evaluations collected at each workshop session as well as post-survey results, the teachers expressed appreciation for hands-on interactive activities and in-person meetings during these workshops. The highest overall rating on the workshop evaluations was for the facilitators, at 4.82 out of a possible 5 followed by high ratings for workshop organization at 4.70. Even the lowest averages were positive, with "The workshop contained content that I will be able to use immediately in my classroom," and "The workshop met my expectations," having ratings of 4.48 and 4.56 respectively. It appears that teachers desired the workshops to have more direct connection to their daily practice which may have stemmed from using content that was not localized but was desired by school administrators. From open-ended comments, teachers liked the trainers, found material that would be useful in their classes, and valued the opportunity to share information among themselves. As one participant noted about what she found most valuable, "going into groups and hearing what other teachers use and how I can use it in the classroom."

In addition to the evaluation ratings collected at each of the workshop sessions, teachers were asked specifically about the workshops on a post-survey which was completed by 14 of the 15 participants in the grant project; one participant left her school before the end of the project. Such follow-up questions provide time for teachers to reflect on their learning and consider whether what may have been an enjoyable session had longer term consequences for teaching practice. Twelve of the teachers agreed or strongly agreed that the workshops met their needs, with two indicating a neutral position. In an open-ended response, one of the neutral teachers suggested that the workshops needed to happen earlier in the year and that she learned more by trying things herself. Both the teachers neutral about the workshops already saw themselves as proficient iPad users. By contrast, two of the teachers who rated the workshops as highly useful argued for more workshops and closer timeframe. In general, those with lower self-rated skill levels and those who found it more challenging to learn new technologies were more positive about the workshops.

Variations were clear in the ways teachers preferred to learn new technologies, with a few indicating they enjoyed workshops for PD, but others liked having someone teach them one-on-one or through informal collaborations. In terms of improvements for future projects and training, teachers had several specific suggestions, although three said the workshops were excellent as presented (i.e., "Nothing much. I felt it was successful!") and all had positive reactions to various aspects of the workshops' delivery and content. Some teachers wanted more training while others wanted less. There was no consistent trend in suggestions for improvements with each teacher generally indicating personal needs and preferences. While large-group workshops may be efficient, these do not necessarily have the flexibility to accommodate variations in pre-existing skills, teaching experience, and learner preferences but can still produce positive results.

Extending PD through a community of learners (CoL). Although the project developers saw a digital "community of learners" as a positive concept for PD based on findings from the pilot 2013 iTEACH grant project as well as recommendations from the literature, it was not a central activity but was more an experimental sideline. The teachers participated in using a private online network through *Instagram* to share events in the classroom as well as new skills they had gained through this project. Although there were several participating teachers who consistently posted images and comments on *Instagram*, not all participating teachers used it. Those who were most invested had indicated in earlier surveys that they were already active users of social media. A second online community and portal for early childhood education resources, the Fred Rogers Center Early Learning Environment (Ele) with forums for sharing with other professionals, was introduced in the digital literacy workshop. The teachers were able to login and review the online discussions as part of the workshop, but follow-up use was limited among the participants. Time and ease of use factors were mentioned in the post-survey as issues in digital social network participation.

What did come out through survey and interview responses is that, while digital community was not seen as very useful, a more personal localized community of learners emerged among project participants that was highly valued. The participants indicated positive impacts of this project from face-to-face interactions among trainers, researchers, and evaluators, and many preschool teachers are eager to learn more about appropriate use in assessing, teaching, and learning. In discussions at the workshops and when meeting with teachers in their schools, many teachers expressed how they appreciated sharing when they met in person rather than online.

These results suggest that these ECE teachers continue to rely more on personal rather than digital professional networks for their learning, although the opportunity for sharing is highly valued as a part of the project. The in-person Community of Learners was a positive experience for the teachers but one that is still in formative stages and, because it requires grant funding, will be more difficult to sustain as the project ends.

Continuing personalized education via specialized resource portals. From the workshop evaluations, teachers appreciated what they learned during the sessions about the Fred Rogers Center Early Learning Environment (Ele) as an informational portal for increasing their knowledge of technology uses in and resources for early childhood education. The two sessions covered not only the use of Ele but also general issues of technology use in pre-school education. However, the interest in the topic did not lead to extensive use of Ele for locating resources. Based on responses on the post-survey, some teachers indicated that they found Ele useful professionally (33%) and helpful for finding resources for their classes (25%), but half indicated a more neutral stance. Of the twelve who responded to the question, all used the site only a few times or rarely, even among those who rated it higher for being useful. One teacher did note that she found it useful in talking about a concern with a parent and recommended it as a way to raise awareness. Issues in using the site described in open-ended responses included lack of time and not easy enough to find what was wanted. While not specifically asked, from other observations and interviews, teachers were seen to seek materials from major generalized internet search engines rather than going to specialized ECE or education portals, even when they knew these existed and could be useful. This suggests web portals such as the Fred Rogers Early Learning Environment with it specialized resources are valued but only explored when identified through a general search or when specifically recommended by another teacher at a time it is needed, with teachers not having time to go looking at multiple possible good sources.

Beyond Content: Changing Attitudes

In a pre-survey to establish baseline information about the teachers, two open-ended questions asked teachers about their attitudes toward technology in early childhood education. In general, their responses paralleled those of earlier studies cited above, noting a mix of positive and negative issues, often with both expressed simultaneously by an individual. Teachers indicated personal concerns such as time management as well as positives such as connecting with others including teachers and parents in terms of technology in their schools. While some had misgivings about taking time away from personal or social interactions for children or using technology as a "baby sitter," several noted the importance of bringing the children into the digital world and using it to engage them and encourage creativity. Safety was a concern while several felt that children could be getting too much screen time. These teachers are aware of the controversies and even the most positive raise questions about appropriate use in ECE and in general, know of issues both pro and con that have been described from other studies and in the media.

By the end of the project on the post-survey, the negative concerns were not mentioned although this does not mean that they were no longer an issue but they were less the focus of the teacher's thinking with a greater focus on action and the potential of iPads. Of particular note is that at the end of the project, all teachers were excited about the possibilities of the iPad for teaching, with eight strongly agreeing and seven agreeing with the statement.

Some comments suggest both increased confidence and more positive attitudes about technology use with young children. For example in open-ended responses on what was most useful to them from the project, they noted,

- At first I was against using the iPad for teaching. Seeing the iPad and devices used in public by parents as a "baby sitter" turned me off but by attending the iPad, GOLD® and ELE workshops my thinking has completely changed.
- It really has made assessment, observations and planning so much easier.
- This project was great. I would never be doing half of the exciting things in the classroom with the iPad had I not been in this project. Although still a bit nervous using the technology I find myself doing more research, sharing great information in class with the children and feeling more confident searching out educational sites for every aspect of learning in our classroom.

What is most interesting is these particular comments were from teachers who initially had numerous concerns and questions about bringing technology into their classrooms, both in terms of their own abilities and in respect to the appropriateness for teaching young children. The one continuing negative response related to use was time, with constraints both in the classroom given other activities required for the children, and in terms of teacher time to learn more. The teacher who began as the most technology novice and who still rated herself as such at the end of the project retained her concerns. She noted,

I was probably not able to do things because of my fear of the iPad. Even though I have become more confident time and fear has kept me from using the iPad in ways I know I should be using it. My co-teacher has been a great help in boosting my confidence and watching her use her iPad in all these great ways is wanting me to keep working on using the iPad to its full potential.

She was also the most junior teacher with the least teaching experience, suggesting that for beginners, PD and related support will need to be more intense to change both attitudes and practice, and again, the importance of personal interaction and modeling in PD.

Discussion and Conclusions

Many of the findings in this study parallel those of earlier studies as well as supporting recommendations for quality professional development. In particular, the study showed teachers valued PD content that made suggestions for increasing student learning and provided clear pathways for use in one's own classroom. Delivering multiple workshops over a longer period of time, and allowing interaction among participants, facilitators, and researchers to share what they learned were seen as important factors in their ability to apply new knowledge and skills and in their satisfaction with the PD.

Several items that have broader implications in the results that have been less well reported from earlier research studies include: the very strong preference for face-to-face contact over digital community; the differing preferences for how to learn the material; and shifting attitudes towards iPad use in early childhood education that were seen by the end of the project. In general, when implementing PD, more consideration will need to be given to customization of learning to accommodate different learning preferences and ranges of knowledge about teaching as well as digital tool use. The use of informal digital professional networks for learning, while an appealing concept, remains an area that requires more exploration among early childhood educators.

Perhaps the most interesting finding related to the shift in attitudes seen by the end of the project indicating fewer stated concerns about negative impacts. It would be easy to automatically presume that the change was the result of effective professional development as is claimed in many similar case studies. The evidence does show that there were different responses by the end of the project, and at least some support for the idea that actual use and better understanding of the technology based on the PD assisted with this change related to increased confidence and knowledge. In particular, seeing positive results in their own classrooms and sharing success stories can be seen as one model for changing teachers' attitudes.

However, following recommendations by Yin (2014) for discussing case study results, it would be preferable to put conclusions in the context of competing hypotheses rather than propose solely a one-to-one relationship between PD and attitude change. As with some more recent research showing efficacy for ECE, iPad technology itself might contribute to changing attitudes. For example, ease of use and mobility have added expanded affordances that help both teachers and young children in applying the technology to learning. But a further factor to consider is that mobile technologies have very rapidly become ubiquitous and popular. As such, from a more social perspective, mobile technologies may not only be more acceptable in multiple societal contexts which teachers recognize extend to their classrooms, but it could also be less socially acceptable to denigrate their use when these trendy technologies are so widely hyped, creating a sort of response bias in what teachers are willing to report about their own thinking. Given changing societal norms, we may be at a "tipping point" in technology integration in ECE which may only be fully understood in retrospect in the future.

References

Beschorner, B., & Hutchison, A. (2013). iPads as a literacy teaching tool in early childhood. *International Journal of Education in Mathematics, Science and Technology, 1*(1), 16-24. Retrieved from http://ijemst.com/issues/2_Beschorner_Hutchison_.pdf

Blackwell, C. K., Lauricella, A. R., & Wartella, E. (2014). Factors influencing digital technology use in early childhood education. *Computers & Education, 77*(0), 82-90. doi: 10.1016/j.compedu.2014.04.013

Blackwell, C. K., Lauricella, A. R., Wartella, E., Robb, M., & Schomburg, R. (2013). Adoption and use of technology in early education: The interplay of extrinsic barriers and teacher attitudes. *Computers & Education, 69*, 310-319. doi: 10.1016/j.compedu.2013.07.024

Desimone, L. M. (2009). Improving impact studies of teachers' professional development: Toward better conceptualizations and measures. *Educational Researcher, 38*(3), 181-199. doi: 10.3102/0013189x08331140

Desimone, L. M. (2011). A primer on effective professional development. [Article]. *Phi Delta Kappan, 92*(6), 68-71.

Ertmer, P. A. (1999). Addressing first- and second-order barriers to change: Strategies for technology integration. *Educational Technology Research and Development, 47*(4), 47-61. doi: 10.1007/BF02299597

Ertmer, P. A., & Ottenbreit-Leftwich, A. T. (2010). Teacher technology change: How knowledge, confidence, beliefs, and culture intersect. *Journal of Research on Technology in Education, 42*(3), 255-284.

Ertmer, P. A., Ottenbreit-Leftwich, A. T., Sadik, O., Sendurur, E., & Sendurur, P. (2012). Teacher beliefs and technology integration practices: A critical relationship. *Computers & Education, 59*(2), 423-435. doi: 10.1016/j.compedu.2012.02.001

Guernsey, L. (2014). Envisioning a digital age architecture for early education. Washington, DC: New America Education Policy Program. Retrieved from http://www.newamerica.org/education-policy/envisioning-digital age-architecture-early-education/

Inan, F. A., & Lowther, D. L. (2010). Laptops in the K-12 classrooms: Exploring factors impacting instructional use. *Computers & Education, 55*(3), 937-944. doi: http://dx.doi.org/10.1016/j.compedu.2010.04.004

Kim, C., Kim, M. K., Lee, C., Spector, J. M., & DeMeester, K. (2013). Teacher beliefs and technology integration. *Teaching and Teacher Education, 29*(0), 76-85. doi: 10.1016/j.tate.2012.08.005

Kopcha, T. J. (2012). Teachers' perceptions of the barriers to technology integration and practices with technology under situated professional development. *Computers & Education, 59*(4), 1109-1121. doi: 10.1016/j.compedu.2012.05.014

Lawless, K. A., & Pellegrino, J. W. (2007). Professional development in integrating technology Into teaching and learning: Knowns, unknowns, and ways to pursue better questions and answers. *Review of Educational Research, 77*(4), 575-614. doi: 10.3102/0034654307309921

Lindahl, M. G., & Folkesson, A.-M. (2012). ICT in preschool: Friend or foe? The significance of norms in a changing practice. *International Journal of Early Years Education, 20*(4), 422-436. doi: 10.1080/09669760.2012.743876

Lynch, J., & Redpath, T. (2012). 'Smart' technologies in early years literacy education: A meta-narrative of paradigmatic tensions in iPad use in an Australian preparatory classroom. *Journal of Early Childhood Literacy*. doi: 10.1177/1468798412453150

McManis, L. D., & Gunnewig, S. B. (2012). Finding the education in educational technology with early learners. *Young Children, 67*(3), 14-24. Retrieved from http://www.naeyc.org/

Mitchell, L., & Cubey, P. (2003). Characteristics of professional development linked to enhanced pedagogy and children's learning in early childhood settings: Best evidence synthesis. Wellington, NZ: New Zealand Ministry of Education. Retrieved from http://www.nzcer.org.nz/

Mueller, J., Wood, E., Willoughby, T., Ross, C., & Specht, J. (2008). Identifying discriminating variables between teachers who fully integrate computers and teachers with limited integration. *Computers & Education, 51*(4), 1523-1537. doi: 10.1016/j.compedu.2008.02.003

NAEYC, & Fred Rogers Center. (2012). Technology and interactive media as tools in early childhood programs serving children from birth through age 8 (Joint position statement). Washington, DC: National Association for the Education of Young Children and the Fred Rogers Center for Early Learning and Children's Media. Retrieved from http://www.naeyc.org/content/technology-and-young-children

Neumann, M. M., & Neumann, D. L. (2014). Touch screen tablets and emergent literacy. *Early Childhood Education Journal, 42*(4), 231-239. doi: 10.1007/s10643-013-0608-3

Ottenbreit-Leftwich, A. T., Glazewski, K. D., Newby, T. J., & Ertmer, P. A. (2010). Teacher value beliefs associated with using technology: Addressing professional and student needs. *Computers & Education, 55*(3), 1321 1335. doi: http://dx.doi.org/10.1016/j.compedu.2010.06.002

Parette, H., Quesenberry, A., & Blum, C. (2010). Missing the boat with technology usage in early childhood settings: A 21st century view of developmentally appropriate practice. *Early Childhood Education Journal, 37*(5), 335-343. doi: 10.1007/s10643-009-0352-x

Penuel, W. R., Fishman, B. J., Yamaguchi, R., & Gallagher, L. P. (2007). What makes professional development effective? Strategies that foster curriculum implementation. *American Educational Research Journal, 44*(4), 921-958. doi: 10.3102/0002831207308221

Snell, M. E., Forston, L. D., Stanton-Chapman, T. L., & Walker, V. L. (2013). A review of 20 years of research on professional development interventions for preschool teachers and staff. *Early Child Development and Care, 183*(7), 857-873. doi: 10.1080/03004430.2012.702112

Venkatesh, V., Morris, M. G., Davis, G. B., & Davis, F. D. (2003). User acceptance of information technology: Toward a unified view. *MIS Quarterly, 27*(3), 425-478.

Wood, E., Specht, J., Willoughby, T., & Mueller, J. (2008). Integrating computer technology in early childhood education environments: Issues raised by early childhood educators. *Alberta Journal of Educational Research, 54*(2). Retrieved from http://ajer.synergiesprairies.ca/ajer/index.php/ajer/article/view/630/613

Yin, R. K. (2014). *Case study research: Design and methods* (5th ed.). Thousand Oaks, CA: Sage Publications.

Zaslow, M., Tout, K., Halle, T., Whittaker, J. V., & Lavelle, B. (2010). Toward the identification of features of effective professional development for early childhood educators. Literature review. Washington, DC: Office of Planning, Evaluation and Policy Development, US Department of Education. Retrieved from https://www2.ed.gov/rschstat/eval/professional-development/literature-review.pdf

"You are Here": Developing Elementary Students' Geography Skills by Integrating Geospatial Information Technologies

Thomas Hammond
Lehigh University
United States
hammond@lehigh.edu

Abstract: This study explores the use of geospatial information technologies to develop third grade students' mastery of latitude and longitude and related geography skills. The researchers worked with teachers and students at three elementary schools to develop and refine a week-long sequence for teaching latitude and longitude—along with map skills and geospatial awareness—incorporating GPS units, Google Earth overlays, and geospatially-embedded social media. Student learning outcomes were assessed before and after the unit, demonstrating large effect sizes, depending upon the level of prior exposure to geography education. Following instruction, student focus groups shared their experiences of geography education, indicating a predominance of traditional methods during in-class instruction but an emerging array of unconventional, non-curricular sources of informal geography education. Implications for geography education and teacher education are addressed, and further research on the use of geospatial tools in elementary geography education is recommended.

Introduction

In 1761, James Harrison completed the first successful test of a precision system for measuring longitude (Sobel, 1995). Ever since then, geographers and cartographers rely upon the increasingly precise measurement of latitude and longitude to locate, identify, and map features of world. The development of the Global Positioning System (GPS) in 1994 has resulted in an ever-expanding list of its applications: In 1997, BMW offered "on-board navigation" as a factory option for $2,800; today, a portable GPS unit is a standard option on rental cars, costing just a few dollars a day. For those who must know their latitude and longitude at all times, they can consult a GPS-enabled wristwatch or use one of dozens of free mobile apps—including full-featuring mobile mapping (O'Neill, 2013).

Despite this significance and emphasis, the actual instruction about latitude and longitude received by K-12 students is not robust. Elementary social studies textbooks typically address the topic in a stand-alone introductory section on "map basics" or a "geography review" sandwiched between other units; suggested lessons for teaching the topic are similarly cursory and de-contextualized. Even National Geographic, publisher of the first national standards *Geography for Life* (Boehm & Bednarz, 1994), present a highly sterile treatment of the topic unlikely to capture student interest:

> Have students find the approximate location of their town and mark it with a dot. Ask students to think about what to do if the location is not on a line but in between lines. Model for students how to figure out the town's latitude and longitude. Next, draw two more dots in other areas of the country and have students work independently or in pairs to figure out the approximate latitude and longitude of those places. Finally, have students figure out what city is at approximately 30°N, 90°W (New Orleans, Louisiana) and what city is at approximately 40°N, 105°W (Denver, Colorado) (National Geographic, n.d., para. 3).

This lesson is only tenuously connected to students' immediate environment and interests and completely fails to take advantage of emerging technologies and their uses of latitude and longitude.

Unsurprisingly, student learning outcomes from these traditional methods of instruction leave much to be desired. For example, the National Assessment of Educational Progress (NAEP) has assessed fourth graders' knowledge of geography—including latitude and longitude and map skills—in 1994, 2001, and 2010. The 1994 and 2001 tests contained items asking students to use maps to identify locations relative to the Equator and/or Prime Meridian. In both cases (1994: Grade 4, Block G7, Question #13; 2001: Grade 4, Block G7, Question #1—see http://nces.ed.gov/nationsreportcard/itmrlsx/search.aspx?subject=geography), less than one third of students—just slightly above the guess-work level—could correctly complete the task.

The current state of instruction and learning outcomes regarding latitude and longitude leave considerable room for improvement. The significance of the concept suggests that geography educators and researchers should search for ways to improve students' mastery of latitude and longitude, linking it to substantive, disciplinary tasks. One route forward would appear to be to integrate emerging geospatial technologies to more fully engage students (Broda & Baxter, 2003) and develop complex spatial understandings (National Research Council, 2006). Researchers and practitioners have already developed models for middle school education to conduct local geospatial inquiries using Google Earth and handheld GPS units (Hammond & Bodzin, 2009); the same tools might be used at the elementary level to enhance existing instruction on the foundational concepts of latitude and longitude and their related, supporting constructs of map skills and geospatial awareness.

The Study

To put this line of reasoning to the test, the author instigated a set of design experiments to explore the possible impacts of integrating geospatial technologies into geography instruction for third grade students. The research questions directing this study were as follows:

1. What effect does a geospatially-enriched instructional sequence have upon third-grade students'
    a. Mastery of latitude and longitude?
    b. Map skills?
    c. Geospatial awareness?
2. What impact does prior traditional instruction have upon students'
    a. Mastery of latitude and longitude?
    b. Map skills?
    c. Geospatial awareness?
3. What are students' formal/curricular and informal/non-curricular experiences of learning and working with geospatial tools, latitude and longitude, map skills, and geospatial awareness?

This study is situated with the design-based research paradigm (Design-Based Research Collective, 2003). Design-based research is conducted in active partnership between researchers and practitioners as they engage in progressive refinement of an educational design and its evaluative mechanisms. According to Collins, Joseph, & Bielaczyc (2004), "the design is constantly revised based upon experience, until all the bugs are worked out" (p. 18). The study was took place in three rounds, with refinements introduced along the way as identified by the researcher or a collaborating teacher.

Settings and participants

The study took place in a mid-sized city in the northeastern United States. Third-grade students and their teachers at three elementary schools participated. Per the state department of education, all three schools serve significant populations of high-need students, with 50% or more of the students classified as "economically disadvantaged". All three schools have recently struggled to meet their mandated targets in reading and math scores: two schools met their Annual Yearly Progress (AYP) goals through safe harbor and/or confidence interval exceptions, and one school failed to make AYP entirely. Each school provided one forty-five minute period for social studies instruction in the spring semester of the school year. The building principals approved the project and identified the teacher to participate in the instruction.

Each group of students received—with modifications for weather—the same five-class sequence, studying latitude and longitude, map skills, and geospatial awareness using a variety of geospatial tools. The instructional sequence is summarized in Table 1 (below). Typically this sequence required one week (Monday-Friday) to complete, with modifications for weather (e.g., rain on day 3 might necessitate moving day 5 up in the sequence) or interruptions in the school schedule (e.g., picture day, testing days, etc.).

Table 1

Sequence of Geospatially-Enhanced Lessons: Topics, Technologies, and Activities

Class session & topic	Geospatial technologies used	Description of instructional activities
Session 1: Orientation to latitude and longitude	Google Earth Flickr map	(Class conducted indoors, whole-class instruction) - Introduction (or re-introduction) to concepts of latitude, longitude - Viewing lat/lon grid in Google Earth - Viewing photos taken on the Equator and Prime Meridian - Locating school in Google Earth, noting position relative to Equator and Prime Meridian
Session 2: Observing changes in latitude and longitude in the schoolyard	Handheld GPS units Google Earth	(Class conducted on school playground in pairs/small groups) - Review of latitude and longitude - Directional orientation: Which way is north? South? In which direction is the Prime Meridian? What local landmarks can we use to orient ourselves? - Orientation Observing GPS unit booting up, finding coordinates - Marking off one second of latitude and one second of longitude - (Time permitting) Observing placemarks for one second-by-one second quadrilateral in Google Earth
Session 3: Experimenting with changes in latitude and longitude in the schoolyard	Handheld GPS units	(Class conducted on school playground in pairs/small groups) - Review of directional orientation, latitude and longitude - Predicting: When we move northeast, what happens to our latitude and longitude? When we move southwest? - Recording latitude and longitude, moving, and then comparing new coordinates to check predictions - (Time permitting) Reviewing observed changes in Google Earth
Session 4: Location-finding with latitude and longitude in a scaffolded geocache (see Hammond, Bodzin, & Stanlick, 2014)	Handheld GPS units Google Earth	(Class conducted on school playground in pairs/small groups) - Given a list of targets, students locate as many as they can during the time allotted - For students who need it, instructor reviews directional orientation, changes in latitude and longitude during movement - (Time permitting) Viewing targets in Google Earth overlay
Session 5: Observing and measuring latitude and longitude with local landmarks	Google Earth	(Class conducted indoors with students using computers one-on-one or in pairs/small groups) - Given a computer loaded with Google Earth, students locate the school and their house, record latitude and longitude of each - Students observe directional orientation of school and home - Students trace a straight line and a path between home and school, observing the differences in length and direction

The research took place sequentially across the three elementary schools and three cohorts of students: at each school, the researcher reviewed the instructional sequence with the cooperating teacher and modified the materials to fit the local context. For example, the cooperating teachers selected local landmarks that students could recognize and use as directional indicators: a nearby convenience store, a park, a major road, etc. Following this consultation, the researcher modified the materials as needed: handouts and Google Earth overlays were edited to show school and local neighborhood, the scaffolded geocache targets were re-assigned, and so forth. The cooperating teacher then reviewed the final versions of the materials. Class sessions were co-taught between the researcher and the classroom teacher, with occasional assistance from a classroom aide or a volunteer.

For all three groups of students, the instruction took place independently of their regularly-scheduled social studies curriculum. For the first two groups, Cohort 1 and Cohort 2, the instruction and assessment took place *before* the students encountered lessons on latitude and longitude in their regular social studies curriculum; for Cohort 3, the instruction took place *after* receiving the standard curricular lesson on latitude and longitude. The researcher observed this lesson, a single 45-minute period discussing the Equator and Prime Meridian and their locations relative to the continents. Following this lesson, the researcher reviewed the lesson with the teacher.

Instrumentation and data collection

Preceding and following the instructional sequence, students took a pretest and posttest. (Available upon request from the author.) The researcher constructed the pre- and posttests to match the targeted constructs of knowledge of latitude and longitude, map skills, and geospatial awareness. Items were modeled on similar concepts from NAEP assessments and refined in consultation with the cooperating teachers. Over the course of the three iterations of the study, the researcher and cooperating teachers introduced further refinements based upon student performance. For example, during the first iteration, many students were unable to locate their homes in Google Earth because they didn't know their home address. The researcher and cooperating teachers subsequently added this item to the assessment to capture this aspect of students' local geospatial awareness. The pretest and posttest contained identical numbers and types of items, but in different versions. For example, on question #1, the pretest map was offset to the north and west; the posttest map was offset to the south and east. On question #8, the pretest asked the direction of travel from home to school; the posttest asked about travel from school to home.

Following these rounds of instruction, the researcher and cooperating teachers conducted three focus groups to learn more about the students' prior and on-going experience of geospatial tools, latitude and longitude, map skills, and geospatial awareness and their impressions of the geospatially-enhanced learning sequence. The focus groups followed a semi-structured protocol, and student responses were analyzed line-by-line to identify themes. To ensure accurate and consistent analysis, the researcher and a graduate assistant independently scored the assessments and coded the focus group responses; all discrepancies were reconciled before findings were identified.

Results

Finding #1: Positive but Varied Effect Sizes Across Constructs

Student outcomes across the three iterations are displayed in Table 2 (see below). Effect sizes between pre- and posttest scores were calculated using Cohen's *d*, following the pooled variance method. Cohorts 1 and 2 had pretest scores ranging between approximately 10% and 30%; Cohort 3 (who received instruction on latitude and longitude before completing the geospatial unit) scored considerably higher on the pretest, about 50% across all three constructs. Posttest results ranged between approximately 40% and 70%. Effect sizes displayed tremendous variability, particularly in map skills. While the effect sizes for latitude and longitude were medium (.52, for Cohort 3) or quite large (above 2.0 for Cohorts 1 and 2), and the effect sizes for geospatial awareness were uniformly large (.9 and above), effect sizes for map skills ranged from quite large (1.4 for Cohort 2) to small (.37 for Cohort 1) to non-existent (.06 for Cohort 3).

Table 2
Student Pre- & Posttest Scores and Effect Sizes

		Latitude & longitude		Map skills		Geospatial awareness	
		pre	post	pre	post	pre	post
Cohort 1	μ =	.29	.66	.32	.44	.31	.69
n = 19	σ =	.17	.17	.34	.36	.24	.20

	$d =$		2.16		.37		1.69
Cohort 2 n = 17	$\mu =$ $\sigma =$	.11 .11	.47 .21	.28 .20	.50 .25	.33 .13	.61 .17
	$d =$		2.33		1.40		2.38
Cohort 3 n = 17	$\mu =$ $\sigma =$	.48 .14	.57 .19	.57 .20	.58 .28	.52 .17	.69 .16
	$d =$		.52		.06		.96

Looking at individual items explained some of the variation. For example, as noted above, the researcher and cooperating teachers added an item requesting students' home address based upon Cohort 1's performance during session #5 (looking at local landmarks in Google Earth – see Table 1, above). The next group, however, appeared to be much stronger on this concept: Cohort 2 pretested on item #7 at 69% and posttested at 88%. Cohort 3 was even stronger, pretesting at mastery level (above 90%) and posttesting at the same. Given the limited number of items in each scale, such disparate performance on pre- and posttests can drastically change the effect size, all other things remaining equal.

Finding #2: Traditional Instruction Can Be Effective

To explore the impact of prior, traditional instruction, we more closely examined the differences between Cohort 3 and Cohorts 1 and 2. As noted above, Cohort 3 had received a previous lesson on latitude and longitude. The researcher observed this lesson and interviewed the teacher to review the lesson and clarify whether the observed lesson was representative of this teacher's standard practice. During the lesson, students observed and interacted with the teacher in placing labels for each continent on a map of the world. As continents were identified, the students copied the labels on wipe-off maps. Next, students cleared their maps as the teacher transitioned to an interactive whiteboard displaying a world map with the latitude-longitude grid displayed. The teacher highlighted the Equator and the Prime Meridian and explained the lines of latitude and meridians of longitude. The teacher then led a discussion of hemispheres (Northern vs. Southern, Eastern vs. Western) as delimited by the Equator and Prime Meridian. The entire lesson took 45 minutes to complete. Students took no permanent notes, and no handouts were used other than the wipe-off maps.

To identify the possible impact of this lesson, the researcher singled out the assessment items that most closely aligned with the teacher's instruction. The researcher compared items #1, #5, and #10a (see Appendix A), which asked students to located and identify the Equator and Prime Meridian, explain latitude and longitude, and draw a compass rose. Cohort 3 displayed significantly different pre- and posttest scores. (See Table 3, below.) For all four items, students in Cohorts 1 and 2 displayed the to-be-expected pattern of some knowledge of the Equator, next to no understanding of the Prime Meridian, no understanding of latitude and longitude, and some knowledge of the compass rose. In contrast, students in Cohort 3 pretested with mastery of the Equator (92%), some understanding of the Prime Meridian (56%), some knowledge of latitude and longitude (15 of 17 students attempted an answer, many of them demonstrating at least partial understanding (e.g., Student C-1, in Table 3, below), and strong understanding of the compass rose (83%).

This pattern suggests that even the single, stand-alone traditional lesson can be effective in developing students' knowledge of latitude and longitude and map skills (i.e., the use of the compass rose). However, no clear pattern emerged regarding Cohort 3's geospatial awareness as compared to the previous groups of students. For example, students in Cohort 3 pretested with very little knowledge of a nearby river that bisects the city— approximately one quarter of the students (27%) could not identify its relative direction, despite the fact that it lies only four blocks to the south of their school. Accordingly, students in Cohort 3 experienced their largest effect size in the geospatial awareness scale, as compared to the latitude and longitude and map skills scales.

Table 3

Selected Latitude and Longitude and Map Skills Items Across Cohorts

	Item 1a: Draw and label the Equator	Item 1b: Draw and label the Prime Meridian	Item 5: What are latitude and longitude?	(Item 5: Sample written responses by selected students)	Item 10a: Draw a compass rose
Cohort 1	pre .42 post .95	pre .11 post .82	pre .00 post .21	Student A-14 pre: (no response) post: "Latitude is the mesher ring of north and south. Longitude is the meshering of East and West"	pre .37 post .82
Cohort 2	pre .53 post .79	pre .00 post .59	pre .00 post .29	Student B-17 pre: "Short and long" post: "Latitude is for the equator and longitude is for the prime meridian."	pre .25 post .77
Cohort 3	pre .92 post .59	pre .56 post .47	pre .26 post .32	Student C-1 pre: "Latitude is a line that goes east and west. Longitude is a line that goes north and south" post: "Latitude is a line that goes west and east and longitude goes north and south"	pre .83 post .76

Finding #3: Ubiquity of Traditional Instructional Methods, With Emerging Non-Curricular Influences

    As mentioned, the researcher and cooperating teachers conducted focus groups following the rounds of instruction (see Appendix B). During these discussions, students characterized the geospatially-enhanced learning activities as "fun" but also "hard". They enjoyed the lessons (particularly going outside!) and liked the opportunity to engage in hands-on use of technology. When asked about previous exposure to latitude and longitude, map skills, and geospatial awareness, students described highly traditional in-class experiences of geography education. For example, the most common instructional methods they identified for learning about latitude and longitude were globes and books. Some students recalled learning about the Equator during the previous year (2nd grade) or in a science class when studying climate; most indicated no prior instruction about the Prime Meridian (with the exception of Cohort 3). However, many students also indicated a wide range of non-curricular sources of information. For example, when asking follow-up questions about the books, some students said that they first learned about latitude and longitude and maps not in a textbook but "on my own" – for example, in the popular press book *There's a Map on My Lap!* (Rabe, 2002). One student ascribed learning about longitude and latitude and maps to watching the Travel Channel's *Mysteries at the Museum* series (http://www.travelchannel.com/tv-shows/mysteries-at-the-museum); another described learning about local landmarks by browsing them in Google Earth while at home. One student had even previously gone on a geocache: his father used a handheld GPS unit as part of his work and regularly brought it home to use for recreational purposes. At one school, students described a teacher using Google Earth during instruction, but only in a whole-class mode and without any student hands-on use.

Discussion & Implications

The findings above showed large but variable effect sizes for third grade students' learning about latitude and longitude, map skills, and geospatial awareness while using a range of geospatial technologies. Part of this variability may be due to the evolving nature of the instruction and the assessment—as items were added to the assessment, for example, it became more robust. A larger part of the variability appears to be due to prior instruction: those students who had received an earlier, traditional lesson on latitude and longitude displayed markedly higher pretest scores on the items most closely related to this instruction. Another part of the variability may be due to the wide range of non-curricular, informal geography education experiences that students reported, from independent reading to watching educational (or edutainment) television shows to personal use of computers and mobile devices.

Given the limitations of the study, all findings should be held tenuously. Data were collected in only one school district, across three elementary schools. Because the research employed intact student groups, the outcomes are vulnerable to selection bias—Cohort 3 may have out-performed the first two groups not only because of previous instruction but also due to tracking or even random chance. Because the research took place sequentially and not simultaneously (i.e., Cohort 1 completed their instruction before Cohort 2 began theirs), student responses may be displaying maturation and not just the impact of prior instruction or extra-curricular activity. Furthermore, as design-based research, this line of inquiry is in the formative stage and bears further replication and verification before being applied broadly to other contexts (Collins, Joseph, & Bielacyzc, 2004).

As indicated by the above findings, student learning about latitude and longitude, map skills, and geospatial awareness is a complex, many-layered process. Elementary students are piecing together a wide set of data about the world and their neighborhood with little or no consistent curricular attention to these constructs. The spatial memory and reasoning required are complex (Loftus, 1978) and can be tenuous—students who confidently drew a compass rose and filled in directional indicators on the pretest could be seen hesitating and second-guessing on the posttest. One student erased a correct compass rose, re-drew an incorrect one (reversing east and west) and proceeded to fill in incorrect answers about the directions to local landmarks. On a different day or given more self-confidence, she may not have had this difficulty. Even during instruction, students tended to reverse "latitude" and "longitude" as they tried to articulate their thinking. Furthermore, spatial reasoning is highly embedded within language and culture (Newcombe & Huttenlocher, 2003); a different treatment or selection of different terms may help struggling students more easily master the interlocking concepts of latitude, longitude, and directional awareness.

While not part of the study design, it is worth noting that none of the cooperating teachers began the project with more than a cursory familiarity with the geospatial tools used. Some had used Flickr recreationally, but never the map feature and never as part of instruction. Some had used Google Earth in instruction, but only for browsing and never for displaying markup (i.e., the overlays displaying the one second-by-one second quadrilateral of latitude and longitude and the scaffolded geocache locations). All cooperating teachers had GPS-based navigation devices in their cars but had never considered using this technology to teach. While each teacher became more comfortable with these tools during the project, only one teacher (who taught instructional technology in addition to social studies) felt comfortable enough to act as lead teacher during the final lessons.

These patterns of initial unfamiliarity and slow-to-develop self-confidence suggest that teachers' learning curve with geospatial tools may be slow, or at least slower than with other, more common technologies. The interface of Google Earth (let alone more complex software such as GIS) is somewhat counter-intuitive and has no close parallels in more familiar productivity software (e.g., MS Word, PowerPoint, Excel, or even Adobe PhotoShop). GPS units also have an unfamiliar interface and may require switching among different coordinate systems (degrees-minutes-seconds vs. degrees-decimal minutes, for example). Teacher educators interested in geospatial technology integration should consider introducing geospatial tools during pre-service instructional technology and/or social studies education classes; professional development instructors can feature these tools during workshops or seminars. The teacher-learners, however, should not be expected to master these technologies quickly but may instead require repeated exposure and even coaching opportunities before they are able to independently design and implement instruction using geospatial tools.

Conclusion

This study showed the promise of integrating geospatial tools into elementary geography education, particularly for addressing the foundational concepts of latitude and longitude, map skills, and geospatial awareness. Interested educators should apply the design with caution, however, given the demands on time, resources, and teacher skill level. The trade-offs with traditional instruction—which can be effective for certain aspects of these topics—must be weighed. Interested researchers are encouraged to adapt and continue improve the designs presented here and participate in future research on implementation and teacher training regarding geospatial technology integration.

References

Boehm, R., & Bednarz, S. (1994). *Geography for Life*. Washington, DC: National Geographic.

Broda, H.W., & Baxter, R.E. (2003). Using GIS and GPS technology as an instructional tool. *The Social Studies, 94*(4), 158-160.

Collins, A., Joseph, D., & Bielaczyc, K. (2004). Design research: Theoretical and methodological issues. *Journal of the Learning Sciences, 13*, 15-42.

Design-Based Research Collective. (2003). Design-based research: An emerging paradigm for educational inquiry. *Educational Researcher, 32*(1), 5-8.

Loftus, G.R. (1978). Comprehending compass directions. *Memory and Cognition, 6*, 416-422.

Hammond. T., & Bodzin, A. (2009). Teaching with rather than about Geographic Information Systems. *Social Education, 73*, 119-123.

Hammond, T.C., Bodzin, A.M., & Stanlick, S.E. (2014). Redefining the longitude/latitude experience with a scaffolded geocache. *Social Studies, 105*, 237-244.

National Geographic. (n.d.) *Introduction to Latitude and Longitude*. Retrieved from http://education.nationalgeographic.com/education/activity/introduction-latitude-longitude/?ar_a=1

National Research Council (2006). *Learning to think spatially: GIS as a support system in K-12 education*. Washington, DC: National Academy Press.

Newcombe, N.S., & Huttenlocher, J. (2003). *Making space: The development of spatial representation and reasoning*. Cambridge, MA: MIT Press.

O'Neill, D. (2013, September 3). Maps-app-android released on Github. *ArcGIS Resources*. Retrieved from http://blogs.esri.com/esri/arcgis/2013/09/03/maps-app-android-released-on-github/

Rabe, T. (2002). *There's a map on my lap! All about maps*. New York: Random House.

Sobel, D. (1995). *Longitude*. New York: Walker.

A Structural Equation Model for Understanding Intensive Facebook Uses of Preservice Teachers

Ismail Celik
icelik@konya.edu.tr
Necmettin Erbakan University
Turkey

Ismail Sahin
isahin@konya.edu.tr
Necmettin Erbakan University
Turkey

Mustafa Aydin
maydinselcuk@gmail.com
Necmettin Erbakan University
Turkey

Ahmet Oguz Akturk
aoakturk@konya.edu.tr
Necmettin Erbakan University
Turkey

S. Ahmet Kiray
ahmetkiray@gmail.com
Necmettin Erbakan University
Turkey

Abstract: Along with the increasing popularity of social networks, spending time on these networking sites has become a part of daily activities. In the present study, intensive use of Facebook (FB) and the variables that directly and indirectly affect FB usage are approached as a whole. A concrete model presenting these relationships is introduced. The model proposed in the current study shows approximately 50% of the variance in intensive use of FB is predicted by other variables. This result shows when the information about the frequency of FB use, the time spent on FB, the number of FB friends, and the general use of FB is obtained, the intensive use of FB by individuals can be understood to a large extent. In summary, this model shows that individuals who have more friends on FB use it more frequently and longer. This situation causes them to use it more for general purposes and increases their intensive uses of FB.

Introduction

Facebook (FB) was originally created by Mark Zuckerberg in early 2004 solely for Harvard University students. Now, with one billion users (BusinessWeek, 2012), FB is the most visited social media site in the world (Bicen & Cavus, 2010; Cain, 2008; Mazman & Usluel, 2010; Ross, Orr, Sisic, Arseneault, Simmering, & Orr, 2009). Since FB is essentially an online social networking site, individuals using FB can share photographs, personal information, and join groups of friends with one another (Buckman, 2005). People can search for others on FB and view the user's picture, if available, but by default can only see profiles and photo albums of other users in their own network (Cain, 2008).

In their study entitled "Why do people use Facebook?," Nadkarni and Hofmann (2012) state that FB use is motivated by two primary needs: (1) the need to belong and (2) the need for self-presentation. Hence, the most common purpose for using FB is for social purposes. There are various studies conducted on this aspect of FB use (Clare, Julia, Jane, & Tristram, 2009; Ellison et al., 2007; Valenzuela, 2009). In a study by Mazman (2009), it was determined people generally use FB to establish social relationships, to follow developments related to their area of study or work, and to become informed about daily activities. To clarify, individuals find and contact old friends and acquaintances, and at the same time make new friends through the opportunities FB provides online. Friendships established on FB are generally formed among people from work, school, family, and close associates. Individuals, who are informed about the new events through friends in these circles, at the same time, find the opportunity to follow their fields of study or work related to their jobs (areas of interest).

Along with the increasing popularity of social networks, spending time on these networking sites has become a part of daily activities. Both creating the content that users share on their walls and following the content on friends' walls lead individuals to spend more time on FB and similar social networking sites. Time spent on FB is seen as the predictor of various variables such as student engagement (Heiberger & Harper, 2008). An increase is observed in the time spent on FB with an increase in the opportunities social networks offer. In related studies, it was found the daily average time spent on FB was 10 to 30 min (Ellison, Steinfield, & Lampe 2007), 30 to 60 min (Walther, Van Der Heide, Kim, Westerman, & Tong, 2008), 30 min (Orr, Sisic, Ross, Simmering, Arseneault, & Orr, 2009), 38.93 min (Muise, Christofides, & Desmarais, 2009), 121.2 min (O'Brien, 2011), and 101.09 min (Junco, 2012). Overall, the longer FB has existed, the more minutes on average people have used FB.

Similarly, another term associated with the density of FB use by individuals is frequency of FB use. Frequency of FB use is the number of times users check updates on FB and is also related to time spent on FB. People frequently check FB to follow comments and responses to the contents they share, and to view and respond to newly shared content. When the studies conducted on FB are reviewed, the number of FB friends is identified as a significant variable in these studies. Angwin (2009) points out today, the word *friend* has started to lose the meaning it had before and is described as *people you add on your social network*. Therefore, it is now possible that people maintain contact with their friends easily through social networking sites. The term *friend* on FB is seen as a label that individuals use to describe both persons with which they are acquainted and also the potential size of their friend networks (Tong, Van Der Heide, Langwell, & Walther, 2008).

Average use of the Internet increases expeditiously. Social networks, particularly FB, are seen as the most important factor in intensive use of the Internet. This has led to the emergence of a new term related to FB use— "intensity of FB use." As a behavioral term, FB intensity is defined as the extent to which individuals are invested psychologically in FB (Vitak, Ellison, & Steinfeld, 2011) and the extent to which FB is integrated into their daily activities (Ellison et al., 2007). Because of its importance, intensity of FB use is included as a research variable in different studies (Ellison et al., 2007; Kirschner & Karpinski, 2010; Smock, Ellison, Lampe, & Wohn, 2011; Valenzuela et al., 2009). In the literature, intensity of FB use is determined as a significant predictor of bridging social capital, even after controlling for a range of demographic, general Internet use, and psychological well-being measures (Steinfeld et al., 2008). Also, it is found that FB intensity is a significant predictor of students' tendencies to use FB for collaborations (Ellison et al., 2007). In fact, FB use may vary, depending on the individual's purpose for usage. Hence, multiple types of uses may lead to high FB intensity. For instance, seeing FB as essential for social processes or seeing it as key for collaborations may both lead to reports of high FB intensity (Lampe, Wohn, Vitak, Ellison, & Wash, 2011).

Purpose of the Study

In this case, the dependence of individuals on these social environments, which act as a second (virtual) world they live in, has started to gradually increase. In the literature, the negative effects of intensive use of FB on academic achievement, goal striving and steadiness are indicated (Alexander, 2012). In addition, it is stated that the intensity of the FB use and engagement in risky FB behaviors are related to FB victimization and FB bullying (Kwan & Skoric, 2013). Similarly, it is found that FB intensity has a positive impact on college students' loneliness (Lou, Yan, Nickerson, & McMorris, 2012). Schwartz (2010) reports that the intensive use of FB by university students is correlated with their narcissism behaviors and lowers their self-esteems. As seen from the related studies, the intensive use of FB affects people in many ways. Thus, it is crucial to learn the factors that influence the intensive use of FB. Then, it will be easier to identify individuals using FB intensively and to reduce the negative consequences caused by the intensive use of FB. For this reason, there is a need to clarify the intensive use of FB, the most commonly used social networking site, and the term *FB intensity*. A review of the related literature shows studies conducted in recent years focused on the effects of this term on the individual and endeavored to present results. However, intensive use of FB and the factors that directly and indirectly affect this use have not been comprehensively studied. In the present study, variables that affect intensive use of FB and the relationships among these variables are concretely presented through a model.

Methods

In the current study, the data are collected from undergraduate students at an Anatolian university in Turkey. The participants consist of 1,066 undergraduates. Of these participants, 65% are female ($n = 691$) and 35% male ($n = 375$). The average age for the participants is about 20 years.

Measurement of Variables

Intensive use of FB is measured by the FB intensity scale (Ellison et al., 2007). This measure includes a series of attitudinal questions designed to tap the extent to which the individuals are emotionally connected to FB and the extent to which FB is integrated into their daily activities. For instance, the survey includes the following items: "I would be sad if Facebook shut down" and "Facebook is part of my everyday activity." This 5-point Likert-type scale consists of 6 items with response choices ranging from "*strongly disagree*" to "*strongly agree.*" This one-dimensional scale has a high level of reliability (Cronbach's Alpha = 0.83). Higher scores for this scale indicate more intensive use of FB.

General FB use is measured by a scale originally developed by Mazman (2009). The general FB use questionnaire includes 11 items with response choices ranging from "*none*" to "*always*" on a 5-point Likert-type scale. The scale includes the following three subscales: 1) social relations (items 1, 2, 3, 4, 5, 6, and 8), 2) work-related activities (items 7 and 9), and 3) daily activities (items 10 and 11). In this study, the Cronbach's Alpha coefficients of the subscales are 0.68 for social relations purposes, 0.81 for the work-related purposes, and 0.87 for daily activities purposes. Higher scores for all three subscales indicate a higher perceived use of FB for general purposes.

Number of friends is assessed by the question, "How many friends do you have in your FB profile?" The following are the answer choices for this question and the distribution of the participants according to this variable: 25 or less ($n = 112$), 26-100 ($n = 203$), 101-200($n = 369$), 201-400 ($n = 313$), and more than 400 ($n = 69$). Higher scores in this measurement scale indicate a higher number of FB friends.

Frequency of FB usage is measured by the question, "How often do you use Facebook?" Participants are provided four response choices, ranging from a few times a year (1) to daily (4). The distribution of the participants based on this measurement is as follows: a few times a year ($n = 117$), a few times a month ($n = 130$), a few times a week ($n = 380$), and daily ($n = 439$). Higher scores in this variable indicate more frequent use of FB.

Time spent on FB is assessed by the question, "When signing in Facebook, how long do you stay connected?" The following are the choice options of the question and the distribution of the participants according to the choices: about 15 min. ($n = 333$), about half an hour ($n = 303$), 1 hour ($n = 274$), 1-3 hours ($n = 121$), more than 3 hours ($n = 35$). Higher scores in this variable indicate more time spent on FB.

Data Analysis

In the present study, structural equation modeling (SEM) with maximum likelihood estimation procedures are used to explore the relationships that exist among the variables. The SEM analysis is a statistical approach to test a theoretical model to reveal the causal relationships between the observed and latent variables (Shumacker & Lomax, 2004). For each endogenous (dependent) variable, an equation is estimated by exogenous (independent) or other endogenous variables from another equation. Both the direct and indirect effects of independent variables on the dependent variables are estimated. The model is tested by examining the path coefficients—the standardized regression coefficients (betas). Statistical analyses are conducted using SPSS (Statistical Package for Social Sciences) 19.0 and AMOS (Analysis of Moment Structures) 19.0 software.

Findings

A structural equation analysis is conducted to test the relationships among the number of FB friends, the frequency of FB use, the time spent on FB, the general use of FB, and the intensive use of FB. The Model for Intensive Use of FB includes three exogenous variables and two endogenous variables. The chi-square estimate with degrees of freedom is still the most commonly used means by which to make comparisons across models (Hoyle & Panter, 1995). The ratio between chi-square and degrees of freedom should not exceed five for models with a good fit (Bentler, 1989). Hu and Bentler (1999) recommend using a cutoff value close to .95 for TLI and the RMSEA close to .06 or less.to evaluate model fit In Table 1, the perfect and acceptable fit indices for a structural equation model are presented (Hu & Bentler, 1999; Jöreskog & Sörbom, 1984; Tanaka & Huba, 1985).

Table 1. Criterion References for Fit Indices of Structural Equation Model

Criterion References	Perfect Fit Indices	Acceptable Fit Indices	Indices of Model for Intensive Use of FB
(χ^2/df)	≤ 3	$\leq 4\text{-}5$	2.424
RMSEA	≤ 0.05	0.06-0.08	0.037
NFI	≥ 0.95	0.94-0.90	0.994
CFI	≥ 0.97	≥ 0.95	0.996
GFI	≥ 0.90	0.89-0.85	0.995
AGFI	≥ 0.90	0.89-0.85	0.982
TLI	≥ 0.95	0.94-0.90	0.989

As depicted in Table 1, the data fit the model perfectly (χ^2 = 16.966, df = 7, $p < 0,018$; GFI = 0.995; AGFI = 0.982; CFI = 0.996; TLI = 0.989; NFI = 0.994; RMSEA = 0.037). The Model for Intensive Use of FB is shown in Figure 1. In the structural equation model, only significant paths are included.

As seen from Figure 1, the general use of FB has three sub dimensions and these can be listed according to their effect sizes as follows: daily use of FB (β = 0.845, $p < 0.001$), social use of FB (β = 0.820, $p < 0.001$), and work-related use of FB (β = 0.496, $p < 0.001$). When the model's predictors are analyzed, the frequency of FB use appears to be the most important independent variable that affects general use of FB (β = 0.396, $p < 0.001$). The second most important independent variable impacting the general use of FB is the number of FB friends (β = 0.217, $p < 0.001$). Also, time spent on FB is the last independent variable influencing FB use for general purposes (β = 0.119, $p < 0.001$). As seen from the model, there is a positive linear relationship between general use of FB, frequency of FB, number of FB friends, and time spent on FB. All three independent variables explain 36% of the variance in the use of FB for general purposes.

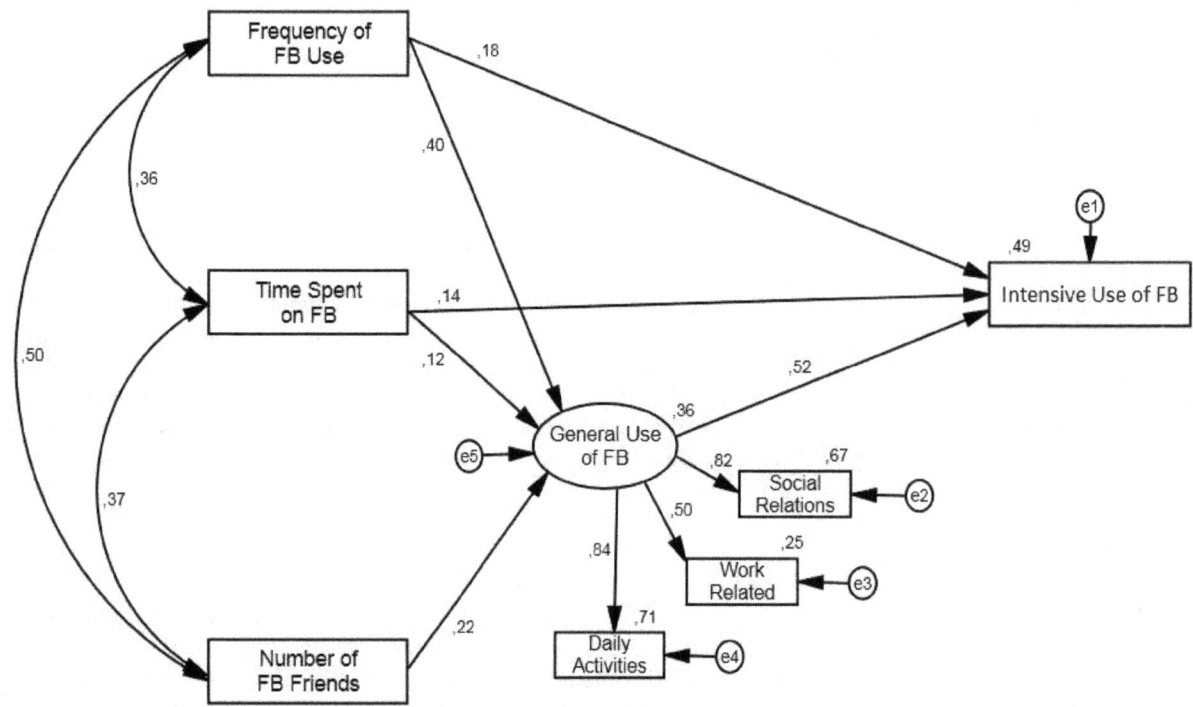

Figure1. Intensive Use of Facebook Model

In Table 2, the total effects are decomposed into direct and indirect effects. When the direct effects are analyzed, general use of FB is determined the most important independent and latent variable influencing intensive use of FB ($\beta = 0.516$, $p < 0.001$). The frequency of FB usage is determined as the second most important variable that affects intensive use of FB ($\beta = 0.178$, $p < 0.001$). The last variable impacting the intensive use of FB is time spent on FB ($\beta = 0.139$, $p < 0.001$).

Table 2. Decomposition of Total Effect for the Model for Intensive Use of FB

Predictor variable	Dependent variable	Total effect [a]	Direct effect	Indirect effect	Standard error	Critical ratio (t)
Time spent on FB	General use of FB	0.119	0.119	0	0.131	3.827**
Frequency of FB use	General use of FB	0.396	0.396	0	0.164	11.493**
Number of FB friends	General use of FB	0.217	0.217	0	0.145	6.496**
Time spent on FB	FB intensity	0.201	0.139	0.062	0.128	5.484**
Frequency of FB use	FB intensity	0.383	0.178	0.205	0.17	5.994**
General use of FB	FB intensity	0.516	0.516	0	0.042	14.760**

[a]: Total effect = Direct effect + Indirect effect, **$p < 0.001$.

As seen from Table 2, the number of FB friends has an indirect effect on intensive use of FB ($\beta=0.112$). When the direct and indirect effects of the independent variables are analyzed, all variables included in the model explain 49% of the variance in intensive use of FB.

Discussion

It is apparent that studies on social networking sites focus on FB, since it is the most commonly used. When studies in the literature on FB are examined, the most significant variables that affect FB use are time spent on FB, number of friends on FB, and frequency of FB use (Acar, 2008; Christofides et al., 2009; Ellison et al., 2007; Joinson, 2008; Lee, Moore, Park, & Park, 2012; Muise et al., 2009; O'Brien, 2011). The examination of the three exogenous variables (frequency of FB use, time spent on FB, and number of FB friends) in the model showed positive and significant relationships among these variables. In the literature, it is found that students spent a substantial amount of time (101.09 min per day) on FB (Junco, 2011). Also, there is a significant correlation found between the number of times FB is checked (a mean of 5.75 times per day) and the time spent on FB. Furthermore, the analysis revealed a highly positive relationship between number of FB friends and frequency of FB use in the model. In their study, Moore and McElroy (2012) also found significant relationships between number of FB friends and frequency of FB use.

Like the Internet, FB use has also become a form of addiction as a result of its prevalent use. For this reason intensive use of FB has been the subject of research studies (Ellison et al., 2007; Kesici & Sahin, 2009; Steinfield et al., 2008; Valenzuela et al., 2009). The aforementioned studies particularly focus on the effects of intensive FB use on the individual. However, it can be concluded that the findings obtained in the present study will facilitate the understanding of intensive use of FB. As seen in the model, the variables of frequency of FB use, time spent on FB, and number of FB friends were found to have a positive relationship among one another, and direct or indirect effects on intensive use of FB. In the present study, the findings show frequency of FB use has both a direct effect on intensive use of FB and an indirect effect through general FB use. In their study, Kayri and Çakir (2010) also found a positive significant relationship between frequency of FB use and intensive use of FB. In the present study, it was seen that intensive FB use showed an increase as frequency of FB use increased.

Similarly, in this study's model, time spent on FB has both a direct effect on intensive use of FB and an indirect effect through general FB use. These findings show that spending longer time on FB is correlated with intensive use of FB. Kayri and Çakir (2010) found a positive significant relationship between time spent on FB and intensive use of FB. Ellison et al. (2007) state the concept of FB intensity is related to amount of time spent on FB and number of FB friends. At the same time, number of FB friends has attracted scholarly attention in SNS research, particularly as an element of a composite measure that assesses intensity of FB use (Ellison et al., 2007; Steinfield et al., 2008; Valenzuela et al., 2009). The model presented in the present study reveals an indirect relationship between number of FB friends and intensive use of FB. Similar to our findings, Lee et al. (2012) also found a positive relationship between intensive use of FB and number of FB friends in their study.

Conclusions

The objective of this study is to explain why university students use FB intensively. In this study, the results show frequency of FB use, time spent on FB, and number of FB friends are significantly and positively correlated. While these three variables affect the general use of FB directly, time spent on FB and frequency of FB use affect intensive use of FB both directly and indirectly. Also, the model proposed in the current study shows approximately 50% of the variance in intensive use of FB is predicted by other variables. This result shows when the information about the frequency of FB use, the time spent on FB, the number of FB friends, and the general use of FB is obtained, the intensive use of FB by individuals can be understood to a large extent. In summary, this model shows that individuals who have more friends on FB use it more frequently and longer. This situation causes them to use it more for general purposes and increases their demanding on FB.

Note

This paper is resulted from the thesis study of the first author.

References

Acar, A. (2008). Antecedents and consequences of online social networking behavior: the case of Facebook. *Journal of Website Promotion, 3*(1/2), 62–83.

Alexander, C. M. (2012). *Facebook usage and academic achievement of high school students: a quantitative analysis*. Ph.D. thesis, Pepperdine University.

Angwin, J. (2009). *How Facebook is making friending obsolete*. Wall Street Journal. Retrieved February 10, 2012 from http://online.wsj.com/article/SB126084637203791583.html?mod=WSJ_hp_mostpop_read

Bentler, M. (1989). *EQS structural equations program manual*. Los Angeles: BMDP Statistical Software.

Bicen, H., & Cavus, N. (2010). The most preferred social network sites by students. *Procedia Social and Behavioral Sciences, 2*(2), 5864-5869.

Buckman, R. (2005). Too much information? Colleges fear student postings on popular Facebook site could pose security risks. *The Wall Street Journal*, p. B1.

Businessweek (2012). *Facebook: The making of 1 billion users*. Retrieved August 30, 2012 from http://www.businessweek.com/articles/2012-10-04/facebook-the-making-of-1-billion-users

Cain, J. (2008). Online social networking issues within academia and pharmacy education. *American Journal of Pharmaceutical Education, 72*(1), 1-7

Christofides, E., Muise, A., & Desmarais, S. (2009). Information disclosure and control on Facebook: Are they two sides of the same coin or two different processes? *CyberPsychology & Behavior, 12*(3), 341–345.

Clare, M., Julia, M., Jane, W., & Tristram, H. (2009). Facebook, social integration and informal learning at university: 'It is more for socialising and talking to friends about work than for actually doing work'. *Learning, Media and Technology, 34*(2), 141-155.

Ellison, N., Steinfield, C., & Lampe, C. (2007). The benefits of Facebook "friends:" Social capital and college students' use of online social network sites. *Journal of Computer-Mediated Communication, 12*, 1143–1168.

Heiberger, G., & Harper, R. (2008). Have you Facebooked Astin lately? Using technology to increase student involvement. *In R. Junco, & D. M. Timm (Eds.), Using emerging technologies to enhance student engagement* (pp. 19–35). San Francisco, CA: Jossey-Bass.

Hoyle, R. H., & Panter, A. T. (1995). Writing about structural equation models. *In R. H. Hoyle (Ed.), Structural equation modeling: Comments, issues, and applications* (pp. 158–176). Thousand Oaks, CA: Sage.Hu, L.-T., & Bentler, P. M. (1999). Cutoff criteria for fit indexes in covariance structure analysis: conventional criteria versus new alternatives. *Structural Equation Modeling, 6*(1), 1-55.

Joinson, A. N. (2008). Looking at, looking up or keeping up with people: motives and use of Facebook. *In Proceedings of the twenty-sixth annual SIGCHI conference on human factors in computing systems* (pp. 1027–1036). New York: ACM Press.

Jöreskog, K., G. & Sörbom, D. (1984*). LISREL- VI user's guide* (3rd ed.). Mooresville, IN: Scientific Software.

Junco, R. (2012). Too much face and not enough books: the relationship between multiple indices of Facebook use and academic performance. *Computers in Human Behavior, 28*(1), 187-198.

Kayri, M. & Çakır, Ö.(2010). An applied study on educational use of Facebook as a web 2.0 tool: The sample lesson of computer networks and communication. *International Journal of Computer Science & Information Technology*, 2(4) 48-58.

Kesici, S., & Sahin I. (2009). A comparative study of uses of the internet among college students with and without internet addiction, Psychological Reports, 105 (3), 1103-1112.

Kirschner, P. A., & Karpinski, A. C. (2010). Facebook and academic performance. *Computers in Human Behavior*, 26(6), 1237–1245.

Kwan, G. C. E., & Skoric, M. M. (2013). Facebook bullying: An extension of battles in school. *Computers in Human Behavior*, 29(1), 16-25.

Lampe, C., Wohn, D. Y., Vitak, J., Ellison, N., & Wash, R. (2011). Student use of Facebook for organizing collaborative classroom activities. *International Journal of Computer-Supported Collaborative Learning, 6*, 329-347.

Lee, J.-E.R., Moore, D.C., Park, E.-A., Park, S.G. (2012). Who wants to be "friend-rich"? Social compensatory friending on Facebook and the moderating role of public self-consciousness. *Computers in Human Behavior*, 28(3), 1036–1043.

Lou, L. L., Yan, Z., Nickerson, A., & McMorris, R. (2012). An examination of the reciprocal relationship of loneliness and Facebook use among first-year college students. *Journal of Educational Computing Research*, 46(1), 105-117.

Mazman, S. G. (2009). *Adoption process of social network and their usage in educational context*. Master thesis, Hacettepe University, Ankara.

Mazman, S. G., & Usluel, Y. K. (2010). Modeling educational usage of Facebook. *Computers & Education*, 55(2), 444-453.

Moore K., & McElroy J. C. (2012). The influence of personality on Facebook usage, wall postings, and regret. *Computers in Human Behavior*, 28(3), 267–274.

Muise, A., Christofides, E., & Desmarais, S. (2009). More information than you ever wanted: Does Facebook bring out the green-eyed monster of jealousy? *Cyber Psychology & Behavior*, 12(4), 441-444.

Nadkarni, A., & Hofmann, S. G. (2012). Why do people use Facebook? *Personality and Individual Differences*, 52(3), 243-249.

O'Brien, S., J. (2011). *Facebook & other internet use & the academic performance of college students*. Doctor Of Philosophy, Temple University.

Orr, E. S., Sisic, M., Ross, C., Simmering, M. G., Arseneault, J. M., & Orr, R. R. (2009). The influence of shyness on the use of Facebook in an undergraduate sample. *CyberPsychology & Behavior*, 12(3), 337–340.

Ross, C., Orr, E. S., Sisic, M., Arseneault, J. M., Simmering, M. G., & Orr, R. R. (2009). Personality and motivations associated with Facebook use. *Computers in Human Behavior*, 25(2), 578–586

Schwartz, M. (2010). The usage of Facebook as it relates to narcissism, self-esteem and loneliness. *ETD Collection for Pace University.* Paper AAI3415681.

Smock, A., Ellison, N., Lampe, C., & Wohn, D. (2011). Facebook as toolkit: A uses and gratification approach to unbundling feature use. *Computers in Human Behavior*, 27, 2322-2329.

Steinfield, C., Ellison, N., & Lampe, C. (2008). Social capital, self-esteem, and use of online social network sites: A longitudinal analysis. *Journal of Applied Developmental Psychology* 29, (6), 434–445.

Tanaka, J. S., & Huba, G. J. (1985). A fit index for covariance structure models under arbitrary GLS estimation. *British Journal of Mathematical and Statistical Psychology*, 38(2), 197–201.

Tong, S. T., Van Der Heide, B., Langwell, L., & Walther, J. B. (2008). Too much of a good thing? The relationship between number of friends and interpersonal impressions on Facebook. *Journal of Computer-Mediated Communication,* 13(3), 531-549.

Valenzuela, S., Park, N., & Kee, K. F. (2009). Is there social capital in a social network site: Facebook use and college students' life satisfaction, trust, and participation. *Journal of Computer-Mediated Communication*, 14, 875–901.

Vitak, J., Ellison, N., & Steinfield, C. (2011). The ties that bond: Re-examining the relationship between Facebook use and bonding social capital. *In Proceedings of the 44th annual hawaii international conference on system sciences*

Walther, J. B., Van Der Heide, B., Kim, S.-Y., Westerman, D., & Tong, S. T. (2008). The role of friends' appearance and behavior on evaluations of individuals on Facebook: Are we known by the company we keep? *Human Communication Research*, 34(1), 28–49.

West, A., Lewis J., & Currie P. (2009). Students' Facebook 'friends': Public and private spheres, *Journal of Youth Studies*, 12(6), 615-627.

Online Mentoring for Secondary Pre-service Teachers in Regional, Rural or Remote Locations

Petrea Redmond
School of Teacher Education and Early Childhood
University of Southern Queensland, Australia
redmond@usq.edu.au

Abstract: This chapter describes a project which investigated qualitative expressions in an online mentoring community involving secondary pre-service teachers and practising teachers. The practising teachers acted as online mentors to the pre-service teachers who were personally, professionally and geographically isolated due to being located in regional, rural or remote areas. The online mentoring enabled rural and remote pre-service teachers to benefit from the ability to engage with practising teachers for both professional and academic purposes. The participants' posts hosted in an invitational online space were coded using a content analysis framework, and outcomes from the online mentoring project are provided.

Introduction

Many teacher education programs are now offered online with pre-service teachers located in many regional, rural and remote areas. Due to a range of circumstances these pre-service teachers are unable to move to locations which offer them less professional isolation. Pre-service teachers located in rural and remote locations do not have the opportunity to interact and engage in a professional learning dialogue with teaching professionals within their disciplines e.g. often there is not a specialist Physics teacher in a small rural high school. An online mentoring project was established to enable rural and remote pre-service teachers to benefit from the ability to engage with practising teachers for both professional and academic purposes. This innovative project provided online mentoring that extended beyond the traditional educational boundaries to enhance support for pre-service educators while developing partnerships with teachers in the field.

Darling-Hammond (2000, 2012) claimed that traditional teacher education programs are not responsive to present-day demands of teaching and are often distant from contemporary practice. She also recommended that the quality of initial teacher preparation and ongoing mentoring could influence teacher competence and reduce attrition from the profession.

The multiple reasons for beginning teachers leaving the profession are well documented (Ashiedu & Scott-Ladd, 2012; Buchanan, 2010; Fetherston & Lummis, 2012; Schuck et al., 2011), however, the crucial reason for leaving the profession is the lack of professional support (Buchanan, 2010; Roberts, 2004; Scheopner, 2010; Schuck et al., 2011). The lack of support is heightened for those located in rural or remote locations where there are fewer experienced teachers in their geographical proximity, and where access to teachers with knowledge in a similar discipline area can be more problematic.

Another significant reason causing beginning teachers to leave the teaching profession is the increased workload and complexity of teachers' work (OECD, 2005). There is additional pressure to gain understanding of an increased volume of knowledge and to be able to apply it in practice (Maher & Macallister, 2013), including the expectation to modify curriculum for diverse learners' needs, and increased technology and pedagogy knowledge and practice. These increased pressures on beginning teachers are exacerbated for those located in rural and remote locations where they are expected to assume additional roles and responsibilities and often teach outside their subject area in their early years in the profession (Roberts & Lean, October, 2005).

Studies show that the key support required by beginning teachers includes mentoring and structured supervision (Buchanan, 2010; Commonwealth of Australia, 2013; Joseph, 2011; Schuck et al., 2011). In their report on attrition of recent graduates, the Queensland College of Teachers (2013) found that providing "adequate support such as structured induction, mentoring from suitable experienced teachers and resources for all graduate teachers, including those employed as casual/relief teachers and on temporary contracts" (p. 47) would have changed their experience and impacted on their decision to leave the profession.

Secondary teachers in rural and remote locations have "decreased contact and networking with teachers in the same subject area from other schools" (Roberts, 2004, p. 10). This project established discipline specific online mentoring for secondary pre-service teachers. The one-to-many discipline specific online mentoring program harnessed the potential of technology to reduce feelings of isolation and to enhance access to information and networking opportunities with experienced teachers. Pre-service teachers were able to access mentors from any location rather than solely within their local area.

Online mentoring

Online mentoring, E-mentoring or virtual mentoring has been described as the "use of e-mail or computer conferencing systems to support a mentoring relationship when a face-to-face relationship would be impractical" (O'Neil, Wagner, & Gomez, 1996, p. 39). It has been suggested by Hunt, Powell, Little and Mike (2013) that "E-mentoring also facilitates a medium of exchange between mentor and mentee that is less threatening and non-confrontational, conducive to building a community of learners" (p. 288).

Technology now makes it possible for mentoring relationships to occur between those within different geographical locations, at a time and place convenient for both parties. It can occur synchronously or asynchronously. Asynchronous mentoring provides the parties with time to create a reflective response, and an opportunity to research prior to responding rather than having an off the cuff response. Asynchronous text mentoring also provides a written and lasting record of the conversations, which can be reviewed over time.

Other advantages online mentoring has over face-to-face mentoring include (Eby, 1997; Ensher, Heun, & Blanchard, 2003; Gutke & Albion, 2008; Mueller, 2004):

- Logistical convenience due to no travel being required and no necessity to be in the same location;
- Flexibility of access as it occurs at time convenient to participants and can occur on a device such as the Smart Phone already in their pocket/handbag;
- Status difference not being obvious in e-mentoring;
- Some degree of anonymity and a less threatening environment, which can encourage mentees to ask questions they are less likely to ask in person;
- Reduced costs with no travel or time away from job;
- Scalability: infrastructure is in place irrespective of number of participants; and
- Group online mentoring has the capacity to contribute to the development of a community of learners.

Some deterrents to online mentoring include those items that are constraints in traditional face-to-face mentoring (Ensher et al., 2003; Mueller, 2004):

- Availability of suitable mentors;
- Ongoing commitment from all parties;
- Ongoing access to ICT resources: may need to re-establish relationships after a long break;
- Potential for miscommunication due to the lack of non-verbal cues; and
- The need for mentoring programs to be managed, planned and implemented, including training and ongoing contact with participants.

Many pre-service teachers study online and don't have access to a teacher with discipline expertise in their local area. The online mentoring project was established to provide all pre-service teachers access to a discipline expert, irrespective of their location. Stanulis and Floden's (2009) study of beginning teachers within the United States, found that mentoring advantages "included an opportunity to share ideas, resources, and advice; an opportunity to hear from other new teachers who were going through similar struggles; and the increased openness to try new things in their practice" (p. 119).

The mentoring in this project, included peer mentoring and group mentoring with an experienced teacher. Lateral or peer mentoring provides job related skill development rather than career related development, and can elicit emotional support, friendship, and feedback through a reciprocal relationship (Eby, 1997). The one-to-many mentoring within the group arrangement provided pre-service teachers an opportunity to hear from other pre-service teachers as well as an opportunity to access the support of an established teacher, all of whom worked in the same discipline area. Dansky (1996) suggested that an important element of group mentoring is the dynamics of the group and the collective behaviours that are not present in a one-to-one relationship. The social dynamics include "polarization, conformity, communication flows, and social networks" (p. 7), which again, are less obvious in one-to-one mentoring relationships.

Computer Conferencing and Content Analysis Conceptual Framework

Online discussions are not constrained by space, location or time. The online environment enables multiple contributions by all learners, unlike face to face environments where it would be "physically impossible for all learners to have their say" (Henri, 1992, p. 118). This adds to the richness and diversity of perspectives within the dialogue.

To understand both the social and cognitive learning processes in online discussions, Henri (1992) developed a Computer Conferencing and Content Analysis framework. This framework has five dimensions:
1. Participative: the number of statements made by participants;
2. Social: statements not related to the formal content;
3. Interactive: statements referring implicitly or explicitly to other statements or participants;
4. Cognitive: statements which demonstrate knowledge and skills related to content and learning processes; and
5. Metacognitive: statements which identify personal characteristics, knowledge and skills which hinder or enhance personal learning processes and task completion.

The cognitive dimension explores the ways people are engaging and learning within the dialogue. It includes clarification questions, making inferences or judgments, and proposing strategies or actions. Henri (1992) suggested that there are two levels of cognition: surface and in-depth. With surface processing including posts that: repeat information without offering interpretation or new ideas; concur with others without adding personal comments; and propose solutions without explanation or offering multiple solutions without judgment of their suitability. In-depth processes are more complex. They include posts that: link ideas, facts etc. to support interpretation and judgment; offer and elaborate on new information; propose solutions with justification; compare and contrast ideas or solutions; provide evidence to support claims; and look at the problem from a big picture perspective.

This framework assists educators to understand the pedagogical and learning outcomes of online discussions. In an effort to explore the depth of discussion within the mentoring relationships in this project, the online discussions have been analysed using Henri's (1992) Computer Conferencing and Content Analysis framework.

Context and Method

Teacher mentors in different disciplines were identified through the researcher's professional networks and the professional experience office. Teachers were invited to volunteer to take on the role of mentor in their discipline area (e.g. Mathematics, English, Science, Business, and Computing). The mentors were identified as effective practitioners and curriculum experts by their peers or academics and came from a range of disciplines. The mentors would either be located in rural or remote schools or have had past experience teaching in such locations. The role of the mentor would be to assist beginning teachers in the ongoing development of their discipline specific pedagogical content knowledge, to answer questions, to share their experiences of issues related to being located in rural or remote locations, and to support the mentees as beginning professionals. The teacher mentors received a small payment for their time from a grant and worked online for approximately one hour per week across two semesters.

The pre-service teacher mentees were volunteers from the Bachelor of Education (BEDU) Secondary specialisation across all year levels and the Graduate Diploma of Learning and Teaching (GDTL) Secondary specialisation, who were completing their professional experience in rural or remote areas.

Data came from archived online discussions within a Wikispace area set up for the project. The asynchronous discussions were analysed to explore the contributions from the mentors and the mentees. After the completion of the year and finalisation of results, the online discussion posts were downloaded and de-identified prior to data analysis. The data were analysed using Henri's (1992) Computer Conferencing and Content Analysis Conceptual Framework, described above. The archived postings in the community online discussion area were coded to identify the dimensions from the framework.

A second data source was interviews with participants. Three student mentees and five teacher mentors were interviewed. The research questions explored in this project were:
- How do pre-service teachers and teachers respond to online mentoring?
- What types of cognitive presence do pre-service teachers show within online mentoring?

Results and Discussion

During this project, mentees and mentors across 10 different curriculum areas generated 578 posts and 12832 views over an eight-month period. There were 10 mentors and 50 mentees, which suggests an average of 9.6 posts and over 213 views of the posts for each participant. The high number of views indicates that the pre-service teachers were very interested in the types of discussions that were occurring, however were hesitant to post their own perspectives. Figure 1 presents the breakdown of the posts over the different dimensions of Henri's (1992) framework.

The most common topics of conversation included homework expectations, student engagement and content relevance, literacy across the curriculum, classroom management, professional experience expectations, and pedagogical approaches, all of which came from the lens of a specific discipline. The topics under discussion were driven by the mentees.

Less than 1% of the posts were social in nature. Given the geographical spread of the mentees, and that the lack of prior relationships between mentees and mentors, this result was surprising. Perhaps the percentage was low because the facilitator did not establish a specific forum or protocol for this purpose. Having said that, there were elements of social activity within many of the posts coded at higher levels.

Interactive posts were those that responded to, or made commentary on other posts without having a significant cognitive element. 15% of the posts were coded as interactive rather than monologic (Gunawardena, Lowe, & Anderson, 1997) where there is no ongoing post/response cycle. This result is similar to the results of Pawan, Paulus, Yalcin and Chang (2003) who also reported low levels of interactive posts. In contrast, McKenzie and Murphy (2000) had 74% of posts coded at the interactive dimension.

Cognitive posts have been further broken down into surface and in-depth, which are seen as different skills connected to the learning process, and which impact on understanding, reasoning, and critical thinking. The posts coded as surface processing are low-level posts, as opposed to in-depth posts, which required the learner to evaluate information, to organise it and to compare it to previous understandings. The majority of the posts (64%) were evaluated as being cognitive surface posts, which shared ideas, experiences or opinions without offering alternatives, justifications or explanations. The second most common type of posts (19%) were cognitive in-depth posts, which were more complex. Again this contrasts with McKenzie and Murphy (2000) who had 22% at the surface level and in-depth processing was three times that.

When completing the data analysis the researcher, an educator within the secondary program, noted that the contributions were at a much higher level than would normally be present within general discussion forums related to a specific course. This raises the question of whether the higher cognitive levels of interaction displayed in the space were due to the perception that participating mentors might be a more authentic audience.

Metacognitive posts made up only 2% of the total. These posts included elements that identified metacognitive knowledge of the self, task or strategies, *or* metacognitive skills of evaluation, planning, regulation and self-awareness. Gunawardena, Lowe, and Anderson's (1997) also found low levels of metacognition, however McKenzie and Murphy (2000) found that 16% of the posts in their study were coded as metacognitive, perhaps because they used prompts within the online weekly activities.

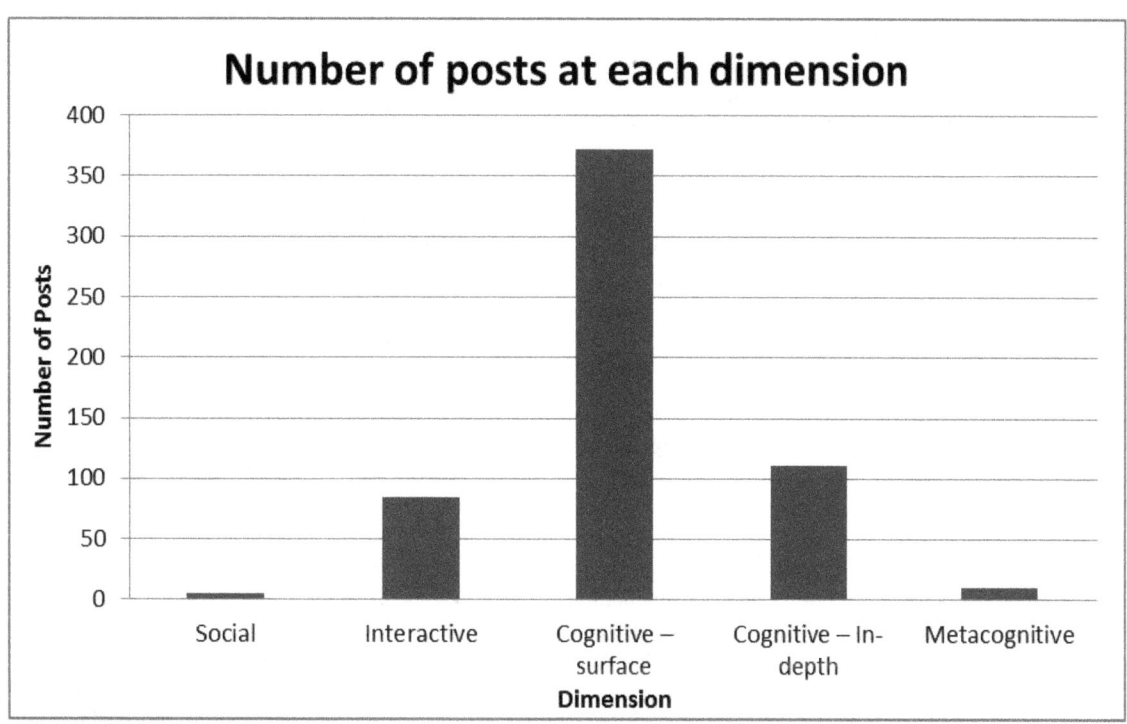

Figure 1: Analysis's of discussion posts a using Henri's (1992) content analysis framework

From the interview data it was clear that both the mentors and the mentees positively responded to the online mentoring. Mentor A commented *I certainly did enjoy it*; supported by Pre-Service Teacher X who stated *I thought it was a good idea*. Mentor E suggested *it was an interesting approach* however was frustrated with the number of "*lurkers*" and questioned how we might *get them to participate rather than observe*. The positive comments from participants support Hew and Knapczyk's (2007) study who found that both the mentors and the mentees benefited from the mentoring relationship.

The pre-service teachers enjoyed the access to others, both peers and experts, who had the same discipline focus but were located beyond their geographical area. Student X revealed *I have been learning to appreciate the extent of experience gained from others outside my geographical area*. Mentor A found that the project was a *good way of communicating with students that you do not normally have contact with*.

The online space provided the flexibility of participation at any time, in any place. Mentor E appreciated the *flexibility of time*, while Mentor B suggested it *wasn't hard to participate but it was time consuming and required an ongoing commitment*. The pre-service teachers also commented on time, Student Y suggesting that *being too busy with assessment and other uni related tasks made me less inclined to spend what little spare time I had pursuing more computer work*.

Some pre-service teachers and mentors engaged in the process more than others. Pre-service teacher Z suggested that *I was a bit more proactive than the mentor, I think*. In contrast, Mentor C suggested that it should *be made compulsory to require an entry every week*. Having an assessment obligation would have increased the number of posts in the mentoring space. Mentor D commented that it was *good to be able to give advice and then have students try out suggestions on prac or reflect that they had seen other do similar things. Basically it was the benefit of reflection and discussion*. Mentor A was *a bit disappointed in terms of the amount of student response*, adding, *I expected more questions*.

The participants agreed that the depth of discussion varied and depended on the topic. Mentor D commented that *I would comment and then other students would also comment on the posts of fellow students, so the conversation became quite focused and specific*. Whiting and de Janaz (2004) also observed the importance of asking effective questions, which should be personally meaningful and open-ended to gain the most comprehensive responses.

Outcomes

A number of outcomes can be identified as a result of this study which explored online mentoring of secondary pre-service teachers. Firstly, online mentoring can occur in an open online space with one-to-many participants. Secondly, secondary pre-service teachers benefit from have access to discipline expertise throughout their program and not just during their professional experience. Thirdly, like online teaching, online mentoring benefits from focus questions or stimulus that requires the pre-service teachers to respond at high cognitive and metacognitive levels.

The results of this study exploring online mentoring are limited to secondary teacher education in one regional university in Australia and this provided limited opportunity for generalisations. Future study in this area could include consideration as to the personal and professional learning of both the mentors and the mentees, and exploration of the differences between mentoring conversations in closed spaces and open spaces.

Conclusion

In an effort to further support the ongoing learning and reduce attrition of rural and remote pre-service teachers, an online mentoring project was established. The goal was to reduce the professional isolation and to enhance the discipline pedagogical content knowledge of the pre-service teachers by providing one-to-to mentors in a range of discipline areas.

In answering the first research question, *How do pre-service teachers and teachers respond to online mentoring?*, pre-service teachers and practicing teachers responded positively to the opportunity to be involved in this online mentoring project. The mentoring questions and concerns were driven by the pre-service teachers rather than by a course, an academic, or the mentors. When exploring the second research question, *What types of cognitive presence do pre-service teachers show within online mentoring?*, it was clear that the majority of the posts by the participants within the online mentoring project were classified as cognitive at the surface level. Perhaps higher levels of participation and depth of conversation would have occurred if stimulus or starter questions seeded the discussions initially rather than having the conversation driven solely by the pre-service teachers' interests and issues.

Mentoring can be used to build pre-service teachers' capacity and to develop competence while they discuss debate, give examples and theorize about their concerns as novice teachers with their peers and experienced teachers. Secondary pre-service teachers in rural and remote areas often have limited opportunity for this interaction at a local level, and online mentoring can provide access to experienced educators, which can leverage effective growth and development for novice educators.

Acknowledgment

This research was supported by a University of Southern Queensland Early Career Researcher grant.

References

Ashiedu, J., & Scott-Ladd, B. (2012). Understanding Teacher Attraction and Retention Drivers: Addressing Teacher Shortages. *Australian Journal of Teacher Education, 37*(11). doi: 10.14221/ajte.2012v37n11.1

Buchanan, J. (2010). May I be excused? Why teachers leave the profession. *Asia Pacific Journal of Education, 30*(2), 199-211. doi: 10.1080/02188791003721952

Commonwealth of Australia. (2013). Teaching and Learning – maximising our investment in Australian schools. In Senate Standing Committee on Education Employment and Workplace Relations (Ed.). Canberra, Australia: Senate Printing Unit.

Dansky, K. H. (1996). The effect of group mentoring on career outcomes. *Group & Organization Management, 21*(1), 5-21. doi: 10.1177/1059601196211002

Darling-Hammond, L. (2000). How teacher education matters. *Journal of Teacher Education, 51*(3), 166-173. doi: 10.1177/0022487100051003002

Darling-Hammond, L. (2012). The right start: Creating a strong foundation for the teaching career. *Phi Delta Kappan, 94*(3), 8-13.

Eby, L. T. (1997). Alternative forms of mentoring in changing organizational environments: A conceptual extension of the mentoring literature. *Journal of Vocational Behavior, 51*(1), 125-144.

Ensher, E. A., Heun, C., & Blanchard, A. (2003). Online mentoring and computer-mediated communication: New directions in research. *Journal of Vocational Behavior, 63*(2), 264-288. doi: 10.1016/S0001-8791(03)00044-7

Fetherston, T., & Lummis, G. (2012). Why Western Australian Secondary Teachers Resign. *Australian Journal of Teacher Education, 37*(4). doi: 10.14221/ajte.2012v37n4.1

Gunawardena, C. N., Lowe, C. A., & Anderson, T. (1997). Analysis of a global online debate and the development of an interaction analysis model for examining social construction of knowledge in computer conferencing. *Journal of Educational Computing Research, 17*(4), 397-431.

Gutke, H., & Albion, P. (2008). Exploring the worth of online communities and e-mentoring programs for beginning teachers. In K. McFerrin, R. Weber, R. Carlsen & D. A. Willis (Eds.), *Society for Information Technology & Teacher Education International Conference* (Vol. 2008, pp. 1416-1423). Chesapeake, VA: AACE.

Henri, F. (1992). Computer conferencing and content analysis. In A. R. Kaye (Ed.), *Collaborative Learning Through Computer Conferencing: The Najaden Papers* (pp. 117-136). Berlin: SpringerVerlag.

Hew, K. F., & Knapczyk, D. (2007). Analysis of ill-structured problem solving, mentoring functions, and perceptions of practicum teachers and mentors toward online mentoring in a field-based practicum. *Instructional Science, 35*(1), 1-40. doi: 10.1007/s11251-006-9000-7

Hunt, J. H., Powell, S., Little, M. E., & Mike, A. (2013). The Effects of E-Mentoring on Beginning Teacher Competencies and Perceptions. *Teacher Education and Special Education, 36*(4), 286-297. doi: 10.1177/0888406413502734

Joseph, D. (2011). Early Career Teaching: Learning to be a teacher and staying in the job. *Australian Journal of Teacher Education, 36*(9). doi: http://dx.doi.org/10.14221/ajte.2011v36n9.5

Maher, M., & Macallister, H. (2013). Retention and Attrition of Students in Higher Education: Challenges in Modern Times to What Works. *Higher Education Studies, 3*(2), 62-73. doi: 10.5539/hes.v3n2p62

McKenzie, W., & Murphy, D. (2000). "I hope this goes somewhere": Evaluation of an online discussion group. *Australian Journal of Educational Technology, 16*(3), 239-257.

Mueller, S. (2004). Electronic mentoring as an example for the use of information and communications technology in engineering education. *European journal of engineering education, 29*(1), 53-63. doi: 10.1080/03043790320001293 04

O'Neil, D. K., Wagner, R., & Gomez, L. (1996). Online mentors: Experimenting in science class. *Educational Leadership, 54*(3), 39-42.

OECD. (2005). Teachers Matter: Attracting, developing and retaining effective teachers. Retrieved from http://www.oecd.org/education/school/34990905.pdf

Pawan, F., Paulus, T. M., Yalcin, S., & Chang, C. F. (2003). Online learning: Patterns of engagement and interaction among inservice teachers. *Language Learning and Technology, 7*(3), 119-140.

Queensland College of Teachers. (2013). Attrition of recent Queensland graduate teachers. Retrieved from http://www.qct.edu.au/Publications/Retention_Research_Report_RP01.pdf

Roberts, P. (2004). *Staffing an Empty Schoolhouse: Attracting and Retaining Teachers in Rural, Remote and Isolated Communities*. Sydney, Australia: NSW Teachers' Federation.

Roberts, P., & Lean, D. (October, 2005). *What does a successful staffing system for rural, remote and isolated schools look like?* Paper presented at the 2005 Society for the Provision of Education in Rural Australia, Darwin, Australia. Retrieved from http://files.eric.ed.gov/fulltext/ED493486.pdf

Scheopner, A. J. (2010). Irreconcilable differences: Teacher attrition in public and catholic schools. *Educational Research Review, 5*(3), 261-277. doi: 10.1016/j.edurev.2010.03.

Schuck, S., Aubusson, P., Buchanan, J., Prescott, A., Louviere, J., & Burke, P. (2011). Retaining Effective Early career Teachers in NSW Schools. *The report of a project commissioned by the NSW Department of Education and Training.* Retrieved from http://www.rilc.uts.edu.au/pdfs/Beginning_Teacher_Retention_Report.pdf

Stanulis, R. N., & Floden, R. E. (2009). Intensive mentoring as a way to help beginning teachers develop balanced instruction. *Journal of Teacher Education, 60*(2), 112-122. doi: 10.1177/0022487108330553

Whiting, V. R., & de Janasz, S. C. (2004). Mentoring in the 21st century: Using the internet to build skills and networks. *Journal of Management Education, 28*(3), 275-293. doi: 10.1177/1052562903252639

Student Engagement: Best Practices in a K-5 Blended Learning Environment

Cindy Prouty
School Psychologist, Arlington School District
Email: cprouty@asd.wednet.edu

Loredana Werth
Associate Professor of Education, Northwest Nazarene University
Email: lwerth@nnu.edu

Abstract: Finding and adopting effective teaching strategies that utilize technology is a matter of exploration and professional development. The purpose of this study was to investigate best practices in a K-5 blended learning environment and to determine if tablet usage in the classroom increases student engagement as observed through on-task conduct, homework completion, increased involvement in class activities, and fewer behavioral incidents. Within a single, rural elementary school in the Pacific Northwest, 250 students were observed in their classrooms and 30 certificated teachers participated in both a survey and interviews. Results of this study suggest that technology eliminates obstacles between casual and more prescriptive education practices. Challenges identified by teachers include: 1) finding time to delve into the apps, 2) effectively implementing digital devices, 3) matching learning targets, 4) aligning work with Common Core State Standards, 5) following district-adopted frameworks, and 6) determining which blended learning techniques are worth utilizing.

Introduction

Educators are utilizing tablets in their classrooms on a daily basis without adequate professional development. The influx of tablets in America's schools has not been well planned, nor have professional development opportunities provided teachers with the necessary training to fully implement and integrate best practice in their classrooms. Blended learning can enrich the elementary school classroom, and data gained from this investigative study highlights those opportunities. Increasing student engagement is a consistent goal in instruction, and one instructional technique being used more frequently toward this goal is the use of technology in the classroom (Sheninger, 2014; Stein & Graham, 2014).

Although educational standardization is trending, a movement toward educational individualization is also strengthening. Researchers forecast that by 2019, the offering of digital high school classes will increase to 50%, and the transformation of education through accessible and custom blended classes has far-reaching potential. (Horn & Staker, 2011; Werth, Werth, & Kellerer, 2013). Of great significance in blended learning is the ability to differentiate instruction for all levels of learners, as well as the ability to reach diverse students (iNACOL, 2013). Educators and families may prefer the fusion of face-to-face traditional instruction with technology-based learning integration rather than purely digital methods (Pointek, 2013; Werth et al., 2013).

Research has shown that although blended learning environments and the integration of technology in classroom activities can be effective for many students, there is a lack of digital transformation in the public school system (Lefton, 2012; Richardson, 2010; Riddle, 2010; Ruiling & Overbaugh, 2009). The term blended learning in the context of this K-5 study means utilizing different technology devices as a means to enhance teaching (Christensen, Horn, & Staker, 2013; Horn & Staker, 2012; Pointek, 2013). An empirical inquiry on the role of technology is required in developing means of instruction that are more effective than traditional methods (Johnson, 2012; Pacansky-Brock, 2013; Yin, 2014). In order for students to be impacted, teachers must first know where technology fits into good pedagogy.

esiring the best way to engage K-5 students through teaching practices in blended learning led to the following three primary questions:
1. What tablet methodology supports best practices in a K-5 blended learning environment?
2. How does tablet use impact student engagement?
3. With an increase in the use of tablets in classrooms, what are teacher perceptions of professional development and needs?

This study is significant as blended learning at the elementary level in a public school setting is not well-recognized or known as a method of best instructional practice. Embedding technology into learning is an ongoing practice that varies greatly depending on funding, leadership, and professional development practices (Shaw, 2010; Velez, 2012), and considerations need to be made in teacher training for exemplary implementation of best teaching practices in blended learning environments. Generalizations from this study may inform other districts about successfully integrating technology devices into the classroom.

Charlotte Danielson's *The Framework for Teaching: Evaluation Instrument, 2013 Edition,* was utilized as the theoretical framework in this study. The application of Danielson's work, in conjunction with best teaching practices including blended learning, should positively impact student outcomes, and higher levels of student engagement would be predicted.

The Study

Both open-ended and close-ended survey questions drawing on multiple sources of data were included in this mixed-method case study (Creswell, 2014). The qualitative aspect of the survey involved open-ended questions intended to explore aspects of blended learning and to measure teacher professional development needs and attitudes toward technology. The quantitative aspect of the research involved multiple choice questions, yes/no questions, and classroom observation. Triangulation was successfully achieved in this study as multiple methods of data collection were employed from numerous viewpoints (Marshall & Rossman, 2011).

By studying the tablet usage and professional development needs in one building, in-depth, a case study design was employed to collect data. The use of a pre-survey was employed to determine the extent to which staff were familiar with the term "blended learning," and whether teachers were knowledgeable about terminology and models associated with blended learning. Upon completion of the pre-survey, certified teachers were directed to work on the online survey. To maintain anonymity, the rural school located in the Pacific Northwest that participated in this study was assigned the pseudonym "Olympic Mountain Elementary School," and data collection for this study occurred at this location from September 2013, to December 2013. Participation in this study was voluntary, and no minors or vulnerable participants were included in the survey or interview portions. Due to the low numbers of males in the site building, gender was removed from the demographic information prior to administration of the survey in order to protect anonymity.

In 2013, the Pew Research Center developed a study titled, *How Teachers Are Using Technology At Home and In Their Classroom* (Purcell, Heaps, Buchanan, & Friedrich, 2013). This study included a questionnaire that was utilized with permission and modified to better meet the needs of this current study and to establish validity with the continuous Likert scale survey tool (Polit & Beck, 2006; Trochim, 2006). The tool was designed to determine benefits of a blended learning environment, measure teacher comfort with tablets as a tool, discover which best teaching practices were incorporated into classrooms, and identify professional development needs. The survey was sent to Olympic Mountain Elementary School, and both the pre-survey and the online survey were completed by 100% of the intended population during a morning staff meeting at the school.

The interview questions were first piloted with four teachers who were not teaching in the district where the research was conducted; the questions were then altered to incorporate the changes suggested by those in the pilot. The survey was then divided into two parts and given to the eight volunteer participants who had been selected based on their digital technology experience. Each participant was asked the questions for interview one, and in a second interview was asked follow-up questions based on information gathered in interview one. This resulted in a total of 16 face-to-face interviews that were recorded and later transcribed by the researcher.

The student engagement portion of the study factored in a compilation of on-task classroom behavior, attendance, and disciplinary referrals. On-task behavior was measured using the *time-sampling* method (Beaty, 2006; Hintze & Shapiro, 1995).

In September 2013, the researcher piloted a classroom observation on-task time sampling. There were two teachers with one-to-one tablets in the elementary site school, strong teaching experience, and strong tablet-integration expertise, and the pilot was a blend of these two individuals. The researcher was introduced as a visitor, and students were told to continue with their regular instruction. Prior arrangements had been made to visit the first grade teacher's classroom for a "tech buddy" instructional time. There were 23 first grade students present. The teacher prepared the students for the arrival of their tech buddies to explore a new app called WordPhoto on their tablets. Twenty-four fifth grade students arrived with their teacher to join their first grade buddies. One student was absent so a different pairing accommodation was made. The 47 students partnered up accessing the Word Photo app on the first graders' tablets. The fifth grade older buddy was to take a picture using the app and then create a collage of common character traits. The fifth grader had a sheet with common character traits and assisted the first grader in choosing words they believed best described them. The fifth grader assisted through the lesson, which was completed in about 15 minutes. Alterations were made to the time-sampling student engagement form based on the pilot observation to include the subject of the lesson being taught, the number of tablets employed during the lesson, and the development of a teacher coding system in order to protect the identity of the teacher.

A time sampling tool was created by the researcher that allowed tallies to indicate the number of students on task within the 30-minute observation, and the data points were arranged in 5-minute intervals. This demonstrated the quantitative data in easily identifiable terms, provided a common understanding relevant to student engagement, and provided a high degree of validity and reliability.

SPSS Statistical Software was used for data analysis, and descriptive statistics were employed to identify features of the data sets (IBM SPSS, 2014; Tanner, 2012). Cronbach's alpha coefficient was inclusively used with the survey instrument through summing the scales for data analysis in each section and for the overall instrument.

As with any case study, there are certain limitations. In this case, the results of the study are limited to one elementary building that may not be representative of urban areas, lower socioeconomic schools, and schools with higher ethnic diversifications. In addition, limitations of a mixed-methods approach include the increased amounts of data collection required to properly conduct a mixed-methods study (Creswell, 2014; Yin, 2014).

Findings

Results indicate that, in this case study, blended learning terminology and models are unfamiliar to rural elementary staff. Quantitative results of the study came from two questions on the pre-survey with teachers, the online teacher survey, and classroom observations. The impetus for the two questions on the pre-survey was the notion that blended learning as a best pedagogical practice is not widely known in the public school elementary setting. The two questions were: 1) Are you familiar with the term blended learning? 2) Are you acquainted with blended learning terminology and models? Three teachers answered "yes" to question 1, indicating some familiarity with blended learning, while 27 participants answered "no." None of the 30 participants, however, were familiar with terminology typically associated with blended learning or models. Based on the results of the pre survey, the following statement was provided to interview participants before moving on with the rest of the study: The term blended learning in the context of this K-5 study means utilizing different technology devices as a means to enhance teaching (Christensen, Horn, & Staker, 2013; Horn & Staker, 2012; Pointek, 2013).

Following the completion of the pre-survey, all 30 participants completed the online survey, which consisted of Likert scale questions followed by open-ended questions. Twenty-eight of the participants defined the methods of professional development they preferred; of the respondents, 17 preferred hands-on, 14 face-to-face, and 8 preferred some type of collaborative effort. This survey was designed to determine the professional development needs of elementary staff in the area of blended learning and for participants to rate how effective the teachers viewed the tablets in their instructional practices. Cronbach's Alpha was employed for reliability, and the results of the study were calculated to be 0783, which would be considered "good" for internal consistency.

The overarching theme from the qualitative portion of the online survey was the need for improvement of the facilitation of technology. Within this overarching theme, three subthemes emerged: 1) professional development, 2) district-level technology supports, and 3) resources. Professional development was the foremost common thread to the enhancement of teacher skills needed to deliver effective instruction to students. District-level supports include having professional development time carved out of teachers' schedules along with the resources needed to be effective in their positions. Most participants identified their building as being in a superior position for building-level supports, though staff appeared to desire a more collaborative and desired to have the full scope of professional development opportunities district wide. Resources identified by participants included district-level professional development opportunities, acquisition of additional equipment/devices, and technology support for equipment not working properly to avoid having to rely on their peers who are busy teaching their own classes.

The classroom observation results were entered into an Excel spreadsheet with each classroom numbered 1-10 and each 5-minute increment numbered 1-6 (totaling 30 minutes). Data included the number of students on task, the percentage of students on task, the number of students off task, the percentage of students off task, and finally the tablet method for each class. One was a special education classroom, and one class had a smaller Title I reading group.

The class with the greatest number of students off task was the class with fewer than 10 tablets. This class had the lowest on task rate of 83%, and its highest on task rate was 92% during the 30-minute observation period. The classes with the highest on-task rates were the two classrooms with one-to-one tablets. Both had 100% on task rates for each 5-minute increment and for the whole 30-minute observation period. The four classrooms with two-to-one tablets had the next highest on task rate with only one 5-minute increment showing a 96% on task rate because one student was off task. All other time sampling for the two-to-one classes reflected a 100% on task rate. The data also showed that the highest on task rates were in classrooms where the teachers had the most experience or familiarity with tablets compared to other teachers in the building, although they had similar or less teaching experience.

There were three different groupings for analysis of the tablet usage: 1) classes with one-to-one tablets, 2) classes with two-to-one tablets, and 3) classes with fewer than 10 tablets. An analysis of variance (ANOVA) was conducted (Tanner, 2012). Statistical tests were conducted at $p = .05$, a 95% confidence interval. Further, a post-hoc test, the Bonferroni, was performed (Guilbaud & Karlsson, 2010; McHugh, 2011; Vialatte & Cichocki, 2008).

A post-hoc assessment encouraged multiple comparisons with the tablet methodology. At the 95% confidence interval, a significant difference was found in two comparisons at the $p = .05$ level. An independent samples t-test analysis was conducted on the subject area of the lesson being taught. Math (1) vs. non-math subjects (2) such as reading, science, and writing, and there were no significant differences ($p = .257$ at the 0.05 level of significance) between math and non-math subjects. A Chi-squared goodness-of-fit test was conducted initially on the classroom observations. The 10 classrooms were averaged to look at proportions for each of the classrooms, and no significant difference was found between the observed and the expected frequency in each class.

From the frequency analysis and coding of the interviews, themes emerge from the data (Creswell, 2014; Marshall & Rossman, 2011). Blended learning, including the integration of technology such as tablet usage into best practice in the classroom, was one of the themes. Professional development was another theme, and factors included both building- and district-level support, the frequency of professional development, and teacher technology support. Finally, the third theme that emerged was the school as the vehicle for teacher collaboration, differentiation for students, and engagement of students. Participants stated that tablet usage was making them better teachers. One participant specified:

> I could see the immediate effect upon the children with just one iPad. Now I find our transition times between activities is quicker than ever. Children have access to apps and websites that allow them to progress at their own pace and learning levels. The tablets are beneficial, especially for struggling students. I use the iPads for both lower students and for higher students.

Maintaining some use of paper and pencil work was important to all participants, as developing handwriting skills is viewed as an emergent skill at the early elementary level. Differentiation for students' varied academic levels and the engagement observed by all interview participants appeared to comprise some of the top reasons for employing tablets in the classroom.

Tools utilized by teachers to support the tablets include the Promethean board, ActivExpressions or ActiVotes (student response system), QR codes, tablets, document cameras, projectors, computers, and a sound system. Teachers reported that utilizing technology in their teaching, such as apps like Tools for Students, Show me, Showbie, and Dropbox, allows their elementary students to send emails directly to the teachers. One teacher sends students feedback by digital audio recordings for each student. Both teachers (and students) like the instant feedback, and more students appear to be showing their parents their work. Some participants use the tablets for all academic subjects to differentiate learning, facilitate student collaboration, provide direct instruction, encourage student practice, manage transition times, and improve writing and sequencing of stories.

Drawbacks of tablet use as reported by participants include the fact that apps get expensive, and some students may think they are a toy *upon initial use.* This latter drawback did not appear to be a factor for teachers who had been using tablets for several months.

Two challenges with blended learning that participants reported were finding time outside of their teaching day to work with them and getting the tablets and apps set up the way they want. Participants wanted to hear from other teachers who have higher numbers of tablets in their classrooms, utilize webinars and blogs, and have adequate charging stations for the iPads. To meet another challenge, they developed a tech buddies program to help students learn how to use apps and manage the iPads. As students practice with tech buddies, they become comfortable with the apps before they experience them on their own. Another challenge is development of adequate technical support to keep the equipment working. Participants also discussed the need for a professional development continuum or menu of options for teachers implementing technology into their pedagogy, and a rating system or evaluation tool to demonstrate growth as a teacher. Some teachers reported they would like more regional or district-level tablet usage classes. Participants want to know how to bring more technology to more kids.

Participants reported that using technology as a tool was motivating for students and enabled students to achieve higher levels of learning. Students are in the classroom right away in the morning, even coming early to work on their projects, and sometimes stay in at recess to work. They are challenged and motivated when they receive immediate feedback and can monitor their learning progress, and this shows in their projects. They are proud of their achievements and empowered to strive for higher goals. Their self-confidence builds as they develop a "can do" attitude because they know how far they have come and see their next step in learning. Younger kids like the visual aspect. Tablets provide extra support that can add on to their learning. When they are done with their work, kids want to explore different apps or learn more about the ones they have been using. Some students are willing to work harder on learning information when it is in a different format.

Conclusions

The results of this study enhance the body of literature in blended learning practices (Creswell, 2014; Marshall & Rossman, 2011). Teachers reported that blended learning facilitated their improvement as professionals, made their students more productive, and resulted in elevated test scores. Teachers indicated they had sufficient access to the tools needed to teach to specific learning targets when utilizing blended learning practices. Results also indicate that educators who have implemented blended learning practices could not imagine going back to traditional classrooms.

Findings from the data in this study support research suggesting that engagement can influence student outcomes (Finn & Zimmer, 2013; Reeve, 2013; Reschly & Christenson, 2013). Teachers in this study engaged students in the blended learning environment as they looked for new apps to meet specific targets, changed their methods to keep learning fresh, promoted student collaboration, worked to engage each individual, allowed students to lead discussions, helped students teach each other and use whole brain learning, and supervised as students videoed their learning process.

Based on the findings in this research study, schools need to define their goals and vision towards effective implementation of technology (Sheninger, 2014; Stein & Graham, 2014). Rather than identifying technology as a separate entity, schools must fully integrate technology into current pedagogical practices.

References

Beaty, J.J. (2006). *Observing development of the young child*. Upper Saddle River, NJ: Pearson Education, Inc.

Christensen, C., Horn, M., & Staker, H. (2013, May). *Is K-12 blended learning disruptive? An introduction of the theory of hybrids*. Retrieved from http://www.christenseninstitute.org/publications/hybrids/

Creswell, J.W. (2014). *Research design: Qualitative, quantitative and mixed methods approaches*. Thousand Oaks, CA: Sage Publications.

Finn, J., & Zimmer, K. (2013). Student engagement: What is it? Why does it matter? In Christenson, S., Reschly, A., & Wylie, C. (Eds.), *Handbook of research on student engagement* (pp. 97-131). New York, NY: Springer.

Guilbaud, O., & Karlsson, P. (2010). Confidence regions for Bonferroni-based closed tests extended to more general closed tests. *Journal of Biopharmaceutical Statistics, 21*(4), 682-707.

Hintze, J.M. & Shapiro, E.S. (1995). Best practices in the systematic observation of classroom behavior. In Thomas, A. & Grimes, T. (1995). *Best practices in school psychology – III*. Washington, DC: National Association of School Psychologists.

Horn, M.B. & Staker, H. (2011). The rise of K-12 blended learning. Retrieved from http://www.innosightinstitute.org/innosight/wp-content/uploads/2011/01/The-Rise-of-K-12-Blended-Learning.pdf

Horn, M.B. & Staker, H. (2012). *Classifying K-12 blended learning*. Retrieved from http://www.innosightinstitute.org/innosight/wp-content/uploads/2012/05/Classifying-K-12-blended-learning2.pdf

IBM SPSS (computer software). (2014). SPSS Statistical software. Retrieved from http://www-01.ibm.com/software/analytics/spss/products/statistics/

iNACOL. (2013). K-12 online learning research database. International Association for K-12 Online Learning (iNACOL). Retrieved from http://www.k12onleresearch.org/

Johnson, D. (2012). *The classroom teacher's technology survival guide*. San Francisco, CA: Jossey-Bass.

Lefton, R. (2012). Digital transformation advances, although slowly. *Educational Marketer, 43*(13), 1-3.

Marshall, C., & Rossman, G. (2011). *Designing qualitative research* (5th ed.). Thousand Oaks, CA: Sage.

McHugh, M. (2011). Multiple comparison analysis testing in ANOVA. *Biochemia Medica, 21*(3), 203-209.

Pacansky-Brock, M. (2013). *Best practices with emerging technologies*. New York, NY: Routledge.

Pointek, J. (2013). *Introduction to blended learning for elementary schools: Personalizing math instruction in the K-5 classroom* [White paper]. Retrieved from http://www.dreambox.com/white-papers/introduction-to-blended-learning-for-elementary-schools

Polit, D. F., & Beck, C. T. (2006). The content validity index: Are you sure you know what's being reported? Critique and recommendations. *Research in Nursing and Health, 29*(5), 489-497. doi: 10.1002/nur.20147

Purcell, K., Heaps, A., Buchanan, J., & Friedrich, L. (2013, February). *How teachers are using technology at home and in their classrooms*. Retrieved from http://www.pewinternet.org/Reports/2013/Teachers-and-technology/Methodology.aspx

Reeve, J. (2013). A self-determination theory perspective on student engagement. In Christenson, S., Reschly, A., & Wylie, C. (Eds.), *Handbook of research on student engagement* (pp. 149-172). New York, NY: Springer.

Reschly, A., & Christenson, S. (2013). Jingle, jangle and conceptual haziness: Evolution and future directions of the engagement construct. In Christenson, S., Reschly, A., & Wylie, C. (Eds.), *Handbook of research on student engagement* (pp. 3-19). New York, NY: Springer.

Richardson, W. (2010). No more one-size-fits all learning: The federal government finally gets 21st century learning right. *District Administration, 46*(7), 85-85.

Riddle, J. (2010). 21 things: Kinder, gentler tips for effective technology integration infusion. *MultiMedia & Internet@school, 17*(2), 25-27.

Ruiling, L., & Overbaugh, R. (2009). School environment and technology implementation in K-12 classrooms. *Computers in the Schools, 26*(2), 89-106.

Shaw, M. (2010). *Teachers' learning of technology: Key factors and processes* (Doctoral dissertation). Retrieved from PQDT Open Dissertations and Theses database. (AAT 3411483)

Sheninger, E. (2014). *Digital leadership: Changing paradigms for changing times*. Thousand Oaks, CA: Sage.

Stein, J., & Graham, C. (2014). *Essentials for blended learning: A standards-based guide*. New York, NY: Routledge.

Tanner, D. (2012). *Using statistics to make educational decisions*. Thousand Oaks, CA: Sage Publications.

Trochim, W. M. K. (2006). Likert scaling. Retrieved from http://www.socialresearchmethods.net/kb/scallik.php

Velez, A. (2012). *Preparing students for the future – 21st century skills* (Doctoral dissertation). Retrieved from PQDT Open Dissertations and Theses database. (AAT 3514336)

Vialatte, F., & Cichocki, A. (2008). Split-test Bonferroni correction for QEEG statistical maps. *Biological Cybernetics, 98*(4), 295-303.

Werth, E., Werth, L., & Kellerer, E. (2013, October). *Transforming K-12 rural education through blended learning: Barriers and practices*. Retrieved from http://www.inacol.org/cms/wp-content/uploads/2013/10/iNACOL-Transforming-K-12-Rural-Education-through-Blended-Learning.pdf

Yin, R. K. (2014). *Case study research: Design and methods* (5th ed.). Thousand Oaks, CA: Sage Publications.

Future Online Faculty, Technology, and Competencies: Student Perspectives

Phillip L. Davidson
University of Phoenix, School of Advanced Studies
Phoenix, Arizona, United States
phil.davidson@phoenix.edu

Abstract: The purpose of this qualitative descriptive study was to acquire a better understanding of the dominant student perceptions of future competencies online faculty might need in the future. This study involved a survey of 500 college-level students who have taken at least one online class. Student college experience included some college and no degree to graduate degrees. Four major themes emerged from a study of the categories and subcategories that evolved from the coding of the surveys. Faculty communication, online and interpersonal, was the most critical aspect for success in future online classes. Technical and computer skills were critical, specifically the need to use visual, auditory, and other multimedia tools to provide as the most effective communication possible. Patience with students will be critical for faculty in the future, as diversity will continue to increase. The themes and their implications to future online teaching and future research are discussed.

Introduction

Learning online, rather than in a traditional classroom, offers students who cannot attend a traditional college or university the opportunity to get a degree. The advent of online education has opened the door to a new group of students who could not previously attend a traditional college or university for a variety of reasons. The introduction of relatively inexpensive personal computers and access to the internet has also made online education easier than the older distance learning options that used conventional mail. The resulting increase and ease of access has introduced a disruptive innovation that has changed the face of education worldwide. A 2013 survey by the Babson Survey Research Group, the Sloan Consortium, and Pearson Publishing made the following important points:

1. "There were 572,000 more online students in fall 2011 than in fall 2010 for a new total of 6.7 million students taking at least one online course" (Allen & Seaman 2013, p. 17).
2. "The most recent estimate, for fall 2011, shows an increase of 9.3 percent in the number of students taking at least one online course" (Allen & Seaman 2013, p. 18).
3. "The proportion of higher education students taking at least one online course now stands at 32 percent" (Allen & Seaman 2013, p. 19) compared to less than 10% in 2003.

However, the world is changing. Distance education has existed in many forms for hundreds of years. The introduction of affordable personal computers and access to the internet was a major disruptive innovation to the educational field. Where older forms of distance education commonly depended on mail service, the ability to instantly post and discuss assignments from and to anywhere in the world fundamentally changed the look and feel of education, as witnessed by the numbers noted above. Online education includes all levels of education from kindergarten to doctorate. While still not the dominant paradigm in education, we see more and more educational programs offering at least a portion of their education online, and the online environment is growing at more than three times the speed of the traditional educational environment (Allen & Seaman 2013).

The high visibility of online classes and the large number of online students raises the question as to whether teaching online can be done in the same fashion as in traditional brick-and-mortar institutions. This paper will not be used to discuss that issue directly, as the evidence over the last 20 years is extensive and clear that online teaching requires additional and different skills and competencies (Goodyear, Salmon, Spector, Steeples, & Tickner 2001). However, technology and the online classroom continue to evolve. While there has been significant progress in defining the skills needed for online teachers today, there is a need to address the future. New tools, such as online social media, are having an effect on teaching and learning, and that is just one issue. The issues evolving from new technologies were the stimulus for this paper, which begins to try and better understand competencies for online teachers *in the future*.

Background to the Study

Access to relatively low cost computers and access to broadband internet fundamentally changed the ability to access educational resources. Private universities evolved to take advantage of this new market. Non-profit and for-profit colleges and universities around the world have added the ability to teach using personal computers. The process has faced a number of hurdles, and a number of vendors have evolved out of this disruptive morass to offer polished learning management systems (LMS), such as Blackboard and eCollege. Some colleges and universities have also developed their own, which is a far better cry from the first days of bulletin boards and newsgroups.

Most LMS vendors continue to change to meet client demands, trying to offer new tools that include more and more different types of media. What has not changed, however, are the methods of instruction. Even with advanced learning management systems, the approach to teaching has remained much the same for centuries. Only the tools have changed. As Cook and Sonnenberg (2014) noted, technology is continuing to evolve and we see an increasing use in mobile technologies. Access to school via smartphones is already a reality and access via wearable devices is certainly likely within the near future. Wearable computers already exist as do devices that allow visualization of the internet while remaining mobile. Demand will continue to push new technologies, which will eventually become practical and reasonably priced. There is also the experiment currently taking place with massive open online courses (MOOCs). Some of these classes can have as many as 250,000 students.

Teachers still facilitate, cajole, encourage, and evaluate students on their knowledge of the subject. Teachers are expected to be subject matter experts. Will those expectations continue and will teachers continue to follow the traditional educational pathways of previous centuries, or will technology create a paradigmatic shift that requires new teacher competencies? That ultimate question is the background for this study. The question, however, cannot be easily answered because there are more stakeholders than just students and faculty. Even students and faculty are not homogeneous groups, so stakeholder opinions might vary considerably within one or both groups.

The point is that online education is not a stable field. Technology is changing rapidly. Students are pushing for the use of more convenient technologies. Students themselves are changing. Community colleges are seeing older students who find that they need to return to school to gain new skills as retirement may be eluding them due to loss of retirement savings (Castillo 2013). Castillo also noted that the number of younger, at risk students, is increasing.

The continuing advancement in technology was the primary stimulus for this research. The question was raised as to what skills and competencies teachers would need *in the future*. The projected research group would be faculty who taught in online environments. This seemed like a relatively easy task. The original question was first researched through literature review, and there are multiple studies that focus on teacher competencies for online educators (Bigatel, Ragan, Kennan, May, & Redmond 2012; Carril, Sanmamed, & Sellés 2013; Williams 2003). However, several considerations became apparent from the research study.

One thing noticed is that almost all studies treat online education as it currently exists. Very few delve into possible future competencies, and even then, the focus is more about curriculum changes. It is difficult to know what technology will look like ten years from now. Additionally, technology is not the only aspect that is changing. The expression of our cultures is changing worldwide, and demands to include cultural aspects in online teaching cannot go ignored (Castillo 2013).

Assumptions

Other issues became apparent as the literature review progressed. One issue is that there are many assumptions related to online learning, online teaching, and student expectations. There is an assumption that faculty are the best at assessing what competencies they will need in the future. A number of studies involved asking faculty what competencies they feel will be needed (Abdous 2011; Bigatel, Ragan, Kennan, May, & Redmond 2012). What about student perspectives? Many studies talk *about* the student, but few actually talk with or interview students to get their perspective on what they believe faculty will need in the future. However, this could be an important perspective.

However, a few studies did seek out the perspective of small groups of students. Bollinger et al. (2010), using a questionnaire available to students (N=302), studied the effects of podcasting as a motivational tool in online learning. Podcasting is reflective of technologies that may become a future competency for faculty. Boling et al. (2012), using a case study method, sought out student and teacher perspectives regarding positive online learning environments (N=15). Kear, Donelan, and Williams (2014) used a survey to study not only the effectiveness in wikis for online learning, but the perspective of students as well (N=74). Each of these three studies focused on the student perspective, particularly concerning technologies that could enhance the online learning environment. Therefore, the literature suggests that the student opinion and insights as to future technologies and teacher competencies are of value in the study of future online learning, and that is an assumption central to this research paper.

The Problem

The general problem is that competencies needed by online faculty ten years in the future are still unclear. Cook and Sonnenberg (2014) focused on the technology involved with online education, but it is still unclear as to the extent technology will play in online education. Most are clear that technology will play a significant role, but will technology define the required competencies needed for online faculty? Not only are future competencies unclear, but much of the research has only addressed the issue of faculty competencies from the perspectives of the faculty themselves (Bigatel, Ragan, Kennan, May, & Redmond 2012; Carrill, Sanmamed, & Sellés 2013). What about students? They are a major stakeholder in online teaching.

Specifically, it is important to understand the student expectations as to what competencies they might need from faculty members in the future (Sander, Stevenson, King, & Coats 2000). While direct associations between student retention and teacher competencies have not been established, it is reasonable to assume that how well a teacher performs has a direct or indirect effect on whether a student progresses or drops from an online teaching program (Omar, Kalulu, & Alijani 2011). This research is not seeking to establish those types of causal relationships, but having a clear picture of student expectations about future online teaching would seem to be important. Not having that clear picture of student expectations creates a void that makes future planning difficult and somewhat arbitrary.

Purpose

The purpose of this qualitative descriptive study was to understand students' beliefs about their expectations for faculty teaching online. The focus was arbitrarily set for ten years into the future. Because we were asking students their opinion, the responses were necessarily subjective. However, it was the belief of this researcher that if enough online students were included in the study, and if there were significant themes developed from the study, then the results would be useful in future online planning.

Significance

Online education has a problem. The online environment is growing exponentially faster than traditional institutions (Allen & Seaman 2013). Universities and faculty experts are projecting what they believe to be the future needs of students as they reshape the online teaching environment. The results of their projections involve new approaches to teaching online such as Massive Open Online Courses (MOOC). MOOCs seem to have become all the rage. These classes can have as many as 250,000 students, and there is controversy as to the effectiveness of MOOC's as well as to whether students will be given credit for taking these courses (Buchanan 2013). MOOC's are only one dramatic example of how faculty and technology are coming together to reshape online education, yet students appear to be left out of the conversation. Without the input of the students who attend these courses, online education might find itself faltering and students could potentially be left with suboptimal choices. Online education offers individuals who work, or who have other responsibilities that prohibit a more traditional education, the possibility of gaining an education. Not listening to their issues and concerns for future online education is a significant concern.

Literature Review

To ignore the changing world of online learning and education makes future planning a guessing game. At the same time, relying only on faculty, even faculty experts, to define what future competencies might be required in may be projecting a false future. In addition, receiving input only from faculty is ignoring a group of major stakeholders in online education – the students. The value students see in online education ultimately defines the market, and competition for online students is intense, so listening to student perspectives is critical. Student perspectives as to the online environment (Boling et al. 2012) as well as perspectives on newer online technologies (Boling et al. 2012; Kear et al. 2014) were noted earlier.

Baran, Correia, and Thompson (2011) noted the importance to understand what is lacking in researching online teaching. There is a "tendency to carry traditional educational practices into the online environment" (p.422). However, the internet is now the basic backbone for instruction and communication online. The internet, however, is not a single "thing." Through the internet, we have a variety of texting tools, multimedia and social networking tools, as well as internet gaming tools, all of which have been used for online education.

Fillion, Limayem, Laferrière, and Mantha (2008) researched the value and perceptions of value of information and communication technologies (ICT) in both onground and online teaching environments. Their study was in a "technology-rich" environment, which suggests that there was already a bias towards significant use of ICT. The findings, however, indicate that communication between students and faculty regarding the use of ICT is better onground, and that communication was important to students. Information and communication technologies influence outcomes, but clarity of communication and instruction between faculty and students was critical. Understanding that the online environment is different is important, however, when students do not have the option of following their educational path onground. "Online teaching experience enables (and sometimes even forces) faculty to reconsider their deep-rooted beliefs about teaching and learning" (Abdous 2011, p. 63).

In a research study by Liu, Chen, Sun, Wible, and Kuo (2010), the researchers noted that when an online course is "interesting, diverse, not too hard, and meets the needs of users at different levels," (p. 608), the students perceive greater value. Comfort with the online technology was directly related to student experience with technology itself, so the inference is that faculty competencies related to making the student more comfortable are of greater value than technological skills by the faculty. Bigatel, Ragan, Kennan, May, and Redmond (2012), in a study involving teachers experienced with online learning, found the highest competency to be "active learning" (p. 65), where the instructor encourages student participation and shows respect for student needs. The authors' research suggested that technology might not be the most important competency.

The study by Allen and Seaman (2013) demonstrated the momentum behind the growth of online education. The number of students suggests a potentially dominant market in higher education and finances cannot be ignored in planning the future design of online education. Competition for students in higher education has been an issue for a decade (Dronholz 2005). Both financial solvency and status are at risk for institutions. In this type of competitive environment (which involves both non-profit and for-profit institutions), planning may be directed towards perceptions rather than needs. As Pak (2013) noted, when "universities compete for faculty, students, funding and so on in their day-to-day operations, all of this is meant to contribute to one final objective, which is to preserve or improve their standing" (p. 280). Pak continued to note that the "competitive game [is] based on elusive and sometimes misleading statistics" (p. 284). It is this perspective that provides the impetus to look elsewhere for better understanding of the competencies that attract students to higher education, and that "elsewhere" is to the students themselves.

Methodology

The goal of this research was to seek the opinions of a large number of students who had taken at least one online class. The participants were all members of Amazon's Mechanical Turk survey group. Mechanical Turk is comprised of individuals who are paid to respond to surveys. The researcher establishes the requirements for the survey with Mechanical Turk, while also establishing the criteria for acceptance and the amount of money that will be paid for each successful survey.

Mechanical Turk is an ideal research environment for many studies as the participants are completely "blind" to the researcher and vice versa. The only identification is an ID established by Amazon to which only they have access. Permission to use the information is implicit in the acceptance by the participants to accept the survey. Mechanical Turk transmits and receives the surveys and the researcher never has contact with the participants.

Based on the use of Amazon's Mechanical Turk resources, the decision was made to focus on a short qualitative descriptive study. Qualitative descriptive research is "categorical, as opposed to [a] 'noncategorical alternative' for inquiry" (Sandelowski 2000, p. 335), and is considered less interpretative. There was no goal to establish a relationship or correlation between student perceptions and faculty competencies, so a quantitative study was inappropriate. Consequently, as the goal was more categorical in discovering an exhaustive list of student opinions on online faculty future competencies, a qualitative descriptive study was deemed the most effective approach.

A contract was established with Amazon's Mechanical Turk to solicit 500 surveys from individuals anywhere in the United States who had taken at least one online class. Each individual was asked demographic questions regarding their age and educational background. One open-ended question was asked. "Thinking about your experience as an online student and thinking about the possible changes in online teaching ten years into the future, what three qualities (competencies) should faculty members incorporate in that future that would be most helpful to students taking online classes? Please include at least three suggestions and explain."

Results

Five hundred surveys were collected, per the contract with Mechanical Turk. Twenty were eliminated as they had at least one piece of information missing, either demographically or in the question response area. Participants could suggest more than three responses and some did, while a few submitted only two suggestions. The net result was approximately 1,450 separate responses (suggestions) and 47 pages of text.

Demographically, the group was approximately 59% male and 41% female. The average age was 29.5 years. Students included those with some college, but no degree as well as students with an associate's degree, a bachelor's degree, or graduate degrees. Table No. 1 provides the exact breakdown.

Table 1.
Demographic breakdown or participant population by age and educational level

College Experience	Average Age	1 Std. Dev.	Gender	Number of Participants	Gender (%)
Some College	26.54	7.37	Female	60	43.50%
			Male	78	56.50%
Associates Degree	29.69	9.73	Male	24	49.00%
			Female	25	51.00%
Bachelor's Degree	29.98	9.13	Male	134	64.40%
			Female	74	35.60%
Graduate Degree	32.72	8.89	Male	46	54.10%
			Female	39	45.90%
			Total	480	
			Male	282	58.75%
			Female	198	41.25%

Analysis and Summary of Responses

There were 47 pages of single-spaced text, which included responses from 480 participants. Twenty individuals were eliminated due to incomplete responses. The first step was to code the text. Saldaña (2009) described codes as "a word or short phrase that symbolically assigns a summative, salient, essence-capturing, and/or evocative attribute for a portion of language-based or visual data" (p. 3). All textual answers related to the questions were analyzed use a software tool called Wordstat 7, a content analysis and text-mining software tool available from

Provalis Research. Wordstat 7 allowed the ability to for patterns of word phrases. The phrases from Wordstat 7 were then input into QDA Miner 4, a qualitative data analysis tool that was used to code and annotate the textual responses from the students. Codes were separated into categories and then subcategories were established under each category. The resulting categorization and subcategorization are shown in table 2.

Table 2.
Top 12 Categories and Subcategories (in order of frequency)

Case Frequency	Category	Subcategory
205	Communication Skills	Online communication skills
		Clear Communication
		Written Communication
		Interpersonal communication
		Email communication
		Knowledge communication
88	Technology Skills	Well versed
		Current
		Ability to master more than basic technology
		Understand where technology fits
		Computer technology
		Emerging technologies
		Technology awareness
79	Computer Skills	Online computer skills
		Skype/video conferencing
		Online communication
58	Patience	Attentiveness
		Empathy
		Patience to explain things
		Patience with students
		Patience in communication
46	Multimedia and Video	Use multimedia and visual resources
		Multimedia presentations
		Reach students with various multimedia
37	Flexibility	Roll with the punches
		Multiple ways to explain subject matter
		Flexibility of schedule
		Communication flexibility
		Flexibility in dealing with issues
32	Clarity	Clarity of words
		Clarity of knowledge
		Clarity of instructions
26	Availability	High availability
		Availability in and out of class
23	Organization	Organizational skills
		Well organized
19	Online Teaching Skills	Interactive teaching
		Technology up-to-date
		Visual and audio learning material
15	Time Management	Clear schedule
		Flexibility as far as assignments
12	Adaptability	Varied skill set
		Adaptability to new technology
		Adaptable schedules

Category frequencies were consistent between both genders. Between the four educational levels, there were few differences. Those with some college focused more on computer skills, while those with associate degrees focused less on video and multimedia. Bachelor degree students preferred clarity to flexibility.

Themes

Four *primary* themes emerged from the categories and subcategories:

1. Faculty communication, online and interpersonal, in all its various forms, is the most critical aspect for success in future online classes. Clarity was a subtheme to communication.
2. Technical and computer skills are critical, specifically the need to use visual, auditory, and other multimedia tools to provide as many different learning tools as possible.
3. Patience with students will be critical for faculty in the future, as diversity will continue to increase. In addition, students experience many different issues, and faculty patience in dealing with those specific needs will be important.
4. Related to patience, future online faculty members need to be flexible in class requirements, schedules, and communication modalities.

Implications and Future Research

There is a strong desire to continue teaching online using the same approaches used in traditional onground educational locations (Baran, Correia, & Thompson 2011). In truth, many of the issues raised in this research are issues long since known to be problematical. Student focus on communications, teacher patience, and flexibility of the curriculum are well-studied issues (Ledbetter & Finn 2013). Ledbetter and Finn also discussed empowerment of students, and we see this theme continuing to grow. While the number of online students continues to grow, the competition to recruit and retain students has also increased. Ignoring the elemental aspects of teaching, as demonstrated in themes 1, 3, and 4 could be a critical mistake.

At the same time, the world and technology is pushing changes to how students learn. Students were very clear in this study that the engagement and relationships established with a communicative, flexible, and patient faculty is critically important. At the same time, students acknowledged that necessity of technical and computer skills, and that need would continue to grow, which is focused in theme #2. What is unclear is how much technology will become requirement in future online classes. Research focused on podcasting and wikis were noted earlier in this paper.

Students mentioned a number of specific technologies such as podcasts and video-conferencing in their specific comments. A number of students mentioned the use of texting as a classroom tool. In addition, in the literature, we are also seeing online tools such as Massive Multiplayer Online Role Playing Games (MMORPGs) appear within education. For example, World of Warcraft, one of the most popular MMORPGs, has also been used as an educational platform in a variety of ways (Curry 2010). Second Life, another MMORPG, has been used for training in businesses as well as offering virtual classrooms (Yoon 2014).

The issue, however, may not be so much the technology, but the mindset of the participants (students and faculty). Students, who tend to be younger than online faculty, see the application of technology different. According to Shah and Meisenberg (2012), we are seeing an age difference of 20+ years between online faculty and online students. Student participants in this study averaged 29.5, which seems about the norm found in the literature. Faculty members tend to average in their late forties (Gibson, Harris, & Colaric 2008). According to Gibson et al., we see the older faculty perceived the use of online technologies as have less value than younger faculty. For students, however, the technologies are part of their everyday life, as the students discussed in their own responses. Texting, video-conferencing (even from smart phones) and playing virtual reality games such as World of Warcraft set the stage for future research and opportunities as best methods to accomplish the softer goals defined by the students in this study.

References

Abdous, M. (2011). A process-oriented framework for acquiring online teaching competencies. *Journal of Computing in Higher Education, 23*(1), 60-77. doi: 10.1007/s12528-010-9040-5

Allen, I. E., and Seaman, J. (2011) *Going the distance: Online education in the United States, 2011.* San Francisco, CA: Babson Survey Research Group and Quahog Research Group, LLC.

Baran, E., Correia, A.-P., & Thompson, A. (2011). Transforming online teaching practice: Critical analysis of the literature on the roles and competencies of online teachers. *Distance Education, 32*(3), 421-439. doi: 10.1080/01587919.2011.610293

Bigatel, P. M., Ragan, L. C., Kennan, S., May, J., & Redmond, B. F. (2012). The identification of competencies for online teaching success. *Journal of Asynchronous Learning Networks, 16*(1), 59-77.

Boling, E. C., Hough, M., Krinsky, H., Saleem, M., & Stevens, M. (2012). Cutting the distance in distance education: Perspectives on what promotes positive, online learning experiences. *The Internet and Higher Education, 15*(2), 118-126. doi: 10.1016/j.iheduc.2011.11.006

Bollinger, D. U., Supanakorn, S., & Boggs, C. (2010). Impact of podcasting on student motivation in the online learning environment. *Computers & Education, 55*(2), 714-722. doi: 10.1016/j.compedu.2010.03.004

Buchanan, W. (2013). Too MOOC or not? *ASEE Prism, 22*(9), 61-62.

Carril, P. C. M., Sanmamed, M. G., & Sellés, N. H. (2013). Pedagogical roles and competencies of university teachers practicing in the e-learning environment. *International Review of Research in Open and Distance Learning, 14*(3), 462-487.

Castillo, M. (2013). At issue: Online education and the new community college student. *The Community College Enterprise, 19*(2), 35-46.

Cook, C. W., & Sonnenberg, C. (2014). Technology and online education: Models for change. *ASBBS eJournal, 10*(1), 43-59.

Curry, K. (2010). Warcraft and civic education: MMORPGs as participatory cultures and how teachers can use them to improve civic education. *The Social Studies, 101*(6), 250-253.

Dronholz, J. (2005). Higher education: More students, higher prices, tougher competition. *The Wall Street Journal*, p. R.4.

Fillion, G., Limayem, M., Laferrière, T., & Mantha, R. (2008). Integrating ICT into higher education: A study of onside vs. online students' and professors' perceptions. *International Jounral of Web-Based Learning and Teaching Technologies, 3*(2), 48-72. doi: 10.4018/jwltt.2008040104

Gibson, S., Harris, M. L., & Colaric, S. M. (2008). Technology acceptance in an academic context: Facultly acceptance of online education. *Journal of Education for Business, 83*(6), 355-359.

Goodyear, P., Salmon, G., Spector, J. M., Steeples, C., & Tickner, S. (2001). Competences for online teaching: A special report. *Educational Technology Research and Development, 49*(1), 65-72.

Kear, K., Donelan, H., & Williams, J. (2014). Using wikis for online group projects: Student and tutor perspectives. *International Review of Research in Open and Distance Learning, 15*(4) Retrieved from http://search.proquest.com/docview/1634290322?accountid=458

Ledbetter, A. M., & Finn, A. N. (2013). Teacher technology policies and online communication apprehension as predictors of learner empowerment. *Communication Education, 62*(3), 301-317. doi: 10.1080/03634523.2013.794386

Liu, I.-F., Chen, M. C., Sun, Y. S., Wible, D., & Kuo, C.-H. (2010). Extending the TAM model to explore the factors that affect intention to use an online learning community. *Computers & Education, 54*(2), 600-610. doi: 10.1016/j.compedu.2009.09.009

Omar, A., Kalulu, D., & Alijani, G. S. (2011). Management of innovative e-learning environments. *Academy of Educational Leadership Journal, 15*(3), 37-64.

Pak, M. S. (2013). Competition and reform in higher education. *USA Business Review, 12*(3), 277-285.

Saldaña, J. M. (2009) *The coding manual for qualitative researchers*, Sage Publications, Thousand Oaks, CA.

Sandelowski, M. (2000). Whatever happened to qualitative description? *Research in Nursing & Health, 23*(4), 334-340. doi: 10.1002/1098-240X(200008)

Sander, P., Stevenson, K., King, M., & Coats, D. (2000). University students' expectations of teaching. *Studies in Higher Education, 25*(3), 309-323. doi: 10.1080/03075070050193433

Shah, S., & Meisenberg, G. (2012). Opinions about teaching modalities: A comparison between faculty and students. *Education Research International, 2012.* Retrieved from http://www.hindawi.com/journals/edri/2012/604052/

Williams, P. E. (2003). Roles and competencies for distance education programs in higher education institutions. *American Journal of Distance Education, 17*(1), 45-57. doi: 10.1207/S15389286AJDE1701_4

Yoon, T. (2014). The application of virtual simulations using Second Life in a foreign language classroom. *Journal of Education and Learning, 8*(1), 78-84. Retrieved from http://journal.uad.ac.id/index.php/EduLearn

Feeling Anxious: Students' Perceptions and Emotions Relative to Online Assessments in College Courses

Catherine F. Brooks
University of Arizona
Tucson, Arizona, USA
cfbrooks@email.arizona.edu

Abstract: Technology-based testing tools are being utilized in a variety of college course types (e.g., online, face-to-face). Though online assessments are often designed to provide students flexibility and ease, students' perceptions of these assessments have not been fully interrogated. Providing student narratives about online testing or quizzing experiences, this research interpretively analyzes student stories about and experiences with online assessments, specifically timed exams and quizzes. The student narratives as data are drawn from across hybrid college courses – those relying on similar online assessment types – on two large, western, public campuses, and this essay presents findings thematically. This research suggests that students enjoy immediate feedback on their performance, but are often concerned about their teacher not being 'there' during online exams and quizzes. Overall, these data show that students experience anxiety relative to online testing events.

Introduction

Students on college campuses are increasingly exposed to a variety of course types, to include those fully online or hybridized across face-to-face and virtual environments. Hybrid courses are often referenced as 'blended' classrooms – those that work across face-to-face and online environments (Mansour & Mupinga, 2007; Rovai & Jordan, 2004). Flipped classrooms, sometimes called 'inverted' classrooms, are hybrid in nature, but they distinctly emphasize online content delivery (e.g., online lectures with face-to-face projects, active knowledge application, or discussion) (Lage, Platt, & Treglia, 2000). Students in flipped courses gain information and content through delivery systems like recorded lectures or podcasts (Berrett, 2012), with face-to-face classroom reserved for interactive activities.

As part of all of these emerging and evolving classroom formats, students are exposed to a variety of online assessment types. Kearns (2012) identifies five categories of online assessments: written assignments, online discussion, fieldwork, quizzes and exams, or presentations. This research focuses on quizzes and exams as a particular type of online assessment, and the ways in which students engage with and perceive these online testing events.

Considering students' experiences with assessments amid the many shifts in classroom format or instructional design is important given scholars' assertions about the degree to which a learner's emotional state can impact educational processes (e.g., Titsworth, Quinlan, & Mazer, 2010). Certainly, we know that student emotions are an important aspect of any learning experience (Brooks & Young, 2015), and "emotional arousal heightens a student's attention, making it easier [for them] to encode more information" (Mazer, 2013, p. 256). In addition to goals for bringing about positive student emotion in classrooms, instructors can deploy approaches that are generally beneficial in educational processes. With regard to assessment, specifically, Beebe (2010) suggests, "promoting sustainable high levels of student performance depends not only on a thorough knowledge of pedagogical content, but also on a well-designed assessment process that concurrently informs teaching and promotes learning" (p. 3). Assessments are thus important in any educational context, and so is an understanding of students' impressions of and emotions tied to their educational experience.

This essay offers a brief review of existing literature on online assessment efforts. As part of that review, the ways online strategies differ from face-to-face efforts are considered. Then, this essay provides a brief discussion of the methodology and research process engaged with this project before the findings are presented. Overall, this research interrogates how students perceive online assessment events.

Online Assessment and Related Literature

Online assessments differ from those taking place in face-to-face environments, depending on the ways in which those assessments are deployed. Online tests or quizzes, for example, can be offered synchronously – mirroring the 'time-certain' nature of face-to-face exams. Online exams also can be timed, similar to the way students are required to complete an assessment during formal course meeting time in a face-to-face environment. At minimum, we know that online assessment "differs from the strategies used in traditional, f2f classrooms [given that] instructor-student interactions in the virtual world are mediated by a computer interface rather than in a f2f setting structured by means of interpersonal exchange" (Beebe, et al., 2010, p. 3). Without interpersonal cues from instructors, students may be missing important social information regarding testing events.

As with most of educational practice, online assessment success can be assumed to be something that works for some students in particular contexts but not others, dependant on a variety of factors such as learning style, course topic, or student level. However, Neuhauser (2002) found social factors like gender, age, or learning preferences and styles had little effect on the type of course a student would take (e.g., online or face-to-face) and had no significant influence on their performance within their course. Similarly, Aragon, Johnson, and Shaik (2002) explored student learning style and success across online and face-to-face courses and found that learning success happened regardless of student preferred learning style. That is, "learners can be just as successful in the online environment as they can in the face-to-face environment, regardless of their learning style preferences" (Aragon, et al., 2002, p. 243). With regard to assessment specifically, research shows comparable student performance and perceptions of fairness across computer-based and face-to-face tests (Escudier, Newton, Cox, Reynolds, & Odell, 2011), with social variables like gender differences having no effect on the success of computer-assisted assessment (Stephens, 2001).

Of particular interest for this project is how students view online assessment and how they may be impacted emotionally or perceptually. Researchers (e.g., Stephens, 2001) have underscored the importance of alleviating computer anxiety when using computer-based assessments, but certainly student behaviors with and perceptions of computers continue to evolve over time and in historic context. So, this research means to interrogate impressions among a set of contemporary students, more than a decade after the Stephens (2001) study, thereby contributing to an ongoing conversation among practitioners and scholars interested in online pedagogies.

Methodology and this Study

This study focuses on students' narratives about online assessments (i.e., quizzes, exams) involving a variety of question or prompt types (e.g., multiple choice questions, essay-type questions). This project focuses on students in hybrid college courses – Gainey and Dukes (2013) describe hybrid courses as those "delivered using various technologies" while some of the class is offered "in a face-to-face classroom setting" (p. 6). In these hybrid courses, students were expected to complete synchronous and timed quizzes and exams online. The student narratives (N = 346), treated as data, are drawn from across eight college-level hybrid college courses on two large, western, public campuses and across three academic departments training large numbers of undergraduate college students. Students were asked to report on their impressions of synchronous, objective, and timed online assessments (i.e., exams and quizzes) in their hybrid classes (a course they were enrolled in at the time).

This study is interpretive in nature, with findings presented thematically. That is, the data were read, then re-read, and organized by 'codes' that emerged during the analysis – these interpretive methods are in line with those suggested by Miles and Huberman (1994) for qualitative data. The findings are ideographic and can speak to students' individualized experiences. Thus, this project is not intended to capture all that happens for students during online assessments of different types, but to instead, offer a set of findings that can inform the deployment of online assessments in college courses. The results offered as part of this project are not generalizable, that is, but rather transferable across similar students in similar learning contexts.

Findings

The narratives of students offer a glimpse of the diverse opinions about online assessments. While some were enthusiastic about the flexibility embedded in online experiences, others voiced tension and anxiety with regard to online tests in their courses. These students highlight some of the main practical and mundane issues tied to online assessments. This section offers the most salient themes derived from the data set, findings that can inform online and instructional practice.

Flexibility: Avoiding Distraction, and Carving a Space

Flexibility and comfort were emphasized by many students who voice happiness about taking exams without being in the presence of their classmates. Pointing to the efficiency and ease with which one could take an online exam, Suzie said, "I woke up an hour and fifteen minutes before the exam so I was able to eat breakfast and do some last minute studying…I was home alone so I had peace and quiet with no possible disruptions. My room was a comfortable temperature, not too hot not too cold" – she expressed pleasure at being able to take time for eating and preparing, as well as at being able to control the testing atmosphere. John, similarly, explained, "I found the environment to be a little more relaxing because we got to choose where to take the test," and Mark said, "I like taking the exams online much better then taking exams in the classroom. It is much less pressure. Even though there is a time frame there is still some flexibility." Mary articulates her view on the testing environment by explaining, "Sitting on a cafe patio near the beach doing classwork is much more relaxing than a plain lecture hall with no windows and 200 other students sitting all around you." Indeed, most students were like Suzie and others, expressing gratitude for the opportunity to ease into the testing experience.

Distractions, though occurring within and beyond the physical classroom, are somewhat minimized with online assessments, depending on timing and student ability to situate themselves in a comfortable location. Brenda explained that she liked taking online exams outside of her classroom because, "sometimes during a test in class, it's hard to focus – you either have someone with a cold sneezing non-stop, or the person next to you presses their pencil very hard." Michelle, however, was more limited and unable to seek comfort: "In the library or study center, I found the environment to be somewhat distracting, but didn't have enough time to go to a more private location in between classes."

Overall, most of these students seemed pleased with the locative possibilities afforded by online assessments. As Daniel mentioned, "The advantages of taking the exams online definitely outweigh any disadvantages. I love the fact that I can be sitting on my couch, in a stress free environment the entire time. Sitting in a classroom, taking a test with a pencil seems so old school." Though students were primarily pleased with the flexibility and lack of distraction tied to their out-of-class testing environment, many voiced both pros and cons tied to some of the practical aspects of online assessments, discussed next.

Practicality: Timing, Question Format, Teacher Presence, and Immediate Results

These students pointed to a number of practical implications of the testing procedure. As opposed to a 'take-home' exam or non-timed experience, these students were expected to engage in synchronous, online, and timed quizzes and exams that allowed roughly one minute per question. Synchronous exams refer to timing of the experience – all students took the exams and quizzes at the same time and typically at the beginning of the course's official start time. These 'multiple choice' style timed quizzes and exams offered one question at a time, questions were randomized, and students were unable to backtrack to questions they had answered previously. These parameters were in place so that students were unable to complete assessments collaboratively or rely on exams of others when taking their own test.

Given these parameters, timing was the issue that was often emphasized in students' narratives about their experiences – indeed, students voiced anxiety tied to being timed. Some, like Shane, voiced frustration with the timing aspect of the experience, "one minute to answer each questions was not enough time for me," and Troy was like many others who explained, "I was a little apprehensive because the exam was timed." Other students sounded more extreme, calling these online assessments a "race against time" or something that can "lead to stress guessing." Indeed, some students reported that they were "constantly looking at the running clock" – and continually worried about the timed nature of the exam. Marti explained a kind of arc of concern: "When the exam began I thought, my gosh, one minute per question! I found myself trying to speed through the questions because I felt like a minute could not possibly be enough for each question. When the test was coming to an end though, though, I noticed I had so much time left on my hands." Marti continued and explained that she thought, "Did I really just speed through that exam when I still have 5 minutes left? I could have gone slower. . . . I need to relax."

In addition to timing issues, students referenced concern about their lack of ability to go back and review questions answered previously in the experience. This issue of 'backtracking' on questions in an exam commonly inspired students to reflect on and compare their online and face-to-face-to-face assessments. Salvatore, for example, compared the online and face-to-face experiences, expressing, "One issue that I had was, during a test in class, you can go back and erase something if you suddenly remember you made a mistake a few questions back. Online when the page changes every question and you cannot go back, it's a bummer when you realize you made a mistake." Brandon similarly compared the online and face-to-face testing experience, "The one question at a time aspect is unfortunate because you can't save troubling questions for the end as I am used to doing." Mae concurred: "Taking an online test is pretty much the same as taking a test in classroom. The only real difference, at least in this class, was not being able to go back and look at my answers. I found that made me a little anxious. Normally if I don't know an answer right away, I skip it and go back to it. That way I don't feel like I'm taking up to much time on one question and feel rushed on the rest of the questions. Then I go back and try to make an educated guess on the question I skipped, thinking through all the possible answers."

Issues tied to the inability to 'backtrack' during assessments were often raised in conjunction with concerns about timing. Indeed, many were like Amy who spoke overall about the online question format, blending concerns about timing and backtracking in this way:

> I found that I usually had more time than needed to finish the exam but felt myself rushing through it to complete it in time. I would often get to the last couple of questions and realize I had more than enough time left. By then I would have rushed through the exam and cannot go back and double check my answers.

Certainly the issue of timing and backtracking were tied together, as Amy suggested, and overall, question format and test deployment strategies among teachers were influential in students' testing experiences. Nicholas, clearly articulated comparisons of face-to-face and online testing that permeated the data:

> I remember contemplating on the fact that if we submitted an answer to a question, that was it! No turning back. What if I didn't submit the right answer? I can't even go back and look them over! This was my biggest problem. I tend to rush and let my nerves take over. So when I'm in a class where I take the exam in person, it gives me the ability to look back and check my answers. My first online exam was definitely a challenge, but as I became more familiar with the process as other exams followed, I became use to it and it became preferred over face-to-face tests.

Timing assessments and removing students' ability to 'backtrack' on questions were pedagogical choices that influenced these students' experiences in profound ways.

Students continually referenced their lack of face-to-face support during their online assessments. Ethan described the thing that distinguishes online experiences with those face-to-face: "When you take an exam in class, if you are unsure of the meaning or wording of a question, the professor is there to clarify for you." Similarly, Ashlee described, "it would be nice to have an instructor present if questions arose." Andy just liked the physical 'feel' of an exam, explaining that "…having an actual physical paper is easier for test taking. Being able to feel the test, write on it, and cross out potential wrong answers is a plus."

Alexia pointed to the stress of 'finishing' her exam, "As I moved onto the last question on the exam, I immediately felt the pit in my stomach, that anxious knot I get before I click "submit. It's torturous to click that button. I loathe that button." However, students like Logan articulated, "I absolutely love that the results of all exams and quizzes are virtually instantaneous. As soon as we hit "submit quiz" we get the gratification of knowing right there and then how we did on the assignment." Griffin too, explained, "The part that I enjoyed the most was the fact that our results were available immediately after the test."

In terms of the practicality of online assessments, then, these students were pleased with certain aspects of online exams and quizzes, and unhappy with others. These students were discomforted by the timed nature of their tests as well as their inability to 'backtrack' to questions or prompts encountered early on in the assessment experience. These students, too, voiced concern about the lack of a teacher 'feel' during the assessment – they noted the ways in which their instructors seemed unavailable for questions or support. Across the data set, however, students raved about the swift marking or grading results – achieving an immediate grade for their work was somehow rewarding and pleasing for these students. The next section will move beyond mundane and practical matters and explore the emergence of anxiety talk in these students' narratives.

Emotion: Anticipatory Anxiety, but the Comfort of Others

Most generally, students voiced initial anxiety with regard to the online assessment process. Andrew, for example spoke of his anxious feelings overall:

> I felt perturbed and anxious. I was hoping no one would distract me, I was hoping the internet would work. I was thinking about so many things that I hardly thought of the exam at all. I stared, eagerly clicking refresh until it was time to take the exam. I try to take it as soon as possible so I can get the torture over with. Immediately the other computer users started talking, I was partially intrigued by their conversation while also being annoyed that the computer lab was so noisy.

Andrew used words like 'torture' and spoke of being 'annoyed' and seemed generally disturbed by the online assessment process. More specifically, Andrew described the waiting-related emotions as he stared at his computer anxiously. Isabella, similarly, talked about the anticipation:

> I always got to the computer early, so I would look over my notes and the book to prepare, and wait for the exam to start. I was always anxious because I was there early and wanted to begin the exam so I could get something else done before my next classes, but because of the time limit I had to wait.

This notion of 'waiting' and experiencing anticipatory anxiety was continually voiced by a wide variety of students. As Carla explained, the moment of 'beginning' the online assessment is an important one:

> I sit in the chair anxiously, my muscles start to tense up, I start to feel butterflies in my stomach. I'm not sure if I have test anxiety but I do know that I get the serious case of the jitters before taking any test. I stare at the screen for a short amount of time, probably around 30 second, until I gather my composure. Then I click start.

Though emotions in the classroom are influential in students' learning processes (Titsworth, et al., 2010), and have been linked to other positive outcomes (e.g., Brooks and Young, 2015), these students offered commentary on some of the major physiological experiences tied to the expectation for and anticipation of online assessments. Indeed, muscle tension alongside 'butterflies' and 'jitters' are serious physiological responses for these students awaiting their tests.

Students who may have otherwise experienced additional anxiety found solace in one another. Though synchronous exams, one minute-per-question, no backtracking, randomized, one-question-at-a-time were designed to help students avoid collaborative test-taking, these students reported shared experiences. Beth explained, "I have had a couple of really hard classes, where I was worried about taking the exam so, in the past, a group of us met up at my apartment. We all used our laptops and helped each other take the exam together." Given that their exam questions differed across students, the 'help' offered by peers was likely emotional in nature. Kara explained, similarly, the importance of sharing the testing experience with others even though questions differ across students: "Although we are not supposed to take the exam with other students, I usually sit with one or two friends in the library while we take the exam individually." Though the exam itself involved randomized questions, timed responses, and did not allow backtracking to early test questions, these students expressed comfort in knowing that other students were simply around for psycho-social support during the exam experience.

These students raised a number of perspectives – both positive and negative – with regard to online testing in their hybrid courses. These findings are in some ways in line with research done more than a decade ago (Stephens, 2001). While Stephens (2001) found potentially more 'dated' concerns among students including the fear of computer crashes – something not particularly salient for these students – other findings were similar: not seeing all questions at once was a concern, but swift turnaround of grades and a relaxed feel to online exams were celebrated among students.

Concluding Reflections

Though these findings are ideographic in nature and cannot be generalized to all students engaging in online assessments, these data are transferrable to similar contexts and can be of use for readers with interests in teacher education. Indeed, this project offers a glimpse of how students are faring amid shifts in pedagogy and trends away from paper-based classroom experiences. Teacher educators as well as those deploying technology-rich pedagogies in their classrooms can consider these data in relation to their own day-to-day work. Contemporary teachers, those working across student levels and institution type, will benefit from considering the importance of student comfort and positive emotion during 'new' types of assessment events and related activities. Alongside changes in praxis are the many implications for students – continual reflection on how these shifts impact students' learning experiences are paramount to good teaching in today's educational environment.

As mentioned previously, these findings are a contribution to an ongoing conversation among practitioners and scholars about online assessment. Given that these students gave of a sense of concern about instructors not being 'there' online, future research ought to examine the ways in which teacher presence (Arbaugh & Hwang, 2006) can be enacted during assessment events in order to mitigate negative student perceptions tied to online activities. Future work might also interrogate the depth of students' anxieties during actual testing events. Given the debilitating power of anxiety, parsing out particularly anxious activities and considering means for addressing students' concerns and fears is paramount to conscientious teaching. It is indeed possible that simply encouraging students to engage in online assessments in groups – when possible – can be beneficial to them; simply allowing others to test nearby or share in an online community while testing might give important comfort to any test taker; future research can explore this notion. In any case, as educators and scholars, we are far from fully understanding the many ramifications of online pedagogies – we have considerable work to do in order to address the needs of contemporary students amid a shifting terrain toward increasing amounts of technology-based activities to include the variety of online assessment types available for use in our classrooms.

References

Aragon, S. R., Johnson, S. D., & Shaik, N. (2002). The influence of learning style preferences on studetn success in online versus face-to-face environments. *The American Journal of Distance Education, 16*(4), 227-244.

Arbaugh, J. B., & Hwang, A. (2006). Does "teaching presence" exist in online MBA courses? . *The Internet and Higher Education, 9*(1), 9-21.

Beebe, R., Vonderwell, S., & Boboc, M. (2010). Emerging patterns in transferring assessment preactices from F2F to online environments. *Electronic Journal of e-Learning, 8*(1), 1-12. Retrieved from http://www.ejel.org/issue/download.html?idArticle=157.

Berrett, D. (2012). How 'flipping' the classroom can improve the traditional lecture. *The Chronicle of Higher Education, Feb. 19, 2012.*

Brooks, C. F., & Young, S. L. (2015). Emotion in online college classrooms: Examining the influence of perceived teacher communication behavior on students' emotional experiences. *Technology, Pedagogy, and Education*, http://dx.doi.org/10.1080/1475939X.2014.995215.

Escudier, M. P., Newton, T. J., Cox, M. J., Reynolds, P. A., & Odell, E. W. (2011). University students' attainment and perceptions of computer delivered assessment; a comparison between computer-based and traditional tests in a 'high-stakes' examination. *Journal of Computer-Assisted Learning, 27*, 440-447.

Gainey, T. W., & Dukes, S. (2013). Examining student perspecctives of the college experience: The impact of on-line learning. *American Journal of Educational Studies, 6*(1), 5-16.

Kearns, L. R. (2012). Student assessment in online learning: Cahllenges and effective practices. *MERLOT Journal of Online Learning and Teaching, 8*(3), online. Retrieved from: http://jolt.merlot.org/vol8no3/kearns_0912.htm.

Lage, M. J., Platt, G. J., & Treglia, M. (2000). Inverting the classroom: A gateway to creating an inclusive learning environment. *The Journal of Economic Education, 31*, 30-43.

Mansour, B., & Mupinga, D. (2007). Students' positive and negative experiences in hybrid and online classes. *College Student Journal, 41*(1), 242-248.

Mazer, J. P. (2013). Student emotional and cognitive interest as mediators of teacher communication behaviors and student engagement: An examination of direct and indirect effects. *Communication Education, 62*(3), 253-277.

Miles, M. B., & Huberman, A. M. (1994). *An expanded resource: Qualitative data analysis* (2nd ed.). Thousand Oaks, CA: Sage.

Neuhauser, C. (2002). Learning style and effectiveness of online and face-to-face instruction. *American Journal of Distance Education, 16*(2), 99-113.

Rovai, A. P., & Jordan, H. M. (2004). Blended learning and sense of community: A comparative analysis with traditional and fully online graduate courses. *International Review of Research in Open and Distance Learning [Online], 5*(2), http://www.irrodl.org/index.php/irrodl/article/view/192/795.

Stephens, D. (2001). Use of computer assisted assessment: Benefits to students and staff. *Education for Information, 19*, 265-275.

Titsworth, S., Quinlan, M. M., & Mazer, J. P. (2010). Emotion in teaching and learning: Development and validation of the classroom emotions scale. *Communication Education, 59*(4), 431-452.

Measuring 21st Century Skills in Technology Educators

Rhonda Christensen
University of North Texas, USA
Rhonda.christensen@gmail.com

Gerald Knezek
University of North Texas, USA
gknezek@gmail.com

Curby Alexander
Texas Christian University, USA
Curby.alex@tcu.edu

Dana Owens
University of Texas at Arlington, USA
danasuzanneowens@gmail.com

Theresa Overall
University of Maine, Farmington, USA
Theresa.overall@maine.edu

Garry Mayes
University of North Texas, USA
Garry.mayes@unt.edu

Abstract: Data gathered from 195 preservice and inservice teachers at four universities during 2014 were used to determine the suitability of the newly revised Technology Proficiency Self Assessment (TPSA C21) for release for wide-scale distribution. Findings were that the four original scales of the TPSA maintained respectable reliability estimates ranging from .73 to .86, while two new scales focusing on emerging technologies yielded Cronbach's Alpha internal consistency reliability estimates of .84 and .91. While university students at all sites generally agreed or strongly agreed that they were proficient in most technology-related skills, one group of accelerated masters students reported less proficiency than anticipated. The authors conclude that the TPSA C21 continues the reliable and valid measurement tradition of the TPSA spanning more than a decade, and extends that tradition with the addition of two scales designed to assess educator skills regarding emerging new technologies. The instrument should continue to be useful as a tool for identifying the professional development needs of an individual teacher or customizing the type of technology-infused professional development inservice needed by a particular school or school district or to assess preservice education students' proficiency in technology for education.

Introduction

In the competency-based environment that surrounds 21st Century education, proficiency in technology itself has also assumed an important role whether it is used to enhance instruction, used for communication between teachers, students and parents or used to assess student learning. The ability to integrate 21st century technology for learning in schools is an expectation for educators. It is important to measure whether or not teachers are confident in their ability to integrate the evolving tools in order to target professional development. Using valid and reliable instruments to assess teachers' perceived proficiency with 21st Century technology tools is an important step in targeting appropriate levels in school-wide training activities, as well as planning meaningful developmental pathways for individual teachers.

This study uses an instrument that measures educators' self-efficacy in their ability to integrate technology into the classroom. Self-efficacy is the concept that provides the underlying rationale for the Technology Proficiency Self Assessment (TPSA). Self-efficacy is based on Bandura's (1977, 1986) social development theory, and is sometimes defined as the expression of beliefs of individuals related to their own capacity to perform a certain behavior (Gencturk, Gokcek, & Gunes, 2010). As reported by Gencturk, Gokcek, and Gunes (2010), teachers with higher self-efficacy are more ambitious and passionate in their teaching (Tuckman & Sexton, 1990), while Collis (1996) observed that these types of teachers shape "... the success or eventual lack of success in any computers-in-education initiative" (p. 22). Henson (2003) found that teacher efficacy is an important component of a classroom teacher's success or failure. The authors of this paper have proposed an operational definition of self-efficacy as *confidence in one's competence*.

Purpose of the Study

The purpose of this study was to determine the usability of the updated TPSA instrument in the 21st century classroom environment. These environments commonly use new information technologies that did not exist when the original TPSA was created. The original Technology Proficiency Self Assessment (TPSA) has been used since 1997 in its original form with only a few minor modifications (changing Alta Vista as a search engine example to Google). The survey instrument has retained its reliability even in the evolving arena of educational technology. An additional 14 items were added to the original TPSA to assess newly emerging technologies such as mobile learning and Web 2.0 tools. These items were added in response to the general trend over time that previously challenging skills became routine for most teachers. The four TPSA subscales were used to gather data over a ten-year period from 2002 to 2011 on preservice and inservice teachers. As shown in Figure 1, teacher confidence in technology proficiency skills increased over the ten-year time frame, likely because of the focus on technology integration in education that grew over that period of time.

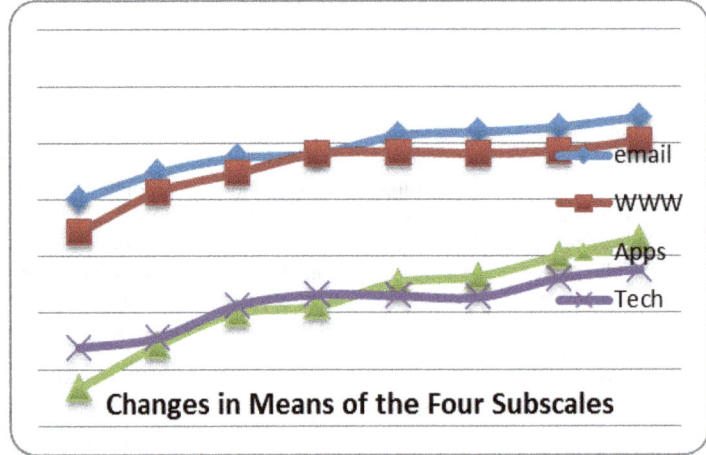

Figure 1. Ten-year trends for the development of educator technology skills.

The new instrument, the Technology Proficiency Self-Assessment for 21st Century Learning (TPSA C21) was used in this study to measure both students from four different universities in educator preparation programs.

Methodology

Participants

Data were gathered from 195 students from four universities at various levels in their teacher education programs. The majority of students were in teacher preparation programs while a few of the students were inservice teachers taking masters' level courses. The mean age of the participants was 24.41 ranging from 18 to 57. As is the case in most education programs in the US, the majority (78%) of the participants responding to the survey were females. The number of students from each university is displayed in Table 1. The groups of students differed in their level of technology instruction. Each of the groups is described in the following section.

Table 1
Number of Participants by University Site

Site	n
University 1 preservice	66
University 2 preservice	19
University 3 preservice	31
University 4 preservice	55
University 3 inservice	18
Other	6
Total	195

University 1 is a mid-size independent university in the southwestern part of the United States. The course in which the data were collected is an Introduction to Education class that is required for every student who plans to enroll in the College of Education. The majority of the students are freshmen and sophomores. The course provides students with a broad overview of many aspects of the U.S. education system, including the attributes and practices of effective teachers. This class is divided into three parts including students' participation in class activities that pertain to a selected topic in education (e.g., philosophies of education), observation in area schools, and small group discussion of class content and observations in small groups. This class serves as a prerequisite for the educational technology class, so most of the students are either concurrently enrolled in both courses or have had no coursework in educational technology.

University 2 is a small public liberal arts university in New England with close to half of the 1700 students in teacher preparation programs. The course in which the data were collected is a sophomore-level, 12-credit block of classes required for all secondary/middle education majors. The classes are curriculum, instruction, and assessment; classroom management; technology integration; and an intense field experience in which students are placed in a classroom in their content area and participate fully with middle or high school students from 7:00am to 2:00pm. After an initial two-week orientation on campus, there are six weeks of course work and 6 weeks in the field during the semester on a three-week rotation. Pre-requisites to the practicum block are a two-credit introduction to secondary/middle education and a two-credit introduction to special education grades 7-12 which includes a service learning mentoring experience at a local middle school. In the introduction courses, faculty utilize instructional technology and require students to use a variety of technologies in their assignments.

University 3 is a large public university serving 36,000 students in a suburban area in the southwestern part of the United States. There were two groups of participants from this university, junior and senior level undergraduate, preservice students enrolled in a technology integration course; and a group of inservice educators who were enrolled in one of the first courses of an online, accelerated-schedule masters' degree program. The preservice students were at the beginning of a technology integration course that teaches the competencies measured by the TPSA. The TPSA will be given again at the end of the semester to measure the change during the semester.

University 4 is a large Hispanic-serving university of over 34,000 students located in an urban area in the southwestern part of the United States. The participants in this study were juniors or seniors enrolled a technology integration course in the College of Education. With no prerequisites for the course, the range of technology skills that students possess varies a great deal. In the course, students learn to use various educational software programs as well as develop lesson plans that include a technology component. Participants must select the most appropriate software and/or technology resources to include in their lesson plans. Each student must produce a website that serves as an electronic portfolio to organize resources for teaching that they have developed during the course.

Instrumentation

The Technology Proficiency Self-Assessment (TPSA) was originally developed to measure preservice and inservice teacher confidence in their competence based on a technology proficiency checklist implemented at

Michigan State University (Ropp, 1999). The instrument included 20 items measuring four subscales: (1) E-mail, (2) World Wide Web, (3) Integrated Applications, and (4) Teaching with Technology. An additional 14 items related to emerging technologies were added to make it a 34-item likert type survey. Factor analysis on a larger set of data revealed the 14 items created two different subscales. One of the additional subscales was related to teaching with emerging technologies and the second subscale was related to emerging technology skills. Internal consistency reliability was run on the data producing Cronbach's Alpha shown in Table 2.

Table 2

Internal Consistency Reliabilities for Six Scales on TPSA 21C

Subscale	Cronbach's Alpha	N of items
Email subscale	.73	5
WWW subscale	.73	5
Integrated Applications subscale	.79	5
Teaching with Technology	.86	5
Teaching with Emerging Technologies	.91	8
Emerging Technologies Skills	.84	6
Entire survey	.96	34

Procedures

The TPSA C21 was administered online to preservice and inservice teachers at four universities in two states during the spring and fall of 2014. The 34-item likert type survey was found to be reliable based on Cronbach's Alpha and valid as tested using factor analysis.

Results

As shown in Table 3, the different groups varied a great deal on each of the subscales. Four out of the five groups rated their highest level of proficiency on the E-mail subscale. As might be expected given that most of the participants are preservice teachers, their lowest level of proficiency was in the two subscales related to teaching with technology (Teaching with Technology and Teaching with Emerging Technologies).

Item analysis was completed on the 34 items on the TPSA to look more closely at the level of difficulty educator groups perceived each item. As shown in Table 4, items were ordered by the level of difficulty from highest mean (least difficult) to lowest mean (most difficult). For each item an asterisk was placed in the column representing the factor in which it belonged. While the original subscales of E-mail (S1) and World Wide Web (S2) contained most of the easiest items, the item rated most difficult (creating a web page) was also on the World Wide Web subscale. Most of the difficult items were found on the Teaching with Emerging Technologies subscale (S5).

Table 3

Mean Scores for Inservice and Preservice Teachers on the TPSA C21

	Univ 1 Preservice	Univ 2 Preservice	Univ 3 Preservice	Univ 4 Preservice	Univ 3 Inservice	All Participants
Email subscale	4.68 (.40)	4.74 (.33)	4.60 (.50)	4.73 (.48)	4.50 (.92)	4.68 (.50)
WWW subscale	4.50 (.46)	4.69 (.38)	4.38 (.55)	4.78 (.42)	4.32 (.98)	4.58 (.55)
Integrated Applications subscale	4.32 (.63)	4.51 (.63)	4.10 (.72)	4.54 (.49)	4.22 (1.10)	4.37 (.68)
Teaching with	4.02 (.77)	4.42 (.55)	4.09 (.83)	4.51 (.54)	4.16 (1.07)	4.24 (.76)

Technology Teaching with Emerging Technologies	4.27 (.60)	4.34 (.92)	4.40 (.64)	4.54 (.55)	4.09 (1.19)	4.37 (.71)
Emerging Technologies Skills	4.48 (.60)	4.63 (.60)	4.55 (.49)	4.57 (.65)	4.36 (.92)	4.52 (.63)

Table 4
TPSA C21 Items Ordered by Difficulty

	Items from Easiest to Most Difficult	Mean (SD)	S1	S2	S3	S4	S5	S6
	I feel confident that I could…							
TP1	send e-mail to a friend.	4.94 (.39)	*					
TP6	use an Internet search engine (e.g., Google) to find Web pages related to my subject matter interests.	4.92 (.39)		*				
TP4	send a document as an attachment to an e-mail message.	4.91 (.42)	*					
TP14	use the computer to create a slideshow presentation.	4.86 (.52)			*			
TP32	send and receive text messages.	4.84 (.61)						*
TP9	keep track of Web sites I have visited so that I can return to them later. (An example is using bookmarks.)	4.76 (.63)			*			
TP33	transfer photos or other data via a smartphone.	4.75 (.66)					*	
TP5	keep copies of outgoing messages that I send to others.	4.74 (.63)	*					
TP7	search for and find the Smithsonian Institution Web site.	4.69 (.75)			*			
TP31	download and view streaming movies/video clips.	4.66 (.73)						*
TP10	find primary sources of information on the Internet that I can use in my teaching.	4.65 (.69)			*			
TP13	save documents in formats so that others can read them if they have different word processing programs (eg., saving Word, pdf, RTF, or text).	4.65 (.75)				*		
TP30	download and read e-books.	4.62 (.79)						*
TP29	download and listen to podcasts/audio books.	4.58 (.80)						*
TP22	use social media tools for instruction in the classroom. (ex. Facebook, Twitter, etc.)	4.54 (.86)					*	
TP16	write an essay describing how I would use technology in my classroom.	4.48 (.86)				*		
TP18	use technology to collaborate with teachers or students, who are distant from my classroom.	4.44 (.81)				*		
TP27	use mobile devices to connect to others for my professional development.	4.43 (.86)					*	
TP3	create a distribution list" to send e-mail to several people at once.	4.42 (.91)	*					
TP2	subscribe to a discussion list.	4.39	*					

			S1	S2	S3	S4	S5	S6
		(1.01)						
TP28	use mobile devices to have my students access learning activities.	4.34 (.95)					*	
TP34	save and retrieve files in a cloud-based environment.	4.34 (1.02)						*
TP21	integrate mobile technologies into my curriculum.	4.28 (.86)					*	
TP11	use a spreadsheet to create a bar graph of the proportions of the different colors of M&Ms in a bag.	4.26 (1.01)				*		
TP25	teach in a one-to-one environment in which the students have their own device.	4.25 (.94)					*	
TP26	find a way to use a smartphone in my classroom for student responses.	4.24 (1.07)					*	
TP24	use online tools to teach my students from a distance.	4.20 (.96)					*	
TP12	create a newsletter with graphics.	4.18 (1.05)				*		
TP17	create a lesson or unit that incorporates subject matter software as an integral part.	4.18 (.97)				*		
TP19	describe 5 software programs or apps that I would use in my teaching.	4.11 (1.05)				*		
TP23	create a wiki or blog to have my students collaborate.	4.09 (1.06)						*
TP20	write a plan with a budget to buy technology for my classroom.	3.99 (1.02)				*		
TP15	create a database of information about important authors in a subject matter field.	3.92 (1.10)				*		
TP8	create my own web page.	3.87 (1.26)			*			

Note. S1-Email, S2-WWW, S3-Integrated Applications, S4-Teaching with Technology, S5-Teaching with Emerging Technologies, S6-Emerging Technology Skills

Discussion

Group mean differences found in Table 3 generally confirm a priori expectations based on known attributes of the different university groups. For example, university #1 students were in one of their first courses for their education degree so it makes sense that they were proficient in E-mail (Mean = 4.68) and using the World Wide Web (Mean = 4.50) but not necessarily confident in their ability to teach with technology (Mean = 4.02) or teach with emerging technologies (Mean = 4.27). For university #2, the students have been introduced to instructional technology and have been required to use technology in their assignments. They rated themselves high in proficiency for emerging technology skills (Mean = 4.63) in addition to E-mail (Mean = 4.74) and World Wide Web (Mean = 4.69). For university #4, the students were juniors and seniors in their education program so they have likely been expected to use technology in their previous classes. This group of students was very high in all six subscales.

One unexpected outcome also shown in Table 3 is the relatively low reported skill level among the university #3 inservice teachers who were enrolled in an online, accelerated-schedule masters degree program. For most of these educators it was their first or second course in the program. This relatively low reported skill level is similar to findings reported by Tyler-Wood, Knezek, & Christensen (2004) when comparing the technology skills of alternative certification teacher preparation candidates to those of traditional preservice teacher candidates completing their preparations in the context of a four-year undergraduate degree program. Tyler-Wood et al., (2004) found that alternative certification teachers completed their required three credit-hour technology course with technology skills still lower on the average than traditional preservice teachers *began* their technology course sequence. The implication is that teacher candidates in alternative programs may need extra training in technology applications and teaching with technology skills.

The distribution of the asterisks in Table 4 give clues regarding how a technology coordinator for a school district (for example) might select skills to be targeted for mastery at a day-long teacher professional development institute. Most of the asterisks in the top half of Table 4 are in the S1 and S2 columns on the left hand side of the table, while most of the asterisks in the bottom half of the table are in the S3-S6 columns to the right of the table. This indicates most of the easy skills already mastered by most teachers are related to email (S1) and the WWW (S2), while the ones not yet mastered by teachers in general are in the areas of integrated applications (S3), teaching with technology (S4), emerging technologies for the classroom (S5) or emerging technology skills (S6). If a school building was able to have all teachers complete surveys and analyze the responses before the training sessions began, then the coordinator should anchor the skill acquisition goals slightly above the self-reported means in each of the six areas. If the technology coordinator does not have the luxury of assessing the teachers before training begins, then he or she might choose skill development activities in each of the six scale categories, and probably with some variety regarding difficulty level. For example, a technology coordinator for a large school or an entire district might make training available for one easy skill, one average skill, and one difficult skill in each of six categories. Teachers could then be required to select one skill workshop from each column to attend during the professional development day. In this way the orchestrated selection of training workshops would be likely to match the professional development skill levels of most teachers.

Collectively, the findings from this study reinforce what researchers have observed for decades regarding educator professional development for emerging technologies. The presence of technology does not guarantee pedagogically sound use in the classroom. Teachers' attitudes towards computers, their self-efficacy, and a general openness to change, are among the factors that are indicative of effective use in K-12 instructional practice (Christensen, 2002; Wang, Ertmer & Newby, 2004; Anderson & Maninger, 2007; Vannata & Fordham, 2004). In light of this body of research that influences the various factors that impact technology infusion, instrumentation must be carefully designed to derive an accurate picture of technology integration into instruction. The Technology Proficiency Self-Assessment instrument has retained high reliability over the past 15 years as shown in various studies (Ropp, 1999; Christensen & Knezek, 2001; Morales, Knezek, & Christensen, 2008; Gencturk, Gokcek & Gunes, 2010; Mayes, Mills, Christensen & Knezek, 2012). The addition of new subscales to the TPSA enables continuing the high relevance (validity) of the TPSA in the emerging classroom environments of the 21st Century.

Conclusion

Findings of this study indicate that the original scales of the TPSA retain acceptable measurement properties more than a decade after the instrument's creation. In addition, findings also illustrate that the new information technology items contribute new knowledge on technology proficiencies in ways that no longer align with specific technologies but rather with the purposes for which the new technologies are used. Specifically, the new constructs added to the original TPSA assess the extent to which new technologies are useful for a teacher's own professional development and for a teacher to enhance student learning. The TPSA C21 continues and extends an established tradition of reliable and valid measurement with the addition of two scales designed to assess educator skills regarding emerging new technologies.

References

Anderson, S.E., & Maninger, R.M. (2007). Preservice teachers' abilities, beliefs, and intentions regarding technology integration. *Journal of Educational Computing Research*, 37(2), 151-172.

Bandura, A. (1977). Self-efficacy: Toward a unifying theory of behavioral change. *Psychological Review, 84*(2), 191-215.

Bandura, A. (1986). *Social foundations of thought and action: A social cognitive theory*. Englewood Cliffs, NJ: Prentice-Hall, Inc.

Christensen, R. (2002). Effects of technology integration education on the attitudes of teachers and students. *Journal of Research on Technology in Education, 34*(4), 411-433.

Christensen, R. & Knezek, G. (2001). Equity and diversity in K-12 applications of information technology. *Key Instructional Design Strategies: KIDS Project Findings for 2000-2001*. Denton, TX: University of North Texas, Institute for the Integration of Technology into Teaching and Learning.

Collis, B. (1996). The internet as an educational innovation: Lessons from experience with computer implementation. *Educational Technology, 36*(6), 21-30.

Gencturk, E., Gokcek, T., & Gunes, G. (2010). Reliability and validity study of the technology proficiency self-assessment scale. *Procedia Social and Behavioral Sciences, 2*, (2010), 2863-2867.

Henson, R. K. (2003). Relationships between preservice teachers' self-efficacy, task analysis, and classroom management beliefs. *Research in the Schools, 10*(1),53-62.

Mayes, G., Mills, L., Christensen, R. & Knezek, G. (2012). Evolution of technology proficiency perceptions: Construct validity for the technology proficiency self assessment (TPSA) Questionnaire from a Longitudinal Perspective. In P. Resta (Ed.), *Proceedings of Society for Information Technology & Teacher Education International Conference 2012* (pp. 1988-1993). Chesapeake, VA: AACE.

Morales, C., Knezek, G., & Christensen, R. (2008). Self-efficacy ratings of technology proficiency among teachers in Mexico and Texas. *Computers in the Schools, 25*(1), 126-144.

Ropp, M.M. (1999). Exploring individual characteristics associated with learning to use computers and their use as pedagogical tools in preservice teacher preparation. *Journal of Research on Technology in Education, 36*(3), 402-424.

Tuckman, B.W. & Sexton, T.L. (1990). The relation between self-beliefs and self regulated performance. *Journal of Social Behavior and Personality*, 5, 465-472.

Tyler-Wood, T., Knezek, G. & Christensen, R. (2004). Barriers to teaching with technology for alternative certification teachers. In L. Cantoni & C. McLoughlin (Eds.), *Proceedings of World Conference on Educational Multimedia, Hypermedia and Telecommunications 2004* (pp. 3209-3214). Chesapeake, VA: AACE.

Vannatta, R. A. & Fordham, N. (2004). Teacher dispositions as predictors of classroom technology use. *Journal of Research on Technology in Education, 36* (3), 253-271.

Wang, L., Ertmer, P. A., & Newby, T. J. (2004). Increasing preservice teachers' self-efficacy beliefs for technology Integration. *Journal of Research on Technology in Education, 36*(3), 231-250.

The Impact of Teacher Observations with Coordinated Professional Development on Student Performance: A 27-State Program Evaluation

Kelly F. Glassett
University of Utah

Steven H. Shaha
Professor, Center for Policy & Public Administration

Aimee Copas
Executive Director, North Dakota Council of Educational Leaders

Abstract: This study examined a large number of schools and districts across the United States in relation to systemic teacher observation and aligned professional development. Current approaches to teacher evaluation provide minimal feedback for improvement and typically are not aligned to professional development. This study describes a systems wherein PD enables teachers to participate in a full range activities from instructional videos on teaching techniques, to communities of other users, to posting and downloading PD-related materials. Results indicate that systemic observation coupled with aligned professional development impacts student achievement in reading and math.

Introduction

Schools and school districts in the U.S. struggle to address critical learning gaps, and to identify ways to improve the quality of teaching for all students (U.S. Department of Education, 2013). Teacher evaluation, which is part of this process, rarely appears to advance learning for teachers (Daley & Kim, 2010). In many schools, evaluations are hit-or-miss and framed by the principal's lens, as opposed to student learning needs or a particular evaluation instrument. The end result of teacher evaluation should be one that fosters improvements in both professional development opportunities and teaching practice (Darling-Hammond, Wise, & Pease, 1983).

Review of the Literature

A large body of research spanning the last 20 years indicates how much impact teachers have on student growth over time compared to other factors. This research indicates that teachers account for the largest differences between students at the end year after controlling for the differences that students bring to the classroom at the beginning of the year (Gordon, Kane, & Staiger 2006; Rivkin, Hanushek, and Kain, 2000; Rockoff, 2004; Rowan, Correnti, & Miller, 2002; Wright, Horn, & Sanders, 1997).

The evaluation of teachers' classroom performance has gone through major changes over the last 100 years. Not only has teacher evaluation changed but, the beliefs and values surrounding the role of teachers, effective teaching, and theories of student learning (Cuban, 1993; Ellett, 1997; Ellett & Teddlie, 2003). Prior to the 1950s, teacher quality was evaluated from an ethical perspective, with evaluations based on the teachers' personal traits (Ellett & Teddlie, 2003; Good & Mulryan, 1990). From the 1950s forward, the influence of scientific management led to measures of performance based on observable behaviors. Over time, the accumulated knowledge from these efforts came to form the criteria used in many teacher evaluation systems (Ellett & Teddlie, 2003). The practice of teacher classroom evaluations came to be predominately structured as at most once or twice yearly occasions, in which an administrator briefly stopped by a classroom to complete a checklist or ratings form (Peterson, 2004). This model has continued to be the dominant approach to teacher evaluation into the 21st century (Weisberg, Sexton, Mulhern, & Keeling, 2009).

The extant literature has recognized the deficiencies of the typical evaluations conducted by administrators, including critique of the rudimentary inventory of teaching skills typically assessed, inadequate time afforded administrators to provide instructional support, poor training, patterns of assigning uniformly high ratings, and weak relationship of principals' impressions of teacher quality to student achievement (Darling-Hammond, 1986; Jacob & Lefgren, 2008; Haefele, 1993; Medley & Coker, 1987; Peterson, 2000).

The school reform efforts of the 1980s and 1990s brought about increased attention to teacher evaluations as a critical lever for improving the quality of teaching (Brandt, 1995; Darling-Hammond, 1990). With the passage of No Child Left Behind in 2001, there continued to be a trend of expanded state oversight and regulation of local evaluation practices, for example by defining teacher quality, setting minimum standards for evaluator training, and requiring data collection (Hazi & Arredondo Rucinski, 2009).

Sadly, the subsequent evaluation procedures have never been geared towards helping teachers, individually or collectively, improve their skills. Evaluations are generally conducted as infrequent and perfunctory events in satisfaction of bureaucratic requirements (Darling-Hammond, 1986; Stiggins & Bridgeford, 1985; Weisberg et al., 2009).

Teacher evaluations can be utilized for the two related purposes of personal growth and accountability (Duke & Stiggins, 1990). Evaluations can be used to convey expectations, assess current abilities, and plan professional development in service of developing higher levels of professional competence. Evaluations also provide defensible and standardized information to use in human resource decisions. In practice, evaluations are rarely used to inform teachers about instructional areas in need of improvement. Studies have established the generally low emphasis given to instructional improvement and the poor quality of feedback made available to teachers as a result of the evaluation (Frase & Streshley, 1994; Stiggins & Bridgeford, 1985).

Method

The data set analyzed included 292 schools in 110 districts within 27 States. School inclusion was defined as a minimum of 15 teachers per school participating in the same commercially-available online, on-demand PD product widely used in the United States (PD 360 ® and Observation 360 ®, School Improvement Network, Salt Lake City). This PD enabled teachers to participate in a full range activities which range instructional videos on teaching techniques, to communities of other users, to posting and downloading PD-related materials.

Student performance was measured by the percentage of students classified as Proficient or Advanced for Math and for Reading/Language Arts collectively by school using percent's of Proficient or Advanced provided a means for normalizing data across the many States and districts using a variety of assessment instruments. Data were captured form publicly available web-based sources. Pre-PD data reflected the 2010-2011 school year, while Post-PD data were for the 2011-2012 school year.

Additional variables beyond student performance were collected PD School participation data analyzed were extracted from the data automatically captured by the PD provider (School Improvement Network) as a result of PD use. Data were summarized by school, resulting in the following variables for analysis:

- Mean number of observations per teacher
- Means observations with assignments per school (i.e. across teachers)
- Average minutes viewed (i.e. PD video time)
- Forums viewed per teacher
- Forums posted per teacher
- Files downloaded per teacher
- Files uploaded per teacher
- Links downloaded per teacher
- Links uploaded per teacher

Schools were classified into Higher versus Lower Observation Rate groups by dividing the schools into two equal groups of 146 schools each based upon the mean number of observations per teacher. The resulting mean number of observations was 8.49 for the schools classified as Higher Observation Rate, versus 2.76 for Lower Observation Rate schools.

All analyses were conducted using SPSS version 17.0 or higher (PASW Statistics, SPSS, 2009) and Excel (Microsoft Office, 2007). Minimum level of statistical significance was determined a priori at $p<0.05$.

Results & Findings

Math

Schools with Higher Observation Rates experienced significantly greater gains in student performance (see Table 1). Interestingly, and not by design, school with the Lower Observation Rates had Pre-PD student performance levels 7% higher than their Higher Observation Rates counterparts. However, the difference flip-flopped by the end of the PD year wherein the Higher Observation Rates schools shared an 11.5% advantage (see Figure 1).

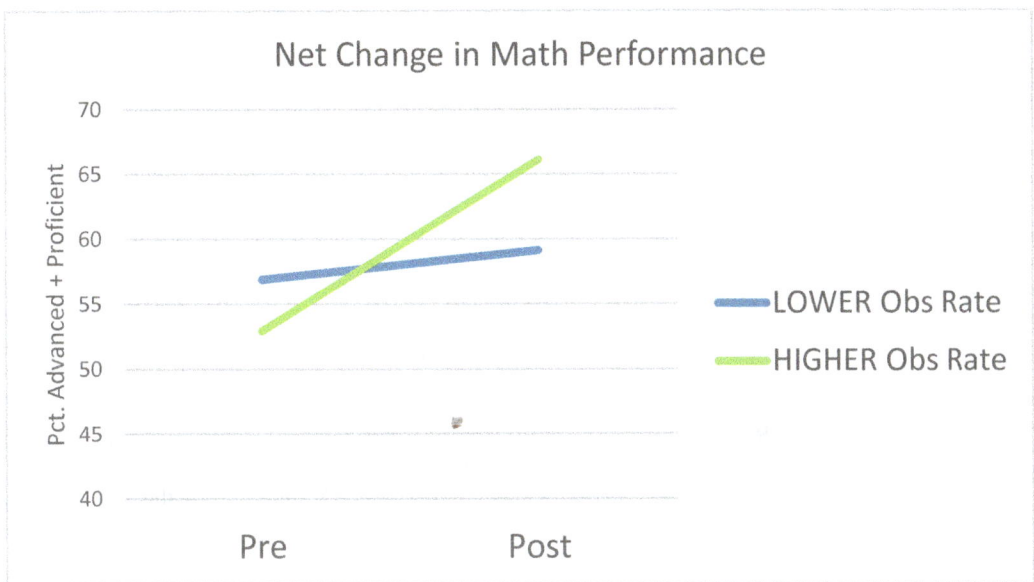

Figure 1. Comparative improvement in student performance for Math.

Schools with Lower Observation Rates collectively experienced 2.22 net gain in students rated as Proficient or Advanced, which represented a statistically significant 3.9% improvement (p=0.016). In contrast, schools with Higher Observation Rates collectively experienced 13.16 net gain in student performance for Proficient or Advanced, representing a statistically significant 24.9% improvement (p<0.001). The comparison reflects 6.37 times the growth in the Higher Observation Rate schools.

Table 1. Comparative Student Gains: Math

	Math Pct. Advanced + Proficient				
	Pre	Post	Net Change	Pct. Change	p-Value
LOWER Observation Rates	56.92	59.14	2.22	3.9%	p=0.016
HIGHER Observation Rates	52.93	66.10	13.16	24.9%	p<0.001
Significant Advantage	p<0.001	p<0.001	p<0.001	p<0.001	

Teachers in Higher Observation Rates schools also experienced significantly higher utilization and engagement within the PD on several of the additional variables measured, which is interpreted as a reflection of the impact of the observations (see Table 2). Teachers in the Higher Observation Rates school had more 31.8% more observations with assignments, 39.5% more minutes of PD viewed and 5.1% more minutes of viewing per target (i.e. module).

Table 2. Engagement and Utilization Comparison for PD Users: Math

	Mean Obs w/ Assignments	Avg Minutes Viewed	Minutes Viewed per Target
LOWER Observation Rates	13.56	55.13	15.49
HIGHER Observation Rates	17.87	76.88	16.28
Significant Advantage	p=0.048	p=0.032	p=0.050

Reading

Schools with Higher Observation Rates experienced significantly greater gains in student performance (see Table 3). Interestingly, and not by design, school with the Lower Observation Rates had Pre-PD student performance levels 12% higher than their Higher Observation Rates counterparts. By the end of the PD year the Higher Observation Rates schools almost closed the gap (see Figure 2).

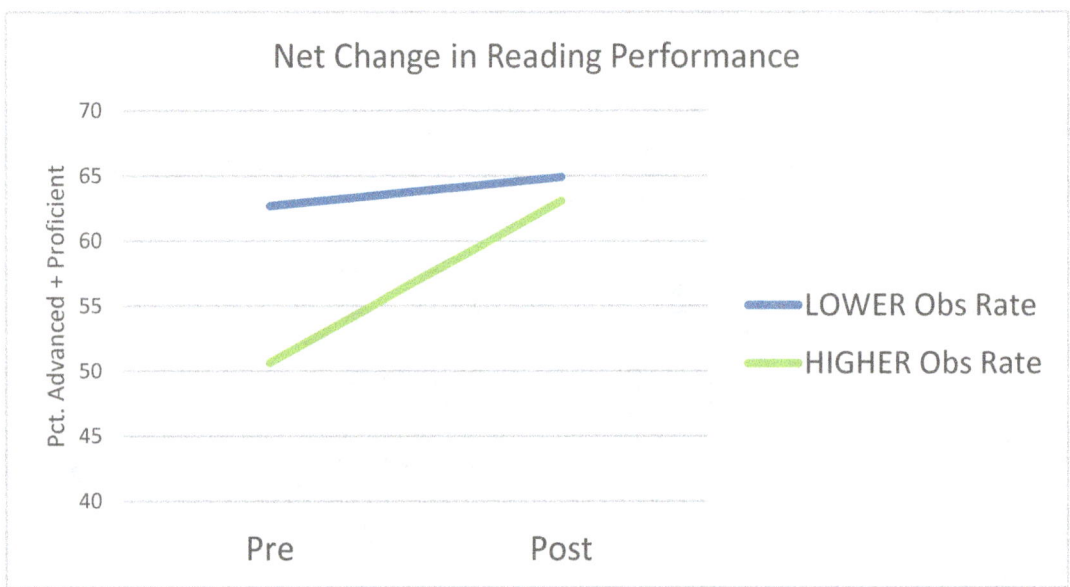

Figure 2. Comparative improvement in student performance for Reading.

Schools with Lower Observation Rates collectively experienced 2.21 net gain in students rated as Proficient or Advanced, which represented a statistically significant 3.5% improvement (p=0.016). In contrast, schools with Higher Observation Rates collectively experienced 12.47 net gain in student performance for Proficient or Advanced, representing a statistically significant 24.6% improvement (p<0.001). The comparison reflects 7.01 times the growth in the Higher Observation Rate schools.

Table 3. Comparative Student Gains: Reading

	Reading Pct. Advanced + Proficient				
	Pre	Post	Net Change	Pct. Change	p-Value
LOWER Observation Rates	62.68	64.89	2.21	3.5%	p=0.016
HIGHER Observation Rates	50.60	63.07	12.47	24.6%	p<0.001
Significant Advantage	p<0.001	ns	p<0.001	p<0.001	

Teachers in Higher Observation Rates schools also experienced significantly higher utilization and engagement within the PD on several of the additional variables measured, which is interpreted as a reflection of the impact of the observations (see Table 4). Teachers in the Higher Observation Rates school had more 3.2% more observations with assignments, 29.9% more minutes of PD viewed and 30.1% more files downloaded.

Table 4. Engagement and Utilization Comparison for PD Users: Reading

	Percent Users w Viewing	Avg Minutes Viewed	Files Downloaded
LOWER Observation Rates	0.79	62.17	24.42
HIGHER Observation Rates	0.82	80.74	31.79
Significant Advantage	p=0.038	p=0.012	p=0.010

Conclusions & Recommendations

The evidence that teachers matter is based on a wide body of research. Research has established that differences in effectiveness between teachers provide the best available explanation for differences in achievement growth between students once student background is controlled for. This study seems to indicate that a useful teacher observation system can reveal the differences between teachers on the basis of their level of involvement with the specified PD in this study. This study also indicates that the observational component of an evaluation system needs to be aligned with purposeful professional development.

These findings have implications for practice and policy. As policymakers work to improve the education in American schools, the central focus of their efforts is the evaluation of teachers. Although teacher evaluation by itself is sometimes criticized as arbitrary, and disconnected from the needs of students, and/or unaligned with professional development opportunities for improvement, this study shows that a well-designed system can be objective, rigorous, differentiated, linked to student learning and supportive of teacher improvement.

References

Brandt, R. M. (1995). Teacher evaluation for Career Ladder and Incentive Pay Programs. In D. L. Duke (Ed.), *Teacher Evaluation Policy: From Accountability to Professional Development* (pp. 13-34). Albany: State University of New York Press.

Cuban, L. (1993). How teachers taught: Constancy and change in American classrooms 1880- 1990 2nd edition. New York: Teachers College Press.

Daley, G., & Kim, L. (2010). *A teacher evaluation system that works.* National Institute for Excellence in Teaching. Retrieved 8/20/2014 from http://www.tapsystem.org/publications/wp_eval.pdf

Darling-Hammond, L., Wise, A. E., Pease, S. R. (1983). Teacher evaluation in the organizational context: A review of the literature. *Review of Educational Research, 53*(3), 285-328.

Darling-Hammond, L. (1986). A proposal for evaluation in the teaching profession. *The Elementary School Journal, 86*(4), 530-551.

Darling-Hammond, L. (1990). Teacher evaluation in transition: Emerging roles and evolving methods. In J. Millman & L. Darling-Hammond (Eds.) *The new teacher handbook of teacher evaluation: Assessing elementary and secondary school teachers.* Newbury Park: Sage.

Duke, D. & Stiggins, R. J. (1990). *Beyond minimum competence: Evaluation for professional development.* In J. Millman & L. Darling-Hammond (Eds.), *The new handbook of teacher evaluation: Assessing elementary and secondary school teachers* (pp. 116-132). Newbury Park: Sage.

Ellett, C. D. (1997). Classroom-based assessments of teaching and learning. In J. Stronge (Ed.) *Evaluating teaching: A guide to current thinking and practice* (pp. 107-128). Thousand Oaks: Corwin.

Ellet, C. D. & Teddlie, C. (2003). Teacher evaluation, teacher effectiveness, and school effectiveness: Perspectives from the USA. *Journal of Personnel Evaluation in Education, 17*(1), 101-128.

Frase, L. E. & Streshly, W. (1994). Lack of accuracy, feedback and commitment in teacher evaluation. *Journal of Personnel Evaluation in Education, 8*(1), 47-57.

Good, T. L. & Mulryan, C. (1990). Teacher ratings: A call for teacher control and self-evaluation. In J. Millman & L. Darling-Hammond (Eds.) *The new teacher handbook of teacher evaluation: Assessing Elementary and Secondary School Teachers.* Newbury Park: Sage.

Gordon, R., Kane, T. J., & Staiger, D. O. (2006). *Identifying effective teachers using performance on the job.* Washington, D.C.: The Brookings Institution.

Haefele, D. L. (1993). Evaluating teachers: A call for change. *Journal of Personnel Evaluation in Education, 7*(1), 21-31.

Hazi, H. M., & Arredondo Rucinski, D. (2009). Teacher evaluation as a policy target for improved learning: A fifty-state review of statute and regulatory action since NCLB. *Education Policy Analysis Archives, 17*(5). Available online at http://epaa.asu.edu/epaa/v17n5/

Jacob, B. A. & Lefgren, L. (2008). Can principals identify effective teachers? Evidence on subject performance evaluation in education. *Journal of Labor Economics, 26*(1), 101-136.

Medley, D. M., & Coker, H. (1987). The accuracy of principals' judgments of teacher performance. *Journal of Education Research, 80*(4), 242-247.

Peterson, K. D. (2000). *Teacher evaluation: A comprehensive guide to new directions and practices 2nd edition.* Thousand Oaks: Corwin Press.

Peterson, K. D. (2004). Research on school teacher evaluation. *NASSP Bulletin, 88*(639), 60-79.

Rivkin, E. A., Hanushek, E. A., & Kain, J. F. (2001). *Teachers, schools, and academic achievement.* Washington, D.C.: National Bureau of Economic Research.

Rockoff, J. E. (2004). The impact of individual teachers on student achievement: Evidence from panel data. *The American Economic Review, 94*(2), 247-252.

Rowan, B., Correnti, R., & Miller, R.J. (2002). What large-scale survey research tells us about teacher effects on student achievement: Insights from the *Prospects* study of elementary schools. *Teachers College Record, 104,* 1525-1567.

Stiggins, R. J., & Bridgeford, N. J. (1985). Performance assessment for teacher development. *Educational Evaluation and Policy Analysis, 7*(1), 85-97.

U.S. Department of Education, For Each and Every Child—*A Strategy for Education Equity and Excellence*, Washington, D.C., 2013.

Weisberg, D., Sexton, S., Mulhern, J., Keeling, D. (2009). *The widget effect: Our national failure to acknowledge and act on differences in teacher effectiveness.* Brooklyn: The New Teacher Project. Available online at http://widgeteffect.org/

Wright, P., Horn, S. P., and Sanders, W. L. (1997). Teacher and classroom context effects on student achievement: Implications for teacher evaluation. *Journal of Personnel Evaluation in Education, 11*(1): 57–67.

A Performance Assessment of Teachers' TPACK Using Artifacts from Digital Portfolios

Joshua M. Rosenberg (jrosen@msu.edu)
Spencer P. Greenhalgh (greenha6@msu.edu)
Matthew J. Koehler (mkoehler@msu.edu)
Michigan State University, United States of America

Abstract: Researchers have employed many different methods of measuring teachers' Technological Pedagogical Content Knowledge (TPACK). Existing measures of TPACK have typically focused on teachers' self-report of their understanding, and relatively few approaches directly measure teacher performances. Moreover, to date, no performance assessments of teachers' TPACK have used teachers' digital portfolios or the work samples (or artifacts) included in teachers' portfolios. In this paper, we build on our initial attempt (Koehler, Rosenberg, Greenhalgh, Zellner, & Mishra, 2014) to test the reliability of a performance assessment of the TPACK present in teachers' portfolio artifacts by focusing on two specific types of artifacts: Dream IT (a type of grant proposal) and a sustainable technology initiative. We report the reliability of our attempts to code levels of TPACK evident in these artifacts and discuss the development of more robust performance measures of teachers' TPACK.

Introduction

Technological Pedagogical Content Knowledge (TPACK) is a framework commonly used in both scholarly and practical settings to describe the knowledge needed to effectively teach with technology. As the influence of this framework has expanded, researchers have developed a number of measures for teachers' TPACK; these measures have contributed to a better understanding of how TPACK can develop over time as a result of experience, resources, interventions, or other mechanisms of change. These measures are varied: Interview protocols, open-ended questionnaires, self-report surveys, observations, and performance assessments have all been used to assess teachers' knowledge (Koehler, Shin, & Mishra, 2011).

Self-reports are a particularly common method for assessing teachers' knowledge (Abbitt, 2011; Koehler, Shin, & Mishra, 2011). They are easy to administer, and the data collected from them is easy to analyze, especially when used in pre-post study designs. However, self-reports may exhibit poor construct validity (Creswell, 2013). That is, researchers may, in fact, be measuring something other than teachers' TPACK, stymying efforts to understand and enhance teachers' capacity to integrate technology. For example, self-reports may assess teachers' confidence about teaching with technology rather than their actual knowledge or behavior (Harris, Grandgenett, & Hofer, 2010). Performance assessments of TPACK are attempts to avoid this problem by measuring teachers' competence based on authentic instances of integrating technology with a specific pedagogy and content area. They can complement self-report and other measures of TPACK because they directly measure the action resulting from knowledge rather than taking indirect measures that may inadvertently capture teachers' confidence instead. However, there is not yet a performance assessment for TPACK for use with either teachers' digital portfolios or the specific work samples or artifacts included in portfolios.

The overarching purpose of this study, then, is to test the reliability of a performance assessment of the TPACK evidenced in artifacts included in teachers' portfolios.

Literature Review

We review four areas of prior research in order to establish the need for this study: First, we examine the TPACK framework; then, we review methods of assessing it. Next, we cover specific attempts to develop performance assessments for it. Finally, we address our initial attempt to use digital portfolios as a performance assessment for teachers' TPACK.

TPACK

The TPACK framework suggests a way of thinking about the knowledge teachers need in order to teach well with technology. It is not enough for teachers to simply know about technology; instead, effectively using technology in teaching and learning requires alignment with the content being taught and the pedagogical practices being used. Mishra and Koehler (2006) suggested that the contemporary importance of digital technologies in education necessitated changes to Shulman's (1986) framework of the knowledge needed by teachers. Shulman identified three bodies of knowledge needed by teachers: knowledge of content, knowledge of pedagogy, and, most importantly, knowledge of how content and pedagogy reciprocally affect each other. Mishra and Koehler argued that the knowledge needed by teachers includes technology in addition to pedagogy and content. Furthermore, just as Shulman considered the interactions between pedagogy and content to be essential, Mishra and Koehler asserted the importance of Technological Pedagogical Content Knowledge, or the interactions between technology, pedagogy, and content. See Figure 1 for a depiction of the components in the TPACK framework and their relationship to one another.

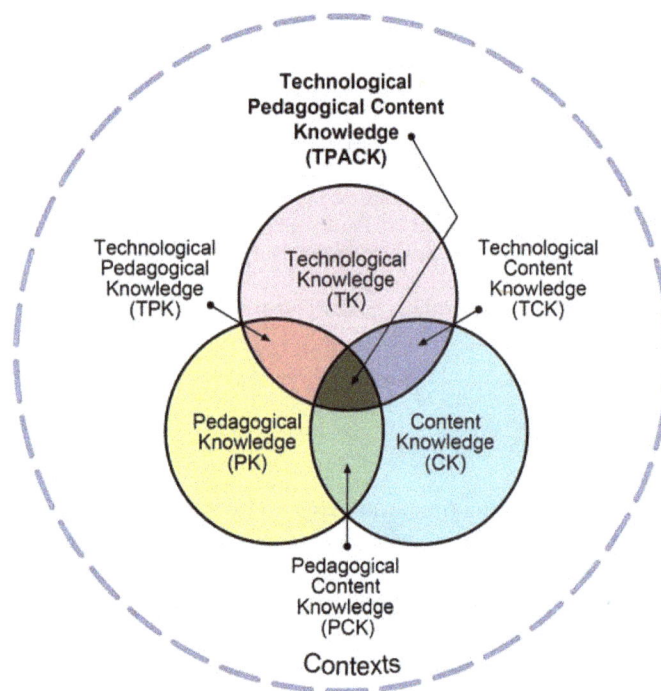

Figure 1. Components of the TPACK Framework. Used with permission from http://tpack.org.

In addition to recognizing three distinct bodies of knowledge and the interactions between them, the TPACK framework also takes context into account (Kelly, 2008; Koehler & Mishra, 2008; Porras-Hernandez & Salinas-Amescua, 2013; Rosenberg & Koehler, 2014). That is, TPACK is not a sterile, theoretical treatment of knowledge so much as a type of knowledge situated in the real-world environments in which teachers work. Students, resources, and supports influence how TPACK develops among teachers as well as how teachers use their TPACK in their planning and instruction.

Methods of Assessing TPACK

Researchers have tried to measure TPACK since its introduction, and there are now multiple methods of assessing teachers' TPACK (Abbitt, 2011; Koehler, Shin, & Mishra, 2012). For example, a number of researchers have explored the potential of using semi-structured interviews to assess teachers' TPACK (Harris, Grandgenett, and Hofer, 2012; Niess, Lee, Sadria, & Suharwoto, 2006). An alternative to interviews is questionnaires, which allow teachers to respond in an open-ended manner. This method has been used by Niess et al. (2006) and by So and Kim (2009). Self-report surveys are also a common measure, with the survey by Schmidt et al. (2009) being widely used. Archambault and Crippen (2009) also developed a self-report survey to assess the TPACK of teachers in online course settings. Observation protocols, such as the one used by Niess et al. (2006), are promising for research as well as practice—administrators and professional development providers can use these to provide ongoing, or formative, assessment.

Finally, some researchers have explored assessing authentic tasks and activities for evidence of teachers' TPACK, a practice referred to as performance assessment. Tasks and artifacts assessed in this way include lesson planning and instruction (Akcaoglu, Kereluik, & Casperson, 2011), instructional plans (Trip, Graham, & Wentworth, 2009), and lesson plans. Harris, Grandgenett, and Hofer (2010) analyzed teachers' lesson plans using a rubric for which they established validity and reliability properties. We discuss this rubric in detail in the next section.

Performance Assessments for TPACK

Performance assessments evaluate teachers' TPACK by directly examining their performance on complex, authentic tasks. Some ask teachers to create and maintain a set of artifacts in a portfolio or journal, while others consist of scenario- or problem-based questions that are assessed by experts. As measures of tasks related to teaching with technology, performance assessments of TPACK can compliment self-report surveys by examining how teachers apply what they know in practice. Furthermore, because they make use of complex, authentic tasks, administrators and professional development providers may make use of performance assessments to provide evaluative feedback, guidance, and support to teachers on the problems of practice they face.

Of six performance assessments of TPACK reviewed by Koehler et al. (2012), only one demonstrated validity and reliability: Harris et al.'s (2010) adaptation of the Technology Integration Assessment Instrument (TIAI; Britten & Cassady, 2005). The TIAI was originally designed for evaluating technology-integrated lesson plans generally, but Harris et al. (2010) modified it for the specific purpose of assessing TPACK. During the modification process, they solicited advice on how closely aligned it was with TPACK from six TPACK researchers and twelve local technology-using teachers and administrators. They then revised the rubric and then asked experienced, in-service, technology-using teachers to assess pre-service teachers' technology-integrated lesson plans across varying grade levels and content areas. They did this by training 15 experienced teachers for a 6-hour period in the use of the rubric, after which the teachers used the rubric to code pre-service teachers' lesson plans.

Unlike many TPACK assessments, Harris et al. (2010) thoroughly demonstrated the validity and reliability of this rubric. The rubric demonstrated construct validity through the approval of the six TPACK experts. It demonstrated face validity in feedback from the 15 experienced teachers, who supported its use to assess TPACK from lesson plans. Harris et al. (2010) demonstrated reliability through the calculation of four statistics. First, they used interrater reliability using a hierarchical linear model. Teachers were the level-2 variable, and their scores were the level-1 variables. An intraclass correlation coefficient explained how the variability across teachers' scores was due to teacher differences. Second, percentage agreement was calculated by pairing raters. Third, Cronbach's alpha demonstrated the internal consistency of participants' scores between each of the four rows of the rubric. Fourth, they computed test-test reliability by having raters code three lesson plans in different content areas and grade levels one month after their initial coding, followed by the calculation of percentage agreement across the two periods.

These validity and reliability measures demonstrated that this rubric could be used with trained raters to assess the levels of TPACK demonstrated in pre-service teachers' lesson plans. Harris et al. (2010) cautioned that the rubric had not yet been used with in-service teachers or with experienced lesson plans. They also suggested that lesson plans considered for coding with this rubric be written in detail so that raters can make well-informed choices. Finally, they suggested that supplementing coded lesson plans with interviews might help triangulate teachers' TPACK. In the next section, we discuss how the research by Harris et al. informed our attempt to evaluate another kind of performance assessment: artifacts or created works in teachers' digital portfolios.

Initial Attempt to Develop Performance Assessment for Teachers' TPACK Using Artifacts from Digital Portfolios

Our experience designing and teaching a master's level teacher portfolio course led us to explore whether we could assess the levels of teachers' TPACK through the portfolios that teachers create. Our initial attempt (Koehler et al., 2014) to test the validity and reliability of Harris et al.'s (2010) performance assessment when applied to portfolio artifacts was guided by four research questions:

1. What skills do teachers choose to represent in their portfolios?
2. Do teachers connect their technology competencies to their content areas or pedagogical approaches?
3. How amenable are the artifacts teachers submit to the TIAI?
4. What levels of TPACK are evidenced by the artifacts teachers submit?

Guided by these research questions, we coded a total of 75 artifacts from 25 portfolios; although each of these portfolios had more than three artifacts, we selected from each one the three that seemed most amenable to analyzing teachers' TPACK through the adapted rubric. We did not analyze "fit," which was part of Harris et al.'s (2010) rubric, because we believed that the TPACK category included the same construct. We trained with the rubric by using it to evaluate a sample of the previously selected teachers' artifacts and then began coding. Because Harris et al. (2010) had already demonstrated the validity of the measure, we concentrated on calculating reliability statistics. We used Cohen's kappa, which takes into account chance agreement and percentage agreement.

Sample	Variable	Percentage Agreement	Cohen's Kappa and Interpretation
n=75 various artifacts	TCK	45.3%	0.234 (slight)
	TPK	41.3%	0.157 (poor)
	TPACK	36.0%	0.120 (poor)

Table 1: Reliability for our initial attempt to infer teachers' TPACK from digital portfolios using Harris, Grandgenett, and Hofer's (2010) rubric; we interpreted Cohen's kappa using guidelines based upon a review of current research by Sim and Wright (2005): 0 - .20 = poor; .21 - .40 = slight; .40 - .60 = moderate; .61 - .80 = substantial; .81 - 1.00 = excellent.

Based on these discouraging results, we identified three potential areas for improvement: we could (1) limit future assessment to common artifacts for coders or artifacts designed to elicit TPACK; (2) use a different rubric or develop a new rubric ourselves; or (3) select different raters, perhaps those with content-area expertise (Koehler et al., 2014).

Purpose and Research Questions

The purpose of this study is to test the reliability of a performance assessment for measuring the TPACK evidenced by artifacts included in teachers' portfolios. We chose to focus on artifacts (rather than the rubric or the raters) as a specific area for improvement because the rubric had already been extensively tested (Harris et al., 2010), and the raters were deemed as competent. Furthermore, this decision aligned with Harris et al.'s (2010) advice that those using their rubric to code lesson plans make sure the artifacts have sufficient detail; we had experienced this problem in our initial attempt, as the artifacts we coded typically did not include detailed information on TPACK. Therefore, we limited our focus to two kinds of artifacts that had more detail than the artifacts we examined in our previous attempt. However, we recognize that this decreases the external validity of the rubric because teachers' portfolios do not consist of just one artifact or one type of artifact: coding only two artifacts limits the generalizability of our results and may mean that those interested in inferring teachers' TPACK from their portfolios may need to require the inclusion of specific artifacts or types of artifacts by teachers. The following research question guides our study: Can the TPACK-adapted TIAI be used to reliably measure the TPACK demonstrated in two types of artifacts designed to elicit teachers' TPACK?

Method

In this section, we describe how we established the reliability of our attempt to code specific artifacts. In doing so, we specifically discuss the sample, the procedure, and the data analysis of this study.

Sample

We analyzed two kinds of artifacts designed to elicit teachers' TPACK, both of which are featured in classes offered by the Master of Arts in Educational Technology program at Michigan State University. This program is designed for in-service teachers and other educators—the students who complete these assignments can therefore also be considered teachers.

- Dream IT: An assignment in a hybrid course (that is, a course with face-to-face and online aspects) on approaches to educational research in which students develop a grant proposal focused on the thoughtful integration of technology into teaching and learning. Students must consider TPACK when describing how the technology will be used in practice as part of their proposal. In addition, the assignment emphasizes the importance of tailoring the grant proposal for the context in which students function.
- Learning Technology Initiative: An assignment in an online course on technology, leadership, and education requiring students to solve a problem of practice, a difficult-to-solve issue that students face in their occupations, through a technology-integrated solution. Students must consider TPACK when

completing a table that specifies what knowledge teachers would need when implementing this solution. This table is organized by the seven components of the TPACK framework (TK, PK, CK, TPK, TCK, PCK, and TPACK). The proposal also emphasizes the contextual factors that need to be considered in order for the initiative to be a success.

Students' Dream IT artifacts were all completed on individual websites; we therefore collected the URLs for the Dream IT artifacts completed during the Summer 2014 and Summer 2013 semesters ($n=35$) and added them to a spreadsheet. We then reviewed the Dream IT artifacts for suitability for coding by checking for broken links and completed assignments; this caused us to remove eight of them, reducing our sample to 27 artifacts. We also collected the Word documents for the Learning Technology Initiative artifacts completed during the Spring 2014 semester ($n=21$) from the course submission system. All of the Learning Technology Initiatives were completed, allowing us to code all 21 artifacts.

To segment the data, we created individual spreadsheets for the Dream IT and Learning Technology Initiative artifacts and then added rows to each spreadsheet for each individual artifact. We then identified the portions of each of the two types of artifacts that were amenable to coding for evidence of teachers' TPACK. For the Dream IT artifacts, we only coded the students' descriptions of TPACK: These segments were typically one to two paragraphs in which students discussed the relationships among technology, pedagogy, and content with respect to their grant proposals. Thus, in the case of the Dream IT artifacts, we inferred teachers' TPK and TCK (as well as their TPACK) from their descriptions of how this framework informed their grant proposals. In the case of the Learning Technology Initiative artifacts, we coded only the table students created to present their descriptions of the knowledge teachers would need with respect to each of the seven areas of TPACK.

Procedure

Two coders evaluated each artifact for three aspects of the TPACK-adapted TIAI rubric from Harris et al. (2010), as shown in Table 2. As in our previous study, we did not analyze "fit"—a part of Harris et al.'s (2010) rubric—because we believed that the TPACK category included the same construct. Also, we added clarifications to the criteria to make explicit their connection to the different aspects of TPACK (e.g., Curriculum Goals & Technologies can be thought of as teachers' TCK). Note that Harris et al. (2010) referred to the content aspect of TPACK as "curricular goals" and the pedagogy aspect of TPACK as "instructional strategies." As an example, if an artifact exhibited strong alignment between the use of technology and curriculum goals it was coded "4" for Curriculum Goals & Technologies. If an artifact exhibited support from technology with respect to instructional strategies, it was coded "3" for Instructional Strategies and Technologies. Finally, if the alignment of technology, instructional strategies, and curriculum goals was exemplary, it was coded "4" for Technology Selections.

Table 2: TIAI-adapted Rubric from Harris et al. (2010)

Criteria	4	3	2	1
Curriculum Goals & Technologies: Curriculum-based technology use (TCK)	Technologies selected for use are strongly aligned with one or more curriculum goals.	Technologies selected for use are aligned with one or more curriculum goals.	Technologies selected for use are partially aligned with one or more curriculum goals.	Technologies selected for use are not aligned with any curriculum goals.
Instructional Strategies & Technologies: Using technology in teaching/learning (TPK)	Technology use optimally supports instructional strategies.	Technology use supports instructional strategies.	Technology use minimally supports instructional strategies.	Technology use does not support instructional strategies.
Technology Selection(s): Compatibility with curriculum goals & instructional strategies (TPACK)	Technology selection(s) are exemplary, given curriculum goal(s) and instructional strategies.	Technology selection(s) are appropriate, but not exemplary, given curriculum goal(s) and instructional strategies.	Technology selection(s) are marginally appropriate, given curriculum goal(s) and instructional strategies.	Technology selection(s) are inappropriate, given curriculum goal(s) and instructional strategies.

Data Analysis

We calculated interrater reliability for both kinds of artifact using two different statistics: percentage agreement and Cohen's kappa. Cohen's kappa is similar to percentage agreement but corrects for chance agreement between coders.

Results

Results for the reliability of our coding of both Dream IT *(n=27)* and Learning Technology Initiative (*n*=21) artifacts are presented in Table 3. Although we coded nearly 50 artifacts, our efforts at coding additional artifacts are ongoing, and so these reliability statistics may not be indicative of the statistics we will report after coding additional artifacts at our presentation.

Sample	Variable	Percentage Agreement	Cohen's Kappa and Interpretation
Dream IT (*n*=27)	TCK	62.9%	0.505 (moderate)
	TPK	51.8%	0.235 (slight)
	TPACK	55.5%	0.337 (slight)
Learning Technology Initiative (*n*=21)	TCK	42.9%	0.131 (poor)
	TPK	47.6%	0.138 (poor)
	TPACK	52.4%	0.163 (poor)

Table 3: Reliability of two coders for Dream IT and Learning Technology Initiative artifacts; we interpreted Cohen's kappa using Sim and Wright's (2005) guidelines as discussed in Table 1.

Discussion

Our reliability using the TPACK-adapted TIAI differed between the Dream IT and Learning Technology Initiative artifacts. For the Dream IT artifacts, we demonstrated some success in reliably coding these artifacts: for TCK, the two coders agreed a majority of the time across the four codes of the rubric, even when accounting for chance agreement. For TPK and TPACK the results were less impressive, especially when chance agreement was taken into account in the calculation of Cohen's kappa. Furthermore, because two raters evaluated each artifact, we cannot speak to the degree to which an additional rater would change the reliability statistics reported in this study. Despite the reliability for TPK and TPACK being less impressive than that for TCK, the percentage agreement and Cohen's kappa for both of these variables was higher than those calculated in our initial attempt (e.g., Koehler et al., 2014). Thus, coding only Dream IT artifacts improved the reliability of our use of the measure. For the Learning Technology Initiative artifacts, while percentage agreement for TPK and TPACK increased from our initial attempt, the Cohen's kappa statistic increased only for TPACK. We demonstrated little improvement in our coding of these artifacts compared to both our initial effort and coding of the Dream IT artifacts. Thus, coding only Learning Technology artifacts did not improve the reliability of our use of the measure.

Differences between the two artifacts may account for the differences in the reliability of our coding. The Dream IT artifacts were written explanations of how students' grant proposals aligned with the TPACK framework, while the Learning Technology Initiatives were students' entries in a table with rows for each of the seven aspects of TPACK. Furthermore, the data we coded for the Dream IT artifacts was focused on just one area of TPACK (TPACK itself—that is, the intersection between technology, pedagogy, and content knowledge), as described in the sample section of the methods. This greater focus, on TPACK itself rather than its constituent areas of knowledge, may have allowed the coders to focus on straightforward responses rather than on extraneous details, thereby achieving greater reliability using the rubric. Taking this into consideration along with Harris et al.'s (2010) suggestion that lesson plans must be written in sufficient detail to be coded, we may only be able to code artifacts with certain characteristics: being written in sufficient detail and also being focused on TPACK.

There are additional steps we can take to improve the reliability of our use of the TPACK-adapted TIAI rubric by continuing to focus on the nature of the artifacts we are coding. First, we can discuss the nature of our disagreements in coding the two types of artifacts. Doing so may reveal differences in how the coders used the rubric that can be reconciled, so that the reliability of the rubric can be improved in future rounds of coding. Second, we can explore different aspects of the two artifacts that we coded in this study: We segmented the Dream IT artifacts so that we coded only descriptions of TPACK and the Learning Technology Initiatives so that we coded only entries in the table about TPACK. Due to our comparative success coding the more-focused descriptions of TPACK among the Dream IT artifacts, making the data segments smaller may enhance the reliability of the rubric as long as they maintain a sufficient level of detail. Finally, we could explore different types of artifacts, from those not explicitly connected to TPACK, to those that make use of different forms of media, such as video, in order to further our understanding of the characteristics of artifacts that are amenable to coding. As our efforts at coding additional artifacts are ongoing, these steps provide direction for our efforts at enhancing the reliability of our use of the rubric.

References

Abbitt, J. T. (2011). Measuring technological pedagogical content knowledge in preservice teacher education: A review of current methods and instruments. *Journal of Research on Technology in Education, 43*, 281-300.

Akcaoglu, M., Kereluik, K. & Casperson, G. (2011). Refining TPACK rubric through online lesson plans. In M. Koehler & P. Mishra (Eds.), *Proceedings of Society for Information Technology & Teacher Education International Conference 2011* (pp. 4260-4264). Chesapeake, VA: AACE.

Archambault, L., & Crippen, K. (2009). Examining TPACK among K-12 online distance educators in the United States. *Contemporary Issues in Technology and Teacher Education, 9*(1), 71-88.

Britten, J. S., & Cassady, J. C. (2005). The Technology Integration Assessment Instrument: Understanding planned use of technology by classroom teachers. *Computers in the Schools, 22*(3-4), 49-61.

Creswell, J. W. (2013). *Research design: Qualitative, quantitative, and mixed methods approaches*. Thousand Oaks, CA: Sage Publications.

Graham, C. R., Tripp, T., & Wentworth, N. (2009). Assessing and improving technology integration skills for preservice teachers using the teacher work sample. *Journal of Educational Computing Research, 41*, 39-62.

Harris, J., Grandgenett, N., & Hofer, M. (2010). Testing a TPACK-based technology integration assessment rubric. In C. Crawford, D. A. Willis, R. Carlsen, I. Gibson, K. McFerrin, J. Price & R. Weber (Eds.), *Proceedings of the Society for Information Technology & Teacher Education International Conference 2010* (pp. 3833–3840). Chesapeake, VA: AACE.

Kelly, M. A. (2008). Bridging digital and cultural divides: TPCK for equity of access to technology. In AACTE Committee on Innovation and Technology (Eds.), *Handbook of technological pedagogical content knowledge (TPCK) for educators* (pp. 30–60). New York, NY: Routledge.

Koehler, M. J., & Mishra, P. (2008). Introducing TPCK. In AACTE Committee on Technology and Innovation (Eds.), *Handbook of technological pedagogical content knowledge (TPCK) for educators* (pp. 3–29). New York, NY: Routledge.

Koehler, M. J., Rosenberg, J. M., Greenhalgh, S., Zellner, A., & Mishra, P. (2014, March). *Can portfolio-based assessments demonstrate teachers' TPACK?* In J. Voogt and P. Fisser (Chairs), Artifacts demonstrating teachers' technology integration competencies. Symposium conducted the Society for Information Technology & Teacher Education International Conference 2014, Jacksonville, FL.

Koehler, M. J., Shin, T. S., & Mishra, P. (2011). How do we measure TPACK? Let me count the ways. *Educational technology, teacher knowledge, and classroom impact: A research handbook on frameworks and approaches*, 16-31.

Mishra, P., & Koehler, M. (2006). Technological pedagogical content knowledge: A framework for teacher knowledge. *The Teachers College Record, 108*, 1017-1054.

Niess, M., Lee, K., Sadri, P., & Suharwoto, G. (2006). *Guiding inservice mathematics teachers in developing a technology pedagogical knowledge (TPCK)*. Paper presented at the Annual Meeting of the American Educational Research Association, San Francisco, CA.

Porras-Hernández, L. H., & Salinas-Amescua, B. (2013). Strengthening TPACK: A broader notion of context and the use of teacher's narratives to reveal knowledge construction. *Journal of Educational Computing Research, 48*, 223-244.

Rosenberg, J. & Koehler, M. (2014). Context and Technological Pedagogical Content Knowledge: A content analysis. In M. Searson & M. Ochoa (Eds.), *Proceedings of Society for Information Technology & Teacher Education International Conference 2014* (pp. 2412-2417). Chesapeake, VA: AACE.

Schmidt, D. A., Baran, E., Thompson, A. D., Mishra, P., Koehler, M. J., & Shin, T. S. (2009). Technological Pedagogical Content Knowledge (TPACK): The development and validation of an assessment instrument for preservice teachers. *Journal of Research on Technology in Education, 42*(2), 123-149.

Shulman, L. S. (1986). Those who understand: Knowledge growth in teaching. *Educational Researcher, 15,* 4-14.

So, H. J., & Kim, B. (2009). Learning about problem based learning: Student teachers integrating technology, pedagogy and content knowledge. *Australasian Journal of Educational Technology, 25,* 101-116.

A "Spot the Different Videos" Training Method to Build Up Teaching Skills Using ICT in Pre-service Teacher Education

Minae Ogawa   Yasuhiko Morimoto   Takeshi Kitazawa   Youzou Miyadera
Tokyo Gakugei University
Japan
m143302w@st.u-gakugei.ac.jp, morimoto@u-gakugei.ac.jp
ktakeshi@u-gakugei.ac.jp, miyadera@u-gakugei.ac.jp

Abstract: The use of information and communications technology (ICT) to apply digitization techniques to advancing education and improving teachers' teaching skills using ICT is in demand. However, it is difficult to teach persons how to acquire teaching skills using ICT and the most effective learning model has not been established. The purpose of this study is to establish an effective learning model for acquiring such teaching skills using ICT in a teacher training course. We established and evaluated a learning model involving problem solving approach through "Spot the different videos" material to acquire the skills. Evaluation results show that the model enables learners using it to think about how ICT can be effectively used and to acquire knowledge about using it.

Introduction

Recently, there has been significant demand for using information and communication technology (ICT) to apply digitization techniques to advancing education and improving teachers' teaching skills using ICT. The Second Basic Plan for the Promotion of Education (MEXT; Ministry of Education 2012) was established "with the aim of enabling all teachers to use ICT in instructing as soon as possible, and to take necessary measures to improve teachers' teaching skills using ICT" in promoting new learning through the use of ICT".

However, there is no one way to use ICT because the scenarios and methods involved in using it will differ according to the child student's learning environment, learning contents, and learning situation. Therefore, it is difficult to instruct persons on how to acquire and improve their teaching skills using ICT, and the best teaching methods have not been established. Morishita (2014) points out that "With regard to acquiring teaching skills using ICT in a teacher training course, it must be clear whether there is the need to expand the curriculum for acquiring these skills and to enrich the environment and subjects", and that it is necessary to know that there is demand for establishing teaching and learning method in this field. Tokyo Gakugei University is now offering a "Using ICT in the Class" course, but a problem that needs to be addressed is how to improve the curriculum it offers for acquiring the necessary teaching skills using it.

The purpose of this study is to establish a learning model for helping leaners acquire teaching skills using ICT in a teacher training course. We established a learning model that involves problem solving approach through a "Spot the different videos" material to acquire the skills and tested it to evaluate whether it is effective as a learning model. We found the model offers several advantages, which are summarized below and discussed in detail in the rest of the paper.

- Its "Learning by making videos" method makes the learner think about how to use ICT in a way that is suitable for the child student's learning environment, learning contents, and learning situation.
- It helps learners understand that they cannot necessarily use ICT effectively by using only knowledge they already have.
- Its "Learning by browsing videos" method can deepen learners' knowledge about how to use ICT.
- Its "Spot the different videos" material may enable learners to think for themselves about how they can make the use of ICT more effective.
- It may make it easier for learners to acquire teaching skills using ICT in a teacher training course.

Teaching Skills Using ICT in a Teacher Training Course: Current Situation

It is said that students in teacher training course do not have a sufficient level of teaching skills using ICT only in classes where having some technical knowledge about ICT is required (e.g., Haugerud 2011).

For the current situation regarding the acquirement of teaching skills using ICT in a teacher training course, previous studies have shown the effectiveness of the class simulation approach. It has been found that with this approach the class practices can effectively help learners to shape their abilities. It has also been found that giving the learners the chance to lecture and train others about the use of ICT can improve their own awareness of its use in the class (Toyoda and Nonaka 2004). However, it is necessary to develop methods that will encourage the learners performing the simulated classes to dig down even more to discover effective ways to use ICT, and to gain insight as to how students would use it in a class. Experience acquired through simulated classes cannot help much in various ICT use scenarios; there are limitations to what mere instruction can achieve and practical experience is needed to solve many of the problems that occur.

Morishita (2014) said that learners in a teaching training course acquired certain abilities regarding information morals education and ICT literacy, but the results he obtained with respect to teaching skills using ICT check list showed they have little experience in applying these abilities. Furthermore, although microteaching is used as part of the instruction process for acquiring teaching skills using ICT, it shows a number of difficult problems occur for a variety of ICT use scenarios.

Taylor (2004) suggested that if students cannot find any problems in using ICT, it is important for them to use their existing knowledge to come up with questions to identify problems. Karagiorgi (2006) said that rather than teach new ways to use ICT as a learning tool, there was a need for perspective of how to adopt ICT into the curriculum in a way that had been expected in classes up to then. Taylor (2003) cited effective skill training methods as "the use of hands-on ICT activities", "the presence of peers or a more skilled user, particularly for beginners" and "learning activities which are relevant and applied to the teaching context and a compulsory element to the activities to provide extrinsic motivation for trainees who are less positive about their use of ICT".

Learning Model for Acquiring Teaching Skills Using ICT

Acquiring Teaching Skills Using ICT through Problem Solving Approach

Recently, in problem solving approaches, learners have been required to find issues themselves and solve them. In this type of learning, the important thing is coordinating the manner in which one's own learning process leads to problem solving, rather than simply being taught given knowledge. It is characterized as a "learn how to learn" approach that encourages a shift from teaching learning to proactive learning. The theory of instruction regarding problem solving learning is based on Dewey's "Reflective Thinking", where problems are solved through a sequence of steps: "Define the Problem", "Analyze the Problem", "Determine Criteria for Optimal Situation", "Propose Solutions", and "Evaluate Proposed Solution".

The well-known General Problem Solver program specifies two sets of thinking process associated with the problem-solving process, understanding processes and search process (Newell & Simon, 1972) and the IDEAL model describes problem solving as a uniform process of identifying potential problems, defining and representing the problems, exploring possible strategies, acting on those strategies, and looking back and evaluating the effects on those activities (Bransford & Stein, 1984) as a model of a problem solving approach. Wood (1974) said that as a problem solving teaching method, the importance of scaffolding that facilitates learning gives a hint to problems that learners cannot find by themselves. Delclos (1991) said that an important instructional method of problem solving for the learner is strategy monitoring, which includes directives such as "Read the problem carefully", "Clarify the problem" and "Think about a similar problem". Hmelo-Silver (2004) showed that "collaborative learning", teaching method teacher act as a facilitator, learner perform in a group to a complex problems with no single solution.

In teacher training, the learning teachers themselves must acquire the professional ability to find and solve problems interspersed within a complex problem. That is, they must learn how to solve problems themselves. Therefore, it is considered that incorporating a problem solving approach to acquire teaching skills using ICT is very advantageous.

"Spot the Different Videos" Material

To satisfy the above requirements, we focused on a "Spot the different videos" approach in developing a learning model for acquiring teaching skills using ICT. "Spot the different videos" material is e-Learning teaching material as "Model type" pairs (commercially available video materials) used in the fields of medicine and nursing. Compared to the "Model type" passive learning mode, with the "Spot the different videos" material learners can learn proactively and have fun while doing so (Iwamoto et al. 2006). Using visual aids to find out about things is said to be effective in helping learners to understand technical aspects. Therefore, with the "Spot the different videos" material we established a learning model comprising a "Learning by making videos" (video making) method and a "Learning by browsing videos" (video browsing) method.

In this way, we expect that the model will help to instill a sense of professionalism in learners learning how to use ICT in the class, by allowing them to use ICT in learning teaching skills. Thus, we adopt the IDEAL model as a step in the problem solving approach process.

Establishing a Learning Model with "Spot the Different Videos"

We thought that the making and browsing of videos in the "Spot the different videos" material would be effective steps in recognizing problems occurring in ICT use scenarios, problems that are important in acquiring teaching skills using ICT. Therefore, for the "Spot the different videos" material we established a learning model comprising "Learning by making videos" (video making) and "Learning by browsing videos" (video browsing) model (Figure 1).

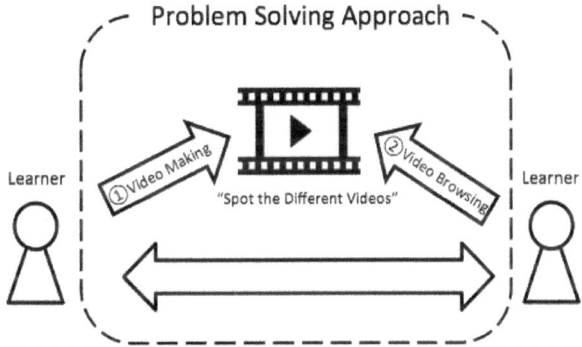

Figure 1: Learning model with "Spot the different videos"

In this learning model the "video making" and "video browsing" methods are performed, enabling teaching skills using ICT to be acquired through the learning process. Figure 2 shows the learning steps in these methods, which are based on the problem solving steps of the IDEAL model.

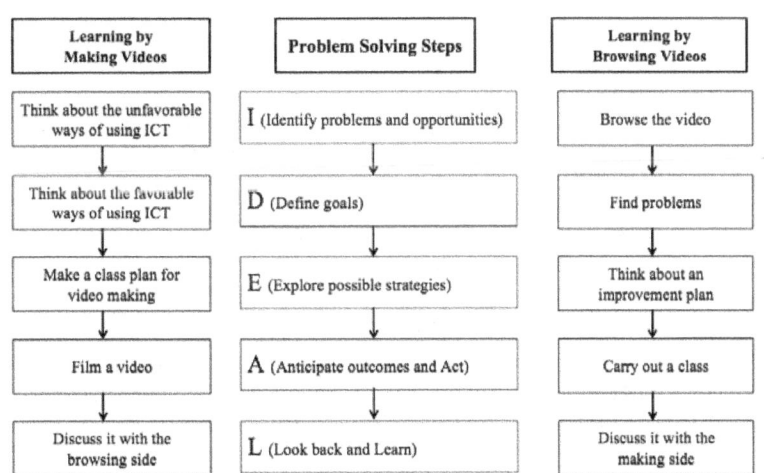

Figure 2: The "Spot the different videos" problem solving approach method

"Learning by Making Videos"

The "Learning by making videos" method is composed of five steps. First, the learners are divided into groups of several people, after which they think together and "brainstorm" about unfavorable ICT use scenarios (Step 1). Second, they think about how to group the favorable and unfavorable scenarios to be used (Step 2). Third, they create a teaching plan by determining the ICT technique, subject, and class unit to be included in the scenario to be used (Step 3). Fourth, they film a "Spot the different videos" video that is based on the teaching plan that they made (Step 4). Finally, they discuss their results with learners using the "Learning by browsing videos" method (Step 5).

"Learning by Browsing Videos"

The "Learning by browsing videos" method is also composed of five steps. First, the learners browse the "Spot the different videos" videos and try to spot the differences among them (Step 1). Second, they comment on those that are unfavorable for ICT use scenarios, browsing repeatedly and adding comments (Step 2). Third, they think about how to develop an improved teaching plan for the unfavorable scenarios (Step 3). Fourth, they conduct a class using the improved plan (Step 4). Finally, they discuss their results with learners using the "Learning by making videos" method (Step 5).

Practice and Evaluation of "Learning by Making Videos"

We evaluated our method to clarify whether it solves problems such as the need to examine effective uses of ICT or the need to use previous studies to establish an effective curriculum for acquiring teaching skills using ICT. We also wished to establish whether the method is useful in helping learners to acquire teaching skills using ICT in classes held in teacher training course. We therefore analyzed it using a statistical technique for the "Learning by making videos" method.

Practice and Analysis

We held a practice session using the "Learning by making videos" method in which seven persons participated: four undergraduate students and three graduate students of Tokyo Gakugei University. After the session we interviewed the students, each of whom had made videos, to get feedback from them for research purposes. They were also asked to fill in a questionnaire on their thoughts concerning the session, in which they were free to answer as they wished. In two of the questionnaire items they were asked if they felt they had learned by making videos and whether the session had made them more aware about the uses of ICT; we analyzed their answers to these in May 2014.

Results and Discussion

Tables 1-2 show the results obtained in interviews with three students who had used the "Spot the different videos" method.

For the "Learning by making videos" method (Table 1), the first student commented that "I understood that even the method of using ICT that I had thought to be favorable was not suitable for some learning situations", and "I was not only able to get an image of a real class using ICT, but also to actually experience it." This shows that the method may help learners to understand the favorable ways of using ICT, not to mention the ways of using ICT devices.

Table 1. Learned by video making

1.	I was able to acquire practice abilities the ways of using ICT devices in the class
2.	It was difficult for me to think about the favorable ways of ICT scenarios and methods
3.	I understood that even the method of using ICT that I had thought to be favorable was not suitable for same learning situation
4.	I could think about many ICT scenarios and methods
5.	I was not only able to get an image of a real class using ICT, but also to actually experience it

For the question about whether using the method had increased the learner's awareness of the uses of ICT (Table 2), the second student commented that "I understood that there were a variety of ways of using ICT with the same ICT device", and "I came to think about how I should be using ICT when the method I had learned in a lecture turned out to be unsuitable for our classes." This shows that going through with the video making in the "Leaning by making videos" method enables the learner to think about ways which ICT scenarios and methods can be made suitable for the child student's learning environment, learning contents, and learning situation. It should be noted that in this case the student had attended lectures about ICT use and thus had prior knowledge about it. It can therefore be expected that using the "Learning by making videos" method may remind such students that they cannot necessarily use ICT effectively by using only knowledge they already have.

Table 2. Whether using the method had increase the learner's awareness of the uses of ICT

1. I understood that there were a variety of ways of using ICT with the same ICT device
2. An imagine a class using ICT became clearer
3. I came to think about using scenarios of ICT by oneself
4. I came to think about how I should be using ICT when the method I had learned in a lecture turned out to be unsuitable for our classes

Practice and Evaluation of "Learning by Browsing Videos"

We evaluated our method to clarify whether it solves problems such as the need to examine effective uses of ICT or the need to use previous studies to establish an effective curriculum for acquiring teaching skills using ICT. We also wished to establish whether the method is useful in helping learners to acquire teaching skills using ICT in classes held in teacher training course. We therefore analyzed it using a statistical technique for the "Learning by browsing videos" methods.

Practice and Analysis

From April through July 2014, Tokyo Gakugei University offered a "Using ICT in the class" course, which 43 students attended. In the course we gave lectures and demonstrations of the use of the "Learning by browsing videos" method. The videos for the browsing sessions were also used for enhancing the students' reflections on ICT use and for eliciting comments from them (Morimoto and Kitazawa 2014). We continued our research during the course by means of questionnaires given to the students before and after the browsing sessions. The questionnaires consisted of five items about the use of ICT in the class and one about the effectiveness of the "Spot the different videos" method. For the latter item, the students rated the method's effectiveness on a 5-point scale (Table 3). Prior to browsing the videos, they were also asked to freely describe their ideas on the use of ICT in the class. After browsing, they were asked to give the reasons they felt or did not feel that the "Spot the different videos" method was effective. In addition, to measure the effectiveness of the "Learning by browsing videos" method we had the students attending the lectures make "mindmaps" for visualizing their image of the use of ICT by students. These were made for two items: "USING", meaning ways of using an electric board in the class, and "IDEA", meaning ideas and considerations to keep in mind when using an electric board in the class.

Table 3. Questionnaire items

Q1.	Can you imagine the using ICT in the class? (Image)
Q2.	Can you explain the merit of the using ICT in the class? (Merit)
Q3.	Can you explain the demerit of the using ICT in the class? (Demerit)
Q4.	Do you understand the using scenarios of ICT in the class? (Using)
Q5.	Do you understand a device and ideas and considerations to keep in mind when using an ICT in the class? (Idea)

After the course was over, we attempted to clarify the degree to which the "Learning by browsing videos" method had improved the students' knowledge about the use of ICT and the degree to which it had increased their awareness of its uses. This was done by making changes to the number of nodes of the mindmaps and performing a *t*-test comparison of the mean of the number of nodes made by the students before and after browsing the videos. We also did a correlation analysis to clarify the correspondence between the aforementioned questionnaire items and the number of nodes.

Results and Discussion

(1) Changing the number of mindmap nodes (*t*-test)

We compared the mean of number of nodes of the mindmaps the learners had made for the "USING" and "IDEA" items before and after browsing (Table 4). Statistical differences among the pre- and post-video browsing mindmaps were determined by performing a two-sided paired *t*-test. These differences suggested that the post-video browsing got significantly higher scores than the pre-video browsing, since the mean for the former was 12.63(USING), 13.50(IDEA) while that for the latter was 3.94(USING), 5.16(IDEA).

Table 4. Changing the number of mindmap nodes

	Pre-video browsing		Post-video browsing		
	M	SD	M	SD	t
USING	3.94	3.79	12.63	4.21	5.12**
IDEA	5.16	3.67	13.50	5.87	9.94**

$**p<.01$

From these results we understood that using the "Learning by browsing videos" method made the learners make mindmaps with a large number of nodes for both the "USING" and "IDEA" items.

(2) Differences in questionnaire items scores

We compared the mean of the scores for the questionnaire items "Image", "Merit", "Demerit", "Using", and "Idea", which the learners answered before and after browsing (Table 5). Statistical differences among the pre- and post-video browsing scores were determined by performing a two-sided paired *t*-test (Image: $t(32)=7.60, p<.01$, Merit: $t(32)=7.96, p<.01$, Demerit: $t(32)=8.11, p<.01$, Using: $t(32)=4.63, p<.01$, Idea: $t(32)=11.75, p<.01$,). The test results showed that all the post-video browsing scores were significantly higher then those for pre-video browsing.

Table 5. Differences in questionnaire items scores

	Pre-video browsing		Post-video browsing		
	M	SD	M	SD	t
Image	2.56	.71	3.78	.55	7.60**
Merit	2.81	.86	3.91	.47	7.96**
Demerit	2.94	.95	4.28	.52	8.11**
Using	2.72	.85	3.47	.57	4.63**
Idea	2.19	.90	3.94	.72	11.75**

$**p<.01$

This shows that the "Learning by browsing videos" method can help learners to more easily get an image of ICT usage and a deeper understanding of it, not only its merits and demerits and the way it is used but also the ideas and considerations that should be kept in mind when using it.

(3) Correlation between number of nodes and questionnaire items answers

Table 6 shows the results we obtained in performing a correlation analysis to clarify the correlation between the number of nodes in the mindmaps the learners made and the answers to questionnaire items about using ICT they provided before and after browsing the videos. Using a coefficient of correlation, we found that there were significant differences in 11 pre-video browsing items (USING and IDEA: ($r=.586$, $p<.01$), Image and Using: ($r=.516$, $p<.01$), Demerit and Idea: ($r=.480$, $p<.01$), Using and Idea: ($r=.479$, $p<.01$), USING and Image: ($r=.440$, $p<.01$), Image and Merit: ($r=.440$, $p<.01$), Merit and Using: ($r=.387$, $p<.05$), USING and Demerit: ($r=.373$, $p<.05$),

USING and Idea: ($r=.367$, $p<.05$), IDEA and Using: ($r=.332$, $p<.05$), Image and Idea: ($r=.325$, $p<.05$)) and eight post-video browsing items (Using and Idea: ($r=.639$, $p<.01$), Image and Using: ($r=.553$, $p<.01$), USING and IDEA: ($r=.549$, $p<.01$), Idea and Effect: ($r=.457$, $p<.01$), Merit and Demerit: ($r=.454$, $p<.05$), IDEA and Idea: ($r=.362$, $p<.05$), Demerit and Using: ($r=.328$, $p<.05$), Merit and Effect: ($r=.086$, $p<.05$)).

Table 6. Correlation between number of nodes and questionnaire items answers

		Nodes		5-point scale					
		USING	IDEA	Image	Merit	Demerit	Using	Idea	Effect
Nodes	USING	— —							
	IDEA	.586** .549**	— —						
5-point scale	Image	.440** .001	.271 -.109	— —					
	Merit	.066 .029	.162 .286	.440** .104	— —				
	Demerit	.373 -.056	.160 .286	.142 .125	.076 .454**	— —			
	Using	.290 -.082	.332* .010	.516** .553**	.387* .288	.202 .328*	— —		
	Idea	.367 .096	.131 .362*	.325* .250	.071 .300	.480** .288	.479** .639**	— —	
	Effect	-.027 -.002	-.050 -.050	.143 .086	-.017 .086**	.015 .305	.043 .415	-.049 .457**	— —

*$p<.05$, **$p<.01$

Note) Upside scores are before browsing the videos and downside scores are after browsing the videos

A significant correlation was obtained for the post-video browsing, even though for five items we tended to focus more on pre-video browsing as a result of the correlation analysis results (Idea and Effect: ($r=.457$, $p<.01$), Merit and Demerit: ($r=.454$, $p<.05$), IDEA and Idea: ($r=.362$, $p<.05$), Demerit and Using: ($r=.328$, $p<.05$), Merit and Effect: ($r=.086$, $p<.05$)). In other words, the possibility was suggested that using the "Learning by browsing videos" method makes the learners more conscious of the connection between merits and demerits in using ICT and also makes them think about the connection between demerits and the way ICT is used. In future we plan to further research this point for items where no significant correlation was obtained for the post-video browsing.

(4) Students' (freely described) reasons they felt that "Spot the different videos" was effective

Table 7 shows some extracts from the replies the 43 students gave in freely describing the reasons they felt that the "Spot the different videos" method was effective. The replies we received included comments such as "I thought it was effective because by using it I was able to imagine a case where I myself was using ICT in a class in a practical manner because it is very thorough method, and because I was able to think about ways to improve the class by comparing the differences between browsing videos and using teaching materials such as textbooks" and "I thought it was effective because it helped me understand certain problems and difficulties and it gave me ideas I would not have considered in an ordinary, desk-type class".

Table 7. Students' reasons they felt that "Spot the different videos" was effective

1. I thought it was effective because by using it I was able to imagine a case where I myself was using ICT in a class in a practical manner because it is very thorough method, and because I was able to think about ways to improve the class by comparing the differences between browsing videos and using teaching materials such as textbooks
2. I thought it was effective because it helped me understand certain problems and difficulties and it gave me ideas I would not have considered in an ordinary, desk-type class
3. I thought it was effective because it easier for me to image a class using ICT
4. I thought it was ineffective because it is too easy for me to try to spot the differences

The replies showed that the method may make it easier for learners to imagine a class using ICT after they have browsed the videos. They also suggest that using the method may help to make learners think about how using ICT can make a class more effective, and how they themselves can think of ways to use it that would suit a child student's learning environment, learning contents, and learning situation.

Conclusion

In this paper, we described a "Spot the different videos" problem solving approach model for acquiring teaching skills using ICT, showed cases of using the model for acquiring teaching skills using ICT, showed cases of using the methods, and presented research analysis and evaluation results. We showed that replies received in interviews with learners using the method's "Learning by making videos" method indicate that it can help learners think about various ways of using ICT and deepen the knowledge they had already had about the uses of ICT.

In addition, we showed that using the method's "Learning by browsing videos" method results in learners significantly increasing the number of nodes of mindmaps they prepare. We also described the correlation between the number of nodes and the answers to questionnaire items about using ICT the learners provided before and after browsing videos.

Certain problems had occurred in previous studies on this topic, such as the need to examine the effectiveness of using ICT and the need to establish an effective curriculum for acquiring teaching skills using ICT in teacher training course. The "Spot the different videos" problem solving approach model we developed in this study is able to solve these problems, which correspond to a variety of ways of using ICT and experiences using it. From this we conclude that this learning model is effective.

In the near future we plan to perform a detailed correlation analysis for all questionnaire items and consider ways to improve the model that will enable it to train not only students in teacher training course but also incumbent teachers.

References

Bransford, J. D. and Stein, B. S. (1993). *The Ideal Problem Solver: A Guide for Improving Thinking, Learning, and Creativity*. NY: Freeman.
Delclos, V. R. & Harrington, C. (1991). Effects of strategy monitoring and proactive instruction on children's problem-solving performance. *Journal of Education Psychology, 83*(1), 35-42.
Hmelo-Silver, C. E. (2004). Problem-based learning: What and how do students learn? *Educational Psychology Review*, 16 (3), 235-266.
Haugerud, T. (2011). Student teachers learning to teach: The mastery and appropriation of digital technology. *Nordic Journal of Digital Literacy*, 6, 226-238.
Iwamoto, Y., Minami. T., Yamauchi, K., & Mizuno, S. (2006). Effectiveness of video learning for aseptic techniques based on mistake identification. *Nursing Journal of Kagawa University, 10*(1), 33-44. (in Japanese)
Karagiorgi, Y. & Charalambous, K. (2006). ICT in-service training and school practice: in search for the impact. *Journal of Education for Teaching, 32*(4), 395-411.
Ministry of Education (MEXT, Japan) (2013). The second basic plan for the promotion of education. http://www.mext.go.jp/english/topics/1338141.htm (accessed on Jun. 20, 2015). (in Japanese)
Morishita, T. (2014). Current status and issue for teacher training around ICT. *Bulletin of the Educational Research and Development, Faculty of Education, Kagoshima University*, 23, 201-208. (in Japanese)

Morimoto, Y., Kitazawa, T. (2014). A development of system for enhancing student reflection using videos of class and an introduction of the system to Tokyo Gakugei University. *The 30th Annual Conference of JSiSE*, 5-6. (in Japanese)

Newell, A. & Simon, H.A. (1972). *Human problem solving*. Englewood Cliffs, NJ: Prentice-Hall.

Ogawa, M., Morimoto, Y., Kitazawa, T. & Miyadera, Y. (2014). Evaluation of problem solving learning with "Spot the Different Videos" to acquire teaching skills using ICT. *Research report of JSET Conferences, 14*(4), 49-56. (in Japanese)

Taylor, L. (2003). ICT skills learning strategies and histories of trainee teachers. Journal of Computer Assisted Learning, 19, 129-140.

Taylor, L. (2004). How student teachers develop their understanding of teaching using ICT. *Journal of Education for Teaching, 30*(1), 43-56.

Toyoda, M. & Nonaka, Y. (2004). A Construction of practical curriculum for teacher training by "Class Simulation" (Teacher Training Class) how to use computer for teaching guideline. *Faculty of Education Wakayama University bulletin of Center for Educational Research and Training*, 14, 217-225. (in Japanese)

Wood, D. J., Bruner, J. S. & Ross, G. (1976). The role of tutoring in problem solving. *Journal of Education for Teaching, 30*(1), 43-56.

A Preservice Secondary Education Technology Course: Design Decisions and Students' Learning Experiences

Dawn Hathaway and Priscilla Norton[1]
George Mason University
USA
dhathawa@gmu.edu
pnorton@gmu.edu

Abstract: Asked to design a technology education course for secondary preservice candidates, the researchers sought to design a course that focused on the interaction of technology and disciplinary teaching not on technology skills. Adopting a design-based research approach, Phase 1 was a review of literature that led to two course design decisions: to situate participants' study of technology in their disciplinary teaching field and to organize modules using disciplinary habits of mind. Phase 2 led to a third design decision: to structure content and activities using a design pattern approach. This paper presents Phase 3 of the research process, examining the influence of course design decisions on candidates' learning experiences. Study participants' course reflections were analyzed to understand the influence of the three course design decisions. Participants' reflections suggested that each course design decision was uniquely successful in focusing participants' learning on the *interaction* of technology integration concepts *and* discipline-specific contexts.

Introduction

Never was the adage "everything old is new again" truer that when we were approached by the secondary education program coordinator after a series of focus group sessions with local administrators. Administrators had endorsed the overall quality of graduates but identified three areas for improvement: working with second language learners, accommodating students with special needs, and using technology in instruction. The program coordinator asked us to help strengthen the program in the domain of technology integration. We were not surprised as his request echoed the findings of the Project Tomorrow & Blackboard (2013) report that stated, "Principals want new teachers to know how to use technology to create authentic learning experiences for students (75 percent) and how to leverage technology to differentiate instruction (68 percent) before they apply for a position at their school" (p. 5). It was also consistent with literature stating that teacher education programs have not taught new teachers how to use technology effectively (e. g., Maddux & Cummings, 2004), that preservice teachers lack the ability and knowledge needed to teach successfully with technology (e. g., Sang, Valcke, van Braak, & Tondeur, 2010), and that teachers feel inadequately prepared to use technology, particularly to support teaching and learning in their disciplines (e. g., Hew & Brush, 2007).

Until 2001, all preservice candidates in the College of Education and Human Development (CEHD) were required to complete a generic, predominantly skills-based, standalone technology course. Beginning Fall 2001, the secondary education faculty removed the technology course requirement and integrated considerations of technology in required methods courses. As the secondary education faculty had discovered, the goal of integrating technology with other program requirements had failed to meet the needs of schools. So, in Spring 2013, we accepted the program coordinator's challenge and began the design and then teaching of a technology integration course for secondary education candidates. Everything old was about to be new again.

The challenge of introducing preservice candidates to the role of technology in support of instruction has plagued teacher education for many years. While many have recommended specific approaches, "There is still the question of how to design the most appropriate technology experiences to intentionally meet the specific technology content goals faculty feel are necessary . . ." (Ottenbreit-Leftwich, Glazewski, & Newby, 2010, p. 23). Given the uncertainties about preservice technology education, we were left to wonder: should we design four, discipline-based courses (social studies, language arts, science, and mathematics) or should we design one course centered on concepts and skills related to technology use and integration? It occurred to us that the answer should be "yes" – the heart of a well-designed course for preservice secondary candidates should center on the *interaction* of technology

---

[1] The authors contributed equally to this work.

integration concepts *and* discipline-specific contents. We set out to design a course whose central goal was to focus participants' attention on this interaction and were guided by a central question: What is an appropriate course design to build secondary candidates' understanding of how technology integration concepts relate to and inform teaching practice in the disciplines? We adopted a design-based research approach in which learning is engineered and systematically studied in context. Design experimentation is concerned with the full, interacting system of learning, kinds of discourse, norms of participation, tools and related materials, and the means by which learners orchestrate relations among these elements. Design-based research has as its goals not the *right* answer but the ability to improve educational practice. Its promise is to provide opportunities to explore possibilities for creating novel learning and teaching environments, to develop contextualized theories of learning and teaching, to construct cumulative design knowledge, and to increase the human capacity for innovation (The Design-Based Research Collective, 2003).

Recognizing that design-based research is a program of research (Bannan-Ritland, 2003) conducted in iterative phases (Cobb, 2001), our first research phase centered on reviewing the literature related to preservice technology education. Results of that review exceed the scope of this paper but led us to two central course design decisions: to situate the course in specific disciplinary areas and to organize content and activities within each disciplinary area using "habits of mind." During the second research phase, we created a design pattern to structure content and activities and an instantiation of the pattern as an online course – EDIT 504 – Educational Technology in Secondary Classrooms. We described this process and the resulting design pattern in a previous paper (Norton & Hathaway, 2014). In this paper, we describe the third phase of the research process. We asked the question, what were the influences of course design decisions on secondary education preservice candidates' learning experiences?

Phase 3 Research Process

Participants

In the CEHD, secondary education is a post-baccalaureate program serving those who seek licensure to teach at the middle and high school levels. Some program candidates seek licensure only while others seek a Master's degree. Candidates are able to obtain teaching licensure in mathematics, English/Language Arts (ELA), social studies, or one of four science disciplines. Once developed, EDIT 504 was offered as a 3 graduate credit hour option toward the 9 credit hour elective requirement. Twenty-six candidates initially enrolled in the course. One candidate received permission to withdraw due to family circumstances. One candidate stopped attending, failed to answer email inquiries, and was not included in this study. One candidate requested and received an Incomplete. Thus, twenty-three candidates completed the course and were identified as participants in the study. Ten participants were ELA candidates; eight were social studies candidates; four were science candidates; and one was a mathematics candidate. Nine of the participants were male, and fourteen were female. No other demographic data were available to the researchers. One of the authors served as the course instructor, and four doctoral students served as content facilitators.

Analysis of Participants' Course Reflections

Data Collection Instrument

Participants were asked to address course content, lesson design, learning with technology, teaching with technology, implications for their practice, and their experiences as an online learner in a written reflection during the culminating course module. They were encouraged to make connections between what they had learned and classroom practice. Participants' synthesis reflections were submitted to the course instructor and content facilitators at the end of the course. These reflections were not graded but were acknowledged as final products and served as a springboard for final closing conversations between individual students, the instructor, and the facilitators. Participants' end of course reflections served as the source of study data.

Data Analysis

We examined participants' reflections for evidence related to course design decisions: a.) to situate participants' study of technology in their disciplinary teaching field, b.) to organize modules using disciplinary habits of mind, and c.) to structure content and activities using a design pattern. Since course reflections were narrative in form, we selected a qualitative approach to data analysis. Qualitative analysis procedures emphasize the views of the participants and interpret the subject of study from their perspective. This process is inductive in that themes emerge during the process of categorizing, coding, and organizing data. We used a categorizing process identified by Maxwell (2013) as coding. In the coding process, we independently examined and coded the reflections using the course design decisions as pre-established organizational topics. Data were fractured (separated from their context) and rearranged into the pre-established organizational topics. When a statement was identified by only one of us, we returned to the reflection, examined the statement in context, and agreed to either include the statement or to eliminate it. When coding of statements differed, we returned to the reflection, examined the statement in context, and agreed upon an appropriate category. When agreement could not be achieved, the statement was eliminated. Collaboratively, we examined each coded category to identify influences on participants' learning experiences. Finally, we collaboratively selected quotations that reflected participants' voices.

Influences of Course Design Decisions

Participants were overwhelmingly upbeat and positive about the course in their end of course reflections. They found the course to be relevant to their practice as well as "challenging," "informative," and "engaging." One science participant wrote, "The course really encouraged me to be creative, reflective and continue to be committed to my own learning as to the learning of my students." An ELA participant stated that the course opened her eyes to "the changing education landscape, the Common Core Standards, the need to use technology to transform education, and an incredible number of tools . . . ."

Decision 1: Situate Participants' Study of Technology in Their Disciplinary Teaching Area

Gonseth, et al. (2010) found that 80% of survey respondents indicated all or some of their teacher education programs required a standalone educational technology course. Brush et al. (2003) found that insufficient effort was made to align technology with discipline-specific pedagogy, and Russell, Bebell, O'Dwyer, and O'Connor (2003) argued for a focus on specific instructional uses of technology instead of general technology skills, and. We decided to situate the course design in participants' disciplinary area and to deemphasize skill-based instruction. The final course consisted of 10 modules. The first module introduced the course topic (technology in education), course processes, and course expectations. Modules 2 through 4 explored four universal concepts (technology integration, technology affordances, authentic learning, and lesson design) and were completed by all participants. With the assistance of four doctoral students each with expertise in one of the four disciplinary content areas, five two week modules (Modules 5 through 9) were designed for each of the disciplinary contents.

Although we viewed the decision to situate the course in participants' disciplinary area as an important course design decision, only one student commented on the discipline-based organization of the course. That ELA participant wrote, "I was surprised that we were divided into content-based groups for this course . . . . Once we began our content-specific modules, however, I came to realize the breadth of opportunities available to us as teachers and how critical it is to choose the technology that best suits our objectives."

Decision 2: Organize Modules Using Disciplinary Habits of Mind

Having made the decision to situate the study of technology in the context of participants' disciplinary area of interest, it was clear that each discipline had many sub-contents. For example, social studies included world history, U. S. History, government, and economics. Given the challenge of addressing all contents within a disciplinary area, we made the decision to design each of the disciplinary modules using disciplinary habits of mind not content topics. Using disciplinary habits of mind to organize the modules acknowledged that a field of practice is governed by a distinctive way of thinking not about facts but evidence, inquiry, and problem-solving (Tishman, Perkins, & Jay, 1995) and that they serve as comprehensive intellectual and critical thinking skills common to a discipline (Charbonneau, Jackson, Kobylski, Roginski, Sulewski, & Wattenberg, 2009). Thus, we organized the ELA modules around the five components of the ELA Common Core Standards (National Governors Association Center for Best Practices & Council of Chief State School Officers, 2010), the social studies modules around the components of historical thinking (Westhoff & Polman, 2008; Wineburg, 2001), the science modules using combinations of the cross cutting concepts identified in the *Next Generation Science Standards* (Achieve Inc., 2013), and the mathematics modules using the standards from the National Council of Teachers of Mathematics (2000).

Analysis of participants' reflections revealed a variety of prior experiences with the concept of disciplinary habits of mind. Regardless of prior experiences, there was a general consensus that the disciplinary habits of mind were relevant to participants' secondary students' future. An ELA participant wrote, "In order to succeed in college and move forward to obtain a successful career, students need to learn skills and competencies applicable to today's economy and digital society throughout every class and subject they are exposed to." Participants also acknowledged habits of mind as relevant for promoting their future secondary students' understanding of thinking in their disciplinary area. A social studies participant stated, "One of the main concepts that I took away from this course was that, as teachers, we should be designing lessons that teach students how to think like historians."

In addition, participants recognized that disciplinary habits of mind can serve as an instructional strategy. For example, a science participant recognized the way in which the habits of mind could connect content with students' lives when she wrote, "Cross-cutting Concepts . . . give the lessons a specific identity . . . a theme and unifying principle. They also allow for students to make the connections between science and their everyday lives." A social science participant recognized that habits of mind could structure classroom discourse when he wrote, "By utilizing this method, a teacher creates a far more meaningful dialogue with students . . . ." Another social studies participant acknowledged the role that habits of mind might play in engaging students with content when he wrote, "I learned technology and historical thinking can work together to get students engaged and excited about learning."

Decision 3: Structure Content and Activities Using a Design Pattern

Peltier, Schibrowsky, and Drago (2007) found that course content was the "number one driver of perceived quality of the learning experience" (p. 149). Acknowledging the need to structure course content, we adopted a design pattern approach. A design pattern approach provides designers with a framework for conceptualizing and expressing design problems and solutions. In this way, designers gain insight into their design problem and are able to capture the essence of the problem and its solution (Hathaway & Norton, 2013). Using this approach, we developed a design pattern for the course during the second phase of our research. That design pattern described a content structure created to build learners' understanding of how general concepts and practice are connected. The design pattern specifies engaging learners in a recurring activity structure that includes a conceptual design challenge, a design experience, analysis of design examples, and a situated design challenge (Norton & Hathaway, 2014).

Even though the design pattern was presented to participants in the introduction to the disciplinary area modules, only one ELA participant explicitly referred to the influence of the design pattern on their learning experience. She wrote, "The structure of having a conceptual design challenge, design experience, design examples, and situated design challenges has taught me about the importance of structure and consistency." One social studies participant did, however, indirectly capture the impact of the design pattern on his learning when he wrote,

> By writing about the [historical] concepts [in the conceptual design challenge] I was able to get an understanding of its importance; and by doing an activity related to the concept [in the design experience] I was able to appreciate the successes and frustrations of the students. Reading about additional activities [in the design examples] and creating my own activities related to the concepts [in the situated lesson design], I could put my newly learned knowledge to work. Together this scaffolding allowed me to better grasp how each historical concept could be used in the classroom.

The first activity in the design pattern was a Conceptual Design Challenge which conceptually linked a disciplinary habit of mind with appropriate technology. Participants were challenged to produce a product that demonstrated the ways in which technology concepts and disciplinary habits of mind inform and blend with authentic learning. For example, social studies participants were asked to review readings and web resources to prepare a presentation for colleagues about the ways in which technology can be integrated with historical research.

No explicit references to the conceptual design challenge were made by participants. However, there was indirect evidence of participants' recognition of the importance of linking technology choices and disciplinary habits of mind. An ELA participant reflected, "It is critical that I can continue to point to these skills and highlight them . . . as they appear and reappear throughout the year. Even beyond technological strategies, that is a lesson I know I will remember going into the new school year." A social studies participant may have summed up the impact of this activity best when he wrote, "This course's emphasis on the connecting between building historical thinking skills and meaningfully integrating technology has changed my perspective."

The second activity in the design pattern was a Design Experience. This activity engaged participants in completing an instance of practice informed by technology integration concepts and disciplinary habits of mind. For example, ELA participants took on the role of 11th grade language arts students and created a podcast as part of a series of podcasts on word usage. Participants' reflections about the design experiences centered on the importance of viewing technology integration from a student's perspective. Wrote an ELA participant, "I have learned the importance of viewing a lesson through a student's eyes to determine how effective the lesson is." A social studies participant reflected, "I think one of the most important parts of the course were [sic] the design experiences, as we were able to put ourselves in the shoes of our students and go through lesson plans that were designed to make connections to the material we were discussing for the week."

Learners need to experience and reflect on models of practice in order to be able to transfer formal learning to applied contexts (Bullock, 2004). Thus, the third activity in the design pattern was a series of Design Examples. These design examples represented case studies of practice connecting technology concepts to habits of mind and were designed to elicit thoughtful examination. For example, ELA participants reflected on a case study about an ELA teacher who challenged her 10th grade students to use *iAnnotate* as part of a lesson on the comprehension of informational text. Participants discussed the ways in which this case study modeled or failed to model the interaction of technology integration concepts and the teaching of the Common Core writing standard.

Participants endorsed the process of analyzing models of practice. They reflected that analyzing the design examples helped them create a vision of practice and develop strategies for analyzing lessons. An ELA participant stated, "The scenarios provided real-life examples of face-to-face lessons. These were great practice for implementing the things we learned even before we have face-to-face time in the classroom." A science participant wrote, "In the design examples we were able to see things that were done well and things that we would improve on in our classrooms . . . . The setting of the classroom was always described well so I was able to see what I wanted my future classroom to look and sound like during hands-on activities, buzzing voices and active bodies." Wrote an ELA participant, "By analyzing various activities I learned to analyze the overall function of a lesson. In the future I will be able to criticize my own lesson ideas to (hopefully) strengthen my approach to a lesson."

The fourth activity, the Situated Design Challenge, required participants to use their emerging knowledge to develop a plan for practice (a lesson design). For example, one science module asked participants to design a biology lesson focusing on the interactions between organisms in an ecosystem. Feedback on the lesson design provided a context for conversation between participants and the content facilitator. Many participants acknowledged the relevance of the lesson design activities. An ELA participant wrote, "The lesson plan portion of the class was by far the largest learning opportunity for me." A social studies participant wrote, "I feel as though I am walking away with more usable material than most of the classes I have taken so far." In completing their lesson designs, participants were able to develop an appreciation of the centrality of lesson goals and objectives. An ELA participant wrote, "The emphasis that this course puts on learning objectives helped me to think about lesson planning in a different way." A mathematics participant stated, "This semester's exploration of technology taught me that no one technology is sufficient to meet all the curricular goals and objectives. Instead teachers must choose technology based on the affordances that support the goals and objectives of the lesson." An ELA participant might have summed it up best when she reflected,

> . . . my 'digitizing' habit was my impulse to use cool technology. I've learned to ask myself: What are the standards guiding this lesson? What do I want my students to learn? Will using this particular technology help them learn better? If not, is there a technology that will do so?

Participants also drew lessons from their lesson design experiences about the role of technology in learning. They acknowledged in their reflections the importance of choosing and using technology to support learning not "just because." A mathematics participant wrote, "So, what this course has taught me is that I should only integrate technology in a lesson plan if the affordances of the technology adds [sic] to the authenticity, outcome, or scaffolding of the lesson." A social studies participant wrote,

> I learned a great deal about how to incorporate technology into a lesson plan. The biggest lesson came not from the utilization of technology, but rather the appropriate appearance and absence of it . . . . It must be used as fits the lesson, not as the primary source of the lesson.

Discussion and Recommendations

In pursuit of our central design goal - to focus participants' attention on the *interaction* of technology integration concepts *and* discipline-specific contents, we made three course design decisions and examined participants' end of course synthesis reflections to understand the influence of these decisions on participants' learning experiences. The first course design decision was to situate participants' study of technology in their disciplinary teaching area. Only one participant remarked about this decision. It is possible that participants did not view this feature of the course as noteworthy because they were accustomed to a disciplinary focus throughout their preservice learning experiences. The second course design decision was to organize modules using disciplinary habits of mind. Participants acknowledged the relevance of disciplinary habits of mind to as relevant to their students' future, their students' ability to understand disciplinary thinking, and as an instructional strategy. The third course design decision was to structure content and activities using a design pattern. Only one participants' reflection referred to the overall design pattern but many wrote about the four pattern elements. The conceptual design challenge influenced participants' understanding of the linkage between technology choices and disciplinary habits of mind. The design experiences influenced participants' ability to view instances of technology integration from a secondary student's perspective. The design examples shaped participants' vision of classroom practice and provided analytical strategies for thinking critically about practice. The situated design challenge was perhaps the most relevant activity as it provided both lesson design experience and usable resources. Our course design decisions succeeded in contributing to participants' understanding of the *interaction* of technology integration concepts *and* discipline-specific contents and suggested that the design of the course was appropriate to support participants' learning experience.

No particular recommendations for course changes in future delivery emerged. However, some general recommendations about the design of preservice technology education courses can be made. One, the efficacy of the design pattern points to the need for a clear structure repeated across course content in order to facilitate preservice teachers' ability to understand expectations and assignments as well as to predict and anticipate course activities. Two, effective teacher technology course design situating course content and activities not in tools and skills but in the interaction of technology and disciplinary teaching is essential as it focuses learners' attention on practice that includes technology rather than on the technology itself. Three, teacher technology education course design should include opportunities for preservice teachers to experience what it is like when technology supports content learning. Equally important, course designs should provide multiple examples of technology-enhanced learning situations to support the development of a vision for practice that integrates standards, technology, disciplinary concepts, and practice. Four, course designs for teacher technology education should provide multiple opportunities to design lessons across multiple standards and disciplinary topics and to receive feedback on those designs. In this way, preservice teachers are able to develop concrete views of teaching with technology in their content areas and to have a set of materials to use when they enter the field.

Phase 4 of our research project now turns to the ways in which course content instantiated by our course design decisions influence candidates' course learning outcomes. What impact does course completion have on candidates' attitudes and beliefs about technology and their practice? Are candidates able to apply course concepts to lesson design? Does their learning transfer to their classroom practice?

References

Achieve Inc., (2013, April). *Next generation science standards*. Retrieved from http://www.nextgenscience.org/

Bannan-Ritland, B. (2003). The role of design in research: The integrative learning design framework. *Educational Researcher, 32*(1), 21-24.

Brush, T, Glazewski, K., Rutowski, K., Berg, K., Stromfors, C., Van-Nest, M. H., ... Sutton, J. (2003). Integrating technology in a field-based teacher training program: The PT$_3$ @ ASU projects. *Educational Technology Research & Development, 51*(1), 57-72.

Brzycki, D., & Dudt, K. (2005). Overcoming barriers to technology use in teacher preparation programs. *Journal of Technology and Teacher Education, 13*(4), 619-641.

Bullock, D. (2004). Moving from theory to practice: An examination of the factors that preservice teachers encounter as they attempt to gain experience teaching with technology during field placement experiences. *Journal of Technology and Teacher Education, 12*(2), 211-237.

Charbonneau, P., Jackson, H., Kobylski, G., Roginski, J., Sulewski, C., & Wattenberg, F. (2009). Developing students' "habits of mind" in a mathematics program. *Primus: Problems, Resources, and Issues in Mathematics Undergraduate Studies, 19*(2), 105-126.

Cobb, P. (2001). Supporting the improvement of learning and teaching in social and institutional context. In S. M. Carver & D. Klahr (Eds.), *Cognition and instruction: Twenty-five years of progress* (pp. 455-478). Mahwah, NJ: Erlbaum.

Gronseth, S., Brush, T., Ottenbreit-Leftwich, A., Strycker, J., Abaci, S., Easterling, W., . . . van Leusen, P. (2010). Equipping the next generation of teachers, *Journal of Digital Learning in Teacher Education*, 27:1, 30-36.

Hathaway, D., & Norton, P. (2013). Designing an online course content structure using a design patterns approach. *Educational Technology, 53*(2), 3-15.

Hew, K., & Brush, T. (2007). Integrating technology into K-12 teaching and learning: Current knowledge gaps and recommendations for future research. *Educational Technology Research & Development, 55*(3), 223-252.

Maddox, C., & Cummings, R. (2004). Fad, fashion, and the weak role of theory and research in information technology in education. *Journal of Technology and Teacher Education, 12*(4), 511-533.

Maxwell, J. (2013). *Qualitative research design: An interactive approach* (3rd ed.). Thousand Oaks, CA: Sage Publications.

Mishra, P., & Koehler, M. J. (2007). Technological pedagogical content knowledge (TPCK): Confronting the wicked problems of teaching with technology. In R. Carlsen, K. McFerrin, J. Price, R. Weber, & D. Willis (Eds.), *Proceedings of Society for Information Technology & Teacher Education International Conference 2007* (pp. 2214-2226). Chesapeake, VA: AACE.

National Council of Teachers of Mathematics. (2000). *Principles and standards for school mathematics online.* Retrieved from http://www.nctm.org/standards/content.aspx?id=16909

National Governors Association Center for Best Practices, & Council of Chief State School Officers. (2010). *Common Core State Standards for English language arts and literacy in history/social studies, science, and technical subjects.* Washington, DC: Authors.

Norton, P., & Hathaway, D. (2014). Using a design pattern framework to structure online course content: Twodesign cases. In *Proceedings of World Conference on E-Learning in Corporate, Government, Healthcare, and Higher Education 2014* (pp. 1440-1449). Chesapeake, VA: AACE.

Ottenbreit-Leftwich, A., Glazewski, K., & Newby, T. (2010). Preservice technology integration course revision: A conceptual guide. *Journal of Technology and Teacher Education, 18*(1), 5–33.

Peltier, J. W., Schibrowsky, J. A., & Drago, W. (2007). The interdependence of the factors influencing the perceived quality of the online learning experience: A causal model. *Journal of Marketing Education, 29*, 140-153.

Project Tomorrow, & Blackboard K-12 (2013). *Learning in the 21st century: Digital experiences and expectations of tomorrow's teachers.* Retrieved from http://www.tomorrow.org/speakup/tomorrowsteachers_report2013.html

Russell, M., Bebell, D., O'Dwyer, L., & O'Connor, K. (2003). Examining teacher technology use: Implications for preservice and inservice teacher preparation. *Journal of Teacher Education, 54*(4), 297-310.

Sang, G., Valcke, M., van Braak, J., & Tondeur, J. (2010). Student teachers thinking processes and ICT integration: predictors of prospective teaching behaviors with educational technology. *Computers & Education, 54*, 103-112

Tishman, S., Perkins, D., & Jay, E. (1995). *The thinking classroom: Learning and teaching in a culture of thinking.* Needham Heights, MA: Allyn and Bacon.

Westhoff, L. M., & Polman, J. L. (2008). Developing preservice teachers' pedagogical content knowledge about historical thinking. *International Journal of Social Education, 22*(2), 1-28.

Wineburg, S. (2001). *Historical thinking and other unnatural acts: Charting the future of teaching the past.* Philadelphia, PA: Temple University Press.

Teacher Comfort and Future Technology Use

Rachel Vannatta Reinhart
rvanna@bgsu.edu

Toni Sondergeld
tsonder@bgsu.edu

Savilla Banister
sbanist@bgsu.edu

Sharon Shaffer
sshaffe@bgsu.edu

College of Education and Human Development
Bowling Green State University, U.S.A.

Abstract: Research has shown that teacher comfort and confidence with technology is significantly related to technology use in the classroom (Buabeng-Andoh, 2012). This study examined teacher technology comfort, value, and pedagogy in relation to classroom technology use through a 1:1 pilot. Pre and post surveys were administered to 45 teachers who participated in a 1:1 pilot program. Multiple regression results indicate that only the pre survey variable of value/importance of learning new technologies for classroom use significantly predicted post (future) classroom use. Pre teacher comfort did not predict post (future) use. In addition, teacher comfort, value, and pedagogy did not significantly change from pre to post.

Introduction

Although research indicates that the best educational technology practices support a student-centered learning environment that promotes critical thinking, creativity, and problem-solving (Ottenbreit-Leftwich, Glazewski, & Newby, 2010), teachers continue to struggle to meaningfully integrate technology in the classroom. "Effective teaching requires effective technology use" (Ertmer & Ottenbreit-Leftwich, 2010, p. 256). Although knowledge and skill in using technology is certainly necessary, a teachers' belief system plays a significant role in classroom technology use (Ertmer & Ottenbreit-Leftwich, 2010). This system includes beliefs of self-efficacy, value, and pedagogy. One aspect of self-efficacy belief is comfort and confidence with technology. For the last decade, numerous studies have supported the relationship between teacher comfort in using technology and their use in the classroom (Buabeng-Andoh, 2012) indicating that the higher the teacher comfort level with technology, the higher the integration rate into the classroom (Mueller, Wood, Willoughby, Ross, & Specht, 2008; Russell et al., 2003). Comfort level often determines how frequently and to what extent the teacher uses technology with their students. If teachers are uncomfortable using technology, they are less likely to use it in the classroom (Russell et al., 2003). Another teacher belief that has shown to influence classroom technology use is the value or importance that a teacher sees in using technology (Zhao & Cziko, 2001). Snoeyink and Ertmer (2001/2002) found that when teachers saw value in using technology for a specific purpose, they were more likely to use technology despite the presence of barriers. Pedagogical beliefs are also intricately tied to effective technology integration. Teachers must understand that that the use of technology in teaching particular content requires new instructional methods (Mishra & Koehler, 2006). Using technology as a substitute for what is already being done in the class is a common mistake among teachers (Puentedura, 2006). Although many studies have examined these teacher beliefs in relation to current technology use, few have examine how these specific beliefs may relate to and predict future use. Consequently, this study sought to examine the relationship of teacher technology belief system of comfort, value, and pedagogy with current and future levels of classroom technology use as a result of a one-to-one (1:1) laptop pilot program.

The Study

The Center of Assessment and Evaluation Services (CAES) conducted the evaluation of a 1:1 laptop pilot a suburban K-12 school districts in Northwest Ohio during 2013-2014 school year. Pre and post surveys were administered to participating teachers and measured technology use, attitudes and beliefs, perceived barriers, and perceived impact of the 1:1 initiative. This correlational study utilized portions of the pre and post survey data to examine the relationship of teacher technology comfort, value, and pedagogy with current and future levels of classroom technology use as a result of a one-to-one (1:1) laptop pilot program. Two research questions guided the study:
1. Does teacher technology comfort, value, and pedagogy significantly relate to classroom technology use among teachers?
2. Which factors (technology comfort, value, pedagogy) best predict future classroom teacher technology use?

The Context

The 1:1 laptop pilot was implemented in 2013-14 in a reputable suburban northwest Ohio district. This district targeted Grades 5, 8, and 9 for the 1:1 pilot with the long-term plan of expanding 1:1 throughout the middle and high schools. The district was also interested in examining laptop differences and therefore piloted the more cost-effective Chromebook with Grades 5 and 8, and Mac Airs with Grade 9. Laptops with cases were purchased specifically for the 1:1. Policies and processes were developed to assigned devices to individual students for the year for school and home use. Training sessions were conducted with students and parents. In addition, an extensive professional development plan on effective technology integration had been implemented with teachers who had had assigned laptops for years. Wireless access was upgraded and technology support was increased throughout the district. The study participants consisted of approximately 45 teachers in grades 5, 8 and 9 and taught approximately 875 students. The district is predominately white (85.35 %) with a high SES; the poverty ratio is 2.81% (Ohio Department of Education, 2013).

Instrumentation

The instrument used to collect pre and post data was the 1:1 Laptop Teacher Survey (1:1TS), which was developed by CAES in conjunction with the participating district. The 1:1TS consists of 74 items. The purpose of the survey was to evaluate and improve the implementation of the 1:1 laptop program within the designated school district. The 1:1TS utilized items from the Maine Learning Technology Initiative (MLTI) Teacher Survey (2004) and the Teacher Technology Integration Survey (TTIS) (Vannatta & Banister, 2009). A draft of the 1:1TS was reviewed by district technology leaders and several teachers. After revisions, the survey was entered into Survey Monkey and again reviewed.

This study utilized data from two 1:1TS subscales and two specific items (see Table 2). Subscales included classroom technology use (frequency of facilitation of student use) and teacher comfort with technology. Classroom technology use was measured by asking teachers to report the frequency that they facilitate student use for various purposes. This subscale was adapted from the MLTI, consisted of 16 items, and utilized a 5-point frequency scale. Examples of classroom/student use items included: creating projects; completing homework; communicating with teachers and other students; and creating documents. The second subscale used was the teacher comfort with technology, which consisted of 8 items and utilized a 4-point Likert scale. Teacher comfort was adapted from the TTIS. This subscale consisted of items that measured comfort and confidence in: learning new technologies, troubleshooting, showing students new technologies, using technology in one's teaching. Three items within this subscale were recoded to create a unidirectional value. Subscale scores were calculated by computing the group means of respective items. Reliability coefficients using Cronbach's alpha were computed for pre and post subscales and produced coefficients ranging from .858 to .932. Two individual items were also include in the analyses. One item measured the importance of learning new technologies for classroom use. The reader should note that the emphasis was on learning new technologies for instruction use and not just using technology in general. This item represented a teachers' value belief around technology and whether learning new technologies to use in the classroom can help teachers achieve their instructional goals (Watson, 2006). A 4-point Likert scale was applied. The second item represented the pedagogy belief as it asked teachers to rate their skill in of using laptops for instruction. Five skill levels were provided and ranged from novice to expert. The 1:1 Teacher Laptop Survey was administered in September 2013 and again in March 2014. Both administrations were conducted via Survey Monkey by the CAES at Bowling Green State University. Of the 45 participants, only 34 teachers completed both the pre and post surveys.

Table 1. 1:1 Technology Factors

Subscale/Item	# of Items	Response Scale	Cronbach's α Pre	Post
Classroom technology use	16	(0-4) 0=never, 1=Less than once a week, 2= once a week, 3= a few times a week, 4=daily	.858	.932
Comfort with technology	8	(1-4) 1=strongly disagree, 2=disagree, 3=agree, 4=strongly agree	.896	.906
Value: Learning new technologies that I can uses in the classroom is important to me.	1	(1-4) 1=strongly disagree, 2=disagree, 3=agree, 4=strongly agree	NA	
Pedagogy: Overall skill in using laptops for instruction.	1	(0-4) 0=novice, 1= beginner, 2=average, 3=advanced, 4=expert	NA	

Data Analysis and Results

After recoding some negatively worded items within teacher comfort, subscale scores were calculated. Descriptive Statistics were calculated for the studied factors (see Table 2). Classroom technology use (facilitation of student use) was quite low at the beginning of the pilot (averaging less than once a week) with post results averaging weekly use. The pre survey mean for teacher comfort was 3.19, which is slightly higher than "Agree" on the 1:1TS subscale and indicates that teachers started the pilot with a moderately high level of comfort. Teachers reported minimal change in comfort from pre to post. The two items—importance in learning new technologies and overall skill in using laptops for instruction—generated high, stable averages for pre and post measures.

Table 2. Means and Standard Deviations of Teacher Beliefs and Technology Use ($n=34$)

	Pre		Post	
	M	*SD*	*M*	*SD*
Classroom Technology Use	1.03	0.63	2.02	0.74
Teacher Comfort	3.19	0.45	3.25	0.52
Value: Importance Learning New Technologies	3.44	0.66	3.44	0.79
Pedagogy: Overall Skill in Using Laptops	3.57	0.90	3.64	1.02

Pearson correlation coefficients were calculated to determine the relationships of classroom technology use (pre, post) with teacher comfort (pre, post), Value: Importance learning new technologies (pre, post), and Pedagogy: Overall skill in using laptops for instruction (pre, post). Table 3 presents these coefficients. Pre classroom technology use was not significantly correlated with any pre survey factors. However, it was significantly related to the post survey value item (Importance learning new technologies for instruction). The lack of significant relationships of pre classroom technology use with any of the pre survey factors is likely due to the low levels of pre classroom technology use. Post classroom technology use was significantly related to the three post factors (comfort, value, and pedagogy) with pedagogy producing the highest coefficient ($r=.652$). However, when examining the pre factors in relation to the post classroom use, only Value: Importance of learning new technologies was significantly related ($r=.626$)

Table 3. Correlation Coefficients of Classroom Technology Use with Comfort, Value, and Pedagogy (*n*=34)

Teacher Beliefs	Classroom Technology Use	
	Pre	Post
Pre		
Teacher Comfort	.253	.223
Value: Importance Learning New Technologies	.291	.626*
Pedagogy: Overall Skill in Using Laptops	.282	.197
Post		
Teacher Comfort	.268	.465*
Value: Importance Learning New Technologies	.433*	.496*
Pedagogy: Overall Skill in Using Laptops	.019	.652*

Note: * $p<.05$

Forward multiple regression was then conducted to determine which of the pre survey factors best predict future (post) classroom technology use. A single factor, Value: Importance of learning new technologies, was entered into the model with a regression equation of Y = .699 - .382X; $F(1, 33)=20.66$, $p<.0001$. This factor accounted for 39.2% of the variance in classroom technology use (post).

Discussion

This study explored the degree to which comfort, value, and pedagogy were related to current and future classroom technology use among teachers participating in a 1:1 pilot. Since the pre survey results of classroom technology use were extremely low with limited variability, it was not significantly related to any of the other pre survey factors. However, post classroom technology use was significantly related with the other post factors. Interestingly, pedagogy (skill in using laptops for instruction) produced the highest correlation. This result indicates that at the conclusion of the 1:1 pilot, teachers who reported high skill levels in using laptops for instruction (technological pedagogy also reported high levels of classroom technology use. This finding reinforces Mishra and Koehler's (2006) TPACK framework that indicates effective technological pedagogy as a critical component of technology integration.

When examining the pre survey factors as predictors of future (post) classroom technology use, we found that neither pre comfort nor pedagogy were significantly related to post use. Rather, the only pre survey variable related to post classroom use was value (the importance of learning new technologies for classroom use). This result is supported by the multiple regression findings that produced the one factor model, indicating that one's value significantly predicts future classroom technology use. These results suggest that current comfort levels may only explain current technology use and cannot be used to predict future levels of use. Such findings are somewhat in conflict with previous studies that have established the link between teacher comfort and technology use (Buabeng-Andoh, 2012; Russell et al., 2003). However, one should note that research has not been conducted on how teacher comfort relates to subsequent reports of technology use. In contrast, the value and importance that a teacher places on learning new classroom technologies was found to significantly predict future classroom technology use. While limited research supports this finding, several scholars note the relationship between the value/importance a teacher places on technology and the likelihood of using technology. Helping teachers make a positive value judgements about technology use often requires training that includes content and grade specific examples so that teachers can see the value in its use, understand the benefits, and integrate it in the classroom (Hughes, 2005; Zhao, Pugh, Sheld, & Byers, 2002). Interestingly, this value item focused not only on the importance of using classroom technology but also the importance of learning new technologies—an essential ingredient when implementing a 1:1 pilot.

Another important finding from this study is that the only variable that significantly increased from pre to post was classroom technology use. Comfort, value, and pedagogy were relatively stable. This result contrasts several studies that indicate personal experiences using technology (Mueller et al., 2008), situated professional development (Cole, Simkins, & Penul, 2002), and working with knowledgeable peers (Ertmer, Ottenbreit-Leftwich, & York, 2006) all help to increase teacher beliefs around technology. For the participating district, these activities were a significant part of the pilot. The lack of growth in these factors may be due to high level of comfort ($M=3.19$) value ($M=3.44$), and pedagogy ($M=3.57$) reported at the beginning of the pilot. Or perhaps the immersion experience of the pilot gave teachers a better understanding of their beliefs such that their pre survey levels were inflated while the post survey levels were more realistic. Finally, another reason may be due to the timing of the post survey, which was administered in early March, when teachers and students were in the thick of the 1:1. Likely, teachers were feeling the pressures of the pilot as well as imminent state testing.

These results have several implications for practice and research within a 1:1 environment. While teacher comfort with technology is related to technology use, administrators cannot assume that a teacher's current comfort level will predict future technology use. Although training efforts should seek to increase teacher comfort with technology, districts should provide context-specific training to increase teachers' value beliefs around using technology and learning new technologies. Finally, technological pedagogy (skill in using laptops for instruction) is essential for meaningful 1:1 technology use. Teachers need opportunities to reflect, discuss, observe, and experiment with effective 1:1 classroom practices (Ertmer & Ottenbreit-Leftwich, 2010). Since technologies are constantly changing, how teachers use such technology in the classroom will also change. Further research on how teacher technology comfort, value and pedagogy changes over time and through various experiences is necessary. Such research should also examine how these factors relate to and predict subsequent teacher technology use.

References

Buabeng-Andoh, C. (2012). Factors influencing teachers' adoption and integration of information and communication technology into teaching: A review of the literature. *International Journal of Education and Development using Information and Communication Technology 8*(1), 136-155.

Cole, K., Simkins, M., & Penuel, W. (2002). Learning to teach with technology: Strategies for inservice professional development. *Journal of Technology and Teacher Education, 10,* 431–455.

Dawson, K., Cavanaugh, C., & Ritshaupt, A. (2006). Florida's EETT leveraging laptops initiative and its impact on teaching practices. *Journal of Research on Technoloogy in Education,41*(2), 143-159.

Ertmer, P., & Ottenbreit-Leftwich, A. (2010).Teacher technology change: How knowledge, confidence, beliefs and culture intersect. *Journal of Research on Technology in Educatiion,42*(3), 255-284. .

Ertmer, P. A., Ottenbreit-Leftwich, A., & York, C. (2006). Exemplary technology-using teachers: Perceptions of factors influencing success. *Journal of Computing in Teacher Education, 23*(2), 55-61

Hughes, J. (2005). The role of teacher knowledge and learning experiences in forming technology-integrated pedagogy. *Journal of Technology and Teacher Education, 13,* 277-302

Mishra, P., & Koehler, M. J. (2006). Technological Pedagogical Content Knowledge: A framework for teacher knowledge. *Teachers College Record, 108*(6), 1017-1054.

Mueller, J., Wood, E., Willoughby, T., Ross, C., & Specht, J. (2008). Identifying discriminating variables between teachers who fully integrate computers and teachers with limited integration. *Science Direct Computers and Education, 51,* 1523-1537.

Ohio Department of Education (2013). Cupp Report 2013. Retrieved from http://education.ohio.gov/Topics/Finance-and-Funding/Finance-Related-Data/District-Profile-Reports/FY2013-District-Profile-Report

Ottenbreit-Leftwich, A., Glazewski, K., & Newby, T. (2010). Preservice Technology Integration Course Revision: A Conceptual Guide. *Journal of Technology and Teacher Education. 18* (1), pp. 5-33. Chesapeake, VA: Society for Information Technology & Teacher Education.

Puentedura, R. R. (2006). Transformation, Technology, and Education. Online at: http://hippasus.com/resources/tte [accessed June 24, 2015]

Russell, M., Bebell, D., O'Dwyer, L., & O'Connor, K. (2003). Examining teacher technology use: Implications for preservice and inservice teacher preparation. *Journal of Teacher Education, 54*(4), 297-310.

Snoeyink, R., & Ertmer, P. A. (2001/2002). Thrust into technology: How veteran teachers respond. *Journal of Educational Technology Systems, 30*(1), 85-111.

The Maine Learning Technology Initiative: The Impact of Maine's One-to-One Laptop Program on Middle School teachers and Students Research Report #1 (2004). Gorham, ME: Maine Education Policy Research Institute, Center for Education Policy Applied Research, and Evaluation, university of Sothern Maine.

Vannatta, R. A. & Banister, S. (2009). Validating a measure of teacher technology integration. In C. Maddux (Ed.), *Research Highlights in Technology and Teacher Education 2009* (pp. 329-338). Chesapeake, Virginia: SITE.

Watson, G. (2006). Technology professional development: Long-term effects on teacher self-efficacy. *Journal of Technology and Teacher Education, 14*(1), 151-165.

Zhao, Y., & Cziko, G. A. (2001). Teacher adoption of technology: A perceptual control theory perspective. *Journal of Technology and Teacher Education, 9*(1), 5-30.

Zhao, Y., Pugh, K., Sheldon, S., & Byers, J. (2002). Conditions for classroom technology innovations. *Teachers College Record, 104*, 482-515.